AN OUTLINE OF

THE RELIGIOUS LITERATURE OF INDIA

AN OUTLINE OF THE RELIGIOUS LITERATURE OF INDIA

J. N. FARQUHAR

MOTILAL BANARSIDASS
Delhi Varanasi Patna Madras

Head Office : Bungalow Road, Delhi 110 007
Branches: Chowk, Varanasi 221 001
Ashok Rajpath, Patna 800 004
6, Appar Swamy Koil Street, Mylapore,
Madras 600 004

By arrangement with the Oxford University Press
First Edition : 1920
Indian Reprint 1967, 1984

ISBN: 0–89581–765–9

Printed in India
by Shantilal Jain, at Shri Jainendra Press
A-45, Phase-I, Naraina, New Delhi 110 028 and published by
Narendra Prakash Jain, for Motilal Banarsidass, Delhi 110 007

TO

MY WIFE

FOREWORD

This book has been written from an overwhelming sense of personal need. On every occasion when I have tried to think my way through the history of any one of the chief Hindu sects or philosophies, or to realize the origin and growth of some doctrine or discipline, I have found my way barred, because the religious literature is so imperfectly known. Numberless friends have expressed in conversation and correspondence the same feeling of helplessness. In order to deal with any one of these subjects it would be necessary for the student to undertake first of all a long and difficult investigation into the sources.

The Vedic literature has been studied with the utmost care by a company of brilliant scholars; certain sections of the philosophical literature have been critically examined; the classical Sanskrit literature is well known; and portions of the literature of Buddhism and of Jainism have been carefully described; but on the mass of the books produced by Hindu sects and on great sections of Buddhist and Jain literature very little labour has yet been expended; while no attempt has ever been made to deal with the religious history as an undivided whole which must be seen as one long process of development before the meaning of the constituent sects or religions can be fully understood.

Consequently, the question arose whether it would not be possible to write a sketch of the whole religious literature of India. I was under no illusions as to the magnitude and the difficulty of the undertaking; and I was very painfully conscious of the slenderness of my own linguistic preparation for the task. On the other hand, I believed that, from the point of veiw of the study of religions, what was wanted was not so much fresh critical study of individual books as a clear comprehensible survey of the literature so far as critical inquiry, translations, and the publication of texts have made it known, so that the student might be able to begin the study of any part of it with intelligence, and to find his way without serious difficulty to all the existing literature, modern as well as ancient, which deals with the section of the field in which he is interested.

It was quite clear that to bring together all that is already known about Hindu, Buddhist, and Jain literature, whether in Sanskrit, Pali, Prakrit, or the modern vernaculars, and exhibit it as one historical development, would be extremely illuminating. The three religions are moments in a single religious movement; and they have reacted on each other throughout their history. Vernacular religious books are as truly a vital part of the growth of the sects as their more formal Sanskrit manuals are. For a full understanding of the history, the whole must be envisaged as one great movement.

I was also conscious that during the last twenty years a very large number of elements in the religious and literary history have been illuminated by fresh discoveries. A good deal of work has been done on the vernacular literatures, and masses of sectarian works in Sanskrit have been unearthed. Yet most of these important advances lie buried in notes in learned journals, in prefaces to texts, in catalogues, in articles in encyclopaedias, or in obscure monographs. They have not yet found their way into any text-book of the literature or of the religions. For example, the problem of the date of the philosophical Sūtras has quite recently been brought much nearer solution, and the result is a general clarifying of the perspective in one of the most important periods. Numerous books, articles, and stray observations have shed welcome rays of light on these systems and their history. Professor Keith's Vedic works contain masses of historical and chronological observations referring to the whole of Vedic and sub-Vedic literature. Professor Hopkins's book, *The Great Epic of India*, throws a flood of light on the religious changes of the time when the epics were gradually being formed. The serried phalanx of details exhibited in Guérinot's splendid thesaurus has never been worked up into a history of Jain literature. Numerous works describe or throw light on sections of the literature of Buddhism; yet no one has reduced them to a single ordered narrative. H. P. Śāstrī's catalogues of Nepalese manuscripts, Vidyābhūshaṇa's volume on mediaeval logic, Bhandarkar's work on the sects, and Schrader's volume on the Vaishṇava Saṁhitās, each contain notable contributions to religious and literary history. Finally, translations from various Indian tongues have in recent years brought many of the more interesting texts within reach of the student of religions.

Another consideration which helped me to get over the feeling that it was extremely rash to undertake such a book was the fact that I have had personal religious intercourse with members of most of the modern sects which come under review, and that, in the ordinary course of my work, I am able to meet Indian scholars and in conversation to receive from them detailed information not otherwise obtainable.

Careful students are well aware that, if the religious history of India is to be understood, each of the leading sects of the three religions must be described by itself. Yet, if each is dealt with in isolation, where will the general movement make itself felt, and how shall we perceive the rise of changes common to all the sects? Clearly the unity of the history in all its length and breadth must be regarded as broken and diversified, on the one hand, by numerous religious communities which, so to speak, lie parallel to each other, and, on the other, by successive waves of change each of which has swept over all the communities in existence at the time of its appearance, and has modified each in some degree. How, then, were these two forms of variation to be exhibited in a continuous narrative? I have attempted to divide the milleniums covered by the growth of the literature into periods corresponding as nearly as possible to the great waves of change in belief and practice, and within each period to group the books, as far as possible, according to the religion, the sect, and the sub-sect to which they severally belong.

The result of this method of procedure is to throw the broad changes marked by the periods into bold relief and to indicate clearly which sects were active within each period; but it has this disadvantage that, in the case of every sect which has been prominent through several periods, the history is cut up into as many pieces. But this disadvantage is more apparent than real; for the student who wishes to deal with a single community will probably find it a rewarding piece of work to study first the whole history throughout a number of periods, and then to re-read consecutively the portions which deal with the particular community.

The reason why the investigation ends with the eighteenth century is this, that from that point Western influence began to act on the Indian mind, and the new forces thereby released are still only in process of being revealed; so that it is not yet possible to write an account of them in any way comparable with the other chapters of the book. In my *Modern Religious Movements in India* an attempt has been made to sketch the religious organizations which have made their appearance since the dawn of the new day.

In preparing the book I have tried to make the narrative readable, if possible, despite the great compression which is necessary, if the subject is to be set forth within the compass of a single volume. I have, therefore, mentioned in the text only volumes of outstanding importance, and have relegated all the rest of the detail involved to the Bibliography. Thus the advanced student had better use the two parts of the book together. The narrative is meant to give an outline of the history and to exhibit the position and influence of the chief masses of the literature and of the leading thinkers and writers, while the Bibliography is meant to supply lists of all the more important religious works, of the best critical books and articles written on these in modern times and of all available translations. For two reasons I decided not to give particulars about editions in the original tongues: these are so numerous that it would take much space to catalogue them, and it is clear that, from the point of view of the average student of religions, books in the original languages are almost useless.

The text of each chapter is divided up by means of headings, so as to exhibit the sectarian relationships, and is then further subdivided into short sections, consecutively numbered, to facilitate reference. In the main part of the Bibliography the books of each sect or school are arranged as far as possible in historical order, and consecutively numbered, the dates and the numbers being printed in emphasized type, so that the chronology may stand out clear and the numbers may readily catch the eye.

It may be well also to point out the unavoidable limitations of the work. First of all, the whole of the secular literature is dropped out of sight. Secondly, since our aim is the study of the religions, the emphasis falls throughout on the religious rather than on the literary aspects of the books. Thirdly, our attention is restricted to the literature as the chief source of knowledge of the religions, and no attempt is made to deal, except in the most incidental way, with other sources, epigraphy, archaeology, art, and what not. Again, while the nature of the task makes it necessary to say a great deal about the religions, the work is not a history of the religions but a sketch of the religious literature. It may also be well to warn readers that large elements of Indian religion scarcely appear in our pages at all. Those cults which have produced no literature are necessarily outside our survey.

I owe a great deal of the most reliable information in the book to the assistance of friends. The subject is so vast and involves so much accurate knowledge that it was clear from the outset that I should have to rely largely on the help of others.

I owe the greatest debt of all to a number of Indian scholars who have most generously given me of their very best. I subjoin a list of my chief helpers with the subjects on which they have given me information:

Mahāmahopādhyāya Vindhyeśvarī Prasād of the Sanskrit Library, Benares: The Vedānta and the Smārtas.

Dr. Gaṅgā Nātha Jhā, Allahabad: The Karma Mīmāṁsā.

Dr. Laḍḍu, the Sanskrit College, Benares: The Bhāgavatas and early Marāṭhī literature.

The Rev. Francis Kingsbury, United Theological College, Bangalore: Tamil literature and the history of the Tamil Śaivas.

A. Govindāchārya Svāmin, Mysore City: the Śrī-Vaishṇavas.

Rao Sahib P. G. Halkatti, Bijapur, and another distinguished Vīra Śaiva: the Vīra Śaivas.

Paṇḍita M. L. Śāstrī, Broach and Poona: the Vallabhāchāryas.

Prof. Bhāgavata Kumāra Gosvāmī[1] Śāstrī, M.A., Hoogly: the Chaitanya sect.

Paṇḍita Rādhā Charaṇa Gosvāmī[2] Vidyāvāgīśa, Honorary Magistrate, Brindāban: the Nimbārkas.

Dr. V. V. Ramaṇa Śāstrī, Tanjore: the later Śaiva literature.

Dr. M. Kṛishṇamāchārya, Tanuku, Kistna dist.: chronological questions.

Mr. Justice J. L. Jainī, Indore: the Digambara Jain Secondary Canon.

Mr. P. P. Subramaṇya Śāstrī,[3] Balliol College, Oxford: Appaya Dīkshita, and Śākta worship among Smārtas.

So many Missionaries have been of service to me that I must not attempt to mention them all.

The late Dr. K. S. Macdonald of the United Free Church Mission, Calcutta, set about gathering material on the Hindu Tantras a few years before his death, and persuaded a number of his friends to analyse or translate one or more Tantras each,

[1] He is a lineal descendant of Vaṁśīvadana, one of the companions of Chaitanya. See p. 308.

[2] He comes of a Mādhva stem.

[3] He is a lineal descendant of Appaya Dīkshita's brother, Āchān Dīkshita.

in order to help him in the study. The MS. material which he left, most obligingly placed at my service by Mrs. Macdonald, has helped me considerably with the later history of the Śākta sect in Bengal. These MSS. may be found on p. 389. of the Bibliography, each described as belonging to the Macdonald MSS.

I owe a special debt to my friend the late Rev. J. J. Johnson of the Church Missionary Society, Benares, who passed suddenly away shortly after my visit to him in December, 1917. It will be something of a consolation for my heavy loss if I bear testimony here to his worth. He was thoroughly well known all over India among Hindu scholars and ascetics for his beautiful Sanskrit speech and his interest in Hindu philosophy. Every one called him Paṇḍit Johnson. How often did the three of us meet—Mr. Johnson, his loved and trusted friend, Mahāmahopādhyāya Vindhyeśvarī Prasād, a scholar of rare judgement who has been already mentioned, and myself. We met so because of my inability to express myself in the classic tongue of India, and our procedure was always the same. I asked my questions in English, and Mr. Johnson expressed them in Sanskrit. I was then usually able to follow the Śāstrī's Sanskrit replies, but if I failed to catch a point Mr. Johnson again interpreted. Now that he is gone Benares can never again be the same to me.

To the Rev. Dr. James Shepherd, of Udaipur—charming host and beloved missionary—I owe the settlement of the date and history of Mīrā Bāī, the Rajput princess whose lyrics of passionate devotion for Kṛishṇa have won her enduring fame.

A pair of Poona friends, the Rev. Dr. N. Macnicol and the Rev. A. Robertson, have given me most generous help toward the interpretation of the religion and the poetry of the Marāṭhā saints and the elucidation of Manbhau problems.

To all others, whether Indians or Missionaries, who have answered my questions, orally or by letter, or who have led me to fresh sources of information, I wish to express my unfeigned gratitude and thanks.

My teacher, Prof. A. A. Macdonell of Oxford, read the first and second chapters of the book in manuscript, and made many valuable suggestions. For the assistance of his ripe Vedic scholarship I am deeply grateful. Prof. A. Berriedale Keith of Edinburgh read the whole manuscript, and sent me a large number of critical notes which have saved me from blunders, from dangerous statements, and from reliance on weak evidence, and have suggested numerous fresh points of view. For such help no thanks can make an adequate return.

But while I owe much precious information and help to these scholars, Indian and European, they must not be held responsible for any statement in the text; for I have not accepted all their conclusions. The final historical judgement in every case is my own. It is therefore quite possible that my suggestions as to what the history behind the evidence is in any particular case may seem to them quite unjustifiable. This is above all likely to happen in the case of the sects. Dr. Berriedale Keith is certainly of opinion that I have been a good deal too optimistic in attempting to assign individual Purāṇas, Tantras, and Upanishads to the chronological periods adopted in the book. I have, however, in each case indicated that the ascription is tentative and at best only probable; and it has seemed wise even to run the risk of being discovered in error, in the hope that the tentative history may stimulate further investigation.

Letters indicating errors or omissions or fresh points of view will be very warmly welcomed.

To Dr. James Morison, Librarian of the Indian Institute, Oxford, who has faithfully carried out the long toilsome task of revising the proofs, I wish to offer my sincere gratitude.

11 FRENCHAY ROAD, OXFORD.
December, 1919.

CONTENTS

ABBREVIATIONS

USED IN THE NOTES AND THE BIBLIOGRAPHY

Acworth, *BM.*	Acworth, *Ballads of the Marāṭhās*, London, 1894.
AMG. II.	Feer, *Analyse du Kandjour, Annales du Musée Guimet*, II, Paris, 1881.
AMG. V.	Feer, *Traductions du Kandjour, Annales du Musée Guimet*, V, Paris, 1883.
AR.	*Asiatic Researches.*
ARAD.	*Annual Report of the Archaeological Department.*
Arunachalam, *STT.*	*Studies and Translations from the Tamil*, by P. A., Madras, 1898.
Avalon, *HG.*	Arthur and Ellen Avalon, *Hymns to the Goddess*, London, 1913.
Avalon, *SP.*	Avalon, *The Serpent Power*, London, 1919.
Avalon, *TGL.*	Avalon, *Tantra of the Great Liberation* (*Mahānirvāṇa T.*), London, 1913.
Avalon, *TT.*	Avalon, *Tāntrik Texts*, London, 1913 ff.
B.	Brāhmaṇa.
Barnett, *HI.*	Barnett, *Heart of India*, a vol. of translations, London, 1908.
Barth, *RI.*	Barth, *Religions of India*, London, 1906.
BEFEO.	*Bulletin de l'École Française d'Extrême-Orient.*
Beng.	Bengālī.
Bhandarkar CV.	*Bhandarkar Commemoration Volume*, Poona, 1917.
Bhandarkar, *EHD.*	Bhandarkar, *Early History of the Deccan*, Bombay, 1884.
Bhandarkar, *R.*	Bhandarkar, *Reports on the Search for Sanskrit MSS.*, Bombay.
Bhandarkar, *VS.*	Bhandarkar, *Vaiṣṇavism, Śaivism &c.*, GRUNDRISS, 1913.
Bhattacharya, *HCS.*	Bhattacharya, *Hindu Castes and Sects*, Calcutta, 1896.
BI.	*Bibliotheca Indica*, a series published by the Asiatic Society of Bengal, Calcutta.
Bloomfield, *AV.*	Bloomfield, *Atharvaveda*, GRUNDRISS, 1899.
Bloomfield, *RV.*	Bloomfield, *Religion of the Veda*, New York, 1908.
BMCTB.	*British Museum Catalogue of Tamil Books*, London, 1909.
BSOSL.	*Bulletin of the School of Oriental Studies*, London.
Chanda, *IAR.*	Chanda, *Indo-Aryan Races*, Rajshahi, 1916.
Chatterji, *HR.*	Chatterji, *The Hindu Realism*, Allahabad, 1912.
Chatterji, *KS.*	Chatterji, *Kashmir Shaivism*, Srinagar, 1914.
Chaukh.	Chaukhamba Series, Benares.

CII.	*Corpus Inscriptionarum Indicarum.*
Colebrooke, *ME.*	Colebrooke, *Miscellaneous Essays*, I. London, 1837.
Comm.	Commentary.
Cowell, *SDS.*	Cowell and Gough, *The Sarva-darśana-saṅgraha of Mādhava*,[3] London, 1908.
CTr.	Chinese translation.
Deussen, *AGP.*	Deussen, *Allgemeine Geschichte der Philosophie*, Leipzig, 1906.
Deussen, *PU.*	Deussen, *Philosophy of the Upanishads*, Edinburgh, 1906.
Deussen, *SUV.*	Deussen, *Sechzig Upanishad's des Veda*, Leipzig, 1897.
Deussen, *SV.*	Deussen, *System of the Vedānta*, Chicago, 1912.
DS.	Dharmasūtra.
Duff, *CI.*	Mabel Duff, *Chronology of India*, London, 1899.
Dutt, *MT.*	Dutt, *A Prose English Translation of the Mahānirvāṇa Tantram*, Calcutta, 1900.
EB.	*Encyclopaedia Brittanica*, XIth ed.
Eggeling, *SMIO.*	*Sanskrit MSS. in India Office*, 1887.
ERE.	Hastings, *Encyclopaedia of Religion and Ethics*, Edinburgh.
ETr.	English Translation.
FTr.	French Translation.
Garbe, *IC.*	Garbe, *Indien und das Christentum*, Tübingen, 1914.
Garbe, *SY.*	Garbe, *Sāṁkhya und Yoga*, GRUNDRISS, 1896.
Getty, *GNB.*	Getty, *Gods of Northern Buddhism*, Oxford, 1914.
Gover, *FSSI.*	Gover, *Folk-songs of Southern India*, London, 1872.
Govindāchārya, *R.*	Govindāchārya, *Life of Rāmānuja*, Madras, 1906.
Govindāchārya, *YMD.*	Govindacharya, ETr. of *Yatīndra Mata Dīpikā*, Madras, 1912.
Grierson, *LH.*	Grierson, *Modern Vernacular Literature of Hindustan*, Calcutta, 1889. References to pages.
Griffis.	Griffis, *Religions of Japan*, New York, 1904.
Griffith, *RV.*	Griffith, *The Hymns of the Ṛigveda Translated*, Benares, 1896.
Growse, *M.*	Growse, *Mathurā*,[3] Allahabad, 1883.
Growse, *R.*	Growse, *The Rāmāyaṇa of Tulsī Dās*,[4] ETr., Allahabad, 1887.
GRUNDRISS.	*Grundriss der Indo-Arischen Philologie und Altertumskunde* (Encyclopaedia of Indo-Aryan Research), Strassburg.
GSAI.	*Giornale della Società asiatica italiana*, Firenze.
GTr.	German Translation.
Guérinot.	Guérinot, *Essai de Bibliographie Jaina*, Paris, 1906. References to pages.
Hall.	Fitzedward Hall, *An Index of the Indian Philosophical Systems*, Calcutta, 1859.
Haug, *AB.*	Haug, *Aitareya Brāhmaṇa*, Bombay, 1863.
Hillebrandt, *RL.*	Hillebrandt, *Ritual-Litteratur, Vedische Opfer und Zauber*, GRUNDRISS, 1897.
Hoernle, *MRBL.*	Hoernle, *Manuscript Remains of Buddhist Literature*, Oxford, 1916.

Holtzmann, *MBH.*	Holtzmann, *Das Mahābhārata*, Kiel, 1892–5.
Hopkins, *GE.*	Hopkins, *The Great Epic of India*, New York, 1901.
Hopkins, *ION.*	Hopkins, *India Old and New*, New York, 1901.
Hopkins, *RI.*	Hopkins, *Religions of India*, Boston, 1908.
Hopkins, *Ruling Caste.*	*JAOS.* 1889.
Hopkins, *YT.*	Hopkins, *Yoga-technique*, *JAOS.* XXIIb, 333.
H. P. Śāstrī.	H. P. Śāstrī, *A Catalogue of Palm-leaf and selected Paper MSS. belonging to the Durbar Library, Nepal*, Calcutta, I. 1905; II. 1915.
IA.	*The Indian Antiquary*, Bombay.
IOC.	International Oriental Congress.
I. St.	*Indische Studien*, 1850 ff.
ITr.	Italian Translation.
Iyengar, *Outlines.*	P. T. Śrīnivāsa Iyengar, *Outlines of Indian Philosophy*, Benares, 1909.
JA.	*Journal Asiatique*, Paris.
Jacob, *EAU.*	Jacob, *Eleven Atharvaṇa Upanishads*, Bombay, 1891.
Jacobi, *AEM.*	*Ausgewählte Erzählungen in Māhārāshṭrī*, Leipzig, 1886.
Jacobi, *R.*	Jacobi, *Das Rāmāyaṇa*, Bonn, 1893.
Jaini, *OJ.*	Jaini, *Outlines of Jainism*, Cambridge, 1916.
JAOS.	*Journal of American Oriental Society.*
JASB.	*Journal of the Asiatic Society of Bengal.*
JBBRAS.	*Journal of the Bombay Branch of the Royal Asiatic Society.*
Jhā, *PSPM.*	Jhā, *Prābhākara School of Pūrva Mīmāṁsā*, Allahabad, 1911.
Jhaveri, *MGL.*	Jhaveri, *Milestones in Gujarati Literature*, Bombay, 1914.
Jolly, *RS.*	Jolly, *Recht und Sitte*, GRUNDRISS, 1896.
JPTS.	*Journal of the Pali Text Society.*
JRAS.	*Journal of the Royal Asiatic Society.*
K. Aiyangar, *AI.*	S. Krishnaswami Aiyangar, *Ancient India*, London, 1911.
Keith, *AĀ.*	Keith, *Aitareya Āraṇyaka*, Oxford, 1909.
Keith, *SS.*	Keith, *Sāṁkhya System*, Calcutta, 1918.
Keith, *TS.*	Keith, *Taittirīya Saṁhitā*, Harvard, 1914.
Kennedy, *HM.*	Kennedy, *Hindu Mythology*, London, 1831.
Kern, *MIB.*	Kern, *Manual of Indian Buddhism*, GRUNDRISS, 1896.
Kingsbury & Phillips.	*Hymns of the Tamil Śaiva Saints*, Calcutta, 1920.
Kṛishṇa Śāstrī, *SII.*	H. Kṛishṇa Śāstrī, *South-Indian Images of Gods and Goddesses*, Madras, 1916.
Krishnasamy Aiyar.	Krishnasamy Iyer, *Śrī Śaṅkarāchārya*, Madras, Natesan.
Macauliffe.	Macauliffe, *The Sikh Religion*, Oxford, 1909.
Macdonald MSS.	See pp. xiv–xv.
Macdonell.	Macdonell, *Sanskrit Literature*, London, 1900.
Macnicol, *PMS.*	Macnicol, *Psalms of Marāṭhā Saints*, Calcutta, 1919.

Mādhava, *SDS.*	Mādhava, *Sarva-darśana-saṅgraha.*
MBH.	*Mahābhārata.*
MBV.	Miśra Brothers, *Miśra Bandhu Vinode*, Allahabad, 1916.
Mitra.	R. L. Mitra, *Sanskrit Buddhist Literature of Nepal*, Calcutta, 1882.
Mitra, *Notices.*	Mitra, *Notices of Sanskrit MSS.*, Calcutta.
Monier Williams, *BH.*	Monier Williams, *Brahmanism and Hinduism*, London, 1891.
Mod. Rev.	*The Modern Review*, a monthly, Calcutta.
Moulton, *EZ.*	Moulton, *Early Zoroastrianism*, London, 1913.
Moulton, *TM.*	Moulton, *Treasure of the Magi*, London, 1917.
Mrs. Rhys Davids, *PEB.*	Mrs. Rhys Davids, *Psalms of the Early Buddhists*, London, *of the Sisters*, 1909; *of the Brethren*, 1913.
Mrs. Stevenson, *HJ.*	Mrs. Sinclair Stevenson, *Heart of Jainism*, London, 1915.
Muir, *OST.*	Muir, *Original Sanskrit Texts*, London, 1858 ff.
Müller, *ASL.*	Max Müller, *Ancient Sanskrit Literature*,[2] London, 1860.
Müller, *SS.*	Max Müller, *Six Systems of Indian Philosophy*, London, 1899.
Nallasvami Pillai, *SJB.*	Nallasvami Pillai, *Śiva Jñāna Bodham*, Madras, 1895.
Nallasvami Pillai, *SSS.*	Nallasvami Pillai, *Studies in Śaiva Siddhānta*, Madras, 1911.
Nanjio.	Bunyiu Nanjio, *The Chinese Buddhist Tripiṭaka*, Oxford, 1883. References to entries.
Oldenberg, *Buddha.*	Oldenberg, *Buddha*, London, 1882.
Oldenberg, *LU.*	Oldenberg, *Die Lehre der Upanishaden und die Anfänge des Buddhismus*, Göttingen, 1915.
Oldenberg, *RV.*	Oldenberg, *Die Religion des Veda*, Berlin, 1894.
OTF.	Oriental Translation Fund of the Royal Asiatic Society.
P.	Purāṇa.
Padmanabhachar, *LTM.*	Padmanabhachar, *Life and Teachings of Madhvacharyar*, Coimbatore, 1909.
Pargiter, *MP.*	Pargiter, *The Mārkaṇḍeya Purāṇa*, translated, Calcutta, 1904.
Pargiter, *PTDKA.*	Pargiter, *The Purāṇa Text of the Dynasties of the Kali Age*, Oxford, 1913.
Peterson.	Peterson, *Reports on the Search for Sanskrit MSS.*, Bombay.
Pischel, *GPS.*	Pischel, *Grammatik der Prākṛit-Sprachen*, Strassburg, 1900.
Pope, *TV.*	Pope, *The Tiruvaśāgam*, Text, Intro., ETr., Oxford, 1900.
Poussin, *Opinions.*	Poussin, *Bouddhisme, Opinions sur l'Histoire de la Dogmatique*, Paris, 1909.
Poussin, *V. & Y.*	Poussin, *Vasubandhu et Yaśomitra*, Troisième Chapitre de *l'Abhidharmakośa*, London, 1914–18.
Poussin, *WN.*	Poussin, *The Way to Nirvāṇa*, Cambridge, 1917.

Powlett, *Ulwur.*	Powlett, *Ulwur, a District Memoir*, Allahabad, 1878.
Prāk.	Prākṛit.
Prasad, *SBS.*	Rai Baleśvar Prasād Bahādur, *Sant Bānī Saṅgraha*, Allahabad, 1915.
Quackenbos, *SPM.*	Quackenbos, *The Sanskrit Poems of Mayūra with Bāṇa's Chandīśataka*, New York, 1917.
Rajagopalachariar, *VRI.*	T. Rajagopalachariar, *The Vaishnavite Reformers of India*, Madras.
R. A. Śāstrī, *Ānandalahirī.*	R. Anantakṛishṇa Śāstrī, *Ānandalaharī*, Palghat, 1899.
R. A. Śāstrī, *Lalitā.*	R. Anantakṛishṇa Śāstrī, *Lalitāsahasranāma*, with Bhāskararāya's comm., in ETr., Madras, 1899.
Rhys Davids, *ALB.*	Rhys Davids, *American Lectures on Buddhism*, New York, 1901.
Rhys Davids, *BBS.*	Rhys Davids, *Buddhist Birth Stories*, London, 1880.
Rhys Davids, *BI.*	Rhys Davids, *Buddhist India*, London, 1903.
Rhys Davids, *DB.*	Rhys Davids, *Dialogues of the Buddha*, London, 1899.
Rhys Davids, *HIB.*	Rhys Davids, *History of Indian Buddhism*, London, 1897.
Rice, *KL.*	Rice, *Kanarese Literature*, Calcutta, 1918.
Russell and Hira Lal.	Russell and Hira Lal, *Tribes and Castes of the Central Provinces*, London, 1916.
S.	Saṁhitā.
S. Aiyaṅgar, *TS.*	M. Śrīnivāsa Aiyaṅgar, *Tamil Studies*, Madras, 1914.
Sansk.	Sanskrit.
Sarkar, *CPT.*	Sarkar, *Chaitanya's Pilgrimages and Teachings*, being the middle part of the *Chaitanya-charitaamṛita* in English, Calcutta, 1913.
SBE.	*Sacred Books of the East*, Oxford.
SBH.	*Sacred Books of the Hindus*, Panini Office, Allahabad.
Schomerus, SS.	Schomerus, *Der Śaiva Siddhānta*, Leipzig, 1912.
Schrader, *IPAS.*	Schrader, *Introduction to the Pāñcharātra and the Ahirbudhnya Saṁhitā*, Madras, 1916.
Schroeder, *ILK.*	Schroeder, *Indiens Litteratur und Kultur*, Leipzig, 1887.
Seidenstücker, *PBU.*	Seidenstücker, *Pali Buddhismus in Uebersetzungen*, Breslau, 1911.
Sen, *CC.*	Sen, *Chaitanya and his Companions*, Calcutta, 1917.
Sen, *HBLL.*	Sen, *History of Bengali Language and Literature*, Calcutta, 1911.
Sen, *VLMB.*	Sen, *Vaiṣṇava Literature of Mediaeval Bengal*, Calcutta, 1917.
Sen, *VSP.*	Sen, *Vaṅga Sahitya Parichaya*, selections from old Bengali literature, Calcutta, 1914.
Seshagiri Rao, *SSTM.*	*Report on the Search for Sanskrit and Tamil MSS.*, Madras.
Siddhānta Dīpikā.	A monthly magazine, Madras, 1897–1913.

SJM.	*Sanskrit Journal of Madras.*
SKPAW.	*Sitzungsberichte der Königlichen Preussischen Akademie der Wissenschaften*, Berlin.
SMIO.	*Sanskrit MSS. in the India Office*, London, 1887.
Suali, *Introduzione.*	Suali, *Introduzione allo Studio della Filosofia Indiana*, Pavia, 1913.
Sukhtaṅkar, *TVR.*	Sukhtaṅkar, *Teachings of Vedānta acc. to Rāmānuja*, Wien, 1908.
Tam.	Tamil.
Tel.	Telugu.
U.	Upanishad.
Vedic Index.	Macdonell and Keith, *Vedic Index of Names and Subjects*, London, 1912.
Vidyābhūshaṇa, *MSIL.*	*Mediaeval System of Indian Logic*, Calcutta, 1909.
V. Smith, *EHI.*	Vincent A. Smith, *Early History of India*,[3] Oxford, 1914.
V. Smith, *HFA.*	V. Smith, *History of Fine Art in India and Ceylon*, Oxford, 1911.
Walleser, *DAV.*	Walleser, *Der ältere Vedānta*, Heidelberg, 1910.
Warren, *BT.*	Warren, *Buddhism in Translations*, Harvard, 1896.
Watters.	Watters, *On Yuan Chwang*, London, 1904.
Weber, *HIL.*	Weber, *History of Indian Literature*, London, 1892.
Westcott, *Kabir.*	Westcott, *Kabir and the Kabir Panth*, Cawnpore, 1907.
Whitney and Lanman, *AV.*	Whitney and Lanman, *Atharva-veda Saṁhitā*, in ETr., Harvard, 1905.
Wilson, *Sects.*	Wilson, *Sketch of the Religious Sects of the Hindus*,[2] London, 1861.
Wilson, *VP.*	Wilson, *Vishṇu Purāṇa*, London, 1864.
Wilson, *Works.*	Wilson, *Select Works*, London, 1861.
Wilson, *TH.*	Wilson, *Theatre of the Hindus*, London, 1871.
Winternitz.	Winternitz, *Geschichte der indischen Litteratur*, Leipzig, Vol. I, 1908, Vol. II. i, 1913.
Woods, *Yoga.*	Woods, *The Yoga-system of Patañjali*, Harvard, 1914.
ZDMG.	*Zeitschrift der deutschen morgenländischen Gesellschaft*, 1847 ff.

CHAPTER I

THE EARLY VEDIC RELIGION: *x* to *y*.

§ 1. The investigations of the past century have shown clearly that the people who conquered India and created the Hindu religion and civilization belonged to that ancient race, now usually called Indo-European, from which sprang the Teutonic, Celtic, Slavonic, Italic, Hellenic, Armenian, Persian, and other peoples. This kinship is visible in the speech of the invaders,[1] in numerous details of their culture,[2] and also in their religion.[3] From a comparison of the beliefs and practices of these many nations it is possible to form some idea of the religion of the parent Indo-European race. The basis of the religion was an animistic belief in a very large number of petty gods, each of which had a special function; but the people had already advanced to the conception of a few glorious heavenly gods (Sanskrit *deva*, Latin *deus*, &c.), each a representative of one of the greater aspects of nature. Sky, thunder, sun, moon, fire, wind, and water were the chief of this new group of great gods. They were worshipped with sacrifice, accompanied with potent formulae and prayer, the offerings being either laid out on grass for the gods to eat or wafted to them on the fire and smoke of the altar. Ancestors were also worshipped as powerful beings who from the other world watched over their descendants. There was thus already some sort of belief in immortality. Magic was highly regarded and much used. The family was patriarchal in

[1] Max Müller, *Lectures on the Science of Language*.
[2] Max Müller, *Biographies of Words*.
[3] Schrader, art. 'Aryan Religion', *ERE.*; Hillebrandt, *RL.* 1–10; Bloomfield, *RV.* 99–149.

character; marriage was universal; and sons were ardently desired.

§ 2. We cannot tell where the home of this ancient race was, nor at what times and places the great historical peoples hived off from it; but we can trace with certainty the invaders of India, in that stage of their life which immediately preceded the invasion.[1] A people, partly nomadic, partly agricultural, lived for a considerable time somewhere in Central Asia, perhaps just to the north of the Hindu Kush. Finally they separated into two groups, perhaps by a process of migration so slow as to leave them unconscious that they had fallen apart, the one moving through Afghanistan into India, the other spreading over the wide territory which bears their racial name, Iran. This word is simply a variant form of Aryan, the name used by their brothers, the invaders of India. We may therefore speak of the period before the separation as the time of Indo-Iranian unity.

There is sufficient evidence available to enable us to form a clearer picture of this period than of the far earlier Indo-European period. Most of our knowledge arises from a comparison of the Veda, the earliest Indian literature, with the earliest literature of the Iranian peoples, viz. the *Avesta*, the sacred book of the Zoroastrians of ancient Persia. A careful comparative study of the two reveals the fact that the Indo-Iranian people had advanced beyond the early Indo-European faith. The religion centres in the heavenly gods and the animistic divinities are far less prominent. There can be little doubt that among the gods reverenced were Varuṇa, Mitra, Soma, Aryaman, Indra, the Aśvins (i.e. the Dioskouroi), and two semi-divine figures, Vivasvant and Yama. All occur in both literatures except Varuṇa, Indra, and the Aśvins. These are not definitely vouched for by the *Avesta*,[2] but they are named in an inscription found by Winckler at Boghaz Keui in

[1] See Keith on *The Early History of the Indo-Iranians*, *Bhandarkar C.V.*, 81.

[2] Yet Indra and Nāsatya (i.e. the Aśvins) occur as demons in the mythology of the *Avesta*.

Asia Minor and believed to date from 1400 B.C.;[1] and there are so many points of resemblance between Ahura Mazdah, the God of Zoroaster, and the Varuṇa of the *Ṛigveda* that one is almost driven to believe the two to be identical in origin.[2] There were three forms of sacrifice in use among the early people, the shedding of oblations of grain and milk on the sacred fire, the setting forth of basins of an intoxicating beverage (Sansk. *soma*, Avestan, *haoma*) for the gods to drink, and the sacrifice of animals. Soma had already been deified, and the priests had begun to sing hymns as an accompaniment to the ritual with which it was offered. The presence in the *Avesta* of a considerable number of ritual terms and designations of priests, which are exact equivalents of technical words and phrases found in the Vedas,[3] proves that the basis of the liturgy and the ritual of the Vedic and the Zoroastrian religions had already taken shape. One most remarkable conception, the idea of law physical and moral as a fixed divine order, was formed at a very early date. It is already found in Persian proper names at a very early date, possibly 1600 B.C., in the form *arta*, and it appears in the *Ṛigveda* as *ṛita*, and in the *Avesta* in the form *asha*.

The time when the people fell into two parts is unknown. Some scholars would give it an extremely early date, while others assign it to the middle of the second millenium B.C.

§ 3. Hindus wrote no formal history at any period; for the early centuries there are no archaeological remains that throw any light on the course of events; nor is any definite information provided by nations outside India; so that the religious and epic literature forms the only sources of information available. Yet, though it is impossible to write the history, it is possible to learn much about the religion of that early time from these ancient books.

[1] It mentions Mitra, Varuṇa, Indra, Nāsatya (i.e. the Aśvins) as gods. Thus the high antiquity of Varuṇa is assured.

[2] Moulton, *EZ.* 61; Bloomfield, *RV.* 132 ff.

[3] Hillebrandt, *RL.* 11; Haug, *AB.* I. 61.

In this chapter we deal with the development of the religion from the moment when the tribes entered India down to the time when the doctrine of transmigration and karma arose, and we divide the whole period into three sections, in order to exhibit more clearly the growth of ideas and institutions.

i. *Rik*, I–IX.

§ 4. The *Ṛigveda*, the earliest literature of India, is a large collection of hymns connected in various ways with the sacrifices, the domestic ceremonies, and the religious speculation of the time. These hymns were composed by the invading Aryan tribes, at last severed from their brothers who were destined to produce Zoroaster and make Persia famous. When the earliest hymns were composed, they were settled in the territories forming the basin of the upper Indus and its tributaries; but thereafter they gradually spread farther east.

But the invading Aryans, tall in stature and of fair complexion, did not form the main population. Scattered about among them and around them and over the plains of North India were innumerable tribes of short, dark people with whom they were frequently at war, and whom they called Dasyus and Dāsas. The hymns of the *Ṛigveda* give no indication that the Aryan tribes thought of themselves as being strangers in India or as being in any way related with another people away to the west. They seem to regard themselves as belonging to the soil on which they live. On the other hand, they are certainly very conscious of the differences between themselves and the Dāsas, and they regard their hostility towards them as not only natural but inevitable. These two races represent the chief elements in the ethnology of India to this day, and from them and the mutual influence they have exercised on each other have come, in the main, the civilization and the religion of India. In the study of the evolution of the religion of India we shall constantly be tempted to give our undivided attention to the Aryan race and community;

but to neglect the large part played throughout the history by the aborigines is to fail to grasp facts of great significance.

§ 5. In the following sentences we combine the few fragments of information given in the hymns about the dark tribes. They are said to have a black skin, and the difference in colour (*varṇa*) between them and the fair Aryans is frequently referred to. They are called *anās*, which probably means 'noseless', i.e. snub-nosed. They were arranged in clans; they had considerable wealth; and they built forts for themselves, frequently on hills; but there is no reason to think that in civilization they were at all comparable with the Aryans. The differences between them and the Aryans on which the hymns lay most stress are religious. The following epithets are applied to them: 'not sacrificing', 'devoid of rites', 'addicted to strange vows', 'god-hating', 'without devotion'; and they are probably the people referred to as *śiśna-devāḥ*, 'those whose god is a phallus'. As many of these people were captured by the Aryans in war and reduced to slavery, the word *dāsa* came to bear the meaning of 'slave'.

§ 6. The picture which the hymns enable us to form of the Aryans shows us an early but not a primitive people; for they had made considerable progress in material civilization. Yet they were still a simple race; for they had neither coinage nor writing, and had little idea of number or measure. Their trade existed only as barter, the cow being the unit of exchange. They lived in wooden houses and built small forts on hills, to which they retired when hard pressed in war.

There was no caste among the Aryan tribes at this time. We certainly find a triple division of the people—warriors, priests, and commons; but there was no hard-and-fast law prohibiting intermarriage and commanding each son to follow his father's occupation. Yet the aristocratic warriors and priests stood out very distinctly from the common people, and it is only of the aristocracy that we have anything like adequate information. Though in race, religion, and language the Aryan tribes were one, they had not reached the idea of forming themselves into a nation; nor had they a sovereign or a war-leader. Each tribe was independent and had its chief, who presided over his people in peace and led them in war. War led occasionally to a coalition of tribes.

Their literature shows that this people had a striking genius for language. Alone among all the languages of Indo-European speech their tongue, with the cultured literary language known as Sanskrit which grew out of it, retains each element in easily recognizable form. It has thus proved of very signal service to the science of philology.

§ 7. The *Ṛigveda*, which is not only the first monument of the Indian genius but the earliest literature produced within the Indo-European family of peoples, is a collection of 1,017 hymns (with eleven extra uncanonical pieces) distributed in ten books. Perhaps we shall find our way into the significance of the collection most readily if we attempt to sketch the way in which it seems to have come into existence.

We have seen above that, already in the Indo-Iranian period, the exhilarating drink made from the soma-plant had been deified, that a special ritual in which this divine drink was offered to the gods was in use, and that the singing of a hymn was an integral part of the ritual. This is the historical tap-root of the *Ṛigveda*. The invaders of India carried these customs with them, and continued the composition of hymns for the Soma-ritual in their new country. Since the hymn was sung, the priest who sang the hymn was called the Singer, *Udgātṛi*. But poetry and the hymn would not be restricted to a single use. Hence a custom arose, probably after the Aryans had entered India, that the leading priest, the Sacrificer, *Hotṛi*, who was responsible for offerings made in the fire and for animal-sacrifice, should recite, in honour of the god he was worshipping, a poem or hymn of praise, *Ṛich*. Then, as the ritual increased in detail, an assistant was appointed to undertake the manual acts of sacrificing (*adhvara*). He was therefore called *Adhvaryu*, and the recitation of praises became the Hotṛi's chief duty.[1] Although the ritual was now divided into three strands, there were no distinct orders of priests corresponding to these divisions. Each officiant was merely called *Hotṛi*, *Udgātṛi*, or *Adhvaryu*, for the time being, according to the duty he undertook at the sacrifice.[2]

§ 8. Men believed that the sacrifices were mighty to influence the gods and bring down gifts from them. Therefore every chieftain and noble among the Aryans was eager to secure the help of a skilled priest, and was glad to pay him handsomely for services which brought victory and wealth from the gods. Hence we find existing among the people a number of priestly families of high standing and influence. The priest taught his sons the precious secret lore which enabled him by conducting sacrifices in the right way to win the favour of the gods for his patrons. It was in these priestly families that the composition of hymns to the gods was practised. Each priest did his utmost to produce as beautiful a hymn as possible, in order to please and move the divinity for whom the sacrifice was held. Then the priest taught his sons the best hymns he had composed; so that in each family there arose a body of hymns which were greatly treasured, and were orally transmitted from father to son, along with the directions for the work of the altar.

Naturally, the priestly families competed for the patronage of the greatest chieftains and the wealthiest nobles, and in the struggle found the quality of their hymns a matter of vital importance. We must therefore picture to ourselves a time of eager poetic emulation, during which metres, stanzas, and refrains were gradually perfected and polished. A very dignified and expressive literary dialect was thus gradually evolved. This dialect is closely related, it is true, to the common vernacular, yet it employs stately words and phrases

[1] Haug, *AB*. I. 17.

[2] Muir, *OST*. V. 350, with a reference to a passage in Yāska; Hillebrandt, *RL*. 13.

which would rise to the lips only in moments of exaltation, and here and there uses well-known and effective archaisms. Thus there arose the first literary dialect of India. As time went on, the influence of the priests tended to increase. The ritual became steadily more complex, and the need of skilled sacerdotal help more pressing. Naturally, hymns were written for the various festivals, anniversaries, and sacrifices. The literature thus tended to become more artificial. The hymn prepared for a special sacrifice, and written so as to fit into its chief incidents or features, would be more appropriate, but probably less inspired than a hymn arising from a spontaneous outburst of religious feeling.

How the father taught his sons the family heritage of technical lore and hymns we do not know. Each experienced priest probably conducted a sort of rudimentary school for the benefit of his sons and nephews, in which he taught them orally all the hymns and priestly lore traditional in the family.[1]

§ 9. The *Ṛigveda*[2] preserves seven groups of hymns which belonged to as many families. Each of these bears the name of a patriarch,[3] and to him in each case most of the hymns in the family collection are ascribed. As authors of hymns these patriarchs are called *Ṛishis*, seers. The names of the eponym Ṛishis of the seven families are: Gṛitsamada, Viśvāmitra, Vāmadeva, Atri, Bharadvāja, Vasishṭha, Kaṇva. There were other families which possessed hymns, but, clearly, these seven were the most famous of all. It seems certain that these family collections grew up gradually and that many singers contributed to each collection; for each family was as it were a distinct school of poetry.

But a moment came when, by some means or other, the hymn-collections belonging to the six families named first

[1] See *ṚV.* VII. 103.

[2] For the growth of the *Ṛik* see Macdonell, 40 ff.

[3] That is, is spoken of as the Atri book, the Vasishṭha book, &c., because the name in each case occurs in many of the hymns of the book as the name of the seer or of the family of which he is the spokesman.

above were all taught together in a single school. Each collection was still kept distinct; but the collections were taught in order, the one after the other, to the same pupils, instead of being each retained and handed down in a single family. There was thus formed the body of poetry now contained in Books II–VII of the *Ṛigveda*. How this unification was effected we do not know. The emergence of a very powerful chieftain, determined at all costs to have the whole of the best poetry at the command of his own chief priest, would account for it; and as the Brahmanic culture first took definite shape in the holy land of Kurukshetra, the land of the Kurus, the modern Sirhind, one is tempted to think that it was some vigorous Kuru prince who commanded that the hymns of the six families should all be taught together; but there is no distinct evidence.

When brought together in the school, the six collections seem to have been taught in ascending order, each succeeding collection containing more hymns than its predecessor: but later interpolations, by increasing the number of the hymns irregularly, have somewhat disturbed the arrangement. The hymns in each of the six collections are in the main arranged according to a common method. They are distributed in groups according to the gods they are addressed to, and within each of these groups they are arranged in descending order according to the number of stanzas each contains.

§ 10. Later, a large number of hymns disposed in nine groups was introduced into the school. Each group was believed to be the work of one poet[1] or family, all the nine being quite distinct from the six already mentioned. These hymns were given the first place in the whole body of literature belonging to the school, being taught before the six original collections. They now form the latter half of Book I of the *Ṛigveda*, beginning with the fifty-first hymn. The whole collection now amounted to Ib + II–VII.

[1] The names are Savya, Nodhas, Parāśara, Gotama, Kutsa, Kakshīvān, Paruchchhepa, Dīrghatamas, Agastya.

Still later two further additions were made to the hymn material of the school. As these two collections each contain a large number of hymns from the last of the seven famous families mentioned above,[1] the family of Kaṇva, and have also a number of common features, it is likely that they had a common origin, and were introduced to the great school at the same time. One group was prefixed to the old material, the other affixed. So that the body of sacred poetry now stood thus: Ia + Ib + II–VII + VIII.

Then the ninth book came into existence. It consists exclusively of Soma hymns dedicated to Soma Pavamāna, 'clearly-flowing Soma'. Hymns which belonged to each of the seven great families represented in Books II–VIII are gathered together here. This collection is thus a sort of preliminary *Sāmaveda*. Though collected later than the hymns of Books I–VIII, the hymns of Book IX are perhaps as early as any in the whole collection.

It is probable that by this time the whole body of hymns of praise (*ṛichas*), regarded by the priests as precious knowledge (*veda*), was called *Ṛigveda*.

We now attempt to understand in outline the religion reflected in Books I–IX of the *Ṛik*.

§ 11. The following are the names of most of the noticeable gods of the Aryans, disposed as the people were accustomed to arrange them, in three categories, according as their function was exercised upon earth, in the region of the air, or in the heaven of light:

Lower gods: Agni, Soma.

Middle gods: Indra, Maruts, Rudra, Parjanya, Vāyu, the Ṛibhus.

Upper gods: Vishṇu, Sūrya, Savitṛi, Pūshan, the Aśvins, Ushas, Aditi and her three sons, Varuṇa, Mitra, Aryaman.

But these three lists are not exhaustive. Several other divinities are named; waters, rivers, and mountains are recognized as divine; and tools and implements, especially the sacrificial

[1] § 9.

implements, receive adoration and are expected to hear and answer prayer.

Indra is the most prominent god in the *Ṛigveda*; for more than one-fourth of the hymns are dedicated to him. He is primarily the regent of the sky. Young and strong, brilliant as the sun, ruddy and golden, he comes riding in his far-shining car to the sacrifice, eats the flesh of bulls and buffaloes, drinks vast quantities of soma, and listens to the hymns recited and chanted in his honour. These stimulate his vital energies and rouse him to his utmost courage. He then assails with thunderbolt and lightning-flash the malevolent demons who keep the rain locked up and swiftly defeats them. The cloud-castles are stormed, and the waters, set free, rush down in fierce torrents on the earth. Naturally this heavenly warrior became the national god of the Aryan invaders. He is praised as the monarch of heaven and earth, the controller of the destinies of men, and the friend and helper of those who offer him sacrifice.

Agni and Soma, who come next after Indra in prominence in the *Ṛigveda*, are also nature-divinities, the one Fire, the other the intoxicating drink made from the soma-plant; but they both owe their great position to their connexion with the ritual. The two chief forms of sacrificing were the offering of milk, butter, grain, and flesh in the altar-fire, and the setting out of great bowls of soma on the sacred grass for the gods to drink. Since through the fire the offerings are presented to the gods, Agni is the great priest of the gods. Soma lives in the divine plant of that name which is the drink of the gods in heaven, and which, transplanted to earth, exhilarates man and delights all the gods at the sacrifices. Both gods are spoken of as doing the work of creator and upholder of the universe. The hymns of the ninth book were sung at the sacrifices in honour of Soma.

Varuṇa is the noblest figure in the *Ṛigveda*. He is connected with the day-sky, the night-sky, and the waters. But he has lofty cosmical functions as well. He upholds heaven and earth, and he is the supporter of all beings. He wields all the powers of *ṛita*, i.e. divine law, both physical and moral; therefore his ordinances are fixed and can never be shaken. All natural things are subject to them, and he watches to see whether men obey his lofty laws. He rewards the righteous, punishes the wrongdoer (frequently with dropsy), and releases the sinner from his sin when he comes with prayer and oblation. He is the wise guardian of immortality.

But the most significant trait in his character is this, that he is always righteous. We have already seen that Varuṇa is the Vedic counterpart of Ahura Mazdah of the religion of Zoroaster. He must have been a god of distinctly ethical character in the period before the Indo-Iranian people fell apart, and in his prominence in the *Ṛigveda* and in the lofty attributes which he wears we must see evidence of an Indian development parallel to Zoroaster's selection of Mazdah to be the one god of his high ethical monotheism. It begins to look as if the two movements may have been roughly contemporaneous; for scholars are more and more inclined to assign to Zoroaster a date about 1000 B.C. rather than the traditional date of 600 B.C.[1] But Varuṇa failed to reach supremacy; the warrior Indra became the leading divinity of the *Ṛigveda*; and India failed to develop an ethical theism.

The religion of the *Ṛigveda* is probably the most interesting polytheism reflected in any literature. It certainly has not the grace and charm of the pantheon of the Homeric poems; but it stands nearer the origin of the gods, and enables us to see them at the most significant stage of their evolution. All the great, and nearly all the minor gods, are deified natural phenomena, and the interest of the presentation springs from the fact that they are still identified with those glorious things and yet are distinguished from them. They are still thought of as being actually dawn, sun, moon, sky, rain, wind, thunder, fire: men actually offer sacrifice to the

[1] Moulton, *TM.* 6, 13; Oldenberg, *LU.* 4.

reddening dawn, to the sun as he mounts the heavens, and to the crackling fire on the hearth; yet each god is conceived as a glorious living being who has his home in heaven, and who comes sailing in his far-shining car to the sacrifice and sits down on the sacred grass to hear his own praises recited and sung and to receive the offerings. Further, each divinity is held to have influence on things far beyond that phase of the physical world which is his source. He is believed to be able to give his worshippers blessings of many kinds, victory, prosperity, cattle, wealth, children. The greatest gods are connected with the creation and upholding of the world, and Varuṇa holds in his hands all divine law, both physical and moral. This ambiguous position then—each glittering god still struggling to release his gorgeous wings from the clinging chrysalis of his natural source—gives them their peculiar charm and interest, and shows us mythology in the making; but it also prevents the development of distinct personality in the gods and makes them natural rather than moral beings.

Though there is much superstition in the *Ṛigveda*, and even the great gods, with the exception of Varuṇa, are not beings of holy character, yet the black arts are held in check, and human sacrifices, cruel rites, eroticism, and other horrors are noticeably absent. The religion is, on the whole, a healthy, happy system. Neither asceticism nor austerity, neither pessimism nor philosophy, disturbs the sunshine of that early day.

§ 12. The worship reflected in the hymns circles round the great sacrifices, which are to be carefully distinguished from the simple oblations which each householder offered in the household fire daily. The great sacrifices were not public acts of worship attended by all the people, like the sacrifices of Israel, of Greece, or of Rome.

A chieftain, a noble, or any other wealthy man simply employed the necessary priests and had the rites carried out for himself. A sacrifice held by a chieftain would have a sort of public significance, if it was intended to secure prosperity for his rule or victory in war; yet, even in that case, it was a personal act, and benefited, in the first instance, the sacrificer and his family alone.

The sacrifices were held in the open air or in a shed erected for the purpose near the house of the sacrificer. No temples or sacred places existed in those days. The word *vedi*, i. e. altar, seems to denote in the *Ṛigveda* the area on which the rite was carried out. It was strewn with sacred grass, that the gods might come and sit down on it. Upon the *vedi* the oblations were laid out; and there also were the sacred fires prepared. The chief oblations were milk, melted butter, grain, and cakes. The Adhvaryu shed them on the fire and muttered his formulae the while. At certain points in the ceremonies the Hotṛi recited hymns.

In the Soma-sacrifice the priests brought the twigs of the soma plant, expressed the juice with the press-stones, purified it, mixed it with milk, and then poured it into basins and set it out on the altar for the gods to drink. The soma-hymns were sung by the Udgātṛi while the Adhvaryu was busy with these ritual acts. The sacrificer, being by the rites admitted to the company of the gods, then drank of the divine beverage, and was thereby made a new man.[1] The priest also drank of the soma.

Animal sacrifice—the goat, the ox, the cow, the ram, or the horse—accompanied both the fire-oblations and the soma-rites. The animals were killed and cut up according to rule, and pieces were laid out on the altar, while certain parts were burned in the fire. The horse-sacrifice had already a highly developed ritual, several hymns specially composed for it being found in the *Ṛik*.[2] The flesh was divided between the sacrificer and the priests.

Without the help of skilled priests, these great sacrifices were quite impossible. Hence an advanced sacerdotal training already existed, and is alluded to in the hymns. By the time the nine books of the *Ṛik* were gathered, the priests

[1] Haug, *AB*. I. 60. [2] I. 162, 163; IV. 38, 39, 40.

formed a distinct profession, though they had not yet developed into a caste.

§ 13. The boons which the worshippers ask for are in most cases material blessings, prosperity, wealth, cattle, rich crops, chariots, wives, children, health, long life, protection from danger, victory in war, and rich spoil. Yet not infrequently immortality is prayed for. There are also numerous prayers for release from sin and its consequences. Usually sacrifice, a hymn, or faithful worship, is made the ground forthe gift of pardon and health, but once or twice something approaching real penitence appears. Yet the overwhelming impression made by the *Ṛigveda* is that the spirit of religion is worldly and indeed tends to be mercenary.

§ 14. There are many passages in which the highest cosmical and divine functions are attributed to Indra, or Agni, or Soma, or some other god. How was it possible to attribute these lofty powers now to one god, now to another? To describe this pose of mind Max Müller coined the word Henotheism, the elevation to supremacy of one god at a time. While the poet invokes the god, he is to him the only possible Supreme, and he does not stint his praises by any thought of another; yet the following day he may ascribe the same lofty powers to a second divinity. To this may be added the thought that, monotheism being the only fully rational faith, the human mind, in proportion to its purity, reverence, and openness, is unconsciously drawn towards it. But we must also recognize that the gods of the *Ṛigveda* do not stand out in clear individuality and distinctness the one from the other. They are personifications of nature, lack character, and tend to melt into one another.

ii. *Ṛik*, X; *Sāman; Early Yajus.*

§ 15. There followed a considerable interval of time during which these nine books were used as the hymn-book of the tribes. The life of the people was expanding, and they were extending their hold on the country. They had now reached the upper waters of the Jumna; and the fertile band of country between the Jumna and the Ganges was being occupied farther and farther south. Many of the better aboriginal tribes had been brought into friendly relations with the Aryans, and were settling down beside them to serve as labourers or as household servants. These accepted aborigines were called Śūdras. The position of the priests was steadily becoming more prominent and assured. In consequence, social distinctions were becoming deeper and more marked. The priests were more and more unwilling to intermarry with the other classes; and the Aryan community as a whole wished to avoid mixture with aboriginals, both those accepted as Śūdras and those excluded as Outcastes.

The power of the priests over the gods was more and more recognized, their services more highly appreciated. Hence they were now frequently asked to assist in marriage and funeral ceremonies, which in earlier days were conducted entirely by the house-father himself, and to perform certain magic rites for individuals, both men and women. Religious unrest was producing philosophical speculation and also a tendency to the practice of austerities. Naturally this varied and growing activity led to the composition of new hymns. Many of them were meant for the old sacrifices, others for use at weddings, funerals, and the feast in commemoration of the fathers; some dealt with those religious and philosophical questions which were beginning to trouble the advancing community; and others were composed for use as incantations in sorcery and magic.

§ 16. Finally, some scholar gathered together a very varied collection of 191 pieces, and it was introduced into the schools and taught as the last section of the oral curriculum of hymns. There were now ten groups of hymns, the ten books of the *Ṛigveda*. As the first book also contains 191 hymns, the whole became a noble series of ten collections, the first and the last balancing each other in the number of their hymns. There can be no doubt that the hymns of the tenth book belong to several different periods. Some of them are quite old; most are clearly subsequent to the hymns of the first nine books; and a few are very late indeed. The ninetieth hymn, usually called the Hymn of Creation, contains a number of developed philosophical concepts, refers to the Caste system, and mentions the names of at least three of the Vedas. Thus we must recognize that, when the collection was completed, the *Sāmaveda* and the *Yajurveda* were already in existence, at least in some primitive form, and that the Caste system was at least taking shape.

§ 17. The interpretation of the *Ṛigveda* is not yet scientifically certain in all respects. No ancient commentary on the whole work has come down to us, though there are manuals dealing with certain groups of phenomena, which date from 500 B.C. or earlier. The earliest commentary preserved on the text as a whole was written in the fourteenth century, by the great scholar Sāyaṇa. Thus there need be no surprise if there are many passages in the hymns which are still incomprehensible.

The age of the *Ṛigveda* is still very uncertain. Max Müller in his *Ancient Sanskrit Literature*, published in 1859, suggested 1200 to 1000 B.C. as the lowest limits that could be postulated for the composition of the Vedic hymns, and 1000 to 800 B.C. for the formation of the collections. Others are inclined to believe that longer time is required for the development; while a few are convinced that the hymns imply the lapse of thousands of years. Scholars seem to incline towards Müller's dates rather than to these extreme figures.[1]

§ 18. With the increasing elaboration of the sacrifices, and the consequent emergence of many new duties for the priests, division of labour became unavoidable. It proved more and more necessary that a man should restrict himself to the functions of a *Hotṛi*, an *Udgātṛi*, or an *Adhvaryu*, instead of

[1] Müller, *ASL.* 572; Macdonell, 11–12; Winternitz, I. 246 ff.; Thibaut, *Hindustan Review*, Jan. 1904; Jacobi, *JRAS.* 1909, 721; Oldenberg, *JRAS.* 1909, 1095; Keith, *TS.* I. clxvi; *JRAS.* 1909, 1100.

attempting to become proficient in all three. Hence the need for a distinct education for each type of priest made itself felt. Perhaps in the formation of the ninth book of the *Ṛik*, which consists exclusively of Soma-hymns, we may trace the beginnings of the movement. But a time came when something more was required.

In the case of the man who sang the strophes at the Soma-sacrifice, the Udgātṛi, two forms of training were required. He had to learn to sing, readily and accurately, all the tunes that were used in the many distinct Soma-sacrifices, and he had also to know which strophes were required for each sacrifice and in what order they were sung. Therefore, that the young priest might master all the tunes thoroughly and have any one at command at any moment, each was connected with a single stanza of the right metre, and the teacher made his pupils sing it over and over again, until tune and stanza were firmly imprinted, in indissoluble association, in the memory. In the Kauthuma school at least, the Udgātṛi student was taught 585 tunes, married to as many single verses. The whole collection of stanzas was called the *Ārchika*, i.e. the book of praises. For mnemonic reasons, the stanzas are arranged in several large groups according to the deities to whom they are dedicated, and the groups are subdivided into sets of ten. Then the strophes used in the ritual of the Soma-sacrifice were arranged in the order in which they were sung, and were taught to Udgātṛi students in this form instead of the *Ṛigveda*. The practical value of this step will be at once apparent. The young priest, in committing the strophes to memory, learnt also at which sacrifices and at what point in each sacrifice they were used. There are 400 strophes in the collection, the great majority consisting of three stanzas each, the whole comprising 1,225 stanzas. This collection was called the *Uttarārchika*, or second praise-book. All the stanzas contained in the two Ārchikas, with the exception of seventy-five, are taken from the *Ṛigveda*; so that, from the point of view of the hymns, these books are of little interest in comparison with the *Ṛik.* These two, the musical collection and the sacrificial liturgy, were taught in special schools; and, since the knowledge, *veda*, which they taught was the songs or chants, *sāmāni*, required for the sacrifice, it was called the *Sāmaveda*, and the schools were called schools of the *Sāmaveda.* In those early days the music, as well as the stanzas, was taught orally; but, at a considerably later date, when writing began to be used in the schools for various purposes, tune-books, called *gānas*, were prepared. In these the tunes were indicated by a system of musical notes, and the words of the hymns were set down precisely as they were sung, with many vowels prolonged, many syllables repeated, and other extra-textual syllables interpolated at various places. These interpolated syllables, called *stobhas*, praises—e. g. *hun*, *hin*, *hai*, *hau*, *hoyi*, *huva*, *hoi*, &c.—are the exact counterpart of the *jubila* interpolated in Plain-song in the ninth and tenth centuries.[1] There were two gānas connected with the *Ārchika*, one *Grāmageyagāna*, for use in the village, the other *Āraṇyagāna*, for use in the case of those texts which, for one reason or another, were held so sacred as to be sung only in the seclusion of the forest.

§ 19. From the earliest days it had been customary for the sacrificer, the Hotṛi, to accompany each ritual-act of the sacrifice with some short phrase, either to indicate its significance, its purpose, or the god for whom it was meant, or to invoke some blessing with it, or to prevent the act from having a dangerous result. The priest muttered these phrases, taking care that he should not be overheard. They were of the nature of incantations and dedications rather than prayer and praise. When the recitation of hymns of praise became the chief duty of the Hotṛi priest, and the working-priest, the Adhvaryu, was appointed to do the manual acts, the latter naturally took over also the duty of muttering these ritual formulae: the name is *yajus*, plural *yajūṁshi.* Rather later still, it became customary for the Adhvaryu to utter, at certain points in the ritual, in addition to the old formulae,

[1] Fox Strangways, *Music of Hindustan*, 255.

praises and prayers consisting of stanzas taken from hymns of the *Ṛigveda* or from other sources.

Probably about the time when the schools of the *Sāmaveda* came into existence, or rather later, the training of the Adhvaryu took a fixed traditional form in special schools conducted for the purpose. The essential part of the tradition was the body of ritual formulae in prose and the prayers in verse which accompanied the ritual acts; but detailed instruction, in one form or another, must have been also given about the ritual acts themselves The mass of material having for its nucleus the formulae, *yajūṁshi*, which accompanied the ritual, gave the Adhvaryu the knowledge, *veda*, necessary for his work, and was therefore called *Yajurveda*.

§ 20. The formation of these special schools for Udgātṛis and Adhvaryus necessarily led to the old schools of the *Ṛigveda* becoming special training-schools for the Hotṛi priests. We must also conclude that, from the time of the rise of these new schools, there were three distinct orders of priests; but there was no rule precluding a priest from exercising the functions of two, or even of all the three orders, provided he had acquired the necessary training. The mass of men, however, would be content with the curriculum of a single school. By this time the priests had become a closed caste and called themselves Brāhmans. Each Brāhman priest received his education in one of the three types of schools and was known thereafter as a member of the school.

§ 21. In our first survey we dealt with the first nine books of the *Ṛik*; so that the fresh literature which we now examine is the tenth book of the *Ṛik*, the *Sāman* and the original *Yajurveda*. For practical purposes we may take Books I–XVIII of the *White Yajus* as representing, with fair accuracy, the extent of the original work. Since nearly the whole text of the *Sāmaveda* is taken unchanged from the *Ṛik*, it is not of so much importance as the other two sources. The most prominent features of the new situation are these: the community is now sharply divided into four groups by caste distinctions—Brāhmans, Kshatriyas, Vaiśyas, Śūdras; and there are three orders of priests, each possessing a Veda taught in schools belonging to the order. The religion reflected in the literature is wider and more varied than it appeared in the glimpse we had in the *Ṛik*, I–IX. The prose formulae muttered by the Adhvaryu in accompaniment to the ritual acts are clearly a very old constituent of the cult, older indeed than the hymns; but the actual formulae contained in the *Yajurveda* are probably of very varied age: some may be very old, others quite new; so that we must be cautious about attributing the whole to very early times. But, although the individual phrases are of indeterminate age, the fundamental thought involved in them, especially the magic character of the whole system, is clearly old. With this agrees the magic power attributed to the tunes sung by the Udgātṛi priests, and to the metres of the hymns. Hence the presence in the tenth book of the *Ṛigveda* of a considerable number of incantations for use in private magic rites probably does not indicate any new access of faith in these operations, but merely an increased willingness on the part of priests trained in the schools to officiate in these ceremonies. The priests are more prominent than ever; for they are now an organized body, the chief of the four castes, and are believed to wield almost limitless supernatural power. The pantheon has not changed materially in the interval; but priestly authority and magical conceptions seem to be gradually weakening the position of the gods, and there is evidence of the existence of considerable religious unrest and scepticism and of various efforts made to cope with it.

The gods and their attributes appear in our source in all essentials the same as they do in the first nine books of the *Ṛigveda*; yet certain changes are visible. A few new gods make their appearance; some divinities, notably *Ushas*, *Varuṇa*, and *Parjanya*, receive less attention than formerly, while others have risen to new prominence. Of these the most noteworthy are *Vishṇu* and *Rudra*, who have already begun that mysterious upward movement, which gradually raised them above all their Vedic compeers, and made them the two supreme divinities of modern Hinduism. So far as our evidence goes, it would seem as if Vishnu owed his first elevation to his being identified with the sacrifice by the Adhvaryu priests. In that sense his name occurs in hundreds of passages in the *Yajurveda*. One of the more prominent elements of the same work is the *Śatarudrīya*, a famous hymn of praise to Rudra, which is decisive evidence of his growing importance.

§ 22. The existence of the three Vedas enables us to get a more vivid idea of the sacrifices which formed almost the whole cult of the gods. The great sacrifices were either obligatory or voluntary. Of the obligatory rites the most noteworthy were the New Moon and the Full Moon sacrifices and the sacrifice to Ancestors observed every month, and a few similar observances which occurred less often. Of the voluntary ceremonies the most elaborate and expensive were the Soma-sacrifices. The Aśvamedha or Horse-sacrifice was meant to secure all blessings for a prince, including even imperial sway. Another type of ceremony, which any wealthy man might undertake, was the Agnichayana, or the building of a fire altar of great elaboration of design.

§ 23. There are a number of hymns in the tenth book of the *Ṛik*, which seem to have been taught in the schools with a view to being used in the contests of wit which closed the sacrifices. There are two collections of riddles, and about a dozen dialogues; but the largest and most interesting group are speculative pieces springing from the new religious situation. One is a hymn in praise of faith, one describes the ascetic, and another deals with *tapas* or self-mortification, while the remainder, eleven in number, form the fountain-head of Indian philosophy. In our first survey we learned that priests trained in the schools had begun to practise private magic and to use certain hymns contained in the *Ṛigveda* as spells. By the time the tenth book was compiled things had gone farther: a large number of incantations are included in it.

There is no hint of the doctrine of transmigration in our sources. Men live and die once. They pray that they may live a hundred autumns. When good men die, Yama guides them to his heavenly home and there they live in immortality and joy. They are then called the Fathers.

iii. *Brāhmaṇas, Atharvan, Āraṇyakas.*

§ 24. We have already seen that a number of spells for use in magic are contained in the *Ṛik.* The character of these poems proves that the old-world incantations which the Aryans, in common with other Indo-European peoples, had been accustomed to use had, in the main at least, given way before a new type of spell, written in polished language and metre, on the model of the hymns to the gods. Doubtless, hundreds of these were being used by sorcerers, exorcists, and magicians, although only a few found their way into the hymn-book of the priests; and the process of composition continued after the canon of the *Ṛigveda* was closed. The incantation-priest had no lack of wealthy clients ready to pay well for his magic arts and poetical charms instinct with supernatural power. Hence numerous hymns from the *Ṛigveda* were turned to these purposes; philosophic poems were perverted to more mysterious uses, their sounding phrases and incomprehensible concepts rendering them most formidable to the ear; and many new incantations were composed to fit into the detailed ritual of magic, both black and white. The man of muttered charms was usually summoned also to do the priestly duties in the domestic ceremonies, which were observed at the time of birth, marriage, death, and such like.

§ 25. Then, during the period of the *Brāhmaṇas*, a school was formed for the training of this class of priests, and quite naturally a great collection of these incantations was made the text-book of the school. This text-book is the *Atharvaveda.* It has come down to us in two recensions, named

Śaunakīya and *Paippalāda*. The former is the text in ordinary use, and it alone has been edited, translated, and examined in detail. A single birch-bark manuscript of the Paippalāda was found in Kashmir in 1874, and a facsimile reproduction has been published. There is a good deal of difference between the two recensions in the way in which the hymns are arranged; and about one-eighth or one-ninth of the contents of the Paippalāda MS. is fresh material, found neither in the Śaunakīya recension nor in any other Vedic collection. Since so little investigation has been carried out on the new text, we shall confine our attention to the Śaunakīya or Vulgate.

It is probable that the *Atharvaveda* was built up to its present proportions in various stages, but we do not know the history. Each of the two recensions consists of twenty books, but the order by no means corresponds. In the Vulgate it is clear that Books XIX and XX are late additions. Books I to XVIII fall into three divisions. The first covers Books I to VII, and consists in the main of short hymns, arranged in accordance with the number of stanzas they contain, and without reference to their subject-matter. The second contains Books VIII to XII and consists of long hymns on miscellaneous subjects. In the third division, Books XIII to XVIII, each book consists of hymns which are marked by essential unity of subject. Various attempts have been made to decide how these three groups were brought together, but no unanimity has yet been reached.

Scholars point out that a number of the shorter spells of the *Atharvaveda* agree in purpose and method, and to some extent also in form, with charms found in the folk-lore of other nations of the Indo-European race; so that the roots of the practices of this Veda go very far back indeed. About 1,200 of the 6,000 stanzas contained in the work are taken from the *Ṛigveda*. But the bulk of the fresh material is of later origin.[1] Part of it is in prose, the rest in verse. The

[1] So Oldenberg, *RV.* 15: Keith agrees.

compilation of the eighteen books took place long after the completion of the *Ṛigveda*, during the period of the Brāhmaṇas.

For a long time the Atharvan collection held a very humble position as compared with the three sacrificial Vedas. It was not accepted as a Veda at all. The *trayīvidyā*, triple knowledge, was all that men recognized. To this day in certain parts of South India it is almost unknown.

§ 26. The priestly schools soon became great and learned associations each with a splendid reputation. The student had first of all to learn the Veda of his school with perfect accuracy from the lips of his teacher. He had then, in the second place, to receive a great deal of instruction as to his duties at the altar, and numerous explanations of the meaning of the hymns, the ritual acts, and such like. The instructions were called *vidhi*, the explanations *arthavāda*. For some time these lectures were given by the teacher in an unfettered way in his own language; but gradually in each school the material took more definite form, and finally was handed down in stereotyped language from teacher to pupil, generation after generation. Naturally, it was in prose. Every piece of instruction of this type was called a *Brāhmaṇa*, either as being the utterance of a *Brāhman*, or as an exposition of religious truth (*brahman*). In contrast with these Brāhmaṇas, the hymns and prose formulae which were recited, sung, or muttered during the sacrifices were called *mantras*. The word *mantra* means originally religious thought, prayer, sacred utterance, but from an early date it also implied that the text was a weapon of supernatural power.

Since these Brāhmaṇa lectures were expositions of the sacrifice, the hymns, and the prayers, the teachers of the *Yajurveda* took the very natural course of inserting them at various points among the material on which they were meant to throw light. In the schools of the *Ṛik* and the *Sāman*, however, this course was not followed. The teachers were probably so impressed with the divine character of the hymn-collections that they felt they could not disturb the sacred arrangement of the text. In any case in both these schools the expository lectures were gathered into a separate collection, which was called *Brāhmaṇa*.

Then the teachers of the Vājasaneya school of the *Yajurveda* were led by this example to a similar course. They separated out all the Brāhmaṇa sections from the sacrificial formulae and the verses of their Veda, and formed a Veda and a Brāhmaṇa out of them. In this way the schools of the *Yajurveda* fell into two groups, and the old mixed collection of mantras and Brāhmaṇas was called the *Black Yajus*, while the new unmixed collection of hymns with its separate Brāhmaṇa was called the *White Yajus*. As the Brāhmaṇa material in each school was constantly growing, the Veda as handed down in the various schools of the *Black Yajus* soon showed considerable differences. It has come down to us in four distinct forms called *Saṁhitās*. See table below.

At a later date one of these schools of the *Black Yajus*, the Taittirīyas, followed the common practice thus far that, on the formation of a fresh body of Brāhmaṇa material, they did not introduce it into the already mixed Veda, but formed it into a separate *Brāhmaṇa*. This new book is really a continuation of the Brāhmaṇa material within the Saṁhitā of the school.

The continued branching of the schools, and the constant addition of fresh Brāhmaṇa material to the old, must have led in the long run to the existence of a very large number of Brāhmaṇas, differing more or less from one another. In the chances and changes of history, much of this literature has been lost. Thus, what survives to-day is but a small part of what once existed. The following table shows the various Saṁhitās of the *Yajurveda* which contain Brāhmaṇa material, and also the ancient Brāhmaṇas:

SAṀHITĀS AND BRĀHMAṆAS

Schools.	*Saṁhitās containing Brāhmaṇa material.*	*Brāhmaṇas.*
A. Ṛigveda		
1. The Aitareyins		1. *Aitareya*
2. The Kaushītakins		2. *Kaushītaki* or *Śāṅkhāyana*
B. Sāmaveda		
1. The Tāṇḍins		1. *a. Pañchaviṁśa* *b. Shaḍviṁśa* *c. Chhāndogya*
2. The Talavakāras		2. *Jaiminīya* or *Talavakāra* (including *Upanishad B.* and *Ārsheya B.*)
C. Yajurveda		
1. The Kāṭhakas	1. *Kāṭhaka*	1. *Kāṭhaka*, preserved in part in the *Taittirīya Āraṇyaka*
2. The Kapishṭhala-Kaṭhas	2. *Kapishṭhala-Kaṭha*	
3. The Maitrāyaṇīyas	3. *Maitrāyaṇī*	
4. The Taittirīyas	4. *Taittirīya*	4. *Taittirīya*
5. The Vājasaneyins		5. *Śatapatha*

§ 27. One's first reading of a Brāhmaṇa is an extraordinary experience. It seems as if the men who composed these interminable gossiping lectures had left realities far behind them, and were living in a dreary realm of shadowy gods and men and topsy-turvy morality and religion, in which nothing belongs to the world we know except the sacrificial meats and drinks and the fees paid to the priestly dreamers. Yet in the midst of this waste of arid ritualism and childish speculation one finds the beginnings of grammar, of astronomy, of etymology, and of the philosophy of the *Ātman*. There are also legends and narratives which are forerunners of the Epic, and numerous rules of conduct out of which finally arose the Hindu *dharma*. The Indian mind was by no means dead, although sacerdotalism was drunk with supremacy and in its folly and arrogance was hastening the day of revolt.

§ 28. In addition to the Brāhmaṇa portions of the *Black*

Yajurveda, only the following six Brāhmaṇas are ritual text-books of importance: *Aitareya*, *Kaushītaki*, *Pañchaviṁśa*, *Talavakāra*, *Taittirīya*, *Śatapatha*. The *Shaḍviṁśa* is an appendix to the *Pañchaviṁśa*, and the *Chhāndogya* deals only with domestic rites. It is impossible to set down this mass of material in strict chronological order, because each Brāhmaṇa is a collection of pieces of different age and origin; yet, if we omit the *Kapishṭhala-Kaṭha Saṁhitā* and the *Kāṭhaka B.*, which have survived only in fragments, the following represents, on the whole, the order in which these books arose: 1. The *Maitrāyaṇī*, *Kāṭhaka*, and *Taittirīya* Saṁhitās, which cannot be safely arranged in any chronological order; 2. the *Aitareya Brāhmaṇa*; 3. the *Pañchaviṁśa*; 4. the *Taittirīya*; 5. the *Jaiminīya*; 6. the *Kaushītaki*; 7. the *Śatapatha*.

§ 29. To the Brāhmaṇas there are appended chapters, written in the main in Brāhmaṇa language and style, but differing somewhat in contents. Usually these chapters begin with material scarcely distinguishable from the Brāhmaṇa itself, but gradually shade off through mystic allegory into philosophic speculation. Usually the ritualistic and allegorical parts are called *Āraṇyaka*, and the philosophic, *Upanishad*; but sometimes the whole receives the title *Upanishad*. The Upanishads will be dealt with in our next chapter; for in them first appears the mighty doctrine of transmigration and karma; but we consider the Āraṇyakas here. Parts of these 'Forest-treatises' (from *araṇya*, forest) describe the ritual and give incidental mystic explanations, and are thus indistinguishable from Brāhmaṇa teaching, except that here and there we meet chapters which add stringent rules to the effect that the rites are to be kept secret and carried out only for certain persons. Similar secrecy is sometimes enjoined in the Upanishads. Side by side with these are found chapters which are exclusively given up to allegorical expositions of the ritual, and are clearly meant not for ritual use but for meditation. Finally there are passages which teach the student to practise meditation on the allegorical meaning of certain sacrifices instead of the actual performance of the ritual. In none of these ritualistic or allegorical chapters is the doctrine of transmigration and karma taught.

§ 30. All scholars agree that the Āraṇyakas were meant to be studied in the forest.[1] But who were the men who studied them? During the time when the Brāhmaṇas were coming into being, an order of hermits who resided in the forests of India appeared. They gave up all the business of the world and devoted themselves to a religious life. Their practice in general had three aspects, *tapas*, i.e. austerities, sacrifice, and meditation; but there was more than one rule, so that practice varied considerably. In some cases sacrifice was given up altogether; and the great and elaborate sacrifices must have been always impossible. These facts about the order are taken from the Dharmasūtras.[2] Very vivid pictures of the life occur in the *Rāmāyaṇa*,[3] agreeing perfectly with what has just been said. When a student had completed his education, he was allowed either to remain with his teacher for life, or to marry and settle down as a householder, or to retire to the woods as a hermit.[4] The earliest name used to designate a hermit seems to have been *Vaikhānasa*[5] (from Vikhanas, the traditional author of the rule), but later *Vānaprastha*, forest-dweller, came into use. It was at a much later date that there came into use the ideal rule for the life of the twice-born man, that his life should be lived in four stages, *āśramas* as a student, householder, hermit, and monk.[6]

Now Sāyaṇa makes a remark which seems to mean that the Āraṇyaka was the Brāhmaṇa of the hermit;[7] and certain modern scholars, especially Deussen, have accepted that view. The varied character of the contents of the Āraṇyakas—ritual,

[1] The ancient evidence is conclusive. See Rāmānuja, *Śrībhāshya*, *SBE*. XLVIII. 645, and Sāyaṇa quoted by Keith in his *Aitareya Ār.* 15.
[2] Gautama, *SBE*. II. 195; Vāsishṭha, *SBE*. XIV. 45; Baudhāyana, *SBE*. XIV. 259; 291; Āpastamba, *SBE*. II. 155.
[3] See II. lvi; III. i; v; vi; vii; xi; xii.
[4] *Chhāndogya U.* II. 23, 1.
[5] Gautama, *DS*. III. 26.
[6] Deussen, *ERE*. II. 128 ff.
[7] *Āraṇyavratarūpam brāhmaṇam*: see Deussen, *PU*. 2 n.; Keith *AĀ*. 15.

secret explanation, allegory, and internal instead of external sacrifice—fits perfectly into the varying practice of the hermits of the forest; so that one is tempted at first sight to conclude that these treatises were actually prepared for the Vānaprasthas. But Oldenberg[1] and Berriedale Keith[2] believe that the Āraṇyakas were held to be texts of such sacredness that they could with safety be repeated only in the seclusion of the forest. The *Āraṇyagāna* of the *Sāmaveda* would then be a parallel case. Professor Keith believes that the Āraṇyakas were taught to priests, just as the Brāhmaṇas were. The difference lay in the secrecy necessary for the forest treatises.

For our purpose, however, it is unnecessary to decide the question. We require merely to distinguish those chapters which separate themselves from the Brāhmaṇas by their stress on allegory, secrecy, and meditation, and from the philosophic Upanishads by the absence of the doctrine of transmigration, whatever their original purpose may have been. The chief texts are:

Ṛigveda: { *Aitareya Āraṇyaka.* / *Kaushītaki Āraṇyaka.*
Black Yajus: *Taittirīya Āraṇyaka*, I–VI.
White Yajus: *Bṛihadāraṇyaka* = *Śatapatha B.* XIV, i–iii.

§ 31. The point at which we take our third survey is just before the appearance of the doctrine of transmigration and karma in the literature. The literature in existence at that time and surviving to our day comprises the four Vedas, the six old Brāhmaṇas, and the Āraṇyakas. Since we have already dealt with the *Ṛik*, the *Sāman*, and the early *Yajus*, the literature which forms the source for this survey is:

1. The later portions of the *Yajurveda.*
2. The *Atharvaveda.*
3. The six old Brāhmaṇas.
4. The Āraṇyakas.

[1] *LU.* 148 ff.
[2] *AĀ.* 15, 257 n. 10.

By the time to which our survey refers the Aryans had spread over North India at least as far as Behar, but the district between the Jumna and the Ganges was still the centre of Brahmanical culture. Probably all the books of our source arose in that region.[1] We cannot fix the date of our survey chronologically; for the estimates of scholars show considerable variation. At the time we seek to envisage there were already many petty princedoms in North India, containing numerous towns, and wealth and culture were growing. While the country between the Jumna and the Ganges was recognized as the central hearth of the religion and education of the time, there were seats of civilization in the Punjab, in the far North-West, and as far east as the modern Patna. Not only the four great castes but many of the modern mixed castes and sub-castes were already in existence. The Brahmanical schools had greatly increased in number. Each Veda had its own multitude of schools, divided into subordinate groups according to the recension of the Veda they used, and further subdivided according to the Brāhmaṇa they recognized. At some quite unknown date, but certainly before the end of the period, the work of the Vedic schools had become widened, so as not only to provide a specialized training for priests but also to give a religious education to all boys of the Brāhman, Kshatriya, and Vaiśya castes. Every boy belonging to these castes went to school immediately after undergoing the ceremony of initiation. Since this ceremony thus became the entrance to a spiritual training, it was called the boy's second birth. Hence these three castes came to be spoken of as twice-born, and wore the sacred thread. Śūdras and women were excluded from the schools; and only Brāhmans could teach.

The priest and the sacrifice were now supreme and omnipotent, and in consequence the religion had become pitifully degraded. The sacrifice was conceived as a magic system irresistibly wielding all powers in earth and heaven, and the

[1] *Vedic Index*, I. 165.

priests who held the system in their hands were regarded as gods on earth. Hence, though the gods nominally retain their old place, they have become of very little account, stripped of nearly all their real power by the priests and the sacrifice. Like the demons, they sacrifice, when they want to obtain anything. Vishṇu, Rudra-Śiva, and Prajāpati alone are prominent, because of their relations with the new sacerdotalism. Magic is supreme everywhere, in the sacrifice, in the Atharvan rites in the home, and in the discipline of the Vānaprastha in the forest. Morality has almost altogether lost its hold in the cult. The result could not but be an unbearable inner dissatisfaction in the best men. Hence we find some eagerly pressing forward towards new light along philosophic lines, following the lead given by the poets of the speculative hymns mentioned in our second survey. Two concepts of great importance, the *Brahman* and the *Ātman*, were separately evolved and then identified, thus forming together a most significant philosophic term for the absolute.[1] There were other conceptions also which were undergoing modification: in the Brāhmaṇas there are a number of passages[2] in which there is reference to the possibility of repeated death in the other world, and men shudder at the thought.

[1] Oldenberg, *LU.* 44–59.

[2] Ib. 27 ff.

CHAPTER II

TRANSMIGRATION AND RELEASE: *y* to 200 B.C.

i. *Transmigration and Karma.*

§ 32. The immense influence which the doctrine of transmigration and karma has exercised on almost every element of Indian thought renders its appearance an event of such extreme significance as to make it the natural starting-point of a new period. The date is not known even approximately. Indian history in the stricter sense opens only with Alexander the Great's invasion of the Punjab in 326 B.C.; so that all previous events possess only a relative chronology. The life of the Buddha, now approximately dated 560–480 B.C., forms the starting-point for the conjectural dating of earlier occurrences. Behind his activity we can descry the rise of the philosophy of the Upanishads, and behind that again the emergence of the belief in transmigration and karma.[1] The whole of the literature of the chapter shares this uncertainty; only a relative chronology is possible.

It is a very remarkable fact that the belief of the early people with regard to birth, death, and the other world underwent such a complete change at this period in their history. There is no trace of transmigration in the hymns of the Vedas; only in the Brāhmaṇas are there to be found a few traces of the lines of thought from which the doctrine arose. In the Upanishads, however, and in all later Hindu literature, the doctrine is universally accepted, and enters as an active force into almost every element of Hindu thought.

[1] See Keith, *JRAS.* 1909, 574; *SS.* 15; Oldenberg, *LU.* 288; Poussin, *WN.* 10 ff.; Waddell, *JRAS.* 1914, 661 ff.

Through the spread of Buddhism the doctrine was accepted by the population of the centre, the east, and the south of Asia. It is thus impossible to exaggerate the importance of the change with which this chapter opens.

It has been clearly demonstrated that the immediate sources of both the conceptions—transmigration and karma—are to be found in the Brāhmaṇas;[1] yet the two are found linked together in a doctrine of moral requital for the first time in the Upanishads. The creation, therefore, of this master-conception is unquestionably the work of the Aryan mind. Yet the suggestion which many scholars have made, that the idea of transmigration must have come from totemistic aboriginals who believed that after death their souls lived in animal bodies, may be, after all, partly true; for the Aryan people were not only in daily contact with aboriginals but had already suffered large infusions of aboriginal blood.

§ 33. The theory is that souls are born and die many times, and that a man's conduct in one life determines his position in the next, good conduct being rewarded, and evil conduct punished. In the earliest passages[2] in which the doctrine appears, that is all that is stated; but soon it received a more definite form:

> Those whose conduct has been pleasing, will quickly attain a pleasing birth, the birth of a Brāhman, or a Kshatriya, or a Vaiśya; but those whose conduct has been abominable, will quickly attain an abominable birth, the birth of a dog, or a hog, or an Outcaste.[3]

and this form it was which became the basis of the orthodox Hindu belief. Caste is the chief element of the requital of one's action. The word for action, *karma*, is used for the mysterious power which, according to this doctrine, causes all action to work itself out in requital in another life. The conception was soon deepened and broadened. It was recognized that a man's body, mind, and character, and also all the

[1] Oldenberg, *LU.* 26–35.
[2] *Brihadāraṇyaka*, *U.* III. 2, 13; IV. 4, 5.
[3] *Chhāndogya*, *U.* V. 10, 7.

details of his experience were elements of the requital. Men also recognized that, since each life is the requital of foregoing action, and since the actions of each new life demand another for their reward or punishment, the process of birth and death, *saṁsāra*, can have had no beginning, and can have no end. The soul was therefore eternal.

It would be well to notice that the theory took form among polytheists, and included gods, demons, animals, and plants in its sweep as well as men: there was no living being that was not subject to the law of rebirth. Nor was there any divine power that controlled the process: the concept of a Supreme, exalted high above all the gods, had not risen on the minds of the men who created the doctrine.

The doctrine would seem to have met a need of the time, for it steadily spread among cultured men throughout North India. Clearly the belief was a moral advance on earlier ideas; for it gave all conduct a moral meaning, and made every man realize the seriousness of life and his personal responsibility. Its evil effects did not become evident at once. For centuries this conception of the world sufficed for multitudes of thinking Hindus, and it still suffices for the unthinking masses; but for others, very soon, an addition became necessary.

§ 34. We have seen that in the age of the Brāhmaṇas a few men were already struggling to reach philosophic conceptions of the world which might form a more satisfactory basis for the religious life than the gross ritual and magic of the sacrifice. Terror-struck at the prospect of repeated death in the other world (an idea frequently referred to in the Brāhmaṇas), men longed for release from that fate; and some believed they had found it in the conviction that the gods and all the spiritual powers of the world are deathless, and that the man who, knowing this, brings his own spirit into union with these powers, wins a sure immortality.[1] The doctrine of transmigration now seemed to explain the grip which the things of

[1] Oldenberg, *LU.* 31 ff.

sense have on the human spirit; it also quickened the desire for release from the bondage of sense and death; but the unbroken series of births and deaths seemed to make the achievement of immortality and release more difficult than ever. How was escape possible? Hence there arose a passionate desire to find some means of deliverance; and from that passion sprang all the noblest forms of Hindu religious thought, and Buddhism and Jainism as well. Indeed, it is but the simple truth to say that karma and rebirth, with release, have given Indian religious thought its peculiar flavour.

§ 35. One of the chief historical facts to be realized at this point is this, that, during this period, South India was gradually inoculated, and at last thoroughly interpenetrated, with the religion and culture which had been taking shape in the north. Three political events must also be mentioned, the conquest of the Punjab by Darius, Alexander's raid, and the rise of the Maurya empire; for the third, which was a direct reaction from Greek domination and an imitation of the Persian system, proved of very large significance for the history of Buddhism.

ii. *The Twice-born and their Literature.*

§ 36. The three twice-born castes—Brāhmans, Kshatriyas, Vaiśyas—formed now a large educated community, sharply divided among themselves, yet far more deeply cut off from the vast Śūdra community which served them, and from the unclean Outcastes with whom they would have nothing to do. The whole of the literature described in our first chapter was their exclusive possession, and much more was destined to come into existence during the period. But, though they kept themselves rigidly separate from Śūdras in all religious matters, it seems probable that Śūdra worship soon began to exercise an influence on them.

We deal, first of all, with what is, strictly speaking, the literature of the twice-born, namely works written in exposition of the earlier literature. In all these books the doctrine of karma and rebirth is accepted as true, and here and there the Upanishad theory of release also finds reflection.

§ 37. We mention first what is clearly the earliest form of Indian philosophy, although its earliest surviving document cannot be dated earlier than the fourth century after Christ, and although in its inception it was in no sense philosophical It is clear that the Karma Mīmāṁsā in some form came into existence quite early during this period. It is, as will be explained later, a method of Vedic exegesis, dealing primarily with the sacred texts which give injunctions for the sacrifices. Its interest for us at this point is twofold, first because it is to this day the special system of the orthodox twice-born man, and secondly because it retained for many centuries certain features characteristic of the time of its birth, and indeed retains some of them to this day. The Mīmāṁsā reflects the time when the average educated man was frankly polytheistic, and thus atheistic from the point of view of theism or pantheism, when he accepted rebirth and karma but felt no need of release, and when, like the average unreflecting man, he took a realistic view of the world. For the understanding of the developments of this period it is of great importance to realize that this was the state of mind of nearly all educated men[1] in the earlier, and probably of the vast majority in the later, part of the period also.

§ 38. We take next the literature of the Vedic schools. The basis of all the training is still the process of laying up in the memory the hymns of the Veda of one's school and the long chapters of the Brāhmaṇa. But a large amount of ancillary material has now to be mastered by the student as well as the fundamental texts. The sciences of Vedic exposition, phonetics, grammar, metre, etymology, &c., the beginnings of which are found in the Brāhmaṇas, have each grown in width and complexity as well as in accuracy. The sacrifices, both minor and major, have grown steadily more intricate

[1] Cf. Oldenberg, *LU.* 31.

and more numerous, and the *dharma*, i.e. the law of conduct, has become a large body of detailed injunctions. Hence, to enable the student to carry in his mind the vast and varied masses of information which he required to know, a new method of teaching was created, the *sūtra*-method. The essential feature of the method is the committing to memory of a long series of very abbreviated phrases, which serve as a sort of classified index of the particular subject dealt with. The method was of service in proportion to the care with which the subject was arranged, and to the skill with which the mnemonic phrases were composed. A series of sūtras is more or less incomprehensible by itself; it has always a commentary attached to it, either oral or written, which fills up the gaps and expounds the thought.

There are four types of sūtras which are of large significance for the religious life, namely the Śrauta, the Gṛihya, and the Dharma manuals, and the magic-books. The Śrauta-sūtras get their epithet Śrauta from the fact that they are directly founded on the hymns and the Brāhmaṇas, which are *śruti*, i.e. revelation in the highest sense. The Gṛihya manuals are called *gṛihya*, i.e. domestic, because they describe the minor sacrifices and the ritual acts obligatory on the family. The Dharma manuals lay down the rules of the *dharma*, i.e. the Hindu law of conduct. Of the Śrauta-sūtras a dozen survive, of the Gṛihyas also a dozen, or thirteen, if the *Kauśika* be included, and of the Dharma manuals six; while there are four noteworthy books on magic.

It is as yet impossible to give any definite chronology of the sūtras; but all the surviving works of the Śrauta, Gṛihya, and Dharma classes (called as a group the Kalpa-sūtras) probably belong to the fifth, fourth, or third centuries.[1] Nor is it yet possible to set them out in the order of their origin.[2]

§ 39. The Śrauta-sūtras are hand-books prepared for the use of priests with reference to the greater Vedic sacrifices, i.e.

[1] See the discussions by Keith, *AĀ*. 21–5; *TS*. I. xlv–xlvi.
[2] But see Keith, *TS*. I. xlv.

those for which three or more sacrificial fires, and priests belonging to each of the three orders, were necessary. Thus each Śrauta-sūtra depends on one of the three Vedas, and contains instructions only for the order of priests corresponding to that Veda. Hence in order fully to understand the ceremonial of any single sacrifice, it is necessary for the student to read together the sections on that sacrifice in three Śrauta-sūtras. For this certain other manuals, called Paribhāshās, which show how the three strands of the sacrifice fit together, are used.

§ 40. The Gṛihya-sūtras deal with three groups of subjects. The first group contains general and detailed rules for the simpler sacrifices, which were performed on the domestic fire by the householder himself, if he were a Brāhmaṇ, or by a priest appointed by him for the purpose. These offerings are of three types: (*a*) melted butter, oil, or milk poured on the fire; (*b*) cooked cakes; and (*c*) animal sacrifices. The second group of subjects are the eighteen sacraments, solemn ceremonies connected with the great moments of life, such as birth, the first solid food given to the child, his tonsure, his initiation as a religious student, his return home after his education, and marriage. The third is a mixed group, including house-building rites, the funeral ceremony, the śrāddhas, or offerings to the spirits of deceased ancestors, and minor observances. As in all these ceremonies there is but one series of ritual acts and liturgic utterances, the Gṛihya-sūtras of the three Vedas differ very little from each other except in the Vedic stanzas they quote.

The Karma Mīmāṁsā, we may remind ourselves, existed in order that every injunction covered by the Śrauta and Gṛihya sūtras should be faithfully performed. Learned Mīmāṁsakas were usually present at the greater sacrifices to guide everything.

§ 41. The Dharma-sūtras deal not with sacrifice but with conduct. The word *dharma* means that which is obligatory, and is thus similar to the Latin *religio*. It is used in several senses, which vary chiefly in their scope: first, Hinduism as a whole is the *dharma*, just as to Buddhists Buddhism is the *dhamma*; second, the whole religious law, as expressed in the Śrauta, Gṛihya, and Dharma codes; third, the laws of conduct: this is the ordinary meaning, as in the Dharma-sūtras and the later Dharmaśāstras; and fourth, the law of a caste, as in the *Gītā* frequently. The Dharma-sūtras contain regulations for the four *āśramas* or forms of Hindu life, viz. the student, the householder, the hermit, and the ascetic, and the following special subjects: the king, civil law, criminal law, marriage, inheritance, funeral rites, penances, and excommunication. Originally the Dharma-sūtras were each meant to be used only by members of its own school, but later a number of them became recognized as valid for all twice-born men.

The basal principle upon which this law of conduct rests is the supreme obligation of the caste system. By that a man's profession and religious duties are determined, as well as his place in Hindu society. The Brāhman is the priest, teacher, and judge; the Kshatriya is the ruler and warrior; the Vaiśya turns to agriculture, industry, or trade; the Śūdra is the servant of these three twice-born castes. The Outcastes are untouchable and are shut out in their filth and their poverty. All the provisions of the laws of property and crime are conditioned by caste: the higher a man's caste, the greater his rights; the higher the caste of the criminal, the less his punishment; the higher the caste of the wronged party, the greater the penalty. It is well to note that in the time of these sūtras each man chooses his own āśrama, i.e. whether he is to remain a student, or become a householder, a hermit, or a sannyāsī: these modes of life have not yet become a series through which each man is expected to pass. Amongst the fresh regulations, we note two of supreme importance for the family—the rule that a girl should be married before puberty,[1]

[1] *Gautama DS.* XVIII. 21–23; *Vāsishṭha DS.* XVII. 69–70; *Baudhāyana DS.* IV. 1, 11 12.

and the rule that no widow who has borne children should remarry.[1]

§ 42. The religion reflected in the sūtras [2] is polytheistic and ritualistic. There is no trace of divine incarnation in them, and no approach to theism. The philosophy of the Ātman is mentioned as a subject of meditation for the sannyāsī; and in one sūtra it is heartily commended to the student on the ground that there is no higher object than the attainment of the Ātman.[3] Necessarily, the whole of the Vedic religion is represented—the soma-cult, the fire-cult, animal sacrifice, and the numerous magic rites. Temples and images also appear side by side with these ancient methods of worship, but we are told nothing about the temple-cult, the reason seemingly being that it stands outside the Vedic faith. The old pantheon remains, but several new divinities appear, chiefly abstractions—Dharma, religious law; Kubera, wealth; Kāma, Cupid. Brahmā, whom we meet in the Āraṇyakas, has also an honoured place. The worship of snakes, mountains, rivers, and pools is also found; and cow-pens are reckoned among holy places. The doctrine of transmigration and karma is recognized as true by every one, but the old eschatology is still in use; so that there is no unity of treatment. Readers will note how close the resemblance is to the religion of the original Epics.

§ 43. The appearance during this period of the sūtra-texts on Magic shows that the practice of the old methods of magic was still a very living part of the religion; but we must notice that these ceremonies did not form part of the obligatory ceremonial law (*kalpa*), but are extra and voluntary. The chief text, the *Kauśika-sūtra* which belongs to the *Atharvaveda*, is first of all a Gṛihya-sūtra, but also gives a great deal of detailed information about magical ceremonies, and makes much that is far from clear in the *Atharvan* quite compre-

[1] *Gautama DS.* XVIII. 4–17; *Vāsishṭha DS.* XVII. 55–68, 74.
[2] See the careful sketch by Hopkins, *RI.* 242–63.
[3] *Āpastamba DS.* I. 8, 22–3.

hensible. The *Ṛigvidhāna* describes the magical effects produced by the recitation of hymns or single verses of the *Ṛigveda*; while the *Sāmavidhāna Brāhmaṇa* shows how the chants of the Sāmaveda may be used for superstitious practices.[1] The *Adbhuta Brāhmaṇa* also belongs to the *Sāmaveda*, and deals with portents and the means to avert their evil influence. We may also mention here the *Gopatha Brāhmaṇa* of the *Atharvaveda*, which is a late text of very varied character, depending on the *Vaitāna-sūtra*.

§ 44. Subsidiary sūtras also existed on the measurement of altars and were called *Śulva-sūtras*, from the word for a measuring line, on Phonetics, *Śikshā*, Grammar, *Vyākaraṇa*, Etymology, *Nirukta*, Prosody, *Chhandas*, and Astronomy, *Jyotisha*. There were also special forms of the text of the *Ṛigveda* and various ancillary works on minor matters.

A large part of this literature is of no interest for our subject, as, from the modern standpoint, it is purely secular. But there is one of these secular books which we must mention, because of the immense influence it has exerted over language in India, and its consequent importance for Indian history. We refer to the *Ashṭādhyāyī* or Eight Chapters of Pāṇini on *Vyākaraṇa*, Grammar. Pāṇini lived at Taxila in the far north-west, seemingly about the middle of the fourth century B.C.[2] He may have been alive when Alexander and his army were entertained in the city with royal magnificence. In him culminated the movement to make the speech of the Vedic schools a thoroughly musical, trustworthy, intelligible, and polished instrument; and his book has been the norm of the *Saṁskṛita*, i. e. the cultured, speech ever since. Down to his time this language had gradually changed; but from the moment when in the schools of India his book became the standard, Sanskrit became an unchangeable language. By his day great differences had already arisen between the polished tongue and

[1] For the date of these texts, see Keith, *TS.* I. clxvii.

[2] Keith, *TS.* I. clxviii.

the current forms of speech: Sanskrit was becoming incomprehensible to the uneducated man. Herein lay its disadvantage and still lies. But, on the other hand, it remains permanently intelligible to all cultured men throughout India, while each vernacular is restricted to its own domain, and also changes so rapidly that usually in three or four hundred years its best literature is as foreign to the vulgar as Sanskrit itself.

The whole of this sūtra-literature was recognized as revelation of the second grade and was called *smṛiti*, remembrance, in contrast with literature of the highest grade, which, as we have already seen, was called *śruti*.

§ 45. A famous work on politics, Kauṭilya's *Arthaśāstra*, which has recently come to light, though not a religious work, must be mentioned here on account of the large amount of detailed information it affords incidentally as to the condition of religion and morals in Magadha, towards the end of the period. According to tradition, Kauṭilya is another name for Chāṇakya, Chandragupta's Brāhman minister; but critical inquiry tends to lead to the conclusion that the work is the text-book of a school of politics, and that, while probably part of it is the work of Chāṇakya, it has been redacted and interpolated.[1] Yet its evidence is of great value, if we give its date rather wide limits, say from 300 to 100 B.C. It is a work which no one dealing with Hindu ethics can afford to neglect. The information it gives about government, law, crime and its punishment, and the social and economic state of the country is of very great importance. Its evidence with regard to the religion of Magadha is most interesting. The popular belief was a wide and varied polytheism; for not only are the great gods and many of the minor divinities of Hinduism mentioned, but the worship of mountains, rivers, trees and fire, of birds, snakes, and cows and other animals, is regarded as of great value as a prophylactic against pestilence, cattle-disease, demons, fire, floods, drought, famine,

[1] Keith, *JRAS.* 1916, p. 130. But see also K.V. Rangaswami Aiyangar, *Some Considerations on Ancient Indian Polity*, Madras, 1916.

and other calamities. Numerous ceremonies, incantations, and magical arts are recommended for such purposes also. Readers will note how well this fits in with the evidence of the epics and the sūtras. Another aspect of the book is its eschatology. It does not seem to mention transmigration, karma, or release at all. In all these features the work is very similar to the edicts of Aśoka. The following is the basis of the moral and religious teaching of the treatise:

> The observance of one's own duty leads one to heaven (*svarga*) and infinite bliss (*ānantya*). When it is violated, the world will come to an end owing to confusion of castes and duties. Hence the king shall never allow people to swerve from their duties. . . . For the world, when maintained in accordance with the injunctions of the triple Veda, will surely progress, but never perish.[1]

This is precisely the position of the Karma Mīmāṁsā. The work recommends the Sāṅkhya, Yoga, and Lokāyata philosophies. The first and the last of the three are atheistic, and it is practically certain that at this date the Yoga was so also.

iii. *The Epics.*

§ 46. The epics of India, the *Mahābhārata* and the *Rāmāyaṇa*, which were originally heroic narratives, became in the course of their history religious works, and are of extreme importance as evidence on the subject of the religion of the common people and with regard to the rise of the sects of Hinduism. But they are so vast that they are apt to fill the virgin inquirer with utter dismay; and in the case of the *Mahābhārata*, the contents present such an extraordinary medley—explained to us as arising from interminable interpolations and the operations of countless editors each with a policy of his own—that they deepen the feeling to blank despair. Yet, taken in the right way, they ought to prove very fruitful. The parts of each poem must be read at the points of the history where they appeared.

[1] I. iii.

Scholars seem to be coming steadily nearer unanimity as to the three essential moments in the history of the epics. They are practically the same for both. All three stages are very fully represented in the *Mahābhārata*, but it is in the *Rāmāyaṇa* that the first and the second can be most easily studied, while the third, which is only faintly represented in it, attains enormous proportions in the *Mahābhārata*. They are as follows:

A. The epics composed as popular poems: sixth, fifth, or fourth century B. C.

B. The epics changed into sectarian poems by Vaishṇava priests: second century B. C.

C. Vaishṇava theism in both epics: the *Mahābhārata* becomes a huge encyclopaedia of theology, philosophy, politics, and law: first and second centuries A. D.

There is perhaps not quite so much unanimity with regard to the dates suggested as to the three distinct movements.[1] All would acknowledge further that fragments of material found their way into the *Mahābhārata* in still later centuries.

§ 47. In this chapter, then, we deal only with the first stage. The roots of popular epic poetry lie very far back, in dramatic stories in the Vedic hymns and narratives in the Brāhmaṇas;[2] and it is probable that the first attempts at actual epics (possibly indeed a rudimentary *Mahābhārata*, or *Rāmāyaṇa*) go back as far as the age of the Brāhmaṇas; for since the epic is popular, and its language is Sanskrit, it must have originated at a time when the warriors in the chieftain's hall understood heroic songs in Sanskrit, that is, a time when the popular and the cultured speech were still near enough to be practically one. That in India, as in Greece, the epic arose from the song that glorified the noble deed, stands out clearly

[1] Holtzmann, *MBH.* I. 5 ff.; 126 ff.; 152 ff.; Jacobi, *R.* 24 ff.; 60 ff.; 100 ff.; Macdonell, *SL.* 285-6; 305-12; Hopkins, *GE.* 397-8; Winternitz, I. 389 ff.; 423 ff.

[2] Macdonell, 280-1; Keith, *AĀ.* 196 n. 19.

in the ancient evidence. The early songs were sung; and the more elaborate compositions founded on them were either sung or recited with eloquent declamation and dramatic gesture.[1]

Scholars agree that the first rounded *Mahābhārata* and the first completed *Rāmāyaṇa* arose from these earlier efforts, and that they both appeared in the same age, between 600 and 300 B.C.;[2] but unanimity has not yet been reached on the question as to which came first.[3] For our purpose, however, the question is of little importance. We need merely recognize that both were already in existence by 300 B.C. and that both may have arisen a good deal earlier. The features of the two epics, the place where they arose, the way in which they were formed from earlier pieces and other interesting problems, are discussed by the critics.[4] Strictly speaking, the original epics ought not to come into our survey; for they were not composed as religious works, but as heroic poems. Yet their subsequent history changed them into religious works of very great importance, and the original material is a source of religious history all the more valuable because it is indirect.

§ 48. We shall take the shorter epic first, as it is easier to detach the original *Rāmāyaṇa* from its accretions than to reach the genuine *Bhārata* amidst the immeasurable masses of extraneous material in which it is buried. Scholars agree that of the seven books of which the *Rāmāyaṇa* consists, the whole of the first[5] and the seventh books are later additions. Thus Books II–VI represent the genuine old epic. But even

[1] Holtzmann, *MBH.* I. 52 ff.; Hopkins, *GE.* 363–7.
[2] Macdonell, *SL.* 285; 306–7; Hopkins, *GE.* VI; Keith, *JRAS.* 1915, 318 ff.
[3] Jacobi puts the *Rāmāyaṇa* first, *R.* 60 ff.; so Macdonell, *SL.* 306, but see also *ERE.* X. 576; Hopkins sets the Bhārata epic first, then the *Rāmāyaṇa*, then the Pāṇḍu epic, *GE.* 60–1; 238–9.
[4] Jacobi, *R.* 119 ff.; Holtzmann, *MBH.* I. 15 ff.; Macdonell, *SL.* 310; Hopkins, *GE.* 79 and *passim.*
[5] With the exception of verses 5 to 8 of Canto V, which Jacobi, *R.* 55, believes formed the first lines of Vālmīki's work.

in these books there are numerous passages that have been foisted on the text by reciters. Most of them are either variants, which make the details of the story harder to follow, or repetitions, which weary the reader intolerably; so that, before scanning text or translation, it would be well to put up a danger-signal beside each morass.[1] Estimates of the date of Vālmīki's work vary from the sixth to the fourth century B. C.[2]

Vālmīki's poem helps us to understand the religion the more because it is a secular work; for it gives us an undisturbed reflection of some aspects of the popular faith. And we do well to look at it carefully; for from a very early date the work has been read as a mirror of character; and in its enlarged form the *Rāmāyaṇa* is still the first of all Vishṇuite scriptures. Religion, then, in the original work is still frankly polytheistic and external. There are no sects. Every one acknowledges all the gods; and worship is made by means of sacrifice, usually animal sacrifice. There is no mention here of the philosophy of the Ātman. The *sannyāsī* never appears; but at every turn the ancient *vānaprastha*. There is no approach to anything like a theism. The idea of divine incarnation never occurs; Rāma from beginning to end is a man and only a man : he is a great hero, but there is no suggestion that he is in any sense a god. Most of the old gods of the Veda are mentioned; and there is no monarch among them, although Indra may receive a little more recognition than the others. A number of new divinities have taken their places among the famous early gods, especially Kāma, Kubera, Śukra, and Kārttikeya, and the following goddesses: Gaṅgā, the Ganges, with Lakshmī and Umā, the

[1] The following are the chief interpolations recognized by Jacobi: II. 41-9, 66-93, 107, 17-111, 117, 5-119; III. 1-14; IV. 17-18, 40-43, 45-7; V. 41-55, 58-64, 66-8; VI. 23-40, 59-60, 69, 74-5. Besides these, there is one very late canto which would confuse the reader seriously, viz. VI. 119.

[2] Jacobi, *R.* 100-112, inclines to the sixth, or even the eighth century. The latest careful review of the question is by Keith, *JRAS.* 1915, 318. He inclines to the fourth century as the true date, and Macdonell agrees: *ERE.* X. 576.

wives of Vishṇu and Śiva. Semi-divine animals, Śesha, the snake, Hanumān, the monkey, Jambavān, the bear, Garuḍa, the eagle, Jaṭāyus, the vulture, and Nandī, Śiva's bull, are quite prominent. Vishṇu and Śiva, who in the later Vedas and the Brāhmanas are far more important than they are in the *Ṛik*, here maintain that prominence. Snakes, trees, rivers, and lakes are also worshipped. It is of importance to note that temples and images of the gods are common, and that animal sacrifice is the usual offering. There is no allusion to the phallus of Śiva. Innumerable superstitions haunt the religious consciousness. The doctrine of transmigration and karma is everywhere accepted and applied to life, but it is not yet full grown. Men do not understand all its implications, and parts of the old scheme of things still survive.

§ 49. The original heroic *Mahābhārata* is much harder to isolate, chiefly because it was redacted with greater care and persistence by the priests than the companion poem. It is referred to in the epic itself; for in the first section of the first book as it stands to-day, we are told that the *Bhārata* consists of 8,800 verses, of 24,000 verses, and of 100,000 verses. These three computations correspond to the three stadia in the composition of the poem referred to above. Thus the work we are thinking of here contained 8,800 verses. No scholar has yet undertaken to separate out the component passages, and reform the ancient work; so that it cannot be studied precisely in the same way as the original *Rāmāyaṇa*; but the student may form some idea of its character by reading one of the oldest episodes, Nala,[1] or Sāvitrī,[2] or the famous gambling scene,[3] or some of the battle-scenes from Book VIII or IX, though even in these the trail of the redactor will be crossed here and there.

Then scholars are quite able to see the religious characteristics of the old poem, though they cannot extricate it from the clinging mass of fresh growth. The religion is polytheistic and ritualistic through and through; sectarianism has not yet

[1] III. 52 ff. [2] III. 292 ff. [3] II. 46–73.

appeared ; there is no theism in it, no divine incarnation, no exposition of the Ātman doctrine. The three chief gods seem to be Indra, Brahmā, and Agni, but the whole of the old pantheon survives. Dharma, i e. Law, and Kāma, Love, appear as divinities, and Kṛishṇa appears also, but whether as god or man is not yet known with certainty.

Epic society is dominated by caste ; yet there is far more social freedom than at later stages of Hindu history ; and women in particular have a good deal of liberty. Brāhmans, in contravention of the regular rule, often become warriors. Hindus have not yet become vegetarians : everybody eats beef. The polyandry of Draupadī is clearly a historical trait which has persisted in the story, despite its naturally repulsive character.

§ 50. One of the chief problems of this period is the rise of the god Kṛishṇa, who seems to have had as one of his epithets the title Vāsudeva. Some scholars believe that in the original *Mahābhārata* he was a man and only a man,[1] and that he was deified at a rather later date. Others affirm that he is always a god in the *Mahābhārata*.[2] Of these some suppose that he was originally a vegetation-spirit, others that he was a sun-god. It is certainly clear that he was already a god of some sort in the fourth century B.C.; for in Pāṇini's grammar [3] Vāsudeva and Arjuna appear as a pair of divinities. Megasthenes, a Greek ambassador at the court of Chandragupta about 300 B.C., has a sentence which seems to mean that Kṛishṇa was worshipped at Mathurā and Kṛishṇapur. In the *Mahānārāyaṇa Upanishad*,[4] which is probably not later than the third century B.C., there is a litany in which the title Vāsudeva is used as an epithet of Vishṇu, which seems to mean that Kṛishṇa was already in some sense identified with Vishṇu. Finally, in the *Mahābhāshya* [5] of Patañjali, which was probably written about 150 B.C., Vāsudeva is spoken of as a divinity.

[1] Hopkins, *ION*. 105 (but see below) ; Grierson, *ERE*. II. 541 ; Garbe, *IC*. 210.
[2] Keith, *JRAS*. 1915, 548 ; Hopkins, *GE*. 395, *n*. 3 ; *RI*. 467–8.
[3] IV. 3. 98. [4] I. 31. [5] On Pāṇini, IV. 3. 98.

Sir R. G. Bhandarkar[1] has a notable theory of his own on the subject. He distinguishes between Vāsudeva and Kṛishṇa. He believes that Vāsudeva was originally a man belonging to the Sātvata tribe, that he lived in the sixth century B.C., if not earlier, and that he taught the people of his tribe a monotheistic religion. Some time after his death he was deified by his own people and identified with the one personal God whom he had preached. He was thereafter identified, first with Nārāyaṇa, then with Vishṇu, and finally with the cowherd god of Mathurā, Gopāla Kṛishṇa. From the sect which worshipped this god there arose, according to this theory, the famous poem, the *Bhagavadgītā*. Grierson,[2] Winternitz,[3] and Garbe[4] accept the theory, and support it ardently, but Hopkins[5] and Keith[6] hold that it can be shown to be unhistorical; and most scholars seem to follow them. There is certainly no clear evidence of the existence of a monotheistic faith during those early centuries.

§ 51. In the Epics and the Sūtras we meet the first references to Hindu temple-and-image worship. But it is most noteworthy that, by the side of the minute instructions for the sacrifices given in the Kalpa-sūtras, no directions for the temple-cult appear. The latter seems to be merely tolerated by the side of the orthodox cult. Then, at a later date, when the Vaishṇavas and the Śaivas organized themselves as sects, worshipping Vishṇu and Śiva by temple and image, they were condemned as unorthodox; and the taint remains to some extent to the present day. It is also important to realize that from the earliest times at which we catch glimpses of the organization of Hindu temple-worship, there are stringent rules to the effect that the priests must be Brāhmans, and that the temples are open to all men and women of the four castes—Brāhman, Kshatriya, Vaiśya, Śūdra—but to no others. What the history behind these facts is, it is as yet impossible

[1] *VS.* Chaps. IV, VII, VIII, IX.
[2] *ERE.* II. 540 ff. [3] I. 373. [4] *IC.* 215 ff.
[5] *JRAS.* 1905, 384. [6] *JRAS.* 1915, 548; ib. 1917, 173.

to say with certainty.[1] One of the largest interests of the later history of Hindu worship is the slow but steady weakening of the old sacrificial cult under the pressure of the more attractive temple-system.

iv. *Systems of Release.*

§ 52. On the basis of ideas expressed in the philosophic hymns of the *Ṛigveda* and the *Atharvaveda*, there were evolved in the time of the Brāhmaṇas two conceptions of the Absolute, the *Brahman* and the *Ātman*, the Self, the former drawn either from the concept of the supernatural power resident in holy things[2] or from reflection on the outer world,[3] the latter drawn from the subjective life of man. The ideas were then combined, with the result that the Absolute was thought of as both the source of all things and as a spiritual being. The Brahman-Ātman thus came to be the phrase for the one spiritual reality, unchanging, universal, free from all earthly bonds, from birth and death, pain and sorrow; and

[1] So far as the evidence goes, it would seem that for many centuries after their entrance into India the Aryan people used no images, erected no temples, and recognized no sacred places. Their cult consisted of the sacrifices, and these were private and personal, and were carried out within a man's own house or domains, or wherever the performance was desirable. On the other hand, the facts of modern India suggest that the sacred spot, with its local shrine and image or symbol, open to all the people of the tribe, is a very old aboriginal institution. It seems as if the Aryans and the aborigines were very sharply divided in their conceptions of worship as well as in other matters. If this inference then is justifiable, it would be natural to conjecture that, when, at a very early period, masses of the aborigines were admitted to intercourse with the conquering Aryans and called Śūdras, they carried with them into the Aryan community their temple-and-image worship; and that this cult was at some later date regularized, either by the appointment of real Brāhmans as ministrants, or by the recognition of the actual incumbents as Brāhmans. If we could be sure that the second of these alternatives is what actually happened, we should then have a really adequate historical reason for the very curious fact that, to this day and all over India, temple-ministrants are held in much less consideration than other Brāhmans. There is one point which is absolutely clear, namely this, that the essential elements of the temple-cult—the sixteen operations, *shoḍaśa upachāra*—are so distinct in character from the sacrificial cult as to betray an alien origin.

[2] Oldenberg, *LU.* 44-52; Poussin, *WN.* 22.

[3] Deussen, *AGP.* I. 240 ff.

the nobler minds of the time longed to be released from the doom of repeated death in the other world, and to reach immortality and the peace of the Ātman.

A. *The Upanishads.*

§ 53. When the doctrine of rebirth and karma arose, it made the phenomenal world and human life seem much more unsatisfactory and enslaving than before, and therefore created in the best men a deeper desire than ever for release from all earthly conditions, and especially from rebirth.

Then some courageous thinker, conscious to the utmost not only of the kinship and similarity of his own ātman to the universal Ātman, but also of the unlimited outlook and desire of the human spirit, took the bold leap and declared the two identical: 'My ātman is the universal Ātman whole and undivided.' The immediate consequence of this outreach of conviction was necessarily a vivid consciousness of uplift above all merely phenomenal conditions, of community of life and privilege with God, and an immovable conviction of release from transmigration and all its bonds.

The conviction spread to others, and soon there was a company of men who regarded themselves as liberated. In their exaltation of mind, and in their fear lest the old worldly life should rob them of their new-found treasure, they gave up completely the life of the family and the world, and became wandering, homeless, celibate ascetics, without possessions, without responsibilities, devoted altogether to the life of the Ātman. They were called *parivrājakas*, wanderers, *bhikshus*, beggars, *sannyāsīs*, renouncers. They found a life that was a fitting expression of their new experience in a complete renunciation of the world and of all the rules of society. They wandered about, giving their time to meditation, discussion, and teaching, sleeping at the foot of a tree, getting their food by begging. In numerous episodes we see them conversing and discussing in the woods, in the villages, at kings' courts, and at sacrifices.

One of the most remarkable facts about these men is this, that they gave up the old worship completely. This is the point at which they are most clearly distinguishable from the older order of ascetics, the *vānaprasthas*. The sacrifices were meant to induce the gods to grant to their worshippers health, wealth, and all the other pleasures of life. Of what service, then, could they be to men who, having found the Ātman, had therein found full satisfaction and no longer looked to material things for comfort and consolation? The ancient worship, and with it all the learning on which it rested, had thus become worthless to them.[1] The corroding effect of philosophic thought had thus already gone a long way. Yet, though they took no further part in the sacrifices, they still believed in the gods and demigods and the old mythology. These still formed to them part of the totality of things explained by their belief in the Brahman-Ātman.

Some scholars hold that the new teaching arose among the Kshatriyas, the warrior caste, and was only at a later date accepted by the Brāhmans;[2] but most scholars believe that, while Kshatriyas and people of lower castes, and women as well as men, took part in the discussions and rejoiced in the new beliefs, the main part in the evolution of the doctrine was taken by Brāhmans. It is certainly true that the root of every single idea involved in the new philosophy is found in the earlier Brahmanical books.[3]

§ 54. At first the teaching seems to have been carried on exclusively in free discussions anywhere and everywhere, and the new ideas and the new life were open to everybody; but finally the Brahmanical schools began to teach it as the last subject of their curriculum, and there it took root and grew. At first doubtless the teaching was given in extempore freedom, only certain great phrases expressing the central ideas, such as *Tat tvam asi*, 'Thou art that', i.e. 'Thou art

[1] Poussin, *WN.* 9, 29.
[2] Deussen, *PU.* 17, 120, 396; Garbe, *Beiträge*, 23; Winternitz, I. 199.
[3] Oldenberg, *LU.* 166; Keith, *AĀ.* 50, 257; *JRAS.* 1915, 550.

the Brahman-Ātman', being given in fixed form; but gradually the lectures received settled expression; and they were then communicated to the pupils and by them committed to memory, precisely as the hymns and the Brāhmaṇas were handed on. From this time onward, then, only Brāhmans taught the doctrine, and only men of the three twice-born castes were allowed to hear it. From this circumstance, doubtless, the name 'Upanishad', 'secret doctrine',[1] arose.

The outcome of this teaching was the early Upanishads. Each consists of a great many distinct pieces of teaching, of varying value, character, and length, products of the activity of many minds and of many years of advancing thought. They are in simple discursive prose, and show clearly the process of transition from the old sacrificial teaching of the Brāhmaṇas to philosophy. Amidst the prose, brief passages in verse occur in a few places. To this group of early prose works there belong six treatises, distributed as follows among the Vedic schools:

Vedas.	*Schools.*	*Upanishads.*
I. ṚIK	Aitareyins	*Aitareya*
	Kaushītakins	*Kaushītaki*
II. SĀMAN	Tāṇḍins	*Chhāndogya*
	Talavakāras	*Kena*
III. BLACK YAJUS	Taittirīyas	*Taittirīya*
WHITE YAJUS	Vājasaneyins	*Bṛihadāraṇyaka*

Since each Upanishad is a collection of pieces of varying date, it is not possible to arrange these six compilations in order of seniority; yet their relative age may be approximately indicated. Deussen's order is:[2] 1. *Bṛihadāraṇyaka.* 2. *Chhāndogya.* 3. *Taittirīya.* 4. *Aitareya.* 5. *Kaushītaki.*

[1] Such is the usual explanation of the word (Deussen, *PU.* 10-11; Keith, *AĀ.* 239). Oldenberg holds that it means 'reverential meditation' (*LU.* 37, 155).

[2] *PU.* 23.

6. *Kena*; and Macdonell[1] and Winternitz[2] follow him. Keith, however, holds that the *Aitareya* is earlier even than the *Bṛihadāraṇyaka*, and that it does not teach the doctrine of transmigration.[3] If that be so, it does not enter into our discussion here. Oldenberg[4] takes the *Aitareya* along with the *Bṛihadāraṇyaka* and the *Chhāndogya*, and also suggests rather tentatively that the *Īśā*, which other scholars regard as a later text, and the *Jaiminīya Upanishad Brāhmaṇa* should be included among these six early works. In any case it is clear that the *Bṛihadāraṇyaka* and the *Chhāndogya* are by far the most important of the six; for in them all the leading ideas are first clearly developed.

It was mainly in the land of the Jumna and the Ganges, from Kurukshetra to Benares, that the original discussions which created the new thought took place; and in the schools of the same regions the Upanishads took form. Since these treatises were formed by a process of slow growth and accretion, and were preserved, not in writing, but in human memories, it is not possible to fix on any definite dates for their composition. Yet it is clear that the teaching had taken very definite form, and was influencing men's thoughts far and wide, when Gautama, the Buddha, began to teach about 525 B.C.; and scholars believe that we may safely assume that by 500 B.C., this body of literature was already in existence in very much the same shape as it has come down to us.[5]

§ 55. The essential aim of the Upanishads is to explain reality, to discover the Absolute. All the ideas of the teaching circle round the great conception of Brahman-Ātman, the source, the support, and the reality of the universe. The human self is not a part of the divine Self, but is the Brahman-Ātman whole and undivided. It is knowledge that gives release. The man who in his own self

[1] 226. [2] I. 205. [3] *AĀ*. 43; *SS*. 16. [4] *LU*. 341.
[5] Hopkins, *YT*. 336, gives the sixth century as the date. Oldenberg suggests still earlier dates, *LU*. 288, and also Poussin, *WN*. 10.

realizes the truth of the Ātman is thereby liberated from the chains of transmigration and from the slavery of worldly things. He is an emancipated spirit, at death will enter into bliss, and will never be reborn. Through his liberation he enters at once upon a blessed experience; for he then begins to know the peace, immortality, and freedom of the supreme Ātman. These lines of belief run through the Upanishads everywhere; and the mass of the teaching seeks to illustrate these positions and to create the conviction that they are true.

But there is no articulated system taught.[1] Outside the leading ideas, the teaching is by no means uniform. The relation of the Brahman to the material world is expressed in several ways. In many passages the reality of the world is assumed; Brahman created it and entered into it; he pervades it and extends beyond it. In others the reality of the Brahman is stated so forcibly as almost to leave the impression that the world is an illusion. One there is, and there is no second. Only the great spiritual Unity exists; there is no manifold such as our eyes see in nature. He who affirms that the manifold exists does not know the One. In these idealistic passages great stress is also laid on the unknowableness of the Ātman. He is a subject without an object, the universal Subject, far uplifted beyond the need of any object, and therefore far beyond human understanding. Similarly, while the Ātman is usually conceived impersonally, there are many phrases which, if strictly interpreted, imply personality. He is called 'the inner Guide'; at his bidding sun and moon stay asunder; he causes men to do good works and to do evil works. The truth is, these wonderful treatises were not meant to build up a complete philosophical temple for the human mind, but rather to provide materials to stab the spirit awake, to open the eyes to the spiritual world, and to lead men to realization of God and renunciation of the world.

[1] Deussen expounds them as teaching an idealistic system: *PU.* 231, 398; but Oldenberg, *LU.* 59-104 and *passim*, and Keith, *SS.* 5, recognize fully the variant conceptions.

The Ātman is bliss, and the man who realizes his identity with the Ātman enters into peace, but, apart from the Ātman, all else is full of sorrow. All that comes into existence is evil. There is thus in the teaching of the Upanishads a basis for pessimism; but their general tone is by no means pessimistic.[1] Emancipation fills many a passage with a joyous radiance.

There are many strikingly beautiful and effective passages in these works; here a few sentences which recall the Psalms, there a brief paragraph which reminds one of Plato. There is a simple sincerity about them, and a childlike naturalness of vision which are very attractive. There are parts of these works which will take a high and permanent place in the world's best literature. But, after all, the books are but compilations; and, beside these lofty prophesyings which reveal the Indian mind at its noblest and greatest, there are many passages as futile and worthless as the poorest twaddle of the Brāhmaṇas. The Brāhman compiler had not yet learnt to separate the wheat from the chaff.

§ 56. The passion for release and the example of these wandering ascetics stirred many other groups of men to thought and inquiry; so that by the middle of the sixth century there were many leaders, each with his doctrine of release and his ascetic discipline, preaching on the plains of the north. These we merely mention now, for we must follow the school of the Upanishads to the end of the period.

The original Upanishads, which we dealt with above, continued to be taught orally in their respective schools as the source of that knowledge of the Brahman-Ātman which brings release from the bonds of karma and transmigration. But men had begun to realize that many passages in these treatises were worthless for the end in view; and the awkwardness of carrying a long piece of discursive prose in the memory as a spiritual tonic constantly obtruded itself; while the verses interspersed proved potent as teaching and easy to remember.

[1] See Keith, *S.S.* 13; Oldenberg, *I.U.* 115 ff.

Hence arose a new series of short Upanishads in verse, which are the sole surviving product of the teaching given in the schools on the subject of the Ātman during these centuries. Their purpose in the main is, not to introduce fresh teaching, but to express in more convenient form what was now the settled orthodox belief of the sannyāsī schools. We here set them out in the order of their age[1] and in their connexion with the Vedic schools:

Veda.	*School.*	*Upanishad.*
BLACK YAJUS	Kāṭhakas	*Kāṭhaka*
WHITE YAJUS	Vājasaneyins	*Īśā*
BLACK YAJUS		*Śvetāśvatara*
ATHARVAN		*Muṇḍaka*
BLACK YAJUS	Taittirīyas	*Mahānārāyaṇa*

It is impossible to give precise dates for any one of these poems, but most scholars would agree that, if we place the *Kāṭhaka* about 500 B.C.,[2] and the *Mahānārāyaṇa* in the third century,[3] we shall not be far wrong.

While it is true that the purpose of these treatises is rather a restatement of teaching than an advance in thought, yet the changes inevitable in the centuries appear in them. These are in the main in two directions. There is a distinct advance shown in the capacity for sustained thinking, and the subject is developed in more orderly sequence than in the earlier works.[4] There is a tendency towards the exaltation of Vishṇu and Śiva as symbols of Brahman, and an increasing emphasis is laid on self-discipline.

The introduction of Vishṇu and Śiva leads to a movement of thought in the direction of theism. In the *Kāṭhaka* there is little advance, but in the *Iśā* we meet with the word which is used in later literature to denote the personal Supreme in Hinduism, *Īśa*, *Īśvara*, Lord. In the *Śvetāśvatara* and in the *Muṇḍaka* the personal God stands out face to face with

[1] Deussen, *PU.* 24.
[2] Oldenberg, *LU.* 203; 288; 357; Keith, *SS.* 9.
[3] Keith, *JRAS.* 1908, 171 *n.* 2.
[4] Oldenberg, *LU.* 206.

the personal soul; yet the philosophy is monistic, and the full identity of the individual and the universal Ātman is maintained.[1] In the *Śvetāśvatara* Śiva is introduced under his old name Rudra; and, for the first time in Hindu literature, devotional feeling, *bhakti*, is spoken of as due to him. He is said to control the whole process of karma and transmigration.

When God is clearly conceived as a person, He is necessarily distinguished from the material universe as well as from the human soul. But the *Śvetāśvatara*, while it suggests divine personality in several ways, is unwilling to give up the ancient monism. Hence the material world is declared to be *māyā*, illusion, so that Brahman may remain the All as well as the One. This idea is of transcendent importance in the later religion.

In the hermitages of the Vānaprasthas, the austerities which were originally used to win supernatural power were employed to discipline the body and mind for religious purposes, the ends sought through the discipline being intercourse with the gods, purity of character, and an etherealized body;[2] and the word *yoga*,[3] 'yoking', 'restraint', was used to cover the whole range of these regulated methods of physical and mental control. In the verse Upanishads these methods are heartily commended for use in the search for Brahman.[4] In the old Upanishads, when the idea of the Ātman is reached by a rigorous process of abstraction, the result is an idealistic conception, a mind which is a subject without an object, a knower that is unknowable. This led quite naturally to the belief that, in order to apprehend the Unknowable in mystic vision, the soul must be disciplined to perfect stillness; and to this end the restraining methods of yoga were prescribed. In so far also as ethical conditions were regarded as a precondition of the enlightenment which is emancipation, the

[1] See Barnett, *JRAS.* 1910, 1363.
[2] *Chhāndogya U.* V. 10, 1; II. 23, 1; *Rāmāyaṇa*, II. liv; III. i; v; xii.
[3] *Taittirīya U.* II. 4.
[4] Oldenberg, *LU.* 258 ff.; Keith, *SS.* 55.

practice of yoga was regarded as helpful. In the *Kāṭhaka* and in the *Śvetāśvatara* yoga methods are very seriously commended; and we shall find that the early Buddhists were led by similar motives to similar practices. Along with the description of these exercises, a theory which explains them is stated in outline three times over in the *Kāṭhaka*, and it reappears in the *Śvetāśvatara*. It is not discussed in detail; yet the conceptions expressed and the technical terms used make it quite clear that it is the germ of what is known in later literature as the Sāṅkhya philosophy.[1]

In these treatises also the Vedānta first occurs as the name of the philosophy of the Upanishads. Both groups of Upanishads were attached to the Brāhmaṇas of the schools to which they belonged, and were recognized as *śruti*, revelation of the highest grade.

B. *Many Schools.*

§ 57. From the prose Upanishads and the earliest Jain and Buddhist literature it is plain that by the middle of the sixth century many speculative systems were already being taught,[2] each represented by a leader and his following of monks; for asceticism was as essential to the system-teacher in India then as the philosopher's cloak was in ancient Greece. Some of these teachers were not far removed from the sannyāsīs of the Upanishads, many were much more sceptical, while some were thorough-going materialists. It is not possible to sketch the systems clearly, but one significant fact stands out undeniable, that a number of them were distinctly atheistic, like the Karma Mīmāṁsā. The chief were the systems which came to be known as Jainism and Buddhism, but there were others. Clearly for a long time, seemingly for several centuries, the doctrine of the Brahman-Ātman laid hold of only a small proportion of thinking Hindus, while the vast majority re-

[1] For the exposition of these passages, see Deussen, *PU.* 249–53; Oldenberg, *LU.* 203–6; Keith, *SS.* 9–14.

[2] Rhys Davids, *ALB.* 30 ff.; Poussin, *WN.* 60.

tained the ancient Vedic polytheistic outlook. This accounts for the Karma Mīmāṁsā, Jainism, Buddhism, and other early atheisms, and also for the emergence of the Sāṅkhya and the Vaiśeshika at later dates. Two further elements of the intellectual atmosphere of those days render the atheistic attitude of the mass, and the materialistic standpoint of many, more comprehensible, first the world-constraining power credited to the sacrifice in the *Yajurveda*, and secondly the automatic character of the theory of transmigration and karma as usually taught :[1] there seemed to be no need for a ruler of the universe.

It seems most probable that the materialistic school, known in India as Lokāyata for two thousand years, was already in existence.[2]

It is probable that the Sāṅkhya and Yoga systems appeared, in early forms which we cannot now reconstruct, in the fourth or third century B.C. Dates are very doubtful: all we can be sure of is that the Sāṅkhya comes in the main from the philosophy of the early and the verse Upanishads,[3] and that the Yoga, while also indebted to the Upanishads, springs ultimately from popular magic and hypnotism.[4] Śūdras were admitted to the order of Sāṅkhya ascetics as readily as twice-born men, and both Śūdras and Outcastes could become yogīs: so that from the time of the foundation of these schools the pursuit of release was open to these classes within Hinduism itself.

§ 58. Amongst these clashing systems were two, now known as Jainism and Buddhism, whose principles speedily set them outside Hinduism and made them rival faiths. They were both founded by Kshatriyas. While both systems recognized all the gods and demigods of the Hindu pantheon, they spoke of them as of little strength and importance as compared with their own leaders. They therefore taught that it was folly to worship them, that the Veda was untrue, and the

[1] Poussin, *WN*. 58.
[2] Poussin, *WN*. 61; Keith, *JRAS*. 1917, 175, *n*. 2.
[3] Oldenberg, *LU*. 211; Keith, *SS*. Ch. I; Deussen, *AGP*. I. iii. 15.
[4] Garbe, *SY*. 34 ff.; Oldenberg, *LU*. 258 ff.

priestly work of the Brāhmans valueless. Both systems offered release to men of every race and caste. It is true that, in order to win release, it was necessary to become a monk. The laity could make a little progress, but could not expect to reach the goal until they accepted the life of renunciation. Yet, even so, this was a great advance on conditions within the school of the Upanishads, in which only men of the three highest castes could become sannyāsīs and press on to release. Hinduism could not fail to condemn both systems as heresies. Jainism is the earlier of the two, but we take Buddhism first because of it we have far fuller and clearer information than of Jainism.

C. *The Buddhist School.*

§ 59. Gautama, the founder of Buddhism, the most potent and attractive personality among all the sons of India and one of the greatest of men, was born at Kapilavastu, on the borders of Nepal, almost due north of Benares, about 560 B.C., the son of a nobleman of the Śākya clan. When about thirty years of age, he left his wife, his little son, and his father, and renounced the world. He became a disciple of several teachers in succession, but did not find satisfaction in their teaching and resolved to seek truth for himself. Finally, at the spot now known as Buddh-Gayā, in Bihar, his system took shape in his mind. From this time, somewhere about 525 B.C., until his death at the age of eighty (*c.* 480 B.C.), he spent all his energy in teaching his principles. He held that the final truth had appeared in him and therefore called himself the Buddha, the enlightened one. Since he was accepted by his followers as a full authority in matters of faith and life, his death must have been an irremediable loss to them. No one was appointed in his place: his teaching must now be their guide. That teaching, preserved in the memories of his disciples and gradually modified and expanded as time passed, finds expression in the Canon.

§ 60. His was an eminently practical system. He regarded

life as full of suffering and believed that his teaching provided the medicine necessary for the healing of men. He taught that the cause of suffering was desire, and sought to show the way whereby desire might be extinguished and release from karma and transmigration and every other form of suffering might be won. He invited men and women to the monastic life, in which under his guidance, as he believed, the *nirvāṇa*, i.e. the extinction, of desire, might speedily be accomplished. Those who reached nirvāṇa in this life, at death would enter final nirvāṇa,[1] and would not be born again.

He expressed the leading ideas of his system in clear and simple forms, and in the vernacular: all early Buddhist books are in the vernacular. The basis of the whole is given in the Four Noble Truths:

1. *The noble truth of misery.* Birth is misery; old age is misery; disease is misery; death is misery; sorrow, lamentation, misery, grief, and despair are misery; to wish for what one cannot have is misery; in short, all the five attachment-groups are misery.
2. *The noble truth of the origin of misery.* It is desire leading to rebirth, joining itself to pleasure and passion, and finding delight in every existence,—desire, namely, for sensual pleasure, desire for permanent existence, desire for transitory existence.
3. *The noble truth of the cessation of misery.* It is the complete fading out and cessation of this desire, a giving up, a loosing hold, a relinquishment, and a non-adhesion.
4. *The noble truth of the path leading to the cessation of misery.* It is this noble eightfold path, to wit, right belief, right resolve, right speech, right behaviour, right occupation, right effort, right watchfulness, right concentration.[2]

In discussing this path the Buddha explained that it was a middle course which shunned two extremes, the pursuit of worldly pleasures and the practice of useless austerities. The following is the exposition of the eight requirements of the noble path:

1. *Right Belief*: belief in the four noble truths.
2. *Right Resolve*: to renounce sensual pleasures, to have malice towards none, and to harm no living creature.
3. *Right Speech*: abstinence from falsehood, backbiting, harsh language, and frivolous talk.

[1] Warren, *BT.* 380.
[2] From *Dīgha-Nikāya*, 22, as translated in Warren, *BT.* 368–73.

4. *Right Behaviour*: abstinence from destroying life, from taking that which is not given, and from immorality.
5. *Right Occupation*: quitting a wrong occupation and getting one's livelihood by a right occupation.
6. *Right Effort*: the purpose, effort, endeavour, and exertion to avoid and abandon evil qualities, and to produce, preserve, develop, and make perfect meritorious qualities.
7. *Right Watchfulness*: strenuous, conscious, unsleeping watchfulness, as regards sensations, the mind, and the elements of being, so as to rid oneself of lust and grief and remain free.
8. *Right Concentration*: the progressive practice of hypnotic trances through reasoning, reflection, contemplation, tranquillization, intense thinking, and the abandonment of misery and of happiness.[1]

The path may be summed up as faith in the Buddha's teaching, vigorous intellectual effort to understand it and to apply it to life in detail, and an earnest moral life accompanied with regular meditation and the practice of hypnotic trances.

§ 61. Thus far we may be sure of our ground, but as soon as we ask what the Buddha taught about the nature of the world and man, and what happens in release, we find ourselves in difficulties, since it is impossible to make certain that the Sutta Piṭaka, which did not take final form until more than two centuries after his death, really represents his teaching. The prevailing doctrine in the Canon is that everything in the world is transitory, evil, and lacking in an ego,[2] and therefore that man has no soul. But if man has no soul, it would seem to be fair to conclude at once that there can be no rebirth, and further that, even if some shadowy form of continuity can be conceived which might make it possible to believe in transmigration, final release in these circumstances can only be final annihilation. The Canon is by no means consistent in its doctrine. Transmigration is certainly everywhere taught, but, while the existence of a self or immortal spirit is usually denied, there are passages where the soul is said to exist. Then, although in a few places release is said to be annihilation pure and simple, that is not the prevalent doctrine.

[1] From *Dīgha-Nikāya*, 22. Abbreviated from Warren, *BT.* 373-4.

[2] These three epithets are in a sense the watchwords of Buddhism. In Ceylon the monk, as he goes his rounds, may be heard muttering, *anichchha*, *dukha*, *anatta*.

Modern scholars have differed greatly in their reconstruction of the Buddha's teaching. The latest exposition, which is by Professor Poussin,[1] strives to do complete justice to all the evidence. He is inclined to believe that Gautama did deny the existence of a soul or permanent entity in man, but he believes he predicated the existence of a sort of substitute for a soul which may be reasonably conceived as a possible basis for transmigration. It is almost impossible to express the idea accurately and clearly in a sentence, but perhaps the following may suggest it. The exposition runs that in our psychical life there exists only the stream of consciousness, with its partial continuity, its imperfect identity, its continuous change; and it is this phenomenal thing that transmigrates, a something which is so changeable as to be no basis for the belief in a permanent soul, and yet has sufficient continuity to make it possible to speak of the individual as transmigrating. Thus man is altogether phenomenal, a composite of fleeting elements, yet rebirth takes place. But, if this is all that transmigrates, must we not conclude that, when transmigration does not take place, the man is annihilated? That seems to be the only possible conclusion. But the Buddha did not usually speak of deliverance as annihilation. In his teaching he eschewed, as far as possible, metaphysical questions as of no practical utility, and, indeed, as obstructions in the path towards the ideal. Hence nirvāṇa is usually called complete deliverance, and no description or definition of the state is added. Such is Professor Poussin's reconstruction of the history. It would, perhaps, be still better to suppose that the Buddha denied the existence of the soul while he affirmed transmigration and deliverance, and that he refused to enter into any philosophic justification of these positions.

§ 62. Buddhist tradition unanimously declares that a few weeks after the death of the master a great Council was held at Rājagṛiha, the capital of Magadha, and that there the rules for the monastic life, and also the discourses of the Buddha as

[1] *WN.* 34.

contained in the Sutta Piṭaka were rehearsed. All critical scholars agree that the story is unhistorical, and that the growth of the Canon is posterior to the death of the Buddha; but it is quite possible that the disciples assembled after the death of the founder to come to some agreement concerning the principal points of the creed and of the discipline.

Very little is known about the history of the faith or of the community during the next two hundred years. Clearly the movement spread; the literature gradually took shape; and differences of opinion on matters of both faith and practice arose among the monks; but it is not possible to give any comprehensible outline of the events of those years. A tradition is found in the Canon that, one hundred years after the death of the Buddha, a second Council was held at Vaisali, to examine and condemn ten illegitimate practices which the monks of that town claimed to have the right to follow, and a much later tradition declares that the Vinaya and Sutta Piṭakas of the Canon were recited here also. Scholars are ready to believe that a Council was held to discuss certain points of discipline and other questions, but the date remains quite uncertain, and the statements about the Canon are unhistorical.

§ 63. About two hundred years after the Buddha's death, however, light begins to fall on the history. Alexander's raid into the Punjab led to a revolution and change of dynasty in Magadha and to the establishment, under Chandragupta, of the first empire ever known in India. The grandson of Chandragupta, the founder of the Maurya empire, was Aśoka, one of the most remarkable monarchs the world has seen. He seems to have reigned from 273 to 232 B.C. A few years after he became emperor he added Orissa by conquest to his empire. According to his own account, the slaughter and misery which the conquest occasioned caused him such acute distress and repentance that he became a Buddhist and decided to wage no more war. Many scholars believe that at a later date he actually became a monk, at least for a short time.

The conversion of Aśoka made the fortune of Buddhism;

for, being a man of conviction and energy, he set about using the wealth, authority, and influence of his great position for the spread of the religion which he had adopted. He spent vast sums from the imperial revenue in erecting Buddhist buildings. The use of stone for architecture and sculpture seems to have begun in India about this time. Consequently, the earliest stone buildings erected on the soil of India dowered the Buddhist faith with a magnificent series of artistic monasteries, temples, and relic-mounds. He sent out monks as missionaries of the faith throughout the length and breadth of India, and also to Ceylon, to Burmah, to the Himalayas, to Afghanistan, and beyond. Great success followed both within and without the bounds of the empire. Ceylon became a Buddhist country, and along the southern slopes of the Himalayas, in Kashmir, and in eastern Afghanistan the faith took firm root. The emperor also prepared simple sermons for his people and had them cut on rocks by the side of pilgrim and trade routes, or on monumental pillars set up in prominent places, so that he might preach to the millions of his subjects and his neighbours. Laws were made to compel men to live in closer accord with the Buddhist ideal; and Government officials were required to help the imperial propaganda in the ordinary course of their duties.

§ 64. Tradition runs that a Council held at Patna during his reign for the settlement of several questions of faith and discipline, accepted the Tipiṭaka (Sansk. Tripiṭaka), the Buddhist Canon in three baskets, *Piṭaka*, or divisions, as under:

1. The *Vinaya*, or Discipline Basket, containing the rules for the life of monks and nuns.
2. The *Sutta*, or Sermon Basket, consisting in the main of dialogues and sermons.
3. The *Abhidhamma*, or Teaching Basket, containing chiefly manuals for the training of monks and nuns.

Is the tradition credible?

The following facts must be recognized. In the third century B.C., the Canon existed only in the memories of the monks and nuns; and it must have been in Māgadhī, the vernacular of Magadha and of the imperial capital, Patna. No portion of this original Māgadhī Canon survives, but the Ceylonese Canon, from which European scholars obtained their knowledge of early Buddhism, purports to be the identical books accepted at the Council. The language, however, is *Pāli*, a literary tongue which is believed to have been developed at a later date from several vernaculars, but especially from Māgadhī, and which was used by Ceylonese Buddhists for the literature of their faith alone. The Pāli Canon was reduced to writing in Ceylon in the first century B.C.; and in the later history it is but the Canon of the Vibhajjavādin school of Ceylon, and of others dependent on it. It is practically certain that this Pāli Canon and the later Sanskrit Canons of North India were derived independently from the Māgadhī original.

As to the relation of the Pāli Canon to the texts of the third century B.C., the position of advanced scholarship is probably best represented by Poussin, who, while acknowledging that the Vinaya and Sutta Piṭakas which we possess are on the whole very much the same as the early Māgadhī texts, yet holds that numerous changes were probably introduced in the time of oral transmission and in the process of translation into Pāli; and roundly declares that 'the apostolic or conciliar origin of the Abhidharma[1] is a pious fraud'.[2] He points out that, while all the schools acknowledged a Canon in two parts, the Vinaya and Sutta Piṭakas, only two schools, namely the Vibhajjavādins of Ceylon, who used Pāli, and the Sarvāstivādins, who probably belonged to Kashmir, and used Sanskrit, possessed an Abhidhamma Piṭaka, and the two collections are wholly independent. Consequently, we can recognize only the Vinaya and the Sutta Piṭakas as belonging to this period.

Further, if a General Council had been held in Patna, it could have been held only with Aśoka's permission and

[1] Abhidhamma in Pāli. [2] *Opinions*, 44.

co-operation ; and it would then almost certainly have been mentioned in his inscriptions. His silence thus suggests a serious doubt about the whole tradition.

§ 65. The central source of the Vinaya is the *Pātimokkha*. Twice every month the monks of every district met in solemn assembly, and the 227 articles of this Confession were recited aloud one by one, the reciter asking after the repetition of each rule whether any monk had been guilty of any transgression. The Confession with its Commentary forms the first book of the Vinaya, the *Sutta Vibhaṅga*. The second part is the Khandakās, the treatises, i.e. the *Mahāvagga* and the *Chullavagga*, which give rules for every part of the life of the monk and the nun. In both these parts of the Vinaya there are numerous stories and tales which are of extreme interest for the life of the Buddha and the early history of the Order. The third part, the *Parivāra*, is a scholastic list of subjects of little interest, probably a late addition to the Canon.

§ 66. The Sutta Piṭaka is of far greater interest. Here one enters into the life of ancient India and makes friends with people of every type, enjoying the simplicity, the humour, the kindliness of the peasant, listening to teaching of every sect, reverent and coarse, wise and foolish, new and old. Here we see religion in the process of being made and unmade. Everywhere walks the Buddha, supreme in his humanity, his fine gentlemanliness, his caustic wit, his quiet reasonableness, his radiant personality, winning his way among all classes of men by the moderation of his teaching and discipline, his feeling for human need, and his firm conviction that he has actually stormed the citadel of truth. The contents of this Piṭaka fall into five main groups.

I. The most attractive and most valuable of all the groups consists of *dialogues and sermons*. Nearly all are said to come from the Buddha himself, but a few are attributed to his immediate disciples. Each has a brief introduction, telling where and in what circumstances tradition said it had been uttered. These beautiful pieces of literature are to be found mainly in the Dīgha and Majjhima Nikāyas, but many fragments are scattered throughout the other collections. A number of dialogues are so full of the power and simplicity of genius that we can readily believe that they reflect with great faithfulness the teaching of the Master; many of the great phrases which form the basis of the teaching also unquestionably come from him; and probably also some of the brief poems which glow like gems amid the more sober prose; but a very large number of the pieces are clearly of later origin, created at various times to meet the needs of the Order or of the lay community.

II. The next group *centres in the Buddha*. There is no life of the Master in the Canon, but there are many biographical passages in both the Vinaya and the Sutta Piṭakas,[1] which were later combined to form biographies of the Buddha in Ceylon and India. In these narratives he is sometimes regarded as purely human, only exalted to wondrous powers by his enlightenment, but in many places he is spoken of as a demigod, and in others he is raised far above all the gods. The doctrine of karma and rebirth leads to the belief that he was gradually prepared for his final enlightenment in his previous births. Hence in the Book of Lives, the *Jātaka*, we have 550 mythical narratives of previous lives, and in the *Chariyāpiṭaka* 35 more, all set out as edifying stories for the Buddhist reader, a literature of extraordinary variety and interest. Further, since truth does not change, Buddhists began to believe that in the earlier ages the same teaching must have been proclaimed by other Buddhas. The outcome of this was a long series of Previous Buddhas. At first there were only three, then six, then twenty-four, then twenty-seven; but finally they became innumerable.[2] They are parallel

[1] The *Mahāvagga* in the Vinaya Piṭaka; the *Mahāparinibbāna* and *Mahāpadāna* suttas of the Dīgha Nikāya; suttas 26, 36, 123 of the Majjhima Nikāya; and the *Dhammachakkappavattana sutta* of the Samyutta Nikāya.

[2] *Mahāpadāna Sutta*; *Buddhavaṁśa*; *Nidānakathā*; *Lalita Vistara*: Waddell in *JRAS*. 1914, 677.

with the Jain Tīrthakaras and the incarnations of Vishṇu and of Śiva.

III. The third group consists of *short religious poems*, ejaculations, epigrams, psalms. The habit of giving expression in verse to the loftier moods of the monastic life seems to have begun with the Buddha himself, and was cultivated with very great success by many generations of pious monks and nuns. There are four collections of these poems, the *Dhammapada*, the *Udāna*, the *Thera Gāthā*, and the *Therī Gāthā*, but, besides these, numerous examples are scattered throughout the Canon.

IV. The fourth group consists of *edifying narratives and ballads*, which vary very much in literary and didactic worth. They seem to have been exceedingly popular among the Buddhist laity, but for us they have their chief interest as stores of folk-lore. In the *Mahāvagga*, the suttas of the Majjhima Nikāya, the *Apadāna* [1] and also in the *Jātaka*-book are numerous tales, and in the Samyutta Nikāya and the *Sutta Nipāta* many stories in verse and ancient ballads.

V. The fifth group consists of *magic texts*, charms against snakes, evil spirits, demons, &c. The *Khuddakapāṭha* and the 32nd sutta of the Dīgha Nikāya consist of texts of this type.

The early Buddhist church was, essentially, the double monastic order, yet there was a large laity also. The duties laid on them were, in the main, attention to the teaching of the Buddha, a really good moral life, the practice of *ahiṃsā*, i. e. non-injury to animals, and liberality to the monks and nuns. But from a very early date reverence for the Buddha and his chief followers led to the beginnings of a cult.[2] Each stūpa, erected over relics of the Buddha or of a noted preacher, became a place of pilgrimage and adoration. The hall in which the laity heard instruction from the monks had

[1] The word *Apadāna*, Sanskrit *Avadāna*, means a heroic deed, and is used of stories about Buddhist saints. This collection is in verse.

[2] The Buddha's attitude to Hindu priests and their sacrifices was so scornful that we may be certain that he established no ritual cultus among his disciples.

a stūpa set up in it to stir devotional feeling, and many symbols of Buddhist faith and practice received fervent adoration. In the time of Aśoka each great stūpa and chaitya became a splendid work of art; and music, shows, and processions were added to earlier observances; so that Buddhist worship began to rival the spectacular attractions of Hindu temple-worship and sacrifice.

§ 67. The Edicts of Aśoka form one of the most interesting of all Buddhist documents. They may be most conveniently studied in Dr. Vincent Smith's *Asoka*. The great Buddhist Mission carried to so much success during his reign is described in them from the point of view of the Emperor who organized and supported it, while the Chronicles of Ceylon describe it from the standpoint of the monastic community who provided the missionaries. The edicts show the extreme interest which the Emperor took in the expansion of the religion, not only among Hindus but also amongst the jungle-folk of India and foreign nations. They also enable us to see that he made large use of the imperial officials in order to spread amongst the people a knowledge of Buddhism, of the Emperor's faith in the religion, and of his desire that it should be widely adopted. One inscription names seven passages in the Canon which he recommends for study, his favourite texts. He lays very great stress on the virtue of saving animal life, and tells how he has restricted animal sacrifice by law and also the slaughter of animals for food. He was almost a vegetarian himself. Instead of the royal hunt, his Majesty now undertook religious tours to visit religious men and sacred places. One edict gives orders that monks or nuns who seek to create schism in the Buddhist church shall be unfrocked. This was probably published immediately after the Council at Patna, if such a council was held. An inscribed pillar also informs us that the Emperor had enlarged for the second time the Stūpa of Kanakamuni, one of the previous Buddhas.

Very little distinctive Buddhist teaching occurs in these edicts, except the insistence on the sacredness of animal life.

It is peculiarly noticeable that there is no single mention of karma and transmigration in them, and not the slightest allusion to nirvāṇa. Since the *Arthaśāstra* shows the same features, we are probably justified in concluding that karma and rebirth had not as yet laid serious hold of the common people in eastern India. The Emperor urges all men to practise the law of piety, first because of the good results which it produces in this world, but above all things because such conduct creates merit, and secures the other world for the pious man. Ordinary morality stands in the foreground, reverence to parents, relatives, teachers, and all religious men, proper treatment of slaves and servants, truth-speaking, liberality, gentleness to all living creatures. Similarly, toleration of all creeds, and liberality to ascetics and teachers of all denominations, are repeatedly recommended. The edicts thus contain scarcely anything which Brāhmans would not approve. Yet the prohibition of animal sacrifice must have been deeply resented.

D. *The Jain School.*

§ 68. For many years European scholars believed that Jainism was a schism or branch-system derived from Buddhism, but research has made it clear that the two are independent and that Jainism is the earlier of the two. Mahāvīra, who was a contemporary of the Buddha,[1] belonged to a Kshatriya family of good position, and was born in a town a little to the north of the site of Patna. He became a sannyāsī of an ascetic order which had been founded by a man named Pārśva, and developed it into the sect of the Jains. The canonical literature of the sect was not reduced to writing until nearly a thousand years after Mahāvīra's death, and it is as yet impossible to say whether any parts of it come from this period or not; so that it requires much caution to work back

[1] There is much uncertainty about his actual date. Jains themselves give two dates for his death, 527 and 467 B.C., while Buddhist texts represent him as a contemporary of the Buddha, and place his death a few years before the Buddha's nirvāṇa.

even to a bare outline of the founder's faith and discipline. A few features of the system, however, stand out with such distinctness that we should almost be justified in accepting them as primary without further evidence; statements found in early Buddhist books about the founder, his sect, and his teaching corroborate the Jain evidence very clearly on a number of points; and the relation between early Hinduism and early Hindu asceticism, on the one hand, and Jain beliefs and ascetic rules, on the other,[1] is so patent that we need not hesitate to accept the chief lines of the tradition as historical. These are the original atheism of the system, and the beliefs, that there are souls in every particle of earth, air, water, and fire, as well as in men, animals, and plants, and that, for the attainment of release, the practice of certain very severe austerities, *tapas*, the strictest abstinence from the destruction of life in any form, and the keeping of a number of moral rules are necessary. Monks and nuns had to pluck their own hair out by the roots, and were not allowed to drink cold water nor to bathe. After twelve years of rigorous austerities they were encouraged to commit suicide by self-starvation, if they chose to do so. The system is more closely allied to animism, hylozoism, and early ascetic practice than any other belonging to the period. The severe austerities and the rule of *ahiṁsā*, non-injury to both vegetable and animal life, both come from the discipline of the Vānaprasthas.[2] Mahāvīra organized the laymen and the lay-women of the community as well as the monks and the nuns. Only ascetics could hope to win release at once, but a faithful lay-life prepared the soul for becoming an ascetic in a future life. On the laity were laid simple moral rules and easy austerities, and it was their special duty to support the monks and the nuns. Mahāvīra did his work in the vernacular, and the Canon is in an old vernacular to this day. Amongst the many titles conferred on him, *Jina*, conqueror, was one of the most prominent. Hence his followers are called *Jaina*, Jains.

[1] Jacobi, *SBE.* XXII. x; xxii ff.; *ERE.* VII. 465.

[2] See § 30.

We may be certain that Jain worship arose in much the same way in which the Buddhist cult developed; for at later dates the two are absolutely parallel.[1]

§ 69. Of the history of Jainism during these centuries we know very little. There seems, however, to be reason to believe that from an early date a distinction tended to arise among the monks of the community, which finally led in the first century A.D. to a great schism. The question at issue was whether the monks should wear white robes or discard all clothing. This division of opinion disturbed the early life of the community in some degree. When the schism actually came, the Jains fell into two sects, the Śvetāmbara or White-clothed, and the Digambara or Sky-clothed, i.e. naked, and the division remains to-day.

The Jains have a tradition that Chandragupta, the founder of the Maurya Empire, was a Jain, that a famine broke out in Magadha during his reign, and that thereupon he abdicated his throne and went south with a great company of Jains under the leadership of Bhadrabāhu to Śravaṇa Beḷgoḷa in the Mysore country, where he became a monk and finally died by self-starvation. If the story is true, the date of the migration would be about 298 B.C.; for his son Bindusāra succeeded to the throne about that date; but, as its earliest attestation is an inscription at Śravaṇa Beḷgoḷa of rather a late date, scholars are very much divided with regard to its trustworthiness.[2]

§ 70. Tradition also says that, towards the end of the twelve years of famine, the sacred books were collected in a council of monks held at Patna, under the presidency of Sthūlabhadra. They are said to have been twelve in number and to have been called 'Aṅga', i.e. 'limbs', members of the body of scripture. The last Aṅga consisted of fourteen books which contained the utterances of Mahāvīra himself, while the first eleven were composed by his followers. Bhadrabāhu, who is said to have led the

[1] See § 121 and § 123.

[2] V. Smith, *EHI.* 146.

migration to the south, is believed to have been the author of three of the canonical books and of *niryuktis*, i.e. brief comments, on ten of them. The last Aṅga is irretrievably lost; but the Śvetāmbaras declare that the eleven Aṅga, which form the first division of their Canon to-day, are the identical books collected at the Council. The Digambaras, on the other hand, who confess that they no longer possess the original Canon, deny that the eleven Śvetāmbara Aṅga are genuine. All modern scholars acknowledge that there are many archaic elements in these Śvetāmbara books, and in particular that the accounts of Mahāvīra, the early community and its beliefs and practices, which we have already dealt with, are in the main at least historical. It thus seems to be clear that parts of the existing Aṅga must have been handed down orally with considerable fidelity for a thousand years; for they were not reduced to writing until about A. D. 500.

The problem set by the Aṅga is of a very complicated character. Their language is not the original Māgadhī, in which works recited and arranged at Patna in the third century B. C. must have been composed, but a later dialect akin in some respects to Māgadhī, but modified under the influence of the speech of the west of India, where the work of codification and writing was carried out about A. D. 500.[1] Further, there are clear proofs that they have undergone extensive alteration since then. Critical study has not yet gone far enough to make the solution of this most intricate problem possible. Thus, while it is probably true that a number of books were collected and recognized at Patna, no one can yet say what precise relation the canonical books bear to those original works. Weber holds that the existing books were formed between the second and the fifth centuries A. D., but Jacobi is inclined to think that parts of them may have come down from the Patna Council comparatively little changed.[2]

[1] See below, § 181.

[2] Weber in *IA.* XVII. 289, 342; XX. 24; Jacobi, *Kalpa-sūtra*, Intro., *SBE.* XLV, p. xl; Keith, *JRAS.* 1915, 551.

There is certainly no body of Jain literature belonging to this period to place beside the Buddhist Tripiṭaka.

§ 71. That the Jains were an important body in the time of the Maurya emperors is perfectly clear from the way in which Aśoka refers to them in one of his edicts.[1] The community have also a tradition that a grandson of Aśoka named Samprati reigned after him, and treated the Jain community with as much favour and munificence as his grandfather had shown to the Buddhists; but Samprati himself and the whole story are not known from any other source;[2] so that the truth of the narrative is extremely doubtful.

[1] Pillar Edict VII, in V. Smith's *Asoka*, 193. But Hoernle's theory, that the Ājīvikas, who are mentioned in the same edict and who received costly caves from Aśoka and his grandson, were Digambara Jains (*ERE.* I. 259), is probably erroneous (Bhandarkar, *IA.* XLI. 286).

[2] V. Smith, *EHI.* 192–3, 440.

CHAPTER III

THE MOVEMENT TOWARDS THEISM

200 B.C. TO A.D. 200.

§ 72. The Hindu movement towards theism shows two distinct stages, and a corresponding though not identical evolution within Buddhism takes place in two unfoldings also, and also at the same times. Great political changes form the background to those religious events.

Early in the second century B.C. the Maurya empire fell. A Hindu dynasty, the Śuṅga, took its place at the capital, Patna, and doubtless annulled Aśoka's laws against animal sacrifice; while on the now contracted western frontier crouched Bactrian Greeks, Parthians, and Scythians, waiting to spring at the central empire. Under the Hindu dynasty arose new texts of the *Rāmāyaṇa* and the *Mahābhārata* in which Rāma and Kṛishṇa walk the earth as divine incarnations. In Buḍdhist works of the same period the Buddha appears as a semi-divine being with new attributes.

The Scythian race called Kushans seized all the western frontiers of India soon after the Christian era, and about the middle of the century conquered the Hindu government at Patna, and thus formed a vast empire stretching from Central Asia to the Gangetic plain. Not long after these events, as it would seem, the *Bhagavadgītā* arose, in which Kṛishṇa is represented as a full incarnation of Vishṇu and as the eternal Brahman of the Upanishads: Vaishṇava theism was thus formed; and other sects hastened to follow the great example. About the same time, or a little later, Mahāyāna Buddhism was formed, in which the Buddha almost became an eternal god.

It seems clear that the wealth and general culture of the times created a strong and intelligent body of laymen, as distinct from the monastic orders. Literature, philosophy, and art all show great activity; and both Hindus and Buddhists found it necessary to modify their standards and prepare fresh literature to meet the needs of the cultured layman.

One of the greatest happenings of these centuries is the spread of Buddhism to Persia, to Turkestan, and to China.

i. HINDUISM.

A. *The Twice-born and their Literature.*

§ 73. No addition of any importance seems to have been made during this period to the literature of the Vedic schools except a number of new Upanishads. The sacrificial discipline of each school still consisted of Mantra, Brāhmaṇa, and Sūtra, with probably the further help of the Karma Mīmāṁsā system, while the Āraṇyaka and the Upanishad formed special courses. The Upanishads which made their appearance during the period fall into two classes, of which only the first attach themselves quite naturally to the original Vedānta texts. Of these there are three, the *Praśna*, *Maitrāyaṇa*, and *Māṇḍūkya*, the *Maitrāyaṇa* belonging to the *Black Yajus*, the other two to the *Atharvaveda*.

§ 74. It seems to be clear also that already about the middle of our period, there existed a work which summed up the teaching of the Upanishads, and was thus a forerunner of the famous but far later *Brahma-sūtra* of Bādarāyaṇa. That at least seems to be the natural inference from the reference in the *Bhagavadgītā*[1] to *Brahma-sūtras* and from the occurrence of the descriptive phrase *sarvopanishadvidyā*, i.e. 'the science of all the Upanishads', in the nearly contemporary *Maitrāyaṇa Upanishad*.[2] It is most likely that it was the example of the Karma-mīmāṁsā, which undertakes to unify

[1] XIII. 4. [2] II. 3.

and sum up the teaching on sacrifice, that led to the exposition of all Upanishad texts in similar fashion. The ancient Karma-Mīmāṁsā text of those days and also the original Upanishad manual were early lost, eclipsed by the classical documents of the next period.

§ 75. Thus far we have dealt with the legitimate literature of the Vedic schools. The second class of Upanishads have not the same standing. They fall into three groups, each related to a special type of ascetic, but all diverging in some degree from the original Vedānta texts. These are the Sannyāsa, Yoga, and Śaiva Upanishads. All were finally attached to the *Atharvaveda*, but in rather irregular fashion.

§ 76. It is clear that from some early date in the period there existed a document belonging to the Sāṅkhya philosophy. It is also probable that, besides the Yoga Upanishads already mentioned, an orderly exposition of the Yoga system existed. The Vaiśeshika, the Nyāya, and the Chārvāka systems must have each had a fundamental text. But these five all stood outside the Vedic schools and were regarded as more or less aberrant. The growth of the epic, which is discussed below, affords an opportunity of setting these works in historical connexion with the rest of the literature.

§ 77. The increasingly complicated curriculum taught in each Vedic school rendered it impossible for the student to master all the subjects taught ; and the result was that schools for the study of special subjects, such as grammar, law, and politics, were established. The law schools are of especial interest, as their labours were of large practical value for the twice-born layman. Their method seems to have been to take the Dharma-sūtra of some Vedic school and modify it in some degree, so as to make it suitable not for members of that school alone, but for all twice-born men. The Dharma-sūtras of Gautama and of Vāsishṭha, already included in our study of dharma in our last chapter, seem to have undergone this process.

§ 78. But verse was the medium for popular literature

during this period, and many of the old laws in their sūtra-form were ambiguous. Hence in the schools it became customary to express the old sūtras in ślokas. The most famous of all Indian law-books, the code of Manu, is a work of this kind, and took shape during the period. It is probable that it was founded on the Dharma-sūtra of the Mānavans, one of the sūtra-schools of the *Black Yajurveda*. The time of the creative activity of the Mānava law-school seems to have been contemporary with the gradual growth of the didactic epic. About the time when this latter was completed, or rather later, the labours of the school culminated in a great law-book in verse, the text of which thereafter underwent very little change.[1] Law-books in verse, in contradistinction to the older treatises in prose sūtras, are called śāstras. Hence, the full name of the text is the *Mānava Dharmaśāstra*, popularly known as the law of Manu, and usually said to be fabulously old. It is to be noted that this law-book and others of the same class were meant for the twice-born only. They are of special interest here because of their importance for the twice-born householder.

This great code registers several advances in Hindu religious law. Here, and also in the contemporary didactic Epic, the ideal is laid down, though it is not made compulsory, that the twice-born man should pass through the four *āśramas* in order, i. e. the life of the celibate student, the householder, the hermit, and the monk. No widow, not even a virgin child-widow, may remarry: her duty is to live an ascetic life. The twice-born may still eat flesh, but there are many restrictions.

§ 79. During this period there arose among twice-born householders a religious distinction which was destined to last throughout the history of the religion. As we shall see in our study of the Epic, there was a group of the twice-born on whom the worship of Vishṇu by temple and image had laid hold with such force that they tended to refuse to

[1] Hopkins, *GE.* 19.

recognize the other gods of the pantheon. Another group stood in a similar relation to Śiva.[1] Now the ritual of temple-worship had not sprung from Vedic sources, but apparently from ancient forms of worship traditional among Śūdras.[2]

It was thus inevitable that those who remained loyal to the ancient sacrificial worship should condemn the exclusive cult of Vishṇu and of Śiva as doubly heterodox, because its ritual was not Vedic, and because it did not worship all the gods.[3] Doubtless, there were many among the orthodox even at this early date who had a god whom they specially favoured; yet this did not affect their orthodoxy, for they freely acknowledged all the others.

From this time, therefore, we must recognize among the twice-born *the orthodox*, who are faithful to the Vedic pantheon and ritual, and *the sectarians*, who exalt one god to the neglect of the rest, and in his cult use a ritual and liturgy of non-Vedic origin. The position of the sects was greatly strengthened by the appearance of the *Bhagavadgītā*,[4] which provided the Vaishṇava with a theology, and led to the formation of a similar system for the worshipper of Śiva. These devoted sectarians still kept up the Vedic forms of worship in their domestic ceremonies, and observed the rules of caste with great strictness. Indeed, throughout their history they have sought to prove themselves orthodox Hindus, and in some cases with considerable success.

§ 80. It is probable that the mass of Śūdras belonged to no sect, but worshipped now one god, now another. That certainly has been the position of the mass of the Hindu people for many centuries. Doubtless there would be a certain number of intelligent Śūdras who would share the strictly sectarian position with their twice-born brethren, just as there is to-day, but they would scarcely be regarded as heterodox, since they were not allowed to perform the ancient sacrifices.

[1] Patañjali calls them Śivabhāgavatas, devotees of Śiva, and speaks of the stress they lay on the worship of images: *Mahābhāshya* on P.V. ii. 76.
[2] See § 51. [3] Chanda, *IAR.* 99. [4] See § 86.

B. *The Epics.*

§ 81. The movement towards theism within Hinduism has the ancient god Vishṇu for its centre. Two stages are very distinctly visible in the movement, and both are reflected in the growth of the epic poems.

The original heroic poem called the *Mahābhārata*, which celebrated the fall of the Kuru family through the wiles of the Pāṇḍus directed by Kṛishṇa, underwent considerable transformation and enlargement. The leading feature of the epic in this, its second stage, is that the Pāṇḍus are now regarded as the heroes of the epic, and, unlike former kings, they are represented as emperors ruling the whole of India. We also find mention in the poem of Yavanas, Pahlavas, and Śakas, i.e. Greeks, Parthians, and Scythians. The mythical Pāṇḍu empire is probably a reflection of the Maurya empire, while the mention of Greeks, Parthians, and Scythians would seem to point definitely to the time of the Śuṅgas. According to the statement of the epic itself, the poem consisted of 24,000 stanzas [1] at this stage, and modern scholars estimate that the epic kernel of the whole work runs to about 20,000 stanzas.[2]

We now turn for a moment to the *Rāmāyaṇa*. The five books of Vālmīki's original work are to-day preceded by one book and followed by another which are clearly of later date. Here also we meet with Yavanas, Pahlavas, and Śakas; so that these additions cannot be dated earlier than the Pāṇḍu form of the great epic.[3]

§ 82. The religious phenomena of both epics are also significant. In the new parts of both, the religion is still polytheistic and sacrificial, but the prominent divinities are now Brahmā, Vishṇu, and Śiva. It seems as if in the popular mind the three stood on an equality.[4] Still more noteworthy is the fact that Kṛishṇa and Rāma, the heroes of the two

[1] I. i. 81; 101; 105.
[2] Hopkins, *ERE.* VIII. 325 a.
[3] Jacobi, *R.* 28 f.; 50; 64; Macdonell, *SL.* 304 f.
[4] For the old religion at this stage, apart from the incarnation doctrine, see Hopkins, *RI.* ch. xix.

epics, are now represented as partial incarnations of Vishṇu,[1] while ancient deeds of divine might have been transferred from Indra and other old gods to Vishṇu.[2] In these facts we have the first clear indication in Indian literature of the rise of something like an organized sect within Hinduism. Vishṇu has now a group of worshippers who exalt him to a place of special honour, and this group has been able to seize and claim for itself the heroes of both the popular poems. A distinct polemic against Buddhism may also be traced in the new form of the *Mahābhārata*.

§ 83. These facts seem to point to the conclusion that the transformation of both poems took place after the fall of the Maurya empire. It is scarcely likely that a large work glorifying Hindu kings, and describing a triumphant Hindu empire, would have made its appearance under Buddhist emperors, far less that they would have tolerated direct attacks on Buddhism; while the publication of the ancient poems in these new and most attractive forms would be quite natural under the patronage of a Hindu monarch who had restored old liberties and re-established the sacrificial ceremonial.[3]

The two epics thus became religious works, glorifying the god Vishṇu; and ever since that time they have been regarded as Vaishṇava scriptures. But Vishṇu was not yet elevated to the position of the Supreme. A perusal of the first book of the *Rāmāyaṇa* will show that, while his followers praised him as the best of the gods, they still thought of him as one of the old divinities, a being similar in nature to Śiva, Brahmā, and the rest. This is but the first stage of the movement towards theism.

§ 84. We do not know how the Vaishṇavas were led to

[1] Macdonell, *SL.* 286, 305; *Rāmāyaṇa*, I. xix.

[2] Holtzmann, *MBH.* I. 10. The dwarf, Vāmana, is in the *Rāmāyaṇa* said to be an incarnation of Vishṇu, I. xxxi.

[3] Hopkins, *GE.* 399. Inscriptions belonging to the second and first centuries B.C., which mention Vāsudeva, i.e. Kṛishṇa, fit in well with this conception. Bhandarkar, *VS.* 3-4.

develop the doctrine of divine incarnation. The idea appears suddenly in the literature, and there is nothing in earlier Hindu thought that would seem to be a natural and sufficient source of the conception.[1] It may be that they were led to it by the example of the Buddhists, who, as we have seen, had already raised Buddha to divine powers and honours, and had created a series of precedent Buddhas stretching away into the distant past. So Kṛishṇa and Rāma with the Dwarf are now conceived as divine, and they already form a short series; for Rāma is held to have appeared at a much earlier date than Kṛishṇa, and the Dwarf precedes Rāma.

§ 85. We now pass to the consideration of the second stage of the movement toward theism, as reflected in the epics. Scholars believe that, during the first and second centuries of the Christian era, the large masses of didactic matter[2] which are found in certain sections of the *Mahābhārata* as it stands were added to the epic of 24,000 stanzas which we have just discussed. This fresh material consists in the main of discourses on Religion, Philosophy, Politics, and Law.[3] Books XII and XIII of the epic, as we have it to-day, consist almost entirely of this material, and masses of it are found also in Books III, V, VI, XI, and XIV. These numerous pieces of teaching are clearly of various date and authorship, and their critical study has not yet proceeded far enough to enable us to arrange them in chronological order; yet certain differences in date stand out quite clear. This whole mass of new material is usually called the didactic epic,[4] to distinguish it from the real epic and the episodes. Scholars believe that it arose in the eastern section of North India.[5]

[1] Yet the idea that a god may temporarily take the form of an animal or a man was clearly present in early Hindu minds; for in the Brāhmaṇas there occur the stories of the fish and the dwarf. These tales may have helped in the evolution of the new conception. Indeed the Dwarf became one of the recognized avatāras of Vishṇu.

[2] Hopkins, *GE.* 387; 398; *ERE.* VIII. 325 ff.

[3] 'The sacred law, the best manual of polity and a guide to salvation', is what the epic itself says, I. 62, 23.

[4] Hopkins also calls it the Pseudo-epic.

[5] Hopkins, *GE.* 78.

C. *The Bhagavadgītā.*

§ 86. The earliest, and also the greatest, of all the sections that form the didactic epic is the far-famed *Bhagavadgītā*. The date of this poem has caused endless discussion. Its own statement is that it was uttered by Kṛishṇa and Arjuna on the fateful field of Kurukshetra, just before the fighting began; and that is the Hindu tradition to this day. Mr. Justice Telang believed that it belonged to the fourth century B.C.,[1] and Sir R. G. Bhandarkar argues in favour of the same date,[2] but most modern scholars recognize that, in its present form, it can scarcely be earlier than the first or second century A.D. What is perfectly clear is that it is later than the fresh material of the second stage of the two epics, and earlier than the rest of the documents of the didactic epic.[3]

§ 87. The poem is a very remarkable one, and has had an immeasurable influence on religion in India. There is no other piece of literature that is so much admired and used by thinking Hindus; and it has won very high praise from many Western thinkers and scholars. Numberless editions, in the original and in translations in many tongues, fall from the press. But it becomes still more remarkable and interesting when one realizes its historical origin. It is the expression of the earliest attempt made in India to rise to a theistic faith and theology. In order to reach this ideal, the Vaishṇava sect identify their own god Vishṇu, on the one hand with the great Brahman-Ātman of the Upanishads, and on the other with Kṛishṇa, the hero of the Epic. There is a double exaltation here. Until now Vishṇu has been but one of the gods of Hinduism, in nature indistinguishable from the other members of the pantheon, though in the two centuries before our era he held a high position among them beside Brahmā and Śiva. Now he is declared to be the Absolute,

[1] *SBE.* VIII. 34. [2] *VS.* 13.

[3] Holtzmann, *MBH.* II. 121; Hopkins, *GE.* 205, 225, 384, 402; Keith, *SS.* 33, 34.

the One without a second, the source of all things and all beings. Kṛishṇa, who had been recognized as a partial incarnation of Vishṇu in the second stage of the Epic, is now declared to be a full incarnation of Vishṇu-Brahman, and receives the title Bhagavān, blessed Lord. Hence the name of the poem, *Bhagavadgītā*, the Lord's Song. Each of these changes is an advance towards theism. The identification of Brahman with Vishṇu distinctly suggests that the Absolute is personal; and the contention that the same Brahman is fully represented by a being who walked the earth in human form bodies forth the personal idea in the most vivid way possible. The change is most revolutionary. Let the student once more read some of the loftiest passages of the ancient Upanishads with the new thought in his mind.

§ 88. But the poem seeks not only to create a theism but to bring a spiritual religion within the reach of all Vaishṇavas. The Upanishads had taught cultured Hindus to aim in their religion not at rewards on earth or a sensuous heaven, but at release from transmigration; and Buddhism and Jainism had attempted, in their heterodox way, to stimulate all classes to the same high endeavour. The *Gītā* shows us the reconstitution of the Vaishṇava sect under the pressure of these powerful movements. The precise limits within which this is done must also be noticed. The Upanishads as taught in the Vedic schools offered release only to the three highest castes, for these holy texts might not be uttered in the hearing of any but the twice-born; Buddhism and Jainism, on the other hand, offered release to all, to Outcastes and foreigners as well as to Hindus of the four castes, and to women as well as men; but the *Gītā* takes a middle course, offering release to all Hindus, i.e. to men and women of the four castes but to no others. It is noticeable that these are precisely the bounds of the sect; all Hindus of the four castes were admitted to Vaishṇava, as to other Hindu, temples. But there is another and still more revolutionary change. In all earlier systems release was possible only for those who gave up the ordinary life of man and became professional ascetics. In the *Gītā* release is made available for the layman and his wife while they maintain the household and take part in the business of the world. These two radical changes necessitated a fresh book: the *Gītā* was written to become the layman's Upanishad. It may also be said with truth that the *Gītā* is a worthy successor to the old Upanishads.

§ 89. The *Gītā* sets forth three distinct ways in which release may be won. The first is the JÑĀNA MĀRGA, or way of knowledge, as taught in the Upanishads and the Sāṅkhya philosophy, and in a modified way by Buddhism and Jainism. The second is the KARMA MĀRGA, or way of works. The earliest conception of religion in Hinduism was a system of duties, summarized in the word dharma. The most prominent of these works in the early days were the sacrifices; but all the duties of caste and condition, of the family and society, were also included. The *Gītā* doctrine of works, which is called Karma-yoga, is this, that the mere performance of the works ordained in Scripture wins only the transient rewards on earth or in heaven that are promised for them, but that the man who does these works without any desire for the rewards will thereby win release. The word Yoga is used in so many senses in the *Gītā* that it is hard to decide which of them is implied in the phrase Karma-yoga, but it probably comes from the radical meaning 'restraint'. The third, BHAKTI-MĀRGA, the path of devotion, is a new method of winning release. It is simply this: that whole-hearted devotion to Kṛishṇa brings release from transmigration as effectively as philosophical knowledge or the selfless performance of ordained duties.

The method of devotion is the link between the ancient cult of the sect and the new teaching of the *Gītā*. For the whole-hearted devotion which brings release finds its most natural and most vivid expression in the regular worship of Kṛishṇa in the temples of the sect.[1] The cult would have

[1] Cf. IX. 6 with XI. 46.

a new dignity to thinking Vaishṇavas, since it would henceforward be to them not a means merely to health, wealth, and happiness, but also to the great spiritual end of the emancipation of the soul from all the bonds of the phenomenal universe.[1] There is just one change in the cult to be noticed. The *Gītā* recognizes no animal sacrifice. The offerings to Kṛishṇa which it commends are purely vegetarian.[2] Thus we must conclude that, about the time when the new theology came to the birth, animal sacrifice was given up in the chief Vaishṇava shrines. The rule is now universal among Vishṇuites.

§ 90. It is of great importance to notice that the *Gītā* calls upon all Vaishṇavas to keep the Hindu law as taught in the Dharmaśāstras.[3] The rules of caste,[4] the laws of the family, and the regular worship of ancestors,[5] are all to be strictly observed. It has been often said that the *Gītā* is opposed to caste, but that is a complete mistake: the principles and rules laid down in the poem are luminously clear.

§ 91. One of the most startling features of the poem is the transformation of Kṛishṇa. In the genuine epic he is a king and warrior, famous as a grim and powerful fighter, but notorious above all things for his extraordinary cunning and his dirty tricks: in the *Gītā* he plays the philosophical guru, quoting the Upanishads and praising the Sāṅkhya philosophy; from time to time he declares himself to be the supreme Ātman,[6] the source and support of the whole universe, the object of all devotion and the recipient of all sacrifices; and again he displays his indescribable glory before the eyes of his astonished friend.[7]

§ 92. The theology of the poem is a most imperfect theism.[8] The idea of the writer seems to have been that he could form

[1] IX. 34; X. 10; XI. 54; XII. 2. [2] IX. 26.
[3] XVI. 23; 24; XVII. 1; 5. For the Dharmaśāstras see § 78.
[4] I. 43; II. 31-33; 37; III. 23-6; 35; IV. 13; XVIII. 41-8.
[5] I. 40-44.
[6] X. 12, 20; VII. 6; 7; 10; IX. 8; 10; 13; XIV. 3; IX. 23-24.
[7] XI. 9-31. [8] Cf. Keith, *JRAS*. 1915, 548.

a new Vaishṇava system by the mere juxtaposition of the worship of Kṛishṇa and the great philosophies of his day, for he does not attempt to modify and fit together these rather incongruous elements so as to create from them a well-articulated theology.

This is especially true with regard to the relation of the Vedānta to the Sāṅkhya. The latter system was clearly very popular in those days.[1] In contrast with the Upanishads, its chief conceptions seem to have been chiselled and polished to smoothness, and carefully fitted together in a system of metaphysical and psychological ideas which any one could readily understand. Further, in it the external world was regarded as a reality, and the soul and its individuality were frankly acknowledged. Thus, in spite of its atheism,[2] these Sāṅkhya conceptions seemed to fit better into a theistic theology than the monistic conceptions of the Upanishads. The Yoga also was popular, but whether it had yet become a theistic system is not known.

The author brought the three together, declared them identical, and placed them beside Kṛishṇa, the incarnation of Vishṇu viewed as the Absolute. These divergent conceptions are not fused into a higher unity but are superimposed, so that the effect is like a composite photograph. Here and there are theistic passages;[3] from other sections a stark pantheism stares out;[4] and now and then the lines seem to suggest an emanation theory and several gods.[5] Nor is anything done to lessen the gulf that yawns between the actionless Brahman of the Upanishads and the incarnate god, born to slay demons and to teach philosophy.[6]

§ 93. What unquestionably gives the *Gītā* its power is the representation of the Supreme as incarnate and as teaching

[1] Hopkins, *GE.* 99 f.

[2] See *Gītā*, XVI. 8, which certainly alludes to a *nirīśvara* system. So Hopkins, *GE.* 105.

[3] IV. 5–7; VI. 47; IX. 22–34; XI. 36–46; XII. 14–20; XVIII. 55–70.

[4] II. 72; IV. 24; V. 24–26.

[5] III. 15; VII. 30; VIII. 3–4; 20–21; XV. 16–18.

[6] IV. 8.

the loftiest philosophy of India to his friend Arjuna, so that he and other simple laymen may find release. The portrait of the incarnate One is drawn with great skill; the situation in which the teaching is given enforces certain of the lessons taught with great vividness; and the literary qualities of the book are well worthy of the teaching it contains. The *Bhagavadgītā* is a very great work.

§ 94. It is of importance to realize that, though the teaching of the *Gītā* is now the very cream of orthodoxy, it was in some respects heterodox when the poem was written. This comes out most clearly in the section of the second book,[1] where the Vedas are spoken of with some scorn, and in several passages elsewhere in which the opponents of Kṛishṇa are very vehemently criticized. The fact is that the poem sprang from the young Vaishṇava sect, the heterodox position of which is explained above.[2] At a later point an attempt will be made to show how the *Gītā* came to be regarded as orthodox.[3]

§ 95. The poem bears traces of having been rewritten,[4] but two very different theories of its origin are held by scholars. Accepting Bhandarkar's theory of the origin of the worship of Kṛishṇa,[5] Garbe[6] attempts to explain the inconsistent theological teaching of the *Gītā* by the hypothesis that it was originally written, early in the second century B.C.,[7] on the basis of the Sāṅkhya-Yoga system, as a theistic tract to glorify Kṛishṇa, and that it was contaminated with the pantheism of the Upanishads in the second century A.D. He analyses the poem into what he believes to be these two sources. A few scholars[8] have accepted this theory, but most would probably

[1] 41–46. [2] § 79. [3] § 144.
[4] Hopkins, *GE*. 205, 234. [5] See above, § 50.
[6] *Die Bhagavadgītā*, Leipzig, 1905; also *IC*. 228 ff.
[7] This date is partly based on the belief that the *Yoga-sūtra* was written by the grammarian Patañjali in the second century B.C., but since it is now clear that the *Yoga-sūtra* dates from the fourth century A.D. (see below, § 139), the theory seems very improbable. See Keith, *SS*. 30.
[8] Winternitz, I. 373; Grierson, *ERE*. II. 541; and Chanda, *IAR*. 98.

follow Hopkins and Keith[1] in saying that the analysis is altogether unconvincing. It is much more likely that the *Gītā* is an old verse Upanishad, written rather later than the *Śvetāśvatara*, and worked up into the *Gītā* in the interests of Krishnaism by a poet after the Christian era.

A careful comparison of the *Gītā* with the *Saddharma Puṇḍarīka*[2] in ideas, language, and verse would probably help to solve the problems presented by both poems. A number of writers have believed that the *Gītā* distinctly betrays Christian influence, but it seems rather more probable that the poem is purely of Indian origin.[3]

§ 96. The *Bhagavadgītā* is the key to the whole of the didactic epic. Its chief characteristics reappear in nearly all the remaining religious documents added to the great poem in the third stage of its history. Even in the few places where Krishṇa's claim is denied, and Śiva, or Sūrya, or Brahmā is glorified as the one God, the influence of the *Gītā* is still supreme; for the mode of exaltation is borrowed directly from the Song: it is only the name of the god exalted that is altered.

D. *The Philosophies.*

§ 97. The *Maitrāyaṇa Upanishad* probably arose about the same time as the *Gītā* or rather later, and it is certainly earlier than the didactic epic, for in two passages its teaching and language are clearly reflected.[4] We therefore take the Upanishad as standing between the two. Along with it we take the *Praśna* and *Māṇḍūkya* Upanishads. The former is clearly earlier, and the latter later, than the *Maitrāyaṇa*,[5] but probably no long time intervenes in either case: for in their doctrine of the sacred syllable *Om* they are very closely

[1] Hopkins, *JRAS.* 1905, 384; Keith, *JRAS.* 1915, 548. Deussen also rejects the theory.

[2] See *SBE.* XXI. xxvi; xxxiv, and below § 125.

[3] For all the theories and a summary of the evidence, see Garbe, *IC.* 244 ff.

[4] Hopkins, *GE.* 33 ff.

[5] Deussen, *PU.* 25.

connected. The *Maitrāyaṇa* alone is of serious significance for the evolution of religious ideas. Professor Keith thus writes[1]:

> The Upanishad clearly reflects a period when various forms of heresy —probably in no small measure the Buddhist—had attacked the main outlines of the system of the Upanishads, and it endeavours to restate that position with, as is inevitable, many traits borrowed from the doctrine it was refuting, and among these traits are clear marks of the Sāṅkhya. It is characterized by a profound pessimism which is not countenanced by the older Upanishads, which lay no stress normally on that doctrine, but which is characteristic at once of Buddhism and of the Sāṅkhya.

§ 98. Sāṅkhya conceptions, similar to those found in the *Gītā* and the *Maitrāyaṇa*, appear also in the didactic epic, and betray the existence of a formed system, an atheistic dualism, enumerating twenty-five principles, extremely like the classic form of the philosophy presented in the *Sāṅkhya Kārikā*, but not identical with it.[2] The Yoga reflected in the *Maitrāyaṇa* is more detailed than that found in any earlier Upanishad, but the epic shows a still more advanced stage.[3]

§ 99. The Yoga philosophy which appears in the *Artha-śāstra* may not have contained the theistic element which occurs in the classic system; nor do we find any conclusive evidence of the existence of the theistic form in the *Gītā*. But in the latest parts of the didactic epic there is frequent mention of the theistic system of Yoga,[4] though in a form less complete than that of the *Yoga-sūtras*.[5] As the *Chūlikā Upanishad* presents the theistic Yoga in the simplest form which we know, we are justified in assigning it to a place near the *Gītā* and before the latest parts of the epic; and since the Sāṅkhya conceptions of the *Chūlikā* stand in very close relation to those of the *Maitrāyaṇa*, the two Upanishads probably belong to very nearly the same time.[6]

[1] *SS.* 13.

[2] Deussen, *SUV.* 312–13; Hopkins, *GE.* 97–133; Keith, *SS.* 11–13; chap. iii.

[3] Hopkins, *YT.* 335 ff.

[4] Hopkins, *GE.* 97–138; Keith, *SS.* 55.

[5] Hopkins, *YT.* 335; 336.

[6] Deussen, *SUV.* 637.

But the *Chūlikā* is clearly not the only Yoga-manual that existed in our period. Among the many teachers of Sāṅkhya and of Yoga named in the didactic epic two seem to be historical, Pañchaśikha and Vārshagaṇya.[1] Numerous references to them occur in the classic documents belonging to the two schools, and a few quotations are embedded in the *Yoga-bhāshya*,[2] and in Vāchaspatimiśra.[3] The evidence is very confused, so that it is hard to make sure of the truth. Probably the most satisfactory solution is to conclude that both authors belonged to the school of theistic Yoga, that Vārshagaṇya was the author of the *Shashṭitantra* (i. e. the Sixty-treatise), a famous work now lost, which seems to have been in verse,[4] while Pañchaśikha wrote a manual in sūtras,[5] which is also lost. These works and the *Chūlikā* probably belong to the group of Yoga treatises referred to in the epic.[6] Another interesting tradition which appears in the epic is that Pañchaśikha is the teacher of the new Vaishṇava sect, the Pāñcharātras,[7] whom we shall have to deal with below.

§ 100. There are also two groups of short Upanishads of rather later date which were clearly meant to be practical manuals for monks of the Vedānta and Yoga schools. The first group glorify *sannyāsa*, the world-renunciation of the Vedānta, and describe the initiation and the life of the sannyāsī, while the Yoga group describe the six elements of Yoga discipline (later they became eight) and give special attention to meditation on the sacred syllable *Om*. These treatises are clearly posterior to the *Maitrāyaṇa* and the *Chūlikā*, and earlier than the *Vedānta-sūtras* and the *Yoga-sūtras*. They are probably to be regarded as of the same general date as the didactic epic, where many of their features reappear, but some may be still later.

[1] XII. 218; 319 f.
[2] Woods, *Yoga*, 359-60; also *Sāṅkhya-kārikā*, 70.
[3] *Sāṅkhya-tattva-kaumudī*, 206.
[4] Keith, *SS.* Chap. v. Cf. Schrader, *ZDMG.* 1914, 101-10; *JPAS.* 110 ff.
[5] Keith, *SS.* 42.
[6] XII. 301, 57; 340, 67, Hopkins, *GE.* 100, 110.
[7] Hopkins, *GE.* 144; but see Keith, *SS.* 39.

Of the Sannyāsa group[1] which are mostly in prose, the *Brahma* and the *Sannyāsa* are composite, their earliest portions being quite as early as the *Maitrāyaṇa*, if not earlier. The later parts of these tracts and the *Āruṇeya*, *Kaṇṭhaśruti*, *Jābāla*,[2] and *Paramahaṁsa* do not differ much in age, and are probably not later than the chief documents of the didactic epic; while the *Āśrama* may be of later origin.

The Yoga[3] group are all in verse, and all follow the lead of the *Chūlikā*. The earliest seemingly is the *Brahmabindu*, which may be as early as the *Maitrāyaṇa*. The main group, consisting of the *Kshurikā*, *Tejobindu*, *Brahmavidyā*, *Nādabindu*, *Yogaśikhā*, *Yogatattva*, *Dhyānabindu*, and *Amṛitabindu*, run parallel with the main Sannyāsa group and the didactic epic,[4] while the *Haṁsa* is later and of indeterminate date.

§ 101. The Vaiśeshika and Nyāya philosophies were already in existence in the first century A.D. Both are mentioned by Charaka,[5] court physician to king Kanishka; and Aśvaghosha[6] his contemporary, and Nāgārjuna[7] who came later, mention the Vaiśeshika. Both are reflected in the didactic epic, but the evidence is too slender to enable us to see what the form of either system was.

E. *The Didactic Epic.*

§ 102. The main didactic epic is believed to have been practically complete by 200 A.D.[8] It deals with a variety of subjects, but three are of more importance than the rest, Politics, Law, and Religion. Philosophy is included under religion, and ethics partly under law and partly under religion.

§ 103. The compilers of the didactic epic introduced a considerable body of political teaching into their cyclopaedia.

[1] Deussen, *SUV.* 678-715.

[2] This is clearly a shortened and modified form of an early Upanishad belonging to the *White Yajus.* See Deussen, *SV.* 11.; *SUV.* 706.

[3] Deussen, *SUV.* 629-77.

[4] Thus Hopkins, *YT.* 379, says that the Yoga-technique of the epic is on a par chronologically with the *Kshurikā.*

[5] *Saṁhitā*, iii. 8, 26 ff; Keith, *JRAS.* 1914, 1093.

[6] Winternitz, II. i. 209.

[7] Woods, *Yoga*, xviii.

[8] Hopkins, *GE.* 387; *ERE.* VIII. 325.

The first half[1] of the twelfth book is almost wholly given to the subject, and shorter pieces occur elsewhere.[2] The relation of this teaching to Kauṭilya's *Arthaśāstra*,[3] to later political treatises, and to the actual state of affairs at the time of the epic,[4] does not seem to have been yet worked out by scholars.

§ 104. It was natural that the Vaishṇava priests, who in the interests of their sect turned the ancient epic into an encyclopaedia of instruction, should wish to include in it a body of law, and that they should choose the new popular form of law in verse. It is also of interest to remember that their constituency included Śūdras and women as well as twice-born men,[5] and even people lower than Śūdras.[6] The legal material is found chiefly in the thirteenth book[7] of the *Mahābhārata*, and shows a very close relationship to the *Mānava Dharmaśāstra*. Hopkins[8] writes:

> In all probability the code known to the later epic was not quite our present code, but it was a code much like ours and ascribed to Manu, a Śāstra which, with some additions and omissions, such as all popular texts in India suffer, was essentially our present text.

F. *Vaishṇava Material in the Didactic Epic.*

§ 105. Since the transformation of the epic into an encyclopaedia of religion, law, and politics was carried out in the interests of the Vaishṇava sect, nearly all the religious sections are devoted to the exposition of the theology first sketched in the *Bhagavadgītā*, and to the praise of Kṛishṇa. The second half of the twelfth book, known as Mokshadharma, is a sort of corpus of Krishnaite teaching, containing a number of pieces of distinct origin, and there are noteworthy sections also in Books III, V, VI, XIII, and XIV. Four of these

[1] Chaps. 1–173.
[2] I. 87; 140–5; II. 15; 17; 25; 62; III. 32; 33; 159; IV. 4; V. 33–4; 36–9; XIII. 13; XV. 5 ff.
[3] See above, § 45.
[4] See Hopkins, *Ruling Caste*, *JAOS*. XIII.
[5] *Gītā*, IX. 32.
[6] Hopkins, *GE*. 2.
[7] Numerous pieces of legal lore are found elsewhere, especially in the first and twelfth books.
[8] *GE*. 22–3.

portions are of such outstanding philosophic and religious interest that they are frequently selected for separate treatment:

V. 40–45: Sanatsujātīya.
VI. 25–42: Bhagavadgītā.
XII. 174–367: Mokshadharma.
XIV. 16–51: Anugītā.

There is one chapter[1] in the thirteenth book which is greatly treasured by devout Vaishṇavas, because it contains the thousand names of Vishṇu, and one chapter in the third book[2] contains a panegyric of Vishṇu by Bhīma, and another, in the political portion of the twelfth book[3], contains a hymn of praise to Vishṇu sung by the great Bhīshma.

We have already discussed the *Gītā*. One considerable section of the Mokshadharma[4] is known as the Nārāyaṇīya and seems to reflect a later period in the history of the Vishṇuite sect. It will therefore be discussed separately along with a passage from the sixth book,[5] which seems to contain similar teaching. The other portions fall to be considered here.

The leading ideas here are the same as in the *Gītā*. We are taught that the highest religion is the worship of Kṛishṇa as Vishṇu, who is the Brahman of the Upanishads. The Śāṅkhya and the Yoga systems are represented as being essentially the same as the philosophy of Brahman, and all three are taught as philosophic foundations for the Vaishṇava religion. There is no care taken to describe any one of these systems with precision, and no articulated Vaishṇava theology is taught. As in the *Gītā*, there are large pieces of a Sāṅkhyan character, others that teach Yoga, and yet others that reflect the monism of the Upanishads. The Sanatsujātīya (V. 40–45) is the most important monistic section. Numerous passages teach slightly variant philosophic systems in which Sāṅkhya, Yoga, and Upanishad elements intermingle interminably. The student may scan these outlines in Hopkins's

[1] 149. [2] 271. [3] 48. [4] Chaps. 335–52.
[5] Chaps. 65–8.

Great Epic.[1] The *Anugītā* is a direct imitation of the *Gītā*. In these passages theology makes no perceptible advance, but the pictorial myth of Śesha, Vishṇu, and Brahmā appears, and six incarnations of Vishṇu are mentioned, the Boar, the Man-lion, the Dwarf, the Fish, Rāma, and Kṛishṇa.

§ 106. We now take the Narāyaṇīya,[2] which shows a later stage of Vaishṇava teaching. The ancient name Bhāgavata occurs, but Sāttvata,[3] and Pāñcharātra,[4] especially the latter, appear more frequently. There is a Pāñcharātra scripture[5] compiled by the seven Chitraśikhaṇḍin Ṛishis, doubtless the forerunner of the Saṁhitās which we shall discuss later.[6] The origin and meaning of the word Pāñcharātra are not yet known with certainty.[7] We have shown above in what precise respects the sect was heterodox.[8]

In the Nārāyaṇīya occurs the doctrine of Vyūha or expansion, according to which Vishṇu exists in four forms. The doctrine[9] is that from Vāsudeva springs Saṁkarshaṇa, from Saṁkarshaṇa Pradyumna, from Pradyumna Aniruddha, and from Aniruddha Brahmā. Saṁkarshaṇa and the three others are then identified with the cosmic existences posited by the Sāṅkhya philosophy thus:

Vāsudeva . .	the supreme Reality.
Saṁkarshaṇa .	primeval matter, *prakṛiti*.
Pradyumna .	cosmic mind, *manas*.
Aniruddha .	cosmic self-consciousness, *ahaṁkāra*.
Brahmā . .	Creator of the visible world, the *bhūtāni*.

It is very difficult to make out what the idea behind this scheme is.[10] Vāsudeva is Kṛishṇa; Balarāma, or Saṁkarshaṇa,[11] is Kṛishṇa's brother, Pradyumna his son, and Aniruddha one of his grandsons. It is probable that these three were local

[1] Chap. iii. [2] XII. 335-52. [3] XII. 349, 29.
[4] XII. 336, 25; 349, 82; 350, 63.
[5] XII. 336, 28; 349, 82; 350, 67.
[6] § 212. [7] See Schrader, *IPAS.* 24 ff. [8] Above, § 79.
[9] See Schrader, *IPAS.* 35 ff.; Chanda, *IAR.* 109 ff.
[10] See Schrader, *IPAS.* 39 ff.
[11] Saṁkarshaṇa means 'Withdrawn', because he was drawn out of his mother's womb and placed in Rohiṇī.

divinities, that an arrangement was made to bring them into relation with Kṛishṇa so as to form a combined sect, and that the doctrine of the Vyūhas is a theologism created to give them a permanent place in the teaching and the worship of the community.

The Nārāyaṇīya shows also an advanced stage of the incarnation doctrine. There are ten incarnations of Vishṇu recognized here,[1] while in the earlier lists[2] there are four, or six.

Hopkins[3] holds that Pañchaśikha, the teacher of the Sāṅkhya-Yoga, a theistic form of the Sāṅkhya philosophy, as we have seen above,[4] was regarded by the Pāñcharātras as the author of the philosophical teaching of the sect. This is interesting; because the Vaishṇava theology unquestionably rests on a Sāṅkhya-Yoga basis.

This passage, the Nārāyaṇīya, tells a story to the effect that Nārada took a long journey to the north, where he came to the Sea of Milk, in the midst of which was White Island, inhabited by white men who worshipped Nārāyaṇa, i.e. Vishṇu.[5] The men, their beliefs, their sanctity, and their worship are described. A number of scholars have believed they detected distinct traces of Christianity in the passage, and the question has been much discussed, with rather doubtful results.[6]

§ 107. The two epics borrow from each other at this period.[7] There are a number of interpolations in the text of the *Rāmāyaṇa* which are clearly contemporaneous with the didactic epic, one passage containing a copy of the description of the inhabitants of White Island.[8] These latest interpolations are mostly in the seventh book, but the most important of all is a canto in the sixth,[9] in which Rāma is praised as a full incarnation of Vishṇu, and is called the eternal Brahman.

[1] XII. 340, 100. [2] Above, § 84. [3] *GE.* 141.
[4] § 99. [5] XII. 336, 8-9.
[6] See the theories and the evidence, Garbe, *IC.* 191-200.
[7] Hopkins, *GE.* 59, 72. [8] Cf. *R.* VII. 77 with *MBH.* XII. 336.
[9] VI. 119; see Muir, *OST.* IV. 148 ff. The other most noteworthy passages are VII. 6, 17, 57, 75-7, 110.

The same theological conceptions are here applied to Rāma as are applied to Kṛishṇa in the didactic epic. We have already seen that Rāma is recognized as Vishṇu in the Kṛishṇa-epic. Similarly Kṛishṇa is recognized in these late interpolations in the *Rāmāyaṇa*.[1]

§ 108. It is important to notice what stage the Kṛishṇa legend has reached in the didactic epic. We are told that he was born in Mathurā to kill Kaṁsa and other demons, and that after he had done that he went to Dvārikā in Kathiawar.[2] His parents' names, Vāsudeva and Devakī,[3] are given, but the story of his birth and of his being miraculously saved from the wrath of Kaṁsa is not told;[4] and there is nothing to suggest that the child Kṛishṇa was worshipped in those days. Nor is there the slightest hint that he was brought up among the cowherds of Gokul. The stories of his boyish tricks with the cowherds, his youthful sports[5] among the Gopīs, and his killing of the demons in the cow-settlement, which are so prominent in the *Harivaṁśa* and the Purāṇas are absent here, except in a few passages which are manifestly very late interpolations.[6] Rādhā is not mentioned at all.

[1] VI. 119; VII. 50.

[2] II. 14, 34-50; XII. 340, 86-7.

[3] VII. 144; XVI. 7.

[4] We must note carefully, however, that the story of the death of Kaṁsa is very old; for it was already dramatized in the second century B. C., as Patañjali tells us.

[5] But in XIII. 149, 88, one of his names is 'he who sports joyously on the banks of the Jumna'.

[6] Thus II. 68, 41 b to 46 a, which calls Kṛishṇa 'Lord of Vraja' and 'favourite of the milkmaids', is clearly a very late piece interpolated into a very early section; for it makes Draupadī appeal to Kṛishṇa for help in her frightful need, while the original says that Dharma, the god of law and right, stood by and helped her. Garbe's argument (*CI.* 227) is thus of very doubtful value. Similarly, in II. 41, Śiśupāla, in abusing Kṛishṇa, calls him 'the cowherd' and says that Bhīshma has praised him for killing Pūtanā and the vulture and other notable deeds; but, when we turn to Bhīshma's praise of Kṛishṇa in chap. 38, there is no mention of Pūtanā, or the vulture, or any other of these exploits. Thus at least verses 4-11 of chap. 41 are an interpolation: Bhandarkar, *VS.* 35 f. It is probable that these local legends had been long current in Mathurā. The point we emphasize is that they had not been accepted into the official body of Vaishṇava teaching when the didactic epic was formed.

G. *Śaiva Material in the Didactic Epic.*

§ 109. In the didactic epic Śiva takes quite as subordinate a place as he does in the heroic poem. Scholars seem to be agreed that the passages in the late books [1] which exalt and praise him are, on the whole, later than the mass of Vaishṇava teaching; and indeed it seems most probable that the changed Śaiva theology which those passages show was formed in direct and conscious imitation of the New Vaishṇavism.

The Śaiva sections consist, in the main, of narratives,[2] hymns of praise,[3] and expositions of the new Śaiva theology.[4] The narratives, which tell how this or that hero went and praised Śiva, in order to receive from him some heavenly weapon of war of peculiar effectiveness, are of minor interest.

The hymns of praise are valuable because we see the new teaching reflected in them most clearly. The greatest of these hymns [5] sets forth the one thousand and eight names of Śiva, a Śaiva copy of the thousand names of Vishṇu.[6] In these ascriptions of praise one half of the new Vaishṇava theology is transferred in the lump to Śiva: there is only a change of names. Śiva is the Brahman of the Upanishads, the Eternal, the Supreme, the source of all gods, all beings, and all things. The other half of Vaishṇava theology, the doctrine of divine incarnations, is not carried over. In its place we have divine theophanies: Śiva appears in various human disguises or other forms to test, or teach, or gratify his worshippers.[7]

Pāśupata,[8] the name of the new Śaiva theology, is thus

[1] The most important are III. 38-41; VII. 80-1; XII. 284-85; XIII. 14-18; 160-1. The most significant are discussed by Muir, *OST.* IV. 150-70.

[2] III. 38-41; VII. 80-1. Cf. also X. 7, which may be of earlier origin.

[3] VII. 80, 54-63; XII. 285, 3-115; XIII. 14, 283-326; 16, 12-63; 17.

[4] XII. 285, 122-5; 350, 63-6; XIII. 160-1.

[5] XIII. 17.

[6] XIII. 149.

[7] III. 39, 2; VII. 80, 38-40; X. 7, 60; XII. 284, 60; &c.

[8] For the Pāśupata see esp. Hopkins, *GE.* 86; 96; 118; 152-7; 189 *n.* Cf. what he says on the theistic faith in general, 102-3; 106; 115; The chief references in the epic are XII. 285; 321; 350; XIII. 14-18; 160-1.

parallel to Pāñcharātra, the name of the new Vaishṇavism. Pāśupata is formed from Paśupati, lord of flocks, an epithet used of Rudra in early literature.[1] But the sect gave the word a new religious significance. Paśupati is the Lord (pati), and man, his creature [2] (paśu), is bound by the fetter (pāśa) of the world, and requires to be released by the Lord. Pāśupata is scarcely distinguishable from Pāñcharātra as a system. Both use the fundamental conceptions of the Sāṅkhya and Yoga, yet are anxious to be in complete harmony with the teaching of the Upanishads. The similarity goes even further; for both number thirty-one philosophical principles, an enumeration which is associated with the name of Pañchaśikha.[3] There is this difference between the two systems that, while Vishṇu has four forms, Śiva has eight.[4] The Pāśupata is also heterodox, like the Pāñcharātra.[5]

§ 110. There is one further point to note with regard to Śiva. In a few of the more important Pāśupata passages in the thirteenth book, his phallic emblem, the *liṅga*, is made the subject of great laudation. No mention of the liṅga occurs in earlier literature; [6] yet, as is well known, all Śaivas are liṅga-worshippers to-day. The question of its origin has been often discussed, but has not yet been settled.[7] Archaeologists tell us that liṅgas belonging to pre-Christian dates are in existence; so that they must be earlier than the first mention in literature. The explanation probably is that the liṅga is of aboriginal origin, as *śiśnadeva* of the *Ṛigveda* implies, that it passed into popular Hinduism and into sculpture at an early date, but did not receive Brahmanical recognition until after

[1] *White Yajurveda*, XVI. 28; *Atharvaveda*, XI. ii. 28; *Āśvalāyana GS.* iv. 8; *Pāraskara GS.* iii. 8; Barth, *RI.* 164.

[2] The figure comes from the farmer with his beast and the rope with which it is bound. 'Creature' must not be taken literally: the soul is eternal and uncreated.

[3] Hopkins, *GE.* 152 ff.

[4] Hopkins, *GE.* 143.

[5] *MBH.* XII. 285, 124; Hopkins, *GE.* 114.

[6] Except the *śiśnadeva* of the *Ṛik*.

[7] Kittel, *Ueber den Ursprung des Liṅgakultus*; Barth, *RI.* 271; Hopkins, *RI.* 150.

the Christian era. It had been already accepted when the Pāśupata system was formed.

§ 111. In two of these passages[1] the phrase *ūrddhva-liṅga* occurs; in one of them *sthīra-liṅga* is found;[2] in two *ūrddhva-retas* occurs;[3] and in another *mahāśepho nagno.*[4] These phrases clearly refer to the conception of the god which is represented in the images of the Lakulīśa sect;[5] yet the name Lakulīśa does not occur in the epic. Since the name means 'the club-bearing god', Fleet[6] conjectures that the Śiva with a club represented on the coins of the Kushan King Huvishka about A.D. 125–140 is Lakulīśa; but the name may be later than the coins.

§ 112. There is an Upanishad, the *Atharvaśiras*,[7] which is a Pāśupata document, and is probably of about the same date as the Pāśupata passages in the epic. Rudra-Paśupati is here the first principle of all things, and also the final goal; pati, paśu, pāśa, are all mentioned; the yoga method of meditation on the sacred syllable *Om* is recommended; and the use of ashes for smearing the body is called the Pāśupata ordinance. Three other Śaiva Upanishads, the *Artharvaśikhā*,[8] the *Nīlarudra*, and the *Kaivalya*[9] may belong to the same time.

ii. BUDDHISM.

A. *The Hīnayāna.*

§ 113. We must think of Buddhism at the beginning of this period as active and spreading in most parts of India and Ceylon, and also in Burmah, along the Himalayas from Nepal to Kashmir, in Afghanistan, and also in Central Asia. In the first century A.D. the religion found a welcome in China, and

[1] XIII. 17, 46; 161, 17; Muir, *OST.* IV. 344.
[2] XIII. 161, 11.
[3] XIII. 14, 212; 17, 46.
[4] XIII. 14, 157. Muir, *OST.* IV. 160.
[5] See § 165.
[6] *JRAS.* 1907, 419.
[7] Deussen, *SUV.* 716 ff; Muir, *OST.* IV. 298–304. There are variant texts of this work: Bhandarkar, *VS.* III.
[8] Deussen, *SUV.* 726 ff.
[9] See *MBH.* XIII. 160, 4, 22; 161, 23; and above, p. 101, n. 4.

about the same time entered Kuchar and Khotan in E. Turkestan, and also Persia. Naturally we can trace only in very broken outlines the literary work of the Buddhist Church in its various schools scattered over these wide regions.

The community already had numerous schools of thought,[1] but these distinctions did not create sects: all Buddhists still worshipped together. Of these schools we must now distinctly envisage three, if we are to understand the development, the *Sthaviras*, who were phenomenalists, the *Sarvāstivādins*, who were realists, and the *Mahāsāṅghikas*, who were idealists.

a. *Sthavira Literature.*

§ 114. The Sthaviras, the oldest of the schools, were found in North India and predominated in Ceylon. The Pāli books which exist to-day are the Canon of the Sthaviras of Ceylon as reduced to writing there in the first century B.C. Hence, if we accept the critical opinion that the Abhidhamma Piṭaka did not exist in the time of Aśoka,[2] we must conclude that it was formed somewhere between the two dates. The natural conclusion then is that the seven works of that collection were gradually formed and compiled, either in North India or Ceylon, during the first part of our period. This fresh material is not of the same value or interest as the best parts of the Sutta Piṭaka. It consists for the most part of dry, unilluminating classifications and definitions of Buddhist terms and ideas, served up in scholastic fashion for the training of monks.[3]

The Canon was reduced to writing in Ceylon during the first century B.C., but the date cannot be more exactly defined.[4] Since then the text has been preserved with fair, but certainly not with faultless, accuracy.

§ 115. *The Questions of King Milinda* is the name of a famous book, the main part of which was written in North India, probably in the first century B.C., possibly a little later.

[1] Kern, *B.* 110 f., 123; *ERE.* VI. 686.
[2] See § 64.
[3] Winternitz, II. i, 134 ff.
[4] Kern, *B.* 120; Winternitz, II. i. 11.

In what language it was originally written is not known. It has been preserved only in Pāli in Ceylon and in two Chinese translations. It is clear from quotations that the Canon which the author used was the same as the Pāli Canon, yet the readings do not agree precisely. The book is much honoured in Ceylon. Indeed it enjoys a consideration and an authority very little inferior to the Pāli Canon itself. Milinda is the Pāli for Menander, a Greek King who ruled in the Punjab and attacked the empire of Magadha, about 155 B.C. According to tradition he became a Buddhist. The book is a piece of apologetic, a dialogue, in which a monk named Nāgasena answers the king's questions about Buddhist faith and practice.

It seems clear that the original work covered only a fragment of Book I with Books II and III. The subjects discussed in those sections are amongst the most important of all Buddhist questions, e.g. nirvāṇa and karma, individuality and soul, renunciation, faith, perseverance, and meditation; and the style is strikingly beautiful, the expression easy and graceful, and the illustrations exceedingly well chosen. In Books IV to VII a large number of minor questions are dealt with; the style, though still good, lacks the brilliance of Books II and III; and, while the main teaching keeps very close to the Pāli canon, yet the influence of later ideas is visible. A tendency is shown to turn away from the ideal of the Arhat, who wins nirvāṇa by a strenuous discipline at once, to the conception of the Bodhisattva,[1] who reaches release by means of devotion in a long career reaching through countless lives.[2] These last books were probably written much later in Ceylon.

§ 116. All the Buddhist schools of North India which have left literature wrote in Sanskrit or in various forms of what is known as mixed Sanskrit. The origin and history of these literary dialects have not yet been definitely ascertained. Some scholars are inclined to think that they are the work of imperfectly trained men trying to write Paninean Sanskrit,

[1] Lit. 'one whose nature is wisdom', but used technically of one who is destined to become a Buddha.

[2] See § 124 B.

while others think they are literary modifications of local dialects. There are two facts about them which require to be carefully noted: first, each school seems to have its own dialect; secondly, as time went on, pure Sanskrit steadily won its way in all the schools.

b. *Sautrāntika Literature.*

§ 117. The Sautrāntikas[1] were a branch of the Sthavira school who received their name because of their reliance on the Sutta Piṭaka, to the neglect of the Abhidhamma. It thus seems clear that their rise must have coincided with the gradual formation of the Abhidhamma. They formed, in exposition of their teaching, a philosophical system which is called the Sautrāntik philosophy. They believed in the existence of the external world, and held an atomic theory of matter, but taught that perception happens indirectly.[2] Their theory of the self, founded on the original Buddhist conception of man's psychical life,[3] proved a stepping-stone from the phenomenalist position of the Sthaviras to the Mahāyāna Philosophy of Vacuity.[4] The self, they argued, is a long series (*saṁtāna*) of phenomenal elements, each member of which exists only for a moment so infinitesimal that its apparition and destruction may be said to be simultaneous. Each momentary member (*kshaṇa*) of the series is both an effect and a cause, yet possesses no real activity. Birth, existence, old age, death, are all illusions; for the series in uncreated, uninterrupted. Thus there is no identity, no continuous existence. On the other hand, they declared this self, consisting of a phenomenal series, to be autonomous; for 'all we are is the result of what we have thought'. They also hold the self to be self-conscious, conscious directly of self and indirectly of other things. The scholar with whose name this philosophy

[1] *Sautrāntika* is formed from *sūtrānta*, the Pāli form of which is *suttanta*, a variant of *sutta*.

[2] Jacobi, *ERE*. II. 201.

[3] See § 61.

[4] See § 124 c.

is connected is Kumāralabdha,[1] a contemporary of Nāgārjuna,[2] but very little is known about Sautrāntika literature.

c. *Sarvāstivādin Literature.*

§ 118. The home of the *Sarvāstivādin*, i.e. the 'All-things-exist', or realist, school seems to have been Kashmir, but they spread far and wide. Their Canon was in Sanskrit and, apart from the Sthavira, was the only Canon which possessed a third, or Abhidharma, 'basket'. As has been already remarked, the contents of this Abhidharma were absolutely distinct from the Sthavira Abhidhamma. We may be certain that the Vinaya and Sūtra 'baskets' of their Canon were already in existence by the beginning of our period, but it is as yet impossible to say how far they differed from the Sthavira Canon: for we are almost entirely dependent for our knowledge upon Chinese and Tibetan translations, only fragments of the original Sanskrit having survived. They seem to have had also a special literature of their own. Like a number of the other leading schools, they had their own Life of the Master; and it must have been a powerful and popular work, for it was taken over afterwards by the new Buddhism, called the Mahāyāna, and it survives only in its altered form, the most famous of all lives of the Buddha, the *Lalita Vistara*.[3]

The Sarvāstivādin philosophy, an outgrowth from the realistic teaching of the sect, is an atomic doctrine of matter combined with a theory of direct perception.[4] Thus, in their speculative teaching, they stood near the Jains and the Vaiśeshikas, but they denied the eternity of atoms.[5] The foundation-text of their Abhidharma Piṭaka, the *Jñānaprasthāna-śāstra*, is by their most renowned scholar, Kātyāyanīputra. Six ancillary works, called 'the feet' of the Abhidharma, by Vasumitra and other writers, complete the contents of the

[1] Kern, *B.* 127; Poussin, *Opinions*, 178 ff.
[2] See § 128.
[3] Nanjio, 159, 160; Winternitz, II. i. 194 ff.
[4] Jacobi, *ERE.* II. 201.
[5] Ib. 202 C.

Piṭaka. The date of these books is not yet known with certainty. On these works commentaries were then written, which carried the philosophy a step farther. The commentaries were called Vibhāshā, and hence the philosophy was called Vaibhāshika. Tradition suggests that the Vibhāshā arose in the reign of Kanishka.

According to Sarvāstivādin books, a general Buddhist Council was held, under the authority of Kanishka, at some place in Kashmir, and at the Council commentaries on the three baskets of the Canon were composed, those on the Vinaya and Abhidharma being called Vibhāshā and those on the Sūtra Piṭaka Upadeśa. The traditions about this Council are, however, very untrustworthy, so that some scholars doubt whether it was ever held at all. Others think that a Sarvāstivādin council was actually held, and that, in imitation of the story of the Council of Aśoka, they called it a General Council. In any case, the commentaries which in the tradition are associated with the Council are Sarvāstivādin, and a number of them were probably written after the time of Kanishka.

From the Sarvāstivādin Vinaya and the ancient Jātakas there sprang numberless tales of heroic deeds done by Buddhas and saints called Avadānas, precisely like the Apadānas of the Pāli Canon. Two collections belong to this period, the *Avadāna-śataka*[1] or Century of Tales, and the *Karma-śataka*,[2] or Century of Deeds. A third collection of great renown, the *Divyāvadāna*,[3] or Divine Tales, which probably dates from after 200 A.D., calls itself a Mahāyāna work, but is manifestly of Sarvāstivādin origin. From these books sprang an edifying literature which flourished for many centuries.

The famous writer Aśvaghosha was a Sarvāstivādin and probably wrote some of his works before he became a Mahāyānist.[4]

[1] Winternitz, II. i. 216. [2] Ib. 221.
[3] Ib. 221; Mitra, 304. [4] See § 127.

d. *Mahāsāṅghika Literature.*

§ 119. The Mahāsāṅghikas, one of the very earliest schools, were idealists in Metaphysics. They were inclined to raise the Buddha above humanity, and to identify his personality with that of the former Buddhas. They had a Vinaya Piṭaka and a Sūtra Piṭaka, written in a curious mixed Sanskrit. Of the Vinaya two works still exist in Chinese and Tibetan; and the *Ekottarāgama* preserved in the Chinese and the Tibetan Canons is from the Mahāsāṅghika Sūtra Piṭaka.[1] One of the branches of this school was known as the school of the *Lokottaravādins*, or Transcendentalists, because they believed that the Buddha was not a human being enmeshed in the life of the world, but one raised far above it. A book called the *Mahāvastu*, written in the curious Mahāsāṅghika Sanskrit, has come down to us. It arose in the Vinaya of the Lokottaravādins, but very little Vinaya material now remains in it. The book contains a vast amount of matter of different kinds and also of varying dates—a life of the Buddha, tales and sermons, poems and Jātakas, many of them early compositions; so that it forms 'one of the most noteworthy books of Buddhist antiquity'. The Buddha-Biography does not differ in any appreciable degree from the narratives of the Pāli Canon, but its theory of the person of the Buddha is distinctly docetic. 'The Buddha of the Mahāvastu is a superman. He feels neither hunger nor thirst; he lives in ignorance of carnal desires; his wife remains a virgin. It is from consideration for humanity, in order to conform to the customs of the world, that he behaves as a man, or that he gives to men the false impression that he is behaving as a man. In technical terms, he is *lokottara*, superior to the world.' The work lays great stress on the saving power of

[1]

Pāli Sutta Piṭaka:	Sanskrit Sūtra Piṭaka:
1. Dīghanikāya.	1. Dīrghāgama.
2. Majjhimanikāya.	2. Madhyamāgama.
3. Saṁyuttanikāya.	3. Saṁyuktāgama.
4. Aṅguttaranikāya.	4. Ekottarāgama.
5. Khuddakanikāya.	5. Kshudrakāgama.

devotion to him. It also names large numbers of former Buddhas, and believes in the existence of many worlds besides our own, in each of which a Buddha reigns concurrently with the Buddha here. The *Mahāvastu* thus forms the bridge between the Hīnayāna and the Mahāyāna. The chapter called Daśabhūmika,[1] which describes the stages (*bhūmis*) through which a man passes in becoming a Buddha is probably a later interpolation. Much of the book is early.[2]

§ 120. Mātṛicheṭa was born a Brāhman but became a Buddhist. He was invited to the Kushan court, seemingly by Kanishka, but begged to be excused on account of age. He left two hymns of praise, which were used for centuries by Mahayanists as well as Hinayanists, and which served as models for later writers. One has survived, and fragments of the other, along with his letter to the king.[3] He seems to stand between the Hīnayāna and the Mahāyāna.

e. *Buddhist Worship.*

§ 121. From 200 B.C. down to the Christian era the great Buddhist stūpas were enriched with masses of beautiful sculpture. Pious Buddhists were accustomed to walk round the stūpas with reverent steps. Enclosing this path of circumambulation there stood a stone railing with a lofty arched gate at each of the cardinal points. These gates were covered with sculpture, and in certain examples the railing itself was decorated with sculptured plaques and panels. Examples, ruinous or well-preserved, have been found in several places.[4] In this early work no image of the Buddha appears, but in many of the scenes represented his presence is indicated by some symbol, and all the carved work breathes the spirit of

[1] *ERE.* II. 744 f., VIII. 329 f.
[2] Winternitz, II. i. 193.
[3] Thomas, *ERE.* VIII. 495; Winternitz, II. i. 211; Nanjio, 1456; Hoernle, *MRBL.* 58–84. Vidyābhūshaṇa, *JASB.* 1910, 425, refers him to the fourth century.
[4] Notably at Sāñchī in the Bhopal State, at Bharhut in Rewa, at Buddh-Gayā in Bihar, at Amarāvatī on the Kistna and in Ceylon. V. Smith, *HFA.* 65–81; 86–8.

devotion. Here we have the reflection in art of the new spirit which shines out from the literature.

In the first century A.D. a new Indo-Greek art, distinctive above all in its sculptures, arose in Gandhāra, the district of which Peshawar is the centre. Images of the Buddha were for the first time made by these artists; and all the Buddhist schools used them as aids to devotion: this is a noteworthy and far-reaching change.

§ 122. Buddhist monks found it necessary to keep abreast of all the culture of the day, so as to be able to influence the rising laity. We therefore find them well acquainted with Hindu philosophy and with the new forms of religion enshrined in the Epic. In the last quarter of the first century of our era, the strong government of the Kushan empire, extending far to the west and the north of India, opened the doors wide to Buddhist Missions; and the numerous races the missionaries had to teach, coupled with the rich variety of foreign influences which met in the empire, led to great changes in Buddhist thought and practice.

B. *The Mahāyāna.*

§ 123. These movements, coupled with new ideas and practices which had been gaining ground in the old sects for two centuries, found their culmination in the creation of a new Buddhism called the Mahāyāna, or great vehicle, in contrast with the old Buddhism, which was depreciated as the Hīnayāna, or small vehicle.[1] The Mahāyāna is, on one side, the acute Hinduizing of Buddhism, on the other, the humanizing of the old discipline, so as to make Buddhism more suitable for the cultured Indian layman and for the men of many races now crowding into the community. The rise of this system is probably to be placed in the reign of Kanishka (perhaps A.D. 78–123), towards the end of the first and the beginning

[1] It is probable that Hīnayāna was originally used with reference to Arhatship, the mode of individual salvation, as opposed to Bodhisattvaship, the plan for the salvation of many.

of the second century; for all tradition points to that time, and many Mahāyāna texts were translated into Chinese before A. D. 170.[1]

The vast literature created by the Mahāyāna does not survive as a definite Canon in the original tongues. Portions of it have been found in Nepal[2] and fragments elsewhere; but for our knowledge of the mass of the books we have to have recourse to the Chinese[3] and Tibetan[4] Canons.

a. *The Full Mahāyāna.*

§ 124. There are two distinct Mahāyāna systems to be recognized at this time. The first may be called the full Mahāyāna, as it contains all the features of the new Buddhism. They may be summed up under three heads:

A. *Devotion.* Mahayanists recognize that there are innumerable Buddhas, each in his own world, and innumerable Bodhisattvas, the most advanced of which live in the heavens. Buddhas and advanced Bodhisattvas are fit objects of devotion, and devotion brings its rich rewards. One result of this change was that the Buddhas, though they were still thought of as being in nirvāṇa, were regarded as responding in some way to the devotion showered upon them. Their personality and activity consequently became more distinct, until they were thought of almost like Hindu gods. We must recognize here a distinct change in the conception of nirvāṇa.[5] Thus in that most orthodox Mahāyāna book, the *Saddharma Puṇḍarīka*, Gautama is made almost an eternal being of omnipotent power, who from time to time descends to earth, like Vishṇu, to be born in the world of the living. Similarly those Bodhisattvas who are drawing near the stage of final enlightenment

[1] Nanjio, Cols. 381–3.

[2] See especially Mitra, *Nepalese Buddhist Literature.*

[3] Buṅyiu Nanjio, *A Catalogue of the Chinese Translation of the Buddhist Tripiṭaka.*

[4] *ERE.* VII. 785, 789; Feer, *Analyse du Kandjour*, Annales du Musée Guimet, II.

[5] Thomas, *Buddhist Scriptures*, 15.

are now regarded as mighty divinities living in the heavens, helping men, and actually declining to enter nirvāṇa in order that they may help men the more.

The Mahayanists created a showy worship, with processions, music, and incense; and a rich liturgy was prepared for each Buddha. The monks took charge of the cult; so that the old chaitya became a temple and the monk a priest.

B. *The Bodhisattva Life.*[1] The monk of the Hīnayāna sought to become an *arhat*, a man who, by a life of asceticism and meditation in obedience to the precepts of the Buddha, has reached the nirvāṇa of the extinction of all desire; but he regarded himself as a mere pupil, following the directions of the omniscient Buddha, and never dreamt of becoming a Buddha himself. The Mahāyāna now declared that, to reach real release, it was necessary to acquire the perfections and the omniscience of the Buddhas, and that, though the upward struggle would take an incalculable number of ages, the goal was within the reach of every human being. Each person, man or woman, was therefore exhorted to take at once the vow to become a Buddha; and the assurance was given that the power of that vow was sufficient to bear them through the innumerable births and serious sufferings which lay before them. If they began a life of active benevolence, and sought to rouse within themselves the desire to save all creatures, they would pass through the ten stages (*bhūmis*) of the career. Since the end was certain, each person who took the vow at once became a Bodhisattva, one destined to become a Buddha. The influence of the Jātakas, which contain narratives of numerous acts of incredible self-sacrifice done by Gautama in his earlier births, is very manifest in the new conception. Since Gautama was believed to have lived as a householder for countless lives, celibacy was not a necessary element of the discipline. Neophyte Bodhisattvas, both men and women, were encouraged to marry, but they were allowed to acquire merit by living the monastic life for a time, if they cared to do

[1] Poussin, *ERE.* art. 'Bodhisattva', and VIII. 33 f.; *Opinions*, 275 ff.

so. On the other hand, the Mahāyāna prohibited the eating of flesh.

C. *The Mahāyāna Philosophy of Vacuity.*[1] The early denial of the existence of the ego and the Sautrāntika doctrine, that the ego consists of an endless series of infinitesimal moments, led to the formulation of the doctrine that there is no real existence, that all things are but appearance, and are in truth empty. This is the famous doctrine of *Śūnyatā*, Vacuity. The young Bodhisattva cannot see the truth of this doctrine, but in the course of his progress to Buddhahood he will come to realize it; for it is the sum of the wisdom of all the Buddhas.

§ 125. A large literature was produced by this school during our period. Amongst these works is one of the greatest of Buddhist books, the *Saddharma Puṇḍarīka*,[2] 'The Lotus', or, as we should say, 'The Rose of the True Religion'. The book probably appeared towards the end of the first or the beginning of the second century,[3] but six of the chapters of the work as it has come down to us (xxi–xxvi) are of later origin. The original work contains the whole Mahāyāna system. The most noteworthy element is the way in which Gautama the Buddha is represented. According to the old teaching, he has gone to nirvāṇa and can no longer have any relations with the world of men. Here he is represented practically as an omnipotent God, whose life is limitless before and after, in whose hands are the universe and all creatures, who dwells continually in infinite glory. It is true he also teaches the Buddha-laws, but his birth, life, teaching, and death are but an appearance, and his passing away into nirvāṇa is but a device to lead men to accept the Buddha-laws. The influence of the Vedānta and of the *Gītā* are very prominent here. The conception of Kṛishṇa-Vishṇu as the

[1] *ERE.* art. 'Madhyamaka'.

[2] *ERE.* art. 'Lotus of True Law'; Winternitz, II. i. 230–8; Kern, *SBE.* xxi.

[3] Winternitz puts it about A.D. 200; Poussin in the first century, *Opinions*, 259.

Supreme is adapted to Buddhist conceptions. Many of the titles are borrowed unchanged, Supreme Spirit, Self-existent, Great Father, World-Father, Ruler of the Triple World, Creator, Destroyer, Physician. He is Everlasting, All-knowing, All-seeing. He wields magic power, *māyā*, which he uses in sport, *līlā*. He is repeatedly born in the world of the living. When men become unbelieving, he appears in this world to save. Yet, although Buddha in the *Lotus* is practically the Supreme, the language is so carefully guarded throughout that Prof. Poussin can say, 'There is not a single word in the *Lotus* which is not capable of an orthodox, i. e. "atheist" interpretation.'[1] The work had large influence in India, whence it passed to China and Japan, and later to Nepal. It is the most popular of all Buddhist books in Japan to-day.

§ 126. The philosophic doctrine of Vacuity was taught in a large number of books, short and long, called the Prajñā-pāramitā-sūtras,[2] i.e. 'the sūtras of the wisdom-perfections' of the Buddhas. Of these the *Daśasāhasrika Prajñāpāramitā-sūtra*,[3] i. e. the 'Ten-thousand-line Sūtra', belongs to our period. This work also describes the ten stages (*bhūmis*) of the Bodhisattva career. The chapter called Daśabhūmika[4] interpolated into the *Mahāvastu* probably comes from this time also.

§ 127. Aśvaghosha[5] was born of Brāhman parents, but became a Buddhist, first of the Sarvāstivādin school, but finally of the Mahāyāna. His splendid genius proved of signal service to Buddhism; for he is a most notable figure in Sanskrit literature, and one of the greatest of the predecessors of Kālidāsa. He was equally distinguished in epic, dramatic, and lyric poetry. His greatest work is the *Buddhacharita*, an epic poem on the life of Buddha. Part of it is lost, yet enough remains to show his genius and his art. In its delineation of the life and work of the Buddha, it scarcely

[1] *ERE.* VIII. 145.
[2] Nanjio, cols. 1 to 8; *ERE.* IV. 838; VIII. 235.
[3] Nanjio, col. 381; also no. 5. [4] See § 119.
[5] *ERE.* art. 'Aśvaghosha'; *SBE.* xlix; Winternitz, II. i. 201; H.P. Śāstrī, *JASB.* 1909, 47; Nanjio, col. 369.

goes beyond the Pāli Canon, but in freshness and power it stands altogether on another level, the work of a true poet. A second epic, the *Saundarānanda-Kāvya*, which deals with a number of scenes and incidents connected with the life of Buddha, also survives. The *Sūtrālaṁkāra*, of which a Chinese version and a few fragments in Sanskrit are extant, is a collection of avadānas, i.e. Buddhist legends told in mingled prose and verse, the style in common use then for artistic romances. A large number of these stories are old, many are new, but all are graced and heightened by Aśvaghosha's charm. There are two philosophical works ascribed to him, the *Vajrasūchī*, i.e. the 'Diamond-needle', and the *Mahāyānaśraddhotpādaśāstra*, the 'Mahāyāna-faith-awakening Treatise', but serious doubts as to his authorship of both works still remain.

§ 128. Nāgārjuna,[1] a Brāhman convert, who became the greatest authority on Mahāyāna Buddhism, is regarded as a younger contemporary of Aśvaghosha in Buddhist tradition; and modern scholars are inclined to place his activity in the latter half of the second century. His chief service was to think out the new doctrine of Vacuity. In those days a philosopher embodied his teaching in a series of aphorisms, either in prose (*sūtras*) or in verse (*kārikās*), and expounded them in a commentary. Nāgārjuna's work is in verse and, as the system is called the middle teaching, Mādhyamaka, the book is known as the *Mādhyamaka-kārikās*. The system is called Mādhyamaka because its leading idea, 'All things are empty', takes the middle course between existence and non-existence. Two distinct kinds of truth must be recognized, apparent truth, *saṁvṛitisatya*, and real truth, *paramārthasatya*.[2] The world appears to be real, but the appearance is an illusion, as empty as a dream; yet we must live in it and in practice take it as real. The actual truth, that all things are empty, seems to us to be folly, but it is the final truth of the

[1] Winternitz, II. i. 250–4; *ERE.* IV. 838; VIII. 235, 336.
[2] Poussin, *Opinions*, 189 *n.* 1.

world; and when we rise to the wisdom of the Buddhas, we shall see its truth. Thus we need not hope to find the truth by intellectual activity, but must strive to hear the silence which is neither affirmation nor denial. Thus the Mādhyamaka philosopher has no system; he has only a method. The doctrine is thus a guarded nihilism, a faith in the emptiness of all things which does not profess to see the truth of what it believes, but holds hard by its faith, while it frankly lives on that which it declares to be illusion. The early *Prajñā* texts, and a number of other works are said to be by Nāgārjuna. An extraordinary mass of legends gathered round his head.

b. *The Paradise Mahāyāna.*

§ 129. The second type of Mahāyāna doctrine is of a much simpler nature and may be described as the Paradise Mahāyāna.[1] It does not trouble to teach the doctrine of Vacuity, nor does it impose on its followers the long ages of discipline which are required for the career of the Bodhisattva. Every person may easily make certain of being born in his next birth in the Western Paradise, where under the fostering care of a great Buddha named Amitābha he will live for ever in joy and will reach final perfection. One of the chief texts of this school, the longer *Sukhāvatīvyūha*,[2] or 'Description of the Land of Bliss', was translated into Chinese before A.D. 170, and thus belongs to our period. In this book we hear of many hundred thousands of millions of Buddhas, and amongst them of one named Amitābha, 'measureless light', who lives and reigns in Sukhāvatī, a Paradise of glory and bliss far away to the West, beyond the limits of the world where Gautama lives. When this new Buddha was but a monk, he vowed and toiled for this Western Paradise, and prayed that he might never obtain the highest perfect knowledge, unless it should be possible for all creatures to be born in that Land of Bliss and there reach perfection, wisdom,

[1] Poussin, *ERE.* VIII. 331 b. [2] Nanjio, col. 381; *SBE.* xlix.

perfect joy, and release. All has now been realized. Amitābha reigns in the wonderful land of bliss, and whoever struggles forward, seeking to make good karma, praying faithfully, worshipping Amitābha with deep devotional feeling, and uttering his name, will be born in that Western Paradise and will live in bliss for ever. A very large part of the book is given to descriptions of the beauties and pleasures of Sukhāvatī.

Of the numerous Mahāyāna texts translated into Chinese during the second century [1] a number of works, in addition to the longer *Sukhāvatīvyūha*, seem to belong to the Paradise school,[2] but the mass undoubtedly derive from the chief school.

C. *Buddhism in China.*

§ 130. Buddhism does not seem to have made rapid progress in China for some two or three centuries; yet it is clear that large efforts were made to win the people. Some reflection of the activities of the Missionaries may be found in the long lists of translations carried out during the two centuries under review.[3] Most of the sūtras selected for translation are quite short, and deal with the simpler elements of Buddhist teaching or with practical questions touching life and discipline. They are taken from Mahāyāna as well as from Hīnayāna sources, the first text translated, *The Sūtra of Forty-two Sections*,[4] being a compendium of Buddhist teaching drawn from many books. There are only four noteworthy translators during the period, and their extraction is significant; two of them, Kāśyapa Matāṅga and Lokaraksha,[5] were Indians, An Shi-Kao was a Parthian prince, while Ch'Yao was probably a Kushan.

[1] Nanjio, nos. 5, 25, 28, 33, 51, 54, 57, 73, 76, 102, 112, 161, 174, 202, 260, 282, 289, 381, 385–7, 431, 435, 478, 1093, 1326, 1331, 1337, 1338, 1360, 1361, 1368.

[2] Nanjio, nos. 25, 28, 33, 51, 54, 57.

[3] Nanjio, cols. 379–85.

[4] Nanjio, no. 678.

[5] This man seems to have translated only Mahāyāna works: Nanjio, col. 381.

iii. Jainism.

§ 131. The history of Jainism remains extremley obscure throughout this period, yet a few facts of large importance can be discerned.

During the two centuries before our era, and probably in still earlier years, the religion expanded steadily both in the north and in the south. Sculptured remains and an inscription found at Muttra, the ancient Mathurā, and assigned to the first century B.C.,[1] reveal to us the growth of Jainism to the north-west; caves with fragments of sculptured frieze in Orissa may date from about the same time;[2] while the powerful influence which Jainism exerted on Tamil literature from the second century after Christ, if not from an earlier date, shows that the religion had achieved considerable success in the far south. From the Christian era onwards, if not earlier, Jainism spread into Gujarāt; and from the third century the community produced a large popular literature in the vernacular of that part of India.

§ 132. As a result of the long-standing difference of opinion within the community, the Jains at last broke into two sects, Śvetāmbaras and Digambaras, about A.D. 80[3]; so that for the full understanding of the history it is necessary as far as possible to distinguish the writers, books, and practices of the two organizations from this time onward. The main difference between them is the single point, that the Śvetāmbaras hold that monks ought to wear white garments, while Digambaras hold that they ought to give up all clothing. Necessarily nuns are found only among the Śvetāmbaras. The Digambaras explain that women cannot win release until a good life has brought them the privilege of being born as men; so that they need not become ascetics. There are other minor divergences. The great mass of Jains to the north of the Vindhyas were Śvetāmbaras, while in the Kanarese and Tamil districts they were nearly all Digambaras.

[1] V. Smith, *HFA*. 82; 144; Indraji, *VIth Oriental Congress*, 143.
[2] V. Smith, *HFA*. 84.
[3] Jacobi, *ERE*. VII. 473.

§ 133. Jain worship is precisely parallel to Buddhist worship during these centuries. They use stūpas, as the Buddhists do, and the forms of their sculpture are similar, although the art is not so good. The remains, though slight, are sufficient to show the intense religious emotions of the Jain community and the deep devotional feeling with which they thought of their Tīrthakaras.[1] The inscription at Muttra shows that Jains already used temples in the first century B.C., and at rather later dates there is evidence that they had begun to use images. These changes are very closely contemporaneous to the corresponding movements in Buddhism.

§ 134. It is impossible to say how much of their early literature was still retained in the memories of Jain ascetics during these centuries, nor how far the formation of the Aṅgas, now preserved in the Śvetāmbara Canon, had gone. Weber believed that the gradual process of creating the present Aṅgas began in the second century A.D., but it is more probable that portions of the ancient literature have been preserved, though doubtless from the time of the Schism, about A. D. 80, a process of revision in the interest of the sect was carried out by Śvetāmbara monks. Numerous traditions refer certain of these canonical works or comments on them to writers believed to have lived during this period—to Ajjasāma, to Kālakāchārya, to Vīrabhadra—but everything is confused and obscure. As research proceeds, a measure of light will doubtless be thrown on the history.

§ 135. In a sixteenth-century Digambara work, the *Tattvārthasāradīpikā* of Sakalakīrti,[2] it is stated that from very early times the Digambaras had a large Canon, handed down orally, but that it was gradually forgotten, until in the second century A.D. it had all been lost. A list of the books is given,[3] divided into three groups, *Aṅgas*, *Pūrvas*, and *Aṅga-*

[1] The Jains use the word Tīrthakara, precisely as the Buddhists use Buddha, for an omniscient teacher, and they have a long list of them stretching away far back from Mahāvīra, just like the list of the Previous Buddhas.

[2] See § 440.

[3] Bhandarkar, *Report*, 83-4, p. 106 f; Jaini, *OJ.* 135.

bāhyas. A large proportion of the names correspond with books of the Śvetāmbara list, but there are differences.

§ 136. There is also an obscure tradition [1] that Pushpadanta and Bhūtavalya reduced the Canon to writing in the second century A.D., but as these two are the very men who are mentioned as having been the last that knew one Aṅga orally, and with whom all knowledge of the sacred literature died, it looks as if the tradition had been invented at a late date to give the Digambaras the *kudos* of having once possessed a written canon like the Śvetāmbaras. The truth seems to be rather this, that during the time when the differences between the two sects were becoming more sharply defined, the Digambaras took so little interest in the sacred books that the Śvetāmbaras were able to manipulate them in their own interest. The Canon bears clear traces of this process of Śvetāmbara redaction. If this be the truth, we can have no difficulty in understanding why the Digambaras 'lost' the Canon. The traditional date for the loss, the second century A.D., just gives time for the process after the schism.

§ 137. The vernacular of the far south, known as Tamil, developed a varied literature at a very early date, and both Buddhists and Jains took part in the movement. Some of the most famous of early Tamil works are said to be of Jain origin, but they are not distinctively Jain works but belong rather to general literature. No work holds a higher place among the classics of the South than the sacred *Kural*, a poem consisting of 2,660 short couplets, dealing with virtue, wealth, and pleasure. It forms one of a group of eighteen didactic poems, five or six of which are by Jains. There are also two romances in verse, the *Maṇimekhalai* and the *Silappadhikaram*, both noted for their simple and elegant style, which are believed to have been written by Jains.[2]

[1] Bhandarkar, *Report*, 83-4, p. 125.

[2] *BMCTB.* 2, 4.

CHAPTER IV

PHILOSOPHIES AND SECTS.

A.D. 200 TO 550.

§ 138. Hindus, Buddhists, and Jains all sought during this period to give the best possible expression to their philosophies. The foundation texts of the six Hindu systems, of Jain philosophy, and of Vijñānavāda Buddhism were all written now, and numerous commentaries, most of which have been lost, were produced for their elucidation. Hindu sects are now far more numerous than formerly. Each has its own theology, in which its god is identified with the Brahman of the Upanishads; and each seeks to popularize its teaching and its cult by means of an interesting Puranic document.

The history of India during the third century is a blank, but in A. D. 320 the family of the Guptas arose, and soon created an empire which recalled the glory of the old Mauryas, and gave North India a century and a half of strong, enlightened government. The peace and prosperity of these years provided the conditions in which religious literature and culture could do their best. It was then that the philosophic texts already mentioned, the early Purāṇas and a great series of Buddhist Mahāyāna Sūtras were written.

Probably at some time during this period the Syrian Christian Church of Malabar came into existence.

i. HINDUISM.

A. *The Philosophies.*

§ 139. We take the philosophies first, as they are probably the healthiest and most abiding elements of the religion of the time. Their interest to us lies in this, that the classic treatises, which form the foundation of study in all the six orthodox systems, appeared at this time. It is evident that each of these works is built on earlier systematic treatises, and is the result of centuries of thinking. But all earlier manuals are lost, having been rendered obsolete by the greater power, accuracy, and finish of these classic works.

No definite date can yet be assigned for any one of these six books: we must be content to recognize that they arose within certain rather wide limits.[1] Yet the following points seem clear: (*a*) They were edited with reference to each other. There are so many cross-references from each to the others that scholars are satisfied that all six arose in a single period. At the time there must have been a great deal of public discussion, in the course of which the characteristic conceptions of each system were chiselled to the utmost perfection of form. (*b*) All six are clearly later than the didactic epic and Nāgārjuna. On the other hand, the lowest possible limit seems to be A.D. 450; for the oldest surviving commentary[2] comes from about that date. A.D. 200 to 450 would thus seem to be the extremest limits that can be allowed. (*c*) The wealth and intellectual activity of the Gupta Empire would provide the natural atmosphere and environment for the mutual intercourse and public discussion which lie behind the books. (*d*) Scholars are now inclined to believe, on the basis of Chinese evidence, that the author of the *Sāṅkhya Kārikā* flourished about the beginning of the fourth century.[3] Asaṅga, the exponent of the Vijñānavādin school of Buddhism, which in all probability is the idealistic system attacked in the *Yoga-sūtras*, lived about the same time. Thus two out of the six treatises would stand related to the first half of the fourth century. (*e*) If, then, all six were edited with reference to each other, there would seem to be

[1] For this whole problem see Jacobi, *JAOS*. XXXI. 1 ff.; Suali, *EI*.; Keith, *JRAS*. 1914, 1089; 1915, 537.

[2] Vātsyāyana's *Nyāya-bhāshya*. Śabara-svāmin's *Mīmāṁsā-bhāshya* is probably as early.

[3] See § 146.

a number of lines of evidence converging to the fourth century as the most probable period for their emergence.

§ 140. The form of these books is very strange at first sight to the Western student. Five of them are sūtras, and one consists of memorial verses, kārikās. No single document by itself provides anything like a clear, comprehensible account of the philosophy which it represents.[1] The system was expounded by the teacher ; and the sūtra or the kārikā was little more than an index of topics which, committed to memory, enabled the student to carry the instructions of his teacher in his mind.

But the two manuals which we deal with first are much more difficult to understand than the others. In them scarcely one single sūtra is intelligible without a commentary.[2] The method of reasoning[3] also employed in these manuals is always elaborate and difficult, and sometimes obscure.

§ 141. There are six systems which are recognized as orthodox. Each is called a darśana, or view, because it embodies a way of looking at the world. They fall into three pairs and are so arranged because of a close connexion between the pairs. The first pair depend definitely on the Vedas, while in the case of each of the other two pairs, the second philosophy adopted the metaphysics of the first.

The first pair of systems fundamentally are not philosophies, but merely systematic expositions of the two main parts of the Veda. Each is called *mīmāṁsā*, which means investigation, exegesis. The Former Investigation, Pūrva Mīmāṁsā, deals with the sacrificial part of the Veda, and the Later Investigation, Uttara Mīmāṁsā, deals with the Upanishads. These two, then, really form the systematic theology of Hinduism. Since, however, the Upanishads are philosophic works, the Uttara Mīmāṁsā stands in the closest possible relation with the whole history of philosophy in India. The

[1] See Keith, *JRAS.* 1916, 613.
[2] See Thibaut, *SBE.* XXXIV. xiii.
[3] It is explained by Max Müller, *SS.* 203–4.

words Former and Later, as applied to these two mīmāṁsās, do not refer to the historical appearance of these systems, far less to the dates of the Sūtras, but to their place in study and in the life of the pious Hindu.

a. *The Karma Mīmāṁsā.*

§ 142. The purpose of the Pūrva Mīmāṁsā, which is also called Karma Mīmāṁsā, i.e. Action Investigation, is to reach certainty on the subject of *dharma*, i.e. the whole religious duty of Hindus, but as a matter of fact sacrifice receives so much attention as almost to eclipse other elements of duty. All necessary instructions are given in the hymns and the Brāhmaṇas, but these are not systematic works, and in using them for the sacrifices priests met numerous difficulties. The Mīmāṁsā was meant to solve these problems by providing principles which should prove sufficient as guidance in the interpretation of the Vedic texts.

Most of the sūtras of Jaimini's *Pūrva-mīmāṁsā-sūtras* are expositions of single texts or phrases, and are thus of little interest to the modern reader, but here and there great questions arise which are worthy of notice. For example, the absolute authority of the Veda requires for its establishment the doctrine of its eternity, and that leads in turn to the doctrine of the eternity of sound and the indefeasible connexion between the sound of a word and its meaning.[1]

As the Veda contains many promises of rewards for those who perform the actions enjoined therein, and as these results are not seen arising at once from the actions, it seemed necessary to believe that sacrifice produces an invisible, transcendental result (apūrva), which will in time provide the promised fruit.

The Pūrva Mīmāṁsā does not teach a philosophical system, yet certain metaphysical ideas are implied or find incidental expression in it. The existence of God is denied

[1] See *ERE.* VIII. 648.

on the ground that an omniscient being is inconceivable; a realistic conception of the world is implied; the eternity of the world is stated in such terms as practically to preclude the belief in the periodic destruction and re-creation of all things; and the law of Karma is held so rigidly that it scarcely seems possible to believe in release from transmigration; and certainly the doctrine does not occur.[1]

The system came into existence to help the Vedic sacrificer and the priests who acted for him; and it remains to this day the guide of orthodox householders of the twice-born castes. Hence, unlike the Vedānta, the Sāṅkhya, and the Yoga, it does not teach asceticism, and has never had ascetics associated with it.

b. *The Uttara Mīmāṁsā or Vedānta.*

§ 143. The manual of the Uttara Mīmāṁsā, or Later Investigation, is usually called the *Vedānta-sūtras*. *Brahma-sūtras* and *Śārīraka-sūtras* are also used, because the subject is Brahman, who is recognized as being the Śārīraka, or spirit 'embodied' in the universe. The work is attributed to Bādarāyaṇa, but the character of the work itself shows that a long succession of scholars stand behind the author, and the names of seven of these occur in the sūtras.[2]

The work is a manual of exegetics for students of the Classical Upanishads, and is based on the belief that these treatises are in the fullest sense Revelation, and therefore contain a harmonious body of truth. As a matter of fact, although the Upanishads all set forth Brahman, one, spiritual, unknowable, as the basis of all things, they teach no settled system, but fling out guesses at truth from various standpoints. Necessarily, the effort to view the whole as an articulated body of clearly expressed ideas creates numerous difficulties. In so far as the obscurity of the sūtras permits us to judge, it would

[1] For these very early ideas see § 37.
[2] Thibaut, *SBE*. XXXIV. xix.

seem that the following outlines of a system are taught in the work:

Brahman is one and formless, and consists of intelligence. He is the source of scripture (*śruti*) and is therefore omniscient; and he is to be known only from scripture. He is the material as well as the final cause of the universe. He has no purpose to fulfil, and is therefore inactive: his seeming activity is sport. The world, though produced from Brahman from time to time, has had no beginning and will have no end. Scripture also is eternal. The gods exist, and they feed in their own divine way on the sacrifices which the Veda enjoins.

The individual soul is eternal, intelligent, all-pervading. It is a portion of Brahman; it *is* Brahman. Its individuality is but an appearance. Sacrificial works help a man to rise to knowledge of Brahman, but it is knowledge alone that confers release. The life of chastity and meditation on Brahman, as taught in scripture, is the path to knowledge. From Brahman comes the fruit of works, and therefore transmigration; from him comes also release.

§ 144. At a very early date the *Vedānta-sūtras* became revered as an inspired work, and it has since been held by almost all Hindus to be infallible. Yet in spite of that, since no commentary by its author has come down to us, the exact meaning of its enigmatical phrases is in many cases far from clear, and many variant expositions have been formulated by Hindu thinkers. These scholars fall in the main into two groups, those, on the one hand, who follow Śaṅkarāchārya (A.D. 788–850) in taking the identity of the individual soul with God in the strictest possible sense, and in accepting a monism so absolute that the material world is regarded as pure illusion, and the personality of God tends to be crushed out, and those, on the other, who, because they believe Brahman to be personal, regard the world as more or less real and the human soul as more or less distinct from him. The chief representative of this group is Rāmānuja, who flourished about 1100.

Thibaut discusses in considerable detail the question whether Śaṅkara or Rāmānuja comes nearest the teaching of the sūtras and reaches the conclusion[1] that, while the kind of Vedānta represented in the *Vedānta-sūtras* must be left an open question, there is reason to suppose that in some important points their teaching is more closely related to the system of Rāmānuja than to that of Śaṅkara.[2] On the other hand, he is inclined to believe that the teaching of Śaṅkara stands nearer to the teaching of the Upanishads than the *Sūtras* of Bādarāyaṇa do; and he explains this striking fact by the supposition that the teaching of the *Sūtras* was influenced in some degree by the *Bhagavadgītā*.[3]

For many centuries the Upanishads, the *Bhagavadgītā* and the *Vedānta-sūtras* have been recognized as the *Prasthāna-traya*, the Triple Source, of the Vedānta philosophy. It seems probable that in Bādarāyaṇa's day the *Gītā* had already risen to great authority, even if it had not yet received its destined place in the Canon of the school. Being thus placed practically on a level with the Upanishads, the *Gītā* necessarily became recognized as absolutely orthodox.[4]

§ 145. It is of interest to realize that three of the distinct theories of the relation of the individual soul to Brahman which were afterwards embodied in commentaries on these sūtras had already received expression by Vedāntic scholars before the time of Bādarāyaṇa. According to Āśmarathya, the soul is neither absolutely different from God nor absolutely without difference; i. e. he held the theory called Bhedābheda; according to Auḍulomi the soul is altogether different from Brahman up to the time when, obtaining release, it is merged in it; i. e. he held the Satyabheda, or Dvaita, theory; while according to Kāśakṛitsna the soul is absolutely non-different from Brahman, i. e. he held the Advaita theory.[5]

From the date of the earliest Upanishads until now there

[1] *SBE*. XXXIV. cxxvi f.
[2] Cf. Keith, *SS*. 6, 52.
[3] *SBE*. XXXIV. cxxvi.
[4] For its original heterodoxy, see § 94.
[5] *SBE*. XXXIV. xix.

has existed the great order of sannyāsīs who seek to follow this teaching. They are still the most numerous and the most highly respected order of monks in India. There are also a few nuns.

c. *The Sāṅkhya.*

§ 146. The primary authority for the Sāṅkhya system is the *Sāṅkhya-kārikā*,[1] a poem consisting originally of seventy verses and attributed to Īśvara Kṛishṇa. It seems clear from Chinese authorities that this writer was also known as Vindhya-vāsin, and that he was a little senior to Vasubandhu, the famous Buddhist scholar.[2] Until recently it was believed that Vasubandhu's date was the first half of the fifth century, but fresh evidence which has become available has led most scholars to conclude that he lived from about A.D. 270 to 350.[3] If that be so, we must place Īśvara Kṛishṇa towards the beginning of the fourth century.[4]

According to tradition, the *Sāṅkhya-kārikā* is really the *Shashṭitantra* rewritten, which, as we have seen above,[5] was a manual of the theistic Sāṅkhya. The contents of the *Shashṭitantra* as sketched in the *Ahirbudhnya Saṁhitā*[6] seem to justify this tradition.

The poem is an excellent piece of work. Unlike the obscure sūtras of the two mīmāṁsās, its verses are each quite comprehensible, although it would undoubtedly be extremely difficult for a beginner to form an intelligible conception of the system from the treatise by itself.

It is well to recognize that with the Sāṅkhya we enter upon rationalistic speculation. It is held to be throughout consistent with scripture (*śruti*), but it is clear on the very surface that the leading ideas have been evolved not from Vedic texts but from observation and speculative thought. The appeal to

[1] See esp. Keith, *SS.* chap. vii.
[2] *JRAS.* 1905, 162; 355.
[3] *BEFEO.* xi, 356 ff.; Thomas, *JRAS.* 1913, 646; 1031; 1914, 748; Franks, *JRAS.* 1914, 398 ff.; Takakusu, ib. 113; Keith, *SS.* 87.
[4] Keith, *SS.* 43; 57; 63.
[5] § 99.
[6] Schrader, *IPAS.* 110 ff.

scripture is more formal than real; yet the system has in consequence been recognized as orthodox, and therefore superior not only to Buddhism and Jainism but to the sectarian systems.

§ 147. The end in view[1] is the removal of misery, and the means is true knowledge. Three kinds of evidence are available, perception, inference, and right affirmation (which includes scripture). The system is an atheistic dualism: there are two eternal existences, original nature (*prakṛiti*), and spirits (*purusha*). Prakṛiti is one, unconscious, productive; spirits are many, conscious, inactive, each a solitary, passive spectator of the operations of nature. It is implied that spirits transmigrate and suffer misery. Prakṛiti is the universal material cause, unconscious, homogeneous, invisible, impalpable, knowable only from its products. Professor Keith writes:[2]

> The essential conception is that from unconscious nature there is developed for the sake of spirit a whole universe, that the development takes place for each individual spirit separately, but yet at the same time in such a manner that nature and its evolutes are common to all spirits.

Prakṛiti and all its products possess the three constituents, goodness (*sattva*), energy (*rajas*), and darkness (*tamas*), but while they are in equilibrium in prakṛiti, they appear in its products in variant balance. From prakṛiti issues Intellect (*buddhi*) called also the Great (*mahat*), a subtle cosmic substance, which constitutes in the individual his organ of thought and decision. From Intellect is produced Egoism or Individuation (*ahaṁkāra*), a subtle cosmic substance which marks every psychical movement with the word 'mine' and makes each spirit imagine itself an active human individual. From Egoism is produced Mind (*manas*), a subtle cosmic substance which enables the individual to apprehend and pass on to the intellect the impressions of things received by the senses, and to carry out the decisions of the intellect by means of the active organs. From Egoism there are also produced the five organs of sense,

[1] Keith (*SS.* Chap. vii) gives a brilliant exposition and criticism of the system of the *Kārikā*.
[2] *SS.* 78.

the five organs of action, and five subtle elements, or rudiments (*tanmātras*), which in turn produce the five material elements. Prakṛiti, with its three first products and these four fives, make twenty-four principles, and spirit makes the twenty-fifth.

The spirit, intelligent but inactive, is united with nature, unconscious but active, like a lame man carried on a blind man's back, and, misled by the operations of Egoism, imagines himself an active individual, thinking, feeling, willing, acting, while he is but an inactive spectator of the unconscious and inevitable processes of nature. Yet nature is produced, so that she may display herself like a dancer, and so give the individual spirit an opportunity to realize the truth that he is not bound by nature but is a free, inactive spirit. By repeated reflective study of these principles the follower of the Sāṅkhya reaches the knowledge, 'Neither I am, nor is aught mine, nor do I exist.' Possessed of this knowledge, the purusha in peace and inaction contemplates nature, which is thereby precluded from her activity, and the purusha at death attains its true life of Isolation (*kaivalya*).

§ 148. It seems clear that this complicated system was evolved from a number of early conceptions in the Upanishads.[1] It has in turn deeply influenced every form of Indian thought.

The Sāṅkhya offers the knowledge which leads to Kaivalya to Śūdras as well as to twice-born Hindus. It thus stands between the Vedānta, which is restricted to the twice-born, and the Yoga, which is open to all. There has existed since the early centuries an order of Sāṅkhya sannyāsīs, but there are few, if any, left now.

d. *The Yoga.*

§ 149. The manual of the Yoga system, the *Yoga-sūtra*, is attributed to Patañjali, and for centuries it was held that the reference was to the grammarian of the second century B.C., and consequently the *Yoga-sūtra* was believed by European

[1] So Keith, *SS.* Chap. i, and 87.

scholars to be the earliest of the philosophic manuals. But since the sūtra shows a more developed system than anything that appears in the epic or in the Yoga Upanishads, and since the Vijñānavāda of Buddhism is criticized in it,[1] it is now recognized that the author must have been another Patañjali, and that his date cannot be earlier than the middle of the fourth century A. D. It is probable that the writing of the *Sāṅkhya-kārikā* and its great success led to the production of the *Yoga-sūtra*.[2] The rise of the Vijñānavādin, or Yogāchāra,[3] system within Buddhism, about A. D. 300, would also be a challenge; for Yoga holds a large place in it.

The Yoga system accepts the twenty-five principles of the Sāṅkhya and adds to them the Lord (*Īśvara*), thus raising the number to twenty-six. But the interest of the Yoga centres, not in the understanding of these principles, but in the practice of the method of yoga and in devotion to the Lord, which it sets forth as the most efficient means for the attainment of the Isolation (*kaivalya*) of the soul (*purusha* or *ātman*).

The Lord of the *Yoga-sūtras* is attached rather loosely to the main conceptions of the system.[4] He is a special kind of soul (*purusha-viśesha*), omniscient, eternal, perfect, untouched by karma, transmigration, or human weakness. He is the teacher of the Primal Sages; and he helps the man who shows him devotion to reach the concentration which leads to Isolation, but he is not called the Creator nor otherwise related to world-processes. He is expressed by the mystic syllable, *Om*.

Yoga-method seeks to gain complete mastery over the movements of the mind, first by means of moral abstentions, ascetic observances, and exercises both physical and mental, and then by fixed attention and deepening meditation, which lead on to ecstatic contemplation and the final discrimination between soul and nature, which secures Isolation.

[1] Hopkins, *JAOS*. XXII b., 335, 336; Woods, *Yoga*, XV ff.; Keith, *SS*. 57.

[2] Keith, *SS*. 57.

[3] § 178.

[4] Keith, *SS*. 56.

In its earlier stages the school of Yoga was open to all Hindus, and even to Outcastes,[1] precisely like Buddhism and Jainism. Yoga ascetics are called Yogīs.

e. *The Vaiśeshika.*

§ 150. As we have seen above, the Vaiśeshika system already existed in the first century A. D., and it may be still older. The classic treatise, the *Vaiśeshika-sūtras*, is attributed to Kaṇāda Kāśyapa. The Vaiśeshika and the Nyāya systems apparently grew up side by side, and the two sūtra manuals seem to have been edited with close reference to each other.[2]

The Vaiśeshika is an atomistic realism. Nine classes of ultimate realities, *dravyas*, are recognized. There are first four classes of paramāṇus, i. e. minima, or atoms. Each paramāṇu is a changeless, eternal reality, yet invisible and without magnitude. The minima fall into four classes, according as they possess odour, flavour, light, or heat, which are regarded as characteristics of earth, water, air, and fire respectively. Two minima form a dyaṇuka, or binary atom, and a combination of three dyaṇukas forms a tryaṇuka, the smallest entity that possesses magnitude and may be termed a substance. The fifth ultimate reality, *ākāśa*, usually translated 'ether', is an indiscrete and all-pervading continuum, conceived as the medium necessary for the formation of substances from the unsubstantial minima. The sixth reality, *kāla* (lit. 'time') stands for the force which produces all activity, movement, and change, and thus gives the basis for the perception of time-differences. The seventh reality, *dik* (i. e. direction or position), acts so as to balance *kāla*, keeping things in position and preventing their dissolution amid the welter of change. The eighth reality is an infinite number of *ātmans*, the old Vedantic word for the self or soul. Each ātman is eternal, infinite, all-pervading. The ninth ultimate is *manas*, the organ through which the ātman comes into touch with the impressions of the senses. Like the paramāṇus, each manas is eternal and without

[1] Hopkins, *GE.* 114. [2] Keith, *JRAS.* 1914, p. 1085.

magnitude. Like the Karma Mīmāṁsā and the Sāṅkhya, the original Vaiśeshika recognizes the Hindu gods but not the one God.

The sūtras name six padārthas, categories or classes of things that can be named, *dravya* (entity, existence), *guṇa* (quality), *karma* (action), *sāmānya* (the relation of a thing to its genus), *viśesha* (differentia), and *samavāya* (inherence). The knowledge of these categories brings release.

f. *The Nyāya.*

§ 151. The Nyāya system, which can be traced from the first century, has adopted the Vaiśeshika metaphysic, and thus stands related to that system in much the same way as the Yoga stands to the Sāṅkhya; but, as sufficient evidence to enable us to trace the early history of the Nyāya has not come down, we cannot tell how it came into existence. As the special interest of the Nyāya is to prove the truths which lead to bliss and deliverance, one might conjecture that the system was formed by combining the method of an early school of dialectic with the Vaiśeshika metaphysic, or, as an alternative, that two schools seeking deliverance grew up side by side, the one seeking saving knowledge in an accurate scientific account of all things, the other feeling the necessity of presenting a demonstrative proof of the truth of the main positions which were held to be necessary for deliverance, and that, after the elaboration of the proofs, the metaphysic of the scientific school was adopted to complete the world-view. There is one further difference to be noted. Like the Yoga, the Nyāya posits a Lord (*Īśvara*), and is thus theistic, but in the sūtra he is referred to only as administering the fruits of action. The fundamental document is Gautama's *Nyāya-sūtra.*

The sūtra enumerates sixteen topics. They are, 1. Proof, 2. Things to be proved, 3. Doubt, 4. Motive, 5. Example, 6. Conclusion, 7. The members of a syllogism, 8. Reductio ad absurdum, 9. Ascertainment, 10. Thesis, 11. Sophistical wrangling, 12. Cavilling, 13. Fallacious reasoning, 14. Futility,

15. Quibbling, 16. Talk that is beside the point. These subjects of discussion show where the centre of interest lies in the philosophy. In the course of its reasonings the Nyāya developed the logic of India.

§ 152. In both the Nyāya and the Vaiśeshika the conception of the soul (*ātman*) is much richer and fuller than in other systems. Its functions are Involuntary vital action, Voluntary action, Desire, Aversion, Cognition, and Control of the organs of sense and of the *manas* or inner organ.

These two schools seem to have sprung up among the orthodox twice-born householders; for neither demands asceticism, nor have ascetics been associated with them.

It is very noteworthy that the Vaiśeshika was certainly atheistic to begin with, and the Nyāya may have been so also. Thus the ancient Hindu mind, which acknowledged all the gods but not the Supreme, lingered long among the twice-born. But gradually a belief in God won its way. From a very early date the Nyāya became theistic, and the Vaiśeshika followed later. The Nyāya is to this day professed by considerable numbers of orthodox Brāhmans in Bengal; while the Vaiśeshika seems to have been associated with Pāśupata Śaivism from the moment when it recognized the existence of the Supreme.

§ 153. It is probable, though not certain, that each of the classical treatises was accompanied by a commentary prepared by the author; but unfortunately, if these existed, no single one of them has survived. Of all existing commentaries on the six manuals, only two seem to belong to our period, namely, Śabara Svāmin's *Bhāshya* on the *Purva-mīmāṁsā-sūtras*, and Vātsyāyana's *Nyāya Bhāshya*. Jacobi conjectures[1] that both these works belong to the fifth century. It seems clear that Vātsyāyana's *Bhāshya* at least falls within the limits of our period; for he comes before Dignāga,[2] the Buddhist writer, whose date is about A.D. 550,[3] while the archaic

[1] *JAOS.* XXXI. 24; *ERE.* II. 201.
[2] Vidyābhūshaṇa, *MSIL.* 86.
[3] Woods, *Yoga*, xix.

character of Śabara's work is sufficient to justify our inclusion of it within the same limits.

The philosophies of Buddhism and Jainism are discussed elsewhere, but it may be useful to note here that the four Buddhist philosophical systems, Sarvāstivādin, Sautrāntika, Mādhyamaka, Vijñānavādin, are combated in these Hindu manuals, and that the classic treatise of the Vijñānavādins was probably written about the same time as the *Sāṅkhya Kārikā*; while Umāsvāti also, whose *Tattvārthādhigama-sūtra* is the fountain head of Jain philosophy, seems to have lived under the Guptas.[1]

B. *The Purāṇas.*

§ 154. It would be difficult to exaggerate the popularity and importance of the religious poems known as Purāṇas. They are very widely used among the common people, both in the original and in numerous vernacular versions and adaptations. Indeed the epics and the Purāṇas are the real Bible of the common people, whether literate or illiterate, and they are the source of half the vernacular literature. On the other hand, the Purāṇas are of little intrinsic interest as compared with the Vedas, or the philosophic or classical literature; and hence they have been largely neglected by serious students. Wilson's essays laid the foundations for critical study, but little has been done since his time. It is thus impossible at present to give a trustworthy chronology of these poems, or to explain how each arose; yet something may be said to enable readers to grasp the significance of the more important sections of the literature.

Purāṇas are referred to in Vedic literature from the *Atharvaveda* downwards; quotations occur in the Dharmasūtras, and in the Epics; while there are definite references to the *Bhavishya P.* in the *Āpastamba Dharmasūtra* and to the *Vāyu P.* in the *Mahābhārata*. A passage in the *Padma P.* is copied in the *Mahābhārata*.[2] Yet even the earliest existing

[1] See § 185.

[2] Hopkins, *GE*. 47–50.

Purāṇas come from later dates. They contain sections and fragments belonging to early centuries, but as works they are late.

§ 155. The Purāṇas are a second type of popular literature, written in the same verse and open to the people with the same completeness as the epics; but they had a different origin. The word purāṇa means ancient, but as a name in literature it signifies not an ancient book but an ancient subject, Archaica. Indeed, originally a Purāṇa would seem to have been a book of origins, a sort of Hindu Genesis. The tradition is that a Purāṇa has five marks, i.e. it contains teaching on five distinct topics, as follows:

I. Creation.

II. Re-creation, i.e. at the opening of each kalpa, with a description of the Universe, Heaven, Hell, and earth.

III. Genealogies of gods and ṛishis, and an account of the origin of the Veda.

IV. The ages of the world and their regents.

V. Genealogies of kings.

This shows that a Purāṇa was conceived as a book of origins; and to this day the Purāṇas are the source of popular conceptions of creation, time, the universe, the earth, geography, and early history. We shall use the word 'cosmic' to describe this type of teaching as a whole, although considerable sections are rather legendary and historical than cosmic. Some very old material, belonging to this category, occurs in two or three of the earliest of our existing Purāṇas, whence it has been copied, with or without alteration, into most of the others. It can be most conveniently studied in the *Vishṇu*. Further, in the genealogies of kings in the *Vāyu*, *Brahmaṇḍa*, and *Matsya*, there is material which has proved to be of historical value. As the latest kings named in these documents belong to the first half of the fourth century, the documents presumably are not much later.

§ 156. But, like the epics, the Purāṇas were used by the sects as vehicles of sectarian teaching. Each sect and sub-sect sought to foist its own documents upon some popular Purāṇa, so that they might find their way into the hands and hearts of the people. The process seems to have begun, as in the epic, with Kṛishṇa. It was quite natural to append his biography to the genealogies of the ancient kings, as is done in the *Harivaṁśa* and the *Vishṇu P.* Thereafter, sectarian documents of many types found their way into the Purāṇas. As in the epic, the Vaishṇavas here took the lion's share, but the Śaivas did not fall far behind them, while other sects had to be content with slighter support.

Scholars are inclined to believe that the earliest of the existing Purāṇas took shape under the Guptas in the fourth, fifth, and sixth centuries, although all have probably undergone more or less modification since then;[1] and it is probably true that every existing Purāṇa owes its present form and its survival to some sect. Thus we take the golden age of the Guptas as the dividing line. In earlier times there existed real old Purāṇas dealing with origins. They were meant for the whole people, and were a genuine national literature. But only fragments of these 'cosmic' Purāṇas survive. All existing Purāṇas come from the Gupta period or from later dates. Further, the Purāṇas have suffered so much from rewriting and interpolation that they cannot be treated like homogeneous texts. The date of each section must be considered by itself, and in most cases internal evidence alone is available. Most of the results must thus be treated as very tentative.

§ 157. From quite an early time the Purāṇas have been spoken of as eighteen in number; for the phrase, 'the eighteen Purāṇas' occurs in a very late passage in the *Mahābhārata*.[2] What this early canon was like, we have no means of knowing, but it may possibly have included a few of the existing Purāṇas; for the passage referred to is probably not earlier

[1] Pargiter, *JRAS*. 1912, 248; Fleet, ib. 1912, 1046; Keith, ib. 1914, 740; 1915, 331.
[2] XVIII. v. 46; vi. 97; Hopkins, *GE*. 48.

than the fourth century. But the actual number of existing works recognized as Purāṇas is twenty; for the *Harivaṁśa*, which forms the conclusion of the *Mahābhārata*, is one of the earliest and greatest of the Purāṇas, and must be reckoned as such; and both the *Śiva* and the *Vāyu*, one of which is usually excluded from the list, ought to be included. There are besides many secondary documents, known as Upapurāṇas. The twenty recognized works are the following eighteen, as found in the list in the Vishṇu: 1. Brahma, 2. Padma, 3. Vishṇu, 4. Śiva, 5. Bhāgavata, 6. Nāradīya, 7. Mārkaṇḍeya, 8. Agni, 9. Bhavishya, 10. Brahmavaivarta, 11. Liṅga, 12. Varāha, 13. Skanda, 14. Vāmana, 15. Kūrma, 16. Matsya, 17. Garuḍa, 18. Brahmāṇḍa—with the Harivaṁśa and the Vāyu added.

§ 158. Thus the roots of the Purānic literature go back to early dates, but most of the material is late. Even a cursory study shows that there have been innumerable additions, excisions, and alterations made in the course of the centuries. Very few Purāṇas have a settled text: differing recensions exist, and countless fragments of many types are found in MSS., either incorporated in a Purāṇa, or claiming to belong to one. The sectarian Purāṇa is essentially an old text partially rewritten for a sectarian end, or an old text with a sectarian document incorporated in it; and this process of contamination has been continued through all the centuries since the Gupta period. Ancient legends about the sectarian gods, masses of sectarian theology, philosophy, ritual, and art, manuals of politics, war, astrology, medicine, rhetoric, and grammar, and māhātmyas (i.e. panegyrics) of temples and other places of pilgrimage, now form a large part of the contents of the Purāṇas. Thus even if the precise date of the original compilation of each of the twenty Purāṇas were definitely known, we should still be compelled to judge the age and origin of each section on its own merits. But very little of this critical work has yet been done; so that only tentative conclusions can be given at present; and critical study will prove fruitful only if the Puranic material is examined in the closest possible relation to the history of the sects.

We propose to fit Puranic material into our outline of the history in two ways. First, we shall give a list in each chapter of those Purāṇas or sections of Purāṇas which seem to belong to its period; and secondly we shall use those sectarian Puranic documents whose connexions can be discerned to help to complete our sketch of the literature of each period.

§ 159. It is clear that the *Harivaṁśa* belongs to this period, but there is no absolute proof with regard to any other document. Yet we propose, tentatively, to assign the following Purāṇas and parts of Purāṇas to this period, since the evidence in each case seems to favour the ascription. They are briefly discussed below in the sections which deal with the sectarian literatures, and in each case the reasons for ascribing them to this period are stated.

The sect of	Vishṇu:	*Harivaṁśa* and *Vishṇu P.*
,,	Śiva:	Sections in *Vāyu P.*
,,	Brahmā:	First Khaṇḍa of *Padma P.*; portions of *Mārkaṇḍeya P.*
,,	Durgā:	Hymns in *Harivaṁśa*; Chaṇḍī Māhātmya of *Mārkaṇḍeya P.*
,,	Sūrya:	Section of *Mārkaṇḍeya P.*; Brāhma Parvan of *Bhavishya P.*

C. *The Orthodox Twice-born and their Literature.*

§ 160. The slow yet steady weakening of the ancient sacrifices prescribed in the Śrauta-sūtras seems to be one of the chief features of orthodox life during this period, while the simpler rites laid down in the Gṛihya-sūtras were more and more practised and also widened in their scope. The popular gods took their place in the worship of the home, and were honoured with a ritual taken from the Gṛihya-sūtras. At this time also the word *Smārta* began to be used for the orthodox twice-born man who does not offer the Śrauta sacrifices, while

Śrauta became the term for the man who still keeps up several or all of the Śrauta rites. The word Smārta occurs first of all in this sense in the Pariśishṭas to Baudhāyana's *Gṛihya-sūtra.* Smārta comes from *Smṛiti*; and the idea is that the Smārta's worship depends upon smṛiti, i. e. the sūtras, and in particular on the Gṛihya-sūtra of the school to which he belongs.

For the whole group of orthodox twice-born men the final exposition of the Karma Mīmāṁsā, the Nyāya, and the Vaiśeshika in sūtras—all three being systems which orthodox householders favoured—and the codification of the ancient dharma in the lawbooks during those centuries must have been of signal importance; while the writing of the Pariśishṭas now attached to the *Baudhāyana Gṛihya-sūtras* seems to have arisen directly from the emergence of the Smārtas.

The chief works on the sacred law belonging to this period are the *Vishṇusmṛiti*, the *Vaikhānasa Gṛihya* and *Dharma-sūtras*, the *Yājñavalkya Dharmaśāstra* and certain *Pariśishṭas* or appendices tacked on to the *Baudhāyana Gṛihya-sūtra.* The earliest of these works is the *Vishṇusmṛiti*, which is later than the *Harivaṁśa*, and the latest is the *Yājñavalkya Dharmaśāstra*, which borrows passages from the *Vishṇusmṛiti* and speaks of Gaṇeśa. The *Baudhāyana Gṛihya-sūtra* is of peculiar interest for the history of the Smārta community; for it is sometimes called the *Smārta-sūtra* in MSS.;[1] and its Pariśishṭas contain rules for their cult.[2] It would be well if they could be critically edited. The *Yājñavalkya Dharmaśāstra* stands in close relationship to Manu and is also an orthodox work.

The legal material of the *Vishṇusmṛiti* is in prose sūtras, and seems to have been taken over almost unchanged from the Dharma-sūtra belonging to the Chārāyaṇīya-Kāṭhakas, one of the ancient schools of the *Black Yajurveda*; but some rules have been altered and a few new ones added. The

[1] Bühler, *SBE.* XIV. xxx.

[2] I am informed that the worship of the five gods is dealt with in them; see § 207.

reviser has also introduced a short chapter at the beginning, in which we are told that the goddess of the earth received this whole body of law from the lips of the supreme Vishṇu, and added two at the end in praise of Vishṇu and his consort Śrī. Kṛishṇa receives no special mention. The code is thus a Vaishṇava work arranged for the use of some Vaishṇava community, most probably the Bhāgavata, as is suggested at many points by the commentator Nandapaṇḍita.[1] The *Vaikhānasa Sūtras* are also Vaishṇava, and as there are found in the Tamil south to-day Vaishṇava temples in which *Vaikhānasa*, as distinct from *Pāñcharātra*, Saṁhitās[2] are used for the ritual, it is probable that this also was prepared for a special Vaishṇava community.

§ 161. It was seemingly during this period that the worship of Vishṇu and Śiva as equal, or as one, was instituted; for the fullest exposition of the theory on which the cult rests occurs in the *Harivaṁśa*.[3] One might think that the worship of Śiva and Vishṇu as one was a compromise meant to reconcile warring sectaries, but facts suggest another explanation.

The word Bhāgavata has two meanings in modern Hinduism. It is first an epithet used of Vaishṇavas generally, as those who use the Bhagavat-śāstra, or body of works which revere Vishṇu as Bhagavān. It is used, in the second place, of a special community of Vaishṇavas, found to-day in most parts of South India, who really adore Vishṇu, but recognize the equality of the two gods and keep up the use of Vedic rites. They are therefore recognized as Smārtas. It is of great importance to distinguish this community of Vaishṇava Smārtas from the sectarian Vaishṇavas called Pāñcharātras. We may be sure that the passage in the *Harivaṁśa*, which reflects the double worship, comes from the Bhāgavatas. An Upanishad was written later to establish the doctrine of the identity of Vishṇu

[1] *SBE.* VII. pp. 155 *n.*; 208 *n.* 2; 268. [2] See § 211 and § 212.

[3] Chap. 184, lines 10660 ff. Cf. Muir, *OST.* IV.; also Winternitz, I. 386. For the *Harivaṁśa*, see § 159 and § 162.

and Śiva, the *Skanda U.*[1] The godhead conceived in this way is designated *Harihara*, Preserver-Destroyer. An inscription dating from A.D. 528–9[2] shows that the Bhāgavata community was already in existence during this period; for it not only uses the word Bhāgavata but quotes their famous mantra, *Oṁ namo Bhagavate Vāsudevāya.*

The presence in the *Harivaṁśa* of the classical text on the metaphysical equality of Vishṇu and Śiva, and of several other passages which fit in with the theory,[3] naturally suggests the question whether the *Harivaṁśa* may not be a Bhāgavata Purāṇa corresponding to the *Vishṇu P.*, which clearly belongs to the Pāñcharātra Vaishṇavas. The emergence about the same time of two Purāṇas so similar in their attitude to Kṛishṇa would thereby find an explanation. The contents and significance of the *Harivaṁśa* are dealt with below.

D. *Vaishṇava Literature.*

§ 162. The *Harivaṁśa* and the *Vishṇu P.* are Krishnaite works prepared with the utmost care and skill from old materials, so that the popularity and the ancient influence of the Puranic literature may be used to strengthen the cult of Vishṇu. It is suggested above[4] that the *Harivaṁśa* may be a Bhāgavata document, while there is no doubt that the *Vishṇu P.* sprang from the Vaishṇava sect known as Pāñcharātras. They must in any case be considered together. The *Harivaṁśa* clearly cannot be dated later than A.D. 400, and the *Vishṇu P.* is so like it in most of its features that it is probable that it belongs to the same general date. Both contain a good deal of cosmic matter, but it is in their treatment of the Kṛishṇa-legend that they are most significant. They presuppose the whole *Mahābhārata* story, but they tell in great detail the sports and exploits of his youth, which are

[1] See § 210.
[2] The Khoh copper plates of Mahārāja Saṁkshobha, belonging to the year 209 of the Gupta era.
[3] cxxxi. 741 ff.; cxlv. 8199 ff.; cclxvi-cclxxxi; cccxxiv. See Winternitz, I. 384 ff.
[4] § 161.

merely alluded to in the epic. Perhaps three stages in the development of the legend may be detected. The dramatist Bhāsa, who probably dates from the third century A. D., has a play called *Bālacharita*, which tells the story of Kṛishṇa's youth, as its name indicates. In it the *Hallīṣa* sport is merely an innocent dance. In the *Vishṇu P.* there are already various erotic touches which go a good deal further; while in the *Harivaṁśa* the whole story of his youth is told at much greater length and the Hallīśa is treated as involving sexual intercourse.[1]

In any case it is the life of Kṛishṇa, and, above all, the legend of his youth that gives these works their significance; and the fresh material they contain, doubtless drawn from legends which had long been current in and about Mathurā, could scarcely be surpassed in power to attract, to interest, and to amuse the common people. Here we have Kṛishṇa and his brother pictured in a series of feats of strength and cunning, killing giants and circumventing rogues, the whole lighted up with coarse country humour of the broadest type, and, alongside, scenes of rustic merrymaking in which the young god captures the hearts of all the young wives, and keeps up the dance and the revel all night long.

The *Harivaṁśa* had the immense good fortune to be accepted as a fitting close to the *Mahābhārata*, and in consequence has enjoyed unlimited popularity and influence. The *Vishṇu P.* is the best representative of the whole class of sectarian Purāṇas, since it is purely Vaishṇava in its teaching from beginning to end, and yet retains with considerable faithfulness the character of the old unsectarian Purāṇas. It is divided into six books, all of which, with the exception of the fifth, are in the main 'cosmic' in character, though distinctly Vaishṇava in theology. The fifth book tells the story of Kṛishṇa and is the heart of the Purāṇa, as has just been shown. In its theology the *Vishṇu* follows, in the main, the *Gītā* and the other Vaishṇava documents of the didactic

[1] Chanda, *IAR*. 86 ff.

epic, but it speaks of Kṛishṇa as being an incarnation of an exceedingly small portion of Vishṇu.

The appearance of these two great works sufficiently attests the great place which Kṛishṇa held in Hindu thought at the time. Thibaut's conjecture as to the influence of the *Gītā* on the *Vedānta-sūtras*, and the unquestioned fact that about this time the Song rose to a place of authority on an equality with the Upanishads[1] are further proofs of the influence of the Vaishṇava movement.

§ 163. The *Mahā*[2] is a short Upanishad which voices the Vaishṇava conviction that Nārāyaṇa, i.e. Vishṇu, is the eternal Brahman, that from him come the twenty-five principles of the Sāṅkhya system, and that Śiva and Brahmā are subordinate deities, creations of his meditative power. It is the oldest Vaishṇava Upanishad, and probably comes from our period. It is quoted by Rāmānuja.[3]

E. *Śaiva Literature.*

§ 164. In the didactic epic, as we have seen, a theology named Pāśupata is woven round the god Śiva. This system makes its appearance next in the earlier part of the *Vāyu P.* The bulk of the Purāṇa probably belongs to the fourth or fifth century, but the date of this Pāśupata section is not yet known. The material, however, stands so near the Śaiva material of the Epic in character that we are inclined to place it in this period rather than in the next. It contains a good deal of 'cosmic' material very little modified, the philosophy following in the main the teaching of the theistic Yoga. Chapters 11 to 15 deal with Pāśupata Yoga, the various forms of physical and intellectual practice which were traditional in the sect.[4] Here also occurs a Māhātmya of Maheśvara, and a hymn of praise in honour of Nīlakaṇṭha, both names of Śiva.

[1] See § 144. [2] Deussen, *SUV*. 743.
[3] *SBE*. XLVIII. 522.
[4] Pāśupata ascetics are called *ūrddhva-retasaḥ*, *Pāśupatās tapasvinaḥ*, and *bhasmoddhūlitavigrahāḥ*.

§ 165. But there is one passage which introduces us to a sub-sect of the Pāśupatas, viz. the Lakulīśas. After an enumeration of the Kalpas, there comes an account of the ages (*yugas*) which form divisions of the present Kalpa. Of these twenty-eight are enumerated, and Śiva promises to become incarnate in each. The last of the prophecies runs that, when Kṛishṇa shall be incarnate as Vāsudeva, Śiva, by means of his Yoga powers, will enter a dead body left unguarded in a burning-ground at Kāyārohana, and will appear as an ascetic named Lakulī. Kuśika, Gārgya, Mitra, and Kaurashya will be his disciples, and will practise Pāśupata Yoga, smearing their bodies with ashes and dust.[1]

Now an inscription in an old shrine near the temple of Ekliṅgjī, fourteen miles from Udaipur, says that Śiva was incarnate in the country of Broach and carried a rod (*lakula*) in his hand, whence the place was called Kāyāvarohana, i.e. descent in a body. The Cintra praśasti says that Śiva became incarnate at Karohana, in the Lāta country, and that, for the strict performance of Pāśupata vows, there appeared in bodily form four pupils, Kuśika, Gārgya, Kaurushya, and Maitreya. Karwar in the Baroda State is held to be the place, and a temple of Lakulīśa still stands there.

We have then, in the prophecy of the *Vāyu*, the earliest notice of the Lakulīśa-Pāśupatas. The history of the sect has been worked out by Mr. R. D. Bhandarkar. A temple belonging to it was assigned by Fergusson to the seventh century; it can be traced in inscriptions from Rajputana south to Mysore, from the tenth century downwards, and large numbers of Lakulīśa images have been found in Gujarāt and Rajputana. These images are different from all other images of Śiva: in them the god has but two arms, he holds a short club in one of his hands, and the penis is naked and erect. The two arms find an explanation if Lakulī was a human ascetic; the club is the *lakula* from which he takes his name;

[1] Cf. the account of Pāśupata ascetics in *Atharvaśiras U.*: see § 112.

and the penis naked and erect recalls the liṅga-passages of the epic discussed above.[1]

It thus seems likely that the sect was founded by a Pāśupata ascetic named Lakulī, i.e. the club-bearer, who taught a form of Pāśupata doctrine, and was recognized as an incarnation of Śiva. Since the name Lakulī does not occur in the *Mahābhārata*, it is likely that the sect arose after the epic and before the *Vāyu*, perhaps about the third or fourth century.[2] Now, given the belief that Śiva has been incarnate in this, the twenty-eighth, Mahāyuga as Lakulī, attended by four disciples, the schematizing Indian imagination, which created a long series of Vaishṇava incarnations before Kṛishṇa, a long series of Buddhas before Gautama, and a long series of Tīrthakaras before Mahāvīra, would soon discover the names of the other incarnations and of the four disciples of each. The sect would then have a line of divine teachers worthy of comparison with the list of avatāras in the Vaishṇava sect; and that is precisely what we have in the *Vāyu*. It is very noticeable that the doctrine of avatāras, which was not adopted at the time of the epic, is now accepted, and that the very form of the story confesses that it is copied from the Kṛishṇa-incarnation.

§ 166. It is probable that the bulk of Śaivas throughout this period belonged to no sub sect, but continued their worship of the god in accordance with ancient usage, as so many do to-day, without troubling about sects and theology, but our information is very scanty.

About the Tamil Śaivas a little is known, but there is practically no literature to catalogue. Nakkīra Deva, who lived at some time during the period, seems to have been a writer of eminence, but only one of the works attributed to

[1] See § 110. The epithet *Ūrddhva-retas*, which occurs in these passages, is used here of Lakulīśa ascetics in the sense of 'chaste'.

[2] This date is certainly very speculative; for the passage may possibly have been interpolated after the writing of the original Purāṇa; but it is at least more likely to be near the date than Bhandarkar's suggestion, the first century A.D.

him is accepted by scholars as genuine, the *Tirumuruhattup-padai*, a poem in honour of the god Muruha, i.e. Subrahmaṇya.

F. *Brahmā Literature.*

§ 167. A Brahmā sect also appears in the literature. In the *Mārkaṇḍeya P.* and in the first Khaṇḍa of the *Padma P.*[1] he is identified with the eternal Brahman of the Upanishads. There can be little doubt that these passages belong to this period, for only during these centuries was the sect of Brahmā prominent. In the *Mārkaṇḍeya* he is spoken of as unborn, changeless, imperishable, unknowable, the source of prakṛiti and of souls, while in the *Padma*,

> Brahmā and Brahman, the instrument and the first cause of creation, are represented as the same, the primeval, excellent, beneficent, and supreme Brahman in the form of Brahmā and the rest, is the creation and the creator, preserves and is preserved, devours and is devoured, the first immaterial cause being, as is common in the pantheism of the Purāṇas, also the material cause and substance of the universe.[2]

The greater part of the first Khaṇḍa of the *Padma* forms the Pushkara Māhātmya, or panegyric of Pushkara, the holy lake in Rajputana, where stands the one famous temple of Brahmā to-day.

Here we had better also say a word about the doctrine of the Trimūrti, according to which the one supreme Reality is manifested as Brahmā, Vishṇu and Śiva. It appears first in two passages in the *Maitrāyaṇa U.* In the first of these[3] there is merely the statement that the three gods are the highest manifestations of the bodiless Supreme. In the second[4] it takes philosophical form: as *prakṛiti*, the imperceptible base of nature, consists of three strands, *sattva*, *rajas*, and *tamas*,[5] so the one Supreme is manifested in the three gods, Vishṇu being sattva, Brahmā rajas, and Śiva tamas.

[1] The *Padma P.* is named from the lotus in which Brahmā appears at the creation. It was thus a Brahmā Purāṇa from the beginning.
[2] Wilson, *Works*, III. 24.
[3] IV. 5-6. [4] V. 2. [5] See § 147.

Such is the original form of the doctrine. But, since each sect identified its own god with the supreme Brahman, the trimūrti has a distinct form in each. To the Vishṇuite Vishṇu-Brahman is manifested in three gods, Brahmā, a subordinate Vishṇu, and Śiva,[1] while to the Śaiva, Śiva-Brahman is manifested in Brahmā, Vishṇu, and Bhava.[2] A similar scheme was set forth by Sauras,[3] by the worshippers of Brahmā,[4] by Gāṇapatyas,[5] and by Śāktas.[6] The Nimbārkas and other sects identify Kṛishṇa as distinct from Vishṇu with Brahman, and thus have a scheme of their own.[7] The doctrine has never been a living element in the religion of the Hindu, although it often appears in literature and now and then in sculpture. It may be well to notice how utterly unlike the Christian doctrine of the Trinity this unstable theory is. It always involves four gods, one Supreme and three manifestations, and the phrase in the *Matsya P.* which has been often mistranslated 'One God and three persons', really means 'One image, three gods',[8] and it does not cover the one Reality behind these manifestations.

G. *Durgā Literature.*

§ 168. The worship of the goddess Durgā also comes to the surface in the literature at this point. The earliest passage occurs in the *Mahābhārata,*[9] and celebrates Durgā as the slayer of Mahisha, and as a virgin goddess, who dwells in the Vindhya mountains, delights in wine, flesh, and animal sacrifice, and upholds heaven by her chastity, but is also the sister of Kṛishṇa,[10] and like him is dark blue in colour and

[1] *MBH.* III. cclxxii. 46.
[2] *Liṅga P.* I. xviii. 12; Muir, *OST.* IV. 330.
[3] *Rāmāyaṇa,* VI. cvi. 19. Cf. Wilson, *Sects,* I. 19.
[4] *Mārkaṇḍeya, P.* xlv. 19.
[5] *ERE.* VI. 175 f.
[6] See Avalon, *TGL.* xxiv.
[7] Bhandarkar, *VS.* 79; Wilson, *Works,* III. 93.
[8] *Ekā mūrtis trayo devāḥ.* It is suggested by images such as the trimūrti in the Elephanta cave.
[9] IV. vi.
[10] This refers to the story of Yoganidrā, which appears first in the *Harivaṁśa* and the *Vishṇu P.*

wears a crest of peacock feathers. Here, as it would seem, a virgin goddess worshipped by the wild tribes of the Vindhyas has become connected with the Kṛishṇa myth. No connexion with Śiva is suggested.

The next passage is also from the epic,[1] and is noteworthy for this, that while the goddess is still connected with the Kṛishṇa legend, and is represented as delighting in the blood of Mahisha, she is now definitely made the wife of Śiva, and is addressed as Umā. She is also identified with the Vedas, the Vedānta, chastity, and many other things, but is no longer regarded as a virgin.

Two hymns in the *Harivaṁśa*,[2] and the episode in the *Mārkaṇḍeya P.*, known as the *Devī-māhātmya* or *Chaṇḍī-māhātmya*, show a still greater advance. The *Harivaṁśa* probably dates from the fourth, and cannot be later than the fifth, century; and the *Chaṇḍī-māhātmya* almost certainly comes from the sixth century at latest; for it forms the chief background of Bāṇa's *Chaṇḍīśataka*, an ode to Chaṇḍī in a hundred verses which was written at the court of the emperor Harsha early in the seventh century.[3] The narrative of the *Chaṇḍī-māhātmya* celebrates the mighty deeds of the goddess and refers to her daily worship and autumnal festival, while the three hymns contained in it and the hymns from the *Harivaṁśa* contain the theology of the cult.

A Devī-worshipping sect is here formed, and by the same method as we have seen adopted by the Vaishṇavas and the Śaivas: the Devī is identified with the Brahman of the Upanishads, and is thus made the one Reality, and set far above all other divinities. The concept of the divine *śakti*[4] finds here its earliest expression. The idea seems to spring from the conviction that the Supreme, if he is to remain

[1] VI. xxiii.

[2] Chaps. lix and clxvi.

[3] The argument of Mr. R. D. Bhandarkar, *JBBRAS.* XXIII. 74, is scarcely convincing; for the line in question may, conceivably, have been a common ascription of praise, and thus, as it stands in the inscription, may not be a quotation from the *Chaṇḍī* at all.

[4] *Mārkaṇḍeya P.* XCI. 4; 10.

beyond the sway of the law of karma, must be inactive. But if the god is inactive, may not his spouse be his *śakti*, energy, and be extremely active? Hence she is more worthy of worship, and the practical man will be more inclined to apply to her when he wants to get something done for him.

The narrative describes in great detail the furious fights in which the goddess destroyed certain demons who were threatening the gods. Here her limitless power and her terrific appearance find forcible, even ghastly, expression. She devours unnumbered foes and drinks their blood. There is no detailed account given of her cult, but it is clear that animal sacrifice was offered, and flesh and wine were used. It is probable that human sacrifice was also practised. The goddess promises that she will never desert a temple in which the *Devī-māhātmya* is read daily, and this document is still one of the chief works in use among Śāktas. It is also called the *Chaṇḍī*, from one of the names of the goddess, and the *Saptaśatī*, because it runs to seven hundred couplets.

As the story of Yoganidrā is not told in the *Mahābhārata*, but first appears in the *Harivaṁśa* and the *Vishṇu P.*, the hymns in the Epic are probably later than the main sections of the didactic Epic, while the hymn in the *Harivaṁśā* and the *Devī-māhātmya* are still later.[1]

H. *Saura Literature.*

§ 169. The sun was worshipped in several forms in the time of the *Ṛigveda*, and the prominence of the cult may be partially gauged by the supremacy of the Gāyatrī among Vedic prayers. In the form of morning and evening prayer finally arranged for all twice-born men the sun has an established place.[2]

In the great Epic we meet for the first time the sect of Sun-worshippers, the Sauras. When Yudhishṭhira leaves his chamber in the morning, he encounters one thousand

[1] For a full exposition of these early passages see Bhandarkar, *VS*. 142.
[2] Ib., 151 f.

Brāhman Sun-worshippers who have eight thousand followers,[1] and the theology of the sect appears in a number of documents belonging to this period, notably passages in the *Mahābhārata*, the *Rāmāyaṇa*, and the *Mārkaṇḍeya P.*, and an inscription of the fifth century. The character of the passage from the *Mārkaṇḍeya P.*, as compared with the other Saura documents here dealt with, proves that it belongs to this period. Sūrya is the eternal Brahman, the supreme Spirit, the Self-existent, the Unborn, the soul of all creatures, the cause of all things, the foundation of the world. On him ascetics desirous of emancipation meditate. He is the Vedas and all the gods. He is the Lord of Brahmā, Vishṇu, and Śiva. Thus far the sect and its ideas seem to be purely Hindu.

§ 170. But as early as the first century A.D. the Persian sun-god, Mithra (Sanskrit, *Mihira*), was introduced into North India; for his name and effigy appear on coins.[2] Then, at later dates, there is much fuller evidence in the literature of the presence of Persian elements in the cult of the sun. The first fragment is a line which occurs in the *Vishṇu P.* and elsewhere, the original reading of which speaks of Magas as the Brāhmans of Śākadvīpa, i.e. of Magians as the priests of the Scythian country, or Iran.[3] Next in age, probably, comes the Brāhma Parvan of the *Bhavishya P.* Sāmba, the son of Kṛishṇa, according to this authority, was afflicted with leprosy and was cleansed by the help of Sūrya. In gratitude to the god he built a temple in his honour where Multan now stands, and, as a result of instructions received from Nārada, took a miraculous journey to Śākadvīpa, and brought thence Magian priests for the temple. The narrative mentions Zoroaster, the Zoroastrian girdle, *Avyaṅga*, the twigs, *Barsom*, which the Magian priest holds in his hand during worship, and other particulars. The rule is also laid down that the installation and consecration of images and temples of the

[1] *MBH.* VII. lxxxii. 14–16. [2] Chanda, *IAR.* 225.
[3] *Vishṇu P.* II. iv. 69–70: *MBH.* VI. xi. 35–8.

sun should be carried out by Magians. Varāha Mihira, whose name proclaims him a devotee of Mihira, and who was an authority on astronomy and astrology, wrote about A.D. 550.[1] He makes it plain that in his day Sūrya was represented in his images in Persian fashion, and he lays down the rule for the installation and consecration of these images and their temples by Magians, using the very *śloka*[2] which occurs in the Purāṇa. This unique passage then in the *Bhavishya P.*, with its extremely accurate reflection of Zoroastrian practice and ideas, and its agreement with Varāha Mihira, is much more likely to belong to this period than the next. It is probable, as Bloch argues,[3] that the name Sāmba is taken from the ancient Persian tale of Sam, and also that the theory that the sun-god cures leprosy, which was long current in India, comes from Persia. Since, however, the name of the god, Sūrya, and the name of the sect, Saura, are Sanskrit, and since the whole of the theology is, like the Śaiva theology, a reflex of the teaching of the *Gītā*, it is clear that the sect was purely Hindu in origin, and that the Zoroastrian features are secondary.

ii. Buddhism.

§ 171. In India, during the three centuries of this period, the Mahāyāna reached the summit of its strength and splendour, and several branches of the Hīnayāna continued to show great vigour. In Ceylon, during the fourth and fifth centuries, there was a great outburst of literary activity, almost exclusively the work of monks. The religion also continued to make progress in Khotan and Kuchar in Central Asia, where, in addition to Zoroastrian propaganda, it now had to face both Christianity and Manichaeism.[4] In China

[1] Macdonell, 318.

[2] *Brihat S.*, LX. 19. Vasu, *Mayūrabhañja*, 3, assumes that the śloka is quoted from the *Bhavishya P.*, and on that basis dates the passage before A.D. 550, but the *śloka* may have been in common use: we cannot be sure that it is quoted from the Purāṇa by Varāha Mihira.

[3] *ZDMG.* 1910, 733.

[4] *ERE.* art. 'Manichaeism'.

great advances were made. At the beginning of the fourth century the emperor gave permission, for the first time, to his subjects to become Buddhist monks.[1] Henceforward the faith laid a far stronger hold on the people. In A.D. 372 Chinese monks introduced the religion into Korea[2]; and in A.D. 399 Fa Hian, the first Chinese pilgrim to leave home in search of Buddhist learning and texts, arrived in India.

A. *Hīnayāna Literature.*

§ 172. We take Hīnayāna literature first, and begin with Ceylon. The monks there made full use of all the commentaries on the sacred books which were procurable from India, but they soon began to write themselves. At first they translated these Indian works into Sinhalese, leaving only the verses scattered about in the prose untranslated, but at last they began to try what they could do in Pāli, which had become to them the sacred language of their religion. Hence in the fourth century there opened a brilliant period of Pāli literary activity. Amid the numerous works prepared at this time perhaps the most interesting is the *Nidānakathā*, an introduction to the commentary on the Jātaka-book, which shows that devotion for the Buddha was moving forward in Ceylon on the same lines as in North India, though more slowly.

This expository activity culminated in Buddhaghosha. He seems to have been born a Brāhman and to have become an accomplished Hindu scholar; but, converted to Buddhism, he became a monk and laboured in the Mahāvihāra in Anurādhapura, Ceylon, in the first half of the fifth century A.D. He absorbed the whole Buddhist system as taught there with all its learning, and became its classic representative. His first work was the *Visuddhimagga*, or Way of Purity, a systematic exposition of the Buddhism of the Pāli books of very high quality. Thereafter he composed, on the basis of all the Sinhalese and Pāli work done before him, a series of great

[1] Hackmann, 78. [2] Ib. 85.

commentaries on the chief books of the Pāli canon. In these works, while the life of the Buddha as a monk is still clearly realized, he is also thought of as a sort of divine being exercising cosmic powers, as in the Mahāyāna. Dhammapāla, a scholar trained also in the Mahāvihāra, lived on the coast of India opposite Ceylon and wrote Pāli commentaries at a date a little later. His conception and outlook are the same as Buddhaghosha's.

The *Dīpavaṁsa*, the Island Chronicle, and the *Mahāvaṁsa*, the great Chronicle, are Pāli epics, the former an artless work in rough language written in the fourth century, the latter a work of genius, comparable with the great Indian *kāvyas*, composed in the last quarter of the fifth century. Both rest on irregular notes of events kept in the Mahāvihāra and ancient Pāli verses scattered in the commentaries, and both are partly historical but largely legendary.

§ 173. We know very little about the history of the Hīnayāna sects in India or about fresh literature composed by them during the period; but it is quite clear that they were very active in propagating their teaching in China and in Central Asia, for a great deal of their literature was translated. The permission granted at the beginning of the fourth century to the Chinese to become monks led to the translation of the Vinaya texts of four Hīnayāna schools within a period of twenty years, A.D. 404–24.

We take the ancient Canon first. The four leading collections of the Sutra Piṭaka—the Dīrgha, Madhyama, Saṁyukta, and Ekottara Āgamas, as they are called in Sanskrit—were translated into Chinese.[1] Three distinct renderings of the *Dharmapada*[2] are mentioned.

Of Sthavira texts the *Questions of King Milinda*,[3] Buddhaghosha's commentary on the Vinaya Piṭaka,[4] and scores of little tracts were translated into Chinese.[5]

[1] Nanjio, 545, 542, 544, 543.
[2] Ib. 1365, 1353, 1321.
[3] Ib. 1358.
[4] Winternitz, II. i. 152.
[5] Nanjio, 615; 638; 645; 665; 670; 674; 693; 696; 698–700; 703; 707–10; 761; 1113; 1327.

The Sarvāstivādins were probably the most vigorous of the Hīnayāna schools. The influence of their philosophy, known as Vaibhāshika, is shown by Vasubandha's criticism, which Saṅghabhadra attempted to answer in his *Nyāyānusāra-śāstra*. Two of the chief books of their Vinaya were translated into Chinese in A.D. 404,[1] and, probably about the same time, parts were rendered into Kuchean.[2] It is probable that much of their Sutra Piṭaka was translated into Chinese, but it is impossible as yet to identify the texts. Parts of the Sanskrit originals have been found in Central Asia.[3] The chief text of the Sarvāstivādin Abhidharma was translated into Chinese in A.D. 383,[4] and at the same time, or rather later, several of the Abhidharma commentaries.[5] The old Sarvāstivādin Buddha-biography had now become the famous Mahāyāna work, the *Lalita Vistara*.[6]

It was the Mahāsāṅghika Ekottara Āgama that was rendered into Chinese in A.D. 384–5,[7] and their Vinaya followed in A.D. 416.[8]

The Dharmagupta and the Mahīśāsaka schools, which were related to the Sarvāstivādins, were also active. The Dharmaguptas had a famous life of the Buddha, the *Abhinishkramaṇa Sūtra*, which was in use during this period. The Dharmagupta Vinaya was translated into Chinese in A.D. 405,[9] and fragments of Vinaya texts in mixed Sanskrit, written during our period, have been found in Kuchar in Central Asia, which show a close relationship at least with the Dharmagupta texts.[10]

The Mahīśāsaka Vinaya was the last of the four to be rendered into Chinese. It was done in A.D. 424.[11]

Finally we may take here Āryaśūra's famous work, the *Jātakamālā*, which seems to belong to the fourth century.

[1] Nanjio, 1115, 1160. Two of the commentaries on the Vinaya were also translated; 1135, 1136.

[2] Hoernle, *MRBL*. 357 ff.

[3] Ib. 166 ff.

[4] Nanjio, 1273.

[5] Ib. 1264, 1279, 1289.

[6] § 174.

[7] *ERE*. IV. 836; Nanjio, 543.

[8] Nanjio, 1119.

[9] Nanjio, 1117.

[10] Hoernle, *MRBL*. 4, 9.

[11] Nanjio, 1122.

He belonged to the school of Aśvaghosha, and his brilliant series of Buddhist tales has many of the qualities of the *Sūtrālaṁkāra*.

B. *Māhāyana Literature.*

§ 174. We take Mahāyāna literature next. It is quite clear that the Great Vehicle grew and extended during our period more rapidly than the Hīnayāna, thus proving itself better fitted for the circumstances of the time than the older school. The *Lalita Vistara*, one of the greatest of Buddhist books, seems to have reached its present condition at some time during our period. Originally the Buddha biography of the Sarvāstivādins, it was taken over by Mahayanists and rewritten, possibly by several hands. Although written partly in verse and partly in prose, and consisting of material drawn from many sources, early and late, it is yet a unity, a work of genuine epic strength and interest, and charged with religious belief and feeling which carried it to every part of central and eastern Asia.

The Buddha is conceived as the Supreme, boundless in power and wisdom, and he is represented as surrounded by multitudes of Bodhisattvas nearing Buddhahood. In the middle watch of the night, while he sits in profound meditation, there shoots out from the crown of his head a ray of light which passes through the heavens and rouses all the gods to attention. They sing a hymn of praise to the exalted Buddha, and, throwing themselves at his feet, beg him to reveal the *Lalita Vistara* to the world. Yet, though the writers of the Mahāyāna thus raise the Buddha to the place of the Supreme, they do not make him altogether a god: they retain some consciousness of his human life, and recognize that he possessed a real body which has left actual relics on the earth.

A new edition of the *Saddharma Puṇḍarīka*,[1] containing six fresh chapters,[2] appeared, probably early in the third

[1] Nanjio, 138. [2] Chaps. xxi–vi. *SBE.* XXI.

century; for it was translated into Chinese about A. D. 300. One of these chapters, chap. xxi, deals with *dhāraṇīs*, spells, i.e. words, phrases, or prayers believed to be filled with magic power, and marks the time when this particular superstition laid firm hold of the Mahāyāna. The next chapter tells how the Bodhisattva Bhaishajyarāja, i.e. King of Medicine, burnt his body in honour of the Buddha; and young Buddhists are urged to burn a finger, a toe, or a whole limb, in order to win great merit. Thus the old Hindu *tapas*, self-torture, which Gautama condemned utterly, has reappeared in Buddhism. Another chapter describes and explains the transformation which the Bodhisattva Avalokiteśvara undergoes in his efforts to save men. No matter how frightful may be the danger a man stands in, this chapter affirms that, if he but think of Avalokiteśvara, he will be saved. This explains how, transformed into a goddess, he became a divinity of mercy to China and Japan.

§ 175. Several fresh books belonging to the Paradise Mahāyāna seem to have been written during the period. Two of these become very famous, the shorter *Sukhāvatī* and the *Amitāyur-dhyāna-sūtra*. The shorter *Sukhāvatī* is scarcely perceptibly different in teaching from the larger work. The main purpose of the *Amitāyur-dhyāna-sūtra* is to teach people by meditation to see the paradise Sukhāvatī in hypnotic vision, so that through this meditation they may obtain entrance to it at death, but it also shows in some degree the influence of the Mādhyamika school and of the Vedānta. Vasubandhu's *Aparamitāyus-sūtra-śāstra* sums up the texts of the Paradise Mahāyāna.

To the same general type of teaching belong three famous sūtras. The early prose *Kāraṇḍavyūha* glorifies the Bodhisattva Avalokiteśvara, who is made so much of in the *Saddharma Puṇḍarīka*; the *Buddhāvataṁsaka* (or *Gaṇḍavyūha*) is devoted to another Bodhisattva, Mañjuśrī; [1] while the *Karuṇāpuṇḍarīka* tells of a Buddha named Padmottara, i.e. Supreme

[1] *ERE.* I. 95.

Lotus, and his wonderful paradise, Padmadhātu, i. e. Lotus-land.

The *Mahāsannipāta*, of which the writer has no description, gave its name to a class of works in the Chinese Canon. The *Suvarṇaprabhāsa* and the *Samādhirāja* represent the full Mahāyāna teaching verging towards the magic spells, the trances, the goddesses, and the inchoate theism of the Tantras.

All these Mahāyāna works were translated into Chinese.

§ 176. One of the developments of Mahāyāna Buddhology belonging to this period occurs so frequently that it had better be mentioned here. Each Buddha has three bodies, the *dharmakāya*, or body consisting of the law, construed by the Mādhyamakas as the void, by the Vijñānavādins in an idealist sense, the *sambhogakāya*, or body of bliss, which he wears for ever in his supramundane state and which is comparable with the glorious bodies of the great Hindu gods, and the *nirmāṇakāya*, the formed or magical body, which he wore on earth, and which is comparable with the body of a Hindu avatāra.[1]

a. *The Mādhyamakas.*

§ 177. Teachers of the Mādhyamaka philosophy were clearly very active during the period. Āryadeva seems to have followed Nāgārjuna in the first half of the third century. Nanjio gives a list of his commentaries and original works. The last of these, the *Svādhishṭhāna-prabheda*, has recently been found in Nepal. Two of the most famous of the Prajñā texts, the *Vajrachchhedikā Prajñāpāramitā* and the *Prajñāpāramitā-hṛidaya-sūtra*, seem to belong to this period. Max Müller says that the *Vajrachchhedikā* is 'one of the most widely read and most highly valued metaphysical treatises in Buddhist literature', while the *Hṛidaya-sūtra* is 'the most widely read Buddhist text in Japan'. Proof of the popularity of the *Vajrachchhedikā* in Khotan is found in the complete MS. of the original Sanskrit text, and the MS. of the old Khotanese version, both found by Sir Aurel Stein and now published.

[1] Poussin, *ERE*. I. 97.

There is also a famous Mādhyamaka work on the ten stages (*bhūmis*) of the career of the Bodhisattva, called the *Daśabhūmika-sūtra*, on which Vasubandhu wrote a commentary.[1] It was originally a chapter of the *Buddhāvataṁsaka-sūtra*.

b. *The Vijñānavādins.*

§ 178. A new Buddhist philosophy of very great importance arose about A.D. 300, the leading writer being Asaṅga, the eldest of three Brāhman brothers, who became Buddhists of the Sarvāstivādin school. Asaṅga, however, soon passed over to the Mahāyāna. His idealist system has two names: from the side of its metaphysics it is called *Vijñānavāda*, 'Thought-system,' because it teaches that nothing exists except thought, while from the side of its practice it is called *Yogāchāra*, Yoga-practice, because the end can be reached only by the long-continued practice of meditation. The external world is illusion: only thought exists. All individual intellectual products are also mere phenomena, products of the *ālaya-vijñāna*, the storehouse of intellectual impressions and forms in each individual, which is the sole foundation of the false belief in the existence of a self. But even the *ālayavijñāna* itself has but a relative reality as compared with the one and universal *bodhi*, 'Wisdom,' which is held and manifested by all Buddhas. In order to attain bodhi, it is necessary to become a Bodhisattva under the Mahāyāna, and practise yogāchāra through all the *bhūmis*, stages, of the Bodhisattva career. Yet in this intellectual philosophy the use of *dhāraṇīs*, spells, is constantly commended, and the belief that the Bodhisattva attains vast miraculous powers, *vibhutva*, is explicitly taught. The foundation text is Asanga's *Yogāchāra-bhūmi-śāstra*, which survives only in Chinese, and is the chief scripture of the Shin-gon sect of Japan.[2] One chapter, however, called the *Bodhisattvabhūmi*, was used as a separate work and survives in Sanskrit. It deals with the stages of the Bodhisattva career, and is thus the Vijñānavādin work corresponding to

[1] Nanjio, 1194.

[2] Griffis, *RJ.* 249.

the Mādhyamaka *Daśabhūmika-sūtra.*[1] Another work of his, the *Mahāyānasūtrālaṁkāra*, is a set of kārikās, or memorial verses, accompanied by a prose commentary, the commentary as well as the text being by Asaṅga. It is a clear, systematic statement of the philosophy. He left other works[2] also. The famous text-book, *Mahāyāna-śraddhotpāda-śāstra*, attributed to Aśvaghosha, seems to teach Asaṅga's system.

The *Laṅkāvatāra-sūtra*, one of the greatest Mahāyāna texts, represents the Buddha as visiting Rāvaṇa in Ceylon. The teaching is Vijñānavādin, yet in some points it seems to go beyond Asaṅga and to draw very near the teaching of the Vedānta, that the human soul is God. It is a controversial work and attacks the Sāṅkhya, Vaiśeshika, Nyāya, Pāśupata, and other Hindu systems.

§ 179. Vasubandhu,[3] Asaṅga's youngest brother, passed over to the Mahāyāna at a fairly late date. Hence his works are partly Hīnayāna, partly Mahāyāna. His greatest work, the *Abhidharma-kośa* is founded on the Sarvāstivādin Abhidharma, and has very close connexions with its chief scripture, yet he has expressed in this work the fundamental conceptions of Buddhism with so much skill and clearness that it is a standard work with all the sects. Chinese and Tibetan translations survive, but the original Sanskrit is lost. The *Abhidharma-kośa-vyākhyā*, however, a commentary on it in Sanskrit by Yaśomitra, survives, and is much used by modern scholars. Amongst his many works we may mention his *Tarka-śāstra*,[4] the earliest systematic logic by a Buddhist, and the *Paramārthasaptati*, a refutation in seventy verses of the seventy verses of the *Sāṅkhya Kārika*.[5]

§ 180. A very large number of texts, Hīnayāna as well as Mahāyāna, were translated into Chinese during this period. Then, in A.D. 518, almost at the end of the period, the first collection of Buddhist Chinese texts was made by order of

[1] See § 177, and cf. *ERE.* II. 745. [2] Nanjio, 1245, 1184, 1236.
[3] For his date see § 146.
[4] Nanjio, 1252; Vidyābhūshaṇa, *MSIL.* 76. [5] See § 146.

the Emperor, and in 520 a list of the books in the Tripiṭaka as translated was drawn up, which still survives.[1] Chinese Buddhism thus created a sacred canon of its own. Towards the end of our period Chinese Buddhism had become so great that, in A.D. 526, the Patriarch of the Buddhist Church was removed from India to China.[2]

iii. JAINISM.

§ 181. The history of Jainism during this period is not yet well known, but it seems to have continued to make progress in many parts of the country. The Digambaras were active in the Kanarese country[3] and also in Tamil-land. Śvetāmbara Jains were clearly growing in influence and numbers in North India from Bihar in the east to Kathiawar in the west. The collection and publication of the Śvetāmbara Canon at Valabhi at the beginning of the sixth century gives vivid expression to the fact that Kathiawar had now become the leading centre of Jain influence. As the Buddhist sects created from the living vernaculars of the day several literary dialects (e.g. Māgadhī, Pāli, mixed Sanskrit) and used them for their sacred books, so the Jains created their own sacred dialect, which they call Ardha-Māgadhī, i.e. Half-Māgadhī, but which modern scholars usually call Jain Prākṛit. In this ancient speech, then, the books of the Śvetāmbara Canon, and also a number of Digambara works, are written. But in Jain commentaries, tales, and poems we meet with a younger Prākṛit which is called Jain Māhārāshtrī, because, though it is closely related to, it is not yet identical with, Māhārāshtrī, the linguistic ancestor of modern Marāṭhī.[4] But Jain writers from the time of the Gupta empire used Sanskrit when they wanted to appeal to the learned public of India in treatises on philosophic and religious subjects.

[1] Nanjio, p. xxvii.
[2] Hackmann, 80.
[3] See a long series of Digambara inscriptions, Guérinot, 224.
[4] Pischel, *GPS.* p. 19; Winternitz, I. 14; Jacobi, *ERE.* VII. 467.

A. *Śvetāmbara Literature.*

§ 182. We begin with Śvetāmbara literature. Jain tradition tells us that the books of the Canon were collected, edited, and reduced to writing at Valabhi in a Council of which Devarddhi was president, 980 years after the death of Mahāvīra. The initial date may have been held to be either 527 B.C. or 467 B.C. Jacobi is inclined to take the latter, which would give us A.D. 514 as the date of the Council. As the gathering of the Council and the arrangement and publication of the voluminous books of the Canon would involve considerable organization and expense, and as the dynasty of Valabhi rose to power about A.D. 490 or 495,[1] it would seem to be more likely that the great task was undertaken in A.D. 514 than sixty years earlier. It is thus probable that the Śvetāmbara Canon dates from the beginning of the sixth century. It will be remembered that the Canon said to have been arranged at Pataliputra consisted of twelve Aṅga.[2] Tradition runs that the fourteen Pūrva, which formed the contents of the twelfth Aṅga, were gradually lost in the following centuries, but that the eleven were faithfully preserved and incorporated in the new Canon at Valabhi. According to a list in the Canon, there were sixty treatises included in it besides the Aṅga.[3]

§ 183. Jains acknowledge that these sixty books came into existence in the interval between the two Councils; and there are certain traditions about the authorship of several of the documents.[4] Jacobi gives it as his opinion that these sixty books were collected 'probably in the first centuries before our era', and that 'additions or alterations may have been made' down to the time of the Council at Valabhi;[5] while Weber[6] gives it as his opinion that the compilation of the Aṅga as well as the other books took place between the second and the fifth centuries A.D. In any case there must have been

[1] V. Smith, *EHI.* 327; Mabel Duff, *CI.* 308.
[2] See § 70.
[3] In the *Nandisūtra*: Weber, *IA.* XVII. 283.
[4] Weber, *IA.* xvii. 281.
[5] *SBE.* XLV. p. xl.
[6] *IA.* XVII. 289.

a good deal of literary activity between A.D. 200 and 500. It is probable that the *Nandīsūtra* and part of the *Kalpasūtra* are by Devarddhi himself.[1]

§ 184. We must now ask what has happened to the books of the Canon since the beginning of the sixth century, and we are at once confronted with the fact that a very large part of the contents have been lost. The Canon to-day consists of forty-five documents. Weber[2] calculates that of the books other than the Aṅgas edited at Valabhi nearly as many have been lost as there are preserved. But the disappearance of a large number of the books is not the only fact to be noticed. Jacobi and Weber[3] tell us that many of the surviving works consist of incoherent parts, and that the commentaries, based on texts older than those available to-day, show that large sections have disappeared, while numerous passages have been interpolated. The texts are thus in a very unsatisfactory condition.

§ 185. We now turn to extra-canonical literature. Two of the most famous of the early writers were connected with Pāṭaliputra, and apparently flourished during the time of Gupta prosperity. Umāsvāti tells us himself[4] that he wrote the *Tattvārthādhigama-sūtra* at Pāṭaliputra. It is a philosophical work, comparable with the sūtras which lie at the foundation of the Hindu philosophies, and deals with all the main constituents of the Jain system. It has been much used by both the sects. As the work refers to Patañjali's *Yoga-sūtra*,[5] while a commentary on it was written by Siddhasenagaṇi, whose date is the first half of the sixth century, it is probable that Umāsvāti belongs to the fifth or the fourth century. Tradition connects Siddhasena Divākara also with Pāṭaliputra, and he is quoted by Siddhasenagaṇi, so that he too belongs to the time of Gupta dominance, whether to the fourth

[1] Weber, *IA.* XVII. 291; XXI. 213; Jacobi, *SBE.* XXII. lii.
[2] *IA.* XXI. 373.
[3] Jacobi, *Kalpasūtra*, 18 f.; Weber, *IA.* XVII. 287 ff.
[4] Vidyābhūshaṇa, *MSIL.* 9.
[5] Woods, *Yoga*, xix.

or the fifth century. He wrote a hymn of praise in Sanskrit verse, the *Kalyāṇamandirastotra*, which Jains greatly treasure, also the *Nyāyāvatāra*, a Sanskrit poem in thirty-two short stanzas, which forms the earliest Jain work on Logic.

Siddhasenagaṇi seems to have been a contemporary of Devarddhi and to have been one of the earliest of those who wrote bhāshyas[1] in Prākṛit on the books of the Canon. He is also the author of the first commentary on Umāsvāti's great work. He is thus parallel to Vātsyāyana and Śabara Svāmin[2] who wrote their bhāshyas a little earlier.

§ 186. It seems clear that the Jains of Gujarāt began to produce a popular literature in Prākṛit at a very early date; and there is abundant evidence to show that down to the ninth century at least they continued to produce a copious and varied Prākṛit literature, which must have proved of large service to general culture. From our period only one Jain work of importance in Prākṛit seems to have survived; but Jacobi assures us that its statements and its style unite to prove that many Prākṛit works preceded it. It is called the *Paümachariya*, and is a Jain adaptation of the *Rāmāyaṇa* of Vālmīki. The author is said to have been Vimala Sūri. Jacobi is inclined to place it in the third or fourth century.[3] It is thus almost as early as Hāla's famous anthology, the *Sattasaī*.

B. *Digambara Literature.*

§ 187. The Digambaras possess no ancient Canon parallel to the Śvetāmbara books. As we have seen above,[4] they have a list of sacred books which they say they once possessed, but which are now no more. They pronounce the Śvetāmbara books apocryphal, and there is this amount of truth in the charge that the Śvetāmbaras undoubtedly modified the

[1] For the *niryuktis* and *bhāshyas* see Leumann, *ZDMG.* XLVI. 581 ff.
[2] See § 153.
[3] For the whole subject see Jacobi's article in the *Modern Review* (Calcutta), Dec. 1914.
[4] See § 135.

ancient books, after the separation, so as to bring them into full consonance with their own standards. Yet among the books which the Digambaras possess, and which have a place in their Secondary Canon,[1] there are at least two which bear the names of books of the Śvetāmbara Canon, viz. the *Sūrya-prajñapti*, and the *Chandraprajñapti*. The whole problem of the relation of the Digambaras to the early literature needs to be cleared up.

§ 188. But there are two Digambara writers who seem to belong to our period and whose works are well known to-day. One is Vaṭṭakera, author of the *Mūlāchāra*, a work on conduct. It corresponds to the *Āchārāṅga-sūtra* of the Śvetāmbara Canon, and is said to be an adaptation and summary of that work. Another book on conduct, the *Trivarṇāchāra*, is also attributed to him. The other writer is one of the greatest names in early Digambara history, Kuṇḍakuṇḍāchārya. Ten fundamental works of great importance, which have been much expounded and studied, were written by him. They are in Prākrit verse, and deal with the whole Digambara system. It seems to be impossible as yet to fix the dates of these men.

1. See § 257.

CHAPTER V

THE ŚĀKTA SYSTEMS

A. D. 550–900.

§ 189. The date with which our chapter opens is meant to coincide with the time when the Śākta systems began to appear; for they are unquestionably the most noteworthy product of these times. The exaltation and the adoration of goddesses is manifestly the first characteristic of these new theologies; but other forms of faith and practice were very prominent: an immense extension of the use of magic spells; a belief in the existence of occult channels and ganglia in the human frame, and in the presence of the goddess herself—coiled up like a snake and asleep—in the chief ganglion; a new type of hypnotic meditation believed to be potent to wake the goddess; and, in some sects, the inclusion in the cult of foul, gruesome, and degrading practices.

During this period the sects became more highly organized than ever before. In addition to the Śākta element already described, each sect was expected to possess an Upanishad and a manual;—the Upanishad to prove that its teaching had come by revelation and was in full consonance with the Vedānta; the manual to provide a statement of the theology of the sect, a directory of its occult yoga practice, rules of conduct and ritual, and directions for the preparation of images and the building of temples. Each sect had its own order of sannyāsīs. Each was also expected to train a number of gurus for its cultured members. The layman received initiation, *dīkshā*, and regular instruction in the philosophical theology of the sect from his guru, just like an ascetic. Finally, each sect had its own mantra and sect-mark, *tilaka*.

One of the most noticeable features of the period is the great series of philosophic thinkers and exegetes who adorned the seventh, eighth, and ninth centuries, chiefly in the North. Scarcely less important is the great company of itinerant poet-musicians, both Vaishṇava and Śaiva, who filled the temples of the Tamil country with their devotion and their song.

Buddhism was carried to Japan in the sixth, and to Tibet in the seventh century, while long-continued emigration carried both Hinduism and Buddhism to Cambodia, Sumatra, and Java. But India received as well as gave. A company of Persian Zoroastrians, hunted to the death by their Muhammadan conquerors, found asylum in India at the beginning of the eighth century: their descendants are the Parsis of to-day.

i. Hinduism.

A. *The Philosophies.*

a. *The Karma Mīmāṁsā.*

§ 190. During the first half of the period, the Karma Mīmāṁsā produced two famous scholars, Prabhākara, who is known as Guru, and Kumārila, who is called Bhaṭṭa. Both expounded Śabara's *Bhāshya*, but they differed in some degree in their interpretation of the system and founded rival schools. The date of Prabhākara in unknown, but it is clear that he preceded Kumārila. His work, the *Bṛihatī*, is purely an exposition of the *Bhāshya*: he does not criticize Śabara.[1] Kumārila, who seems to have lived in the first half of the eighth century,[2] wrote a commentary on the *Bhāshya* in three parts, in which he frequently differs from Śabara:

a. *Ślokavārtika*: verse: on the first part of Chap. I.

[1] Jhā, *PSPM.* 12.

[2] Pāthak, *JBBRAS.* 1892, 227.

b. *Tantravārtika*: prose: on the rest of Chap. I and Chaps. II and III.

c. *Ṭupṭīkā*: prose: brief notes on Chaps. IV to XII.

Prabhākara's teaching was further expounded by his own disciple, Sālikānātha, while Maṇḍanamiśra, also called Sureśvarāchārya, a disciple of Śaṅkara, wrote several works on Kumārila's system. His *Vidhiviveka* was in turn expounded in the *Nyāya-Kaṇikā* by Vāchaspatimiśra, whose position is explained below.

Both Prabhākara and Kumārila maintain the original atheism of the system, denying that divine action is needed in creation, or in apportioning merit and demerit to souls. Both also hold a realistic view of the universe; but they differ on the question whether the soul is pure consciousness or not, on the nature of perception, of inference, and of logical categories.[1]

Kumārila proved the more potent influence of the two both within the school and without. He attacks Buddhists frequently in his works; and tradition asserts that he used every means to discredit and weaken them wherever he went in his scholarly journeys, and that he invoked the civil power to persecute them. What the historical facts are, we cannot tell; but it is probable that strong action lies behind a tradition so widespread and persistent. His activity is to be explained as the first vigorous manifestation of the spirit of modern Hinduism. He represents the system which takes its stand on the authority of the Vedas and of the Brāhman priests, recognizes a mass of sects within that ample fence, and opposes every other system vehemently..

§ 191. It is of importance to observe that *mukti*, final release, appears in the system for the first time in Prabhākara and Kumārila. During the interval between Jaimini and these thinkers Release had become a matter of such moment to the Hindu mind that it could no longer be evaded. They teach

[1] For both systems see Jhā, *PSPM.* and Keith, *JRAS.* 1916, 369. Also Jhā, *Bhandarkar CV.* 167.

that release is won when both *dharma* and *adharma* disappear, and that he who desires release should therefore perform only necessary duties.[1]

§ 192. It is a most interesting fact that by the time of Kumārila's activity, the ancient Vedic sacrificial system, which the Karma Mīmāṁsā expounds, was steadily decaying. Everywhere temple-worship and the presentation of offerings to images tended to take the place of the ancient ordinances, and the movement went on with increasing force after his day. Yet the Mīmāṁsā maintained its place, because it provided rules for the exposition of the Vedic literature, which all scholars required to use. Although the Karma Mīmāṁsā is the one system recognized by all Smārtas, the changes which have arisen in their practice seem to have left no trace in the system itself.

b. *The Vedānta.*

§ 193. The earliest surviving commentary on the *Vedānta-sūtras* is by the great Śaṅkara, who flourished in the first half of the ninth century; but there is abundance of evidence to show that a long line of writers and students of the Vedānta filled the centuries between the time of the sūtras and his day. We have already seen that three types of theory were current within the school before the sūtras were composed.[2] Various doctrines were also held after that event; for between the sūtras and Śaṅkara there were representatives both of the strict monism which he upholds and of the modified monism taught much later by Rāmānuja.[3] One of the strict monists, Gauḍapāda by name, the teacher of Śaṅkara's teacher, is the author of a very noteworthy poem, which is appended to the *Māṇḍūkya U.* and is known as the *Māṇḍūkya Kārikā.*[4] So far as we know, he wrote no commentary on the sūtras, but

[1] Jhā, *PSPM.* 83 ff.

[2] § 145.

[3] § 284.

[4] Walleser, *DAV.*, contends that the name Gauḍapāda is a mistake, that the writer's name has not been handed down, and that Buddhist evidence proves that the *Kārikā* was already in existence by A. D. 550. Scholars are inclined to think that the balance of evidence is in favour

his *Kārikā* has a very special interest for us as the earliest, or at least the earliest surviving, document of the school of monism and illusion. It is a work of genius, brilliant alike in conception and expression. Deussen[1] compares him to Parmenides. He also wrote commentaries on a number of Upanishads. He must have flourished about the middle of the eighth century. From information found in the works of Śaṅkara and Rāmānuja we are able to give the names of three writers earlier than Śaṅkara who taught a theistic interpretation of the sūtras similar to Rāmānuja's doctrine, namely Bodhāyana, author of a *vṛitti*, Ṭaṅka, author of a *vākya*, and Drāmiḍa, author of a *bhāshya* on the sūtras.[2]

§ 194. Śaṅkara was the name assumed by a sannyāsī born at Kaladi in the north of Travancore, probably in A.D. 788. He became a brilliant scholar and produced a number of philosophical writings characterized by great intellectual capacity and an extremely fine style. He seems to have lived until about A.D. 850.[3] He left bhāshyas on the *Vedānta-sūtras*, the *Gītā* and the chief Upanishads. Besides these, a number of Vedantic writings, mostly in verse, are attributed to him, the chief being the *Upadeśa-sahasrī*, a summary of his doctrine in verse. Until strictly scientific methods of comparison are applied to these works, it will be impossible to say how many are by Śaṅkara. The best scholars usually decide against them all. Numerous Śākta works in prose and verse also bear his name, but there can hardly be a doubt that they are not his offspring. About the *Vedānta-sūtra-bhāshya* fortunately there can be no question.

§ 195. The following is a brief outline of his *advaitavāda*, pure monism. There exists only Brahman, one without a

of the personal name of the writer and of his connexion with Śaṅkara. Certainly the Buddhist evidence cited in favour of the early date of the *Kārikā* does not seem to be cogent. See Barnett, *JRAS.* 1910, p. 131 ff.; Jacobi, *JAOS.* xxxiii. 51, *n.* 1.

[1] *SUV.* 514.

[2] Thibaut, *SBE.* XXXIV. xx ff.

[3] Macdonell, *SL.* 402; Keith, *AĀ.* 11. The date A.D. 805–97, proposed by S. V. Veṅkaṭeśvara in *JRAS.* 1916, 151 ff., is scarcely likely to be right, in view of the date of Vāchaspati's *Bhāmatī.*

second, spiritual, unknowable. The material world is *Māyā*, illusion. The human soul is identical with Brahman: *Tat tvam asi*, 'Thou art that.' But this contradicts all experience, and man must live in his experience. Therefore Śaṅkara distinguishes between supreme truth and the truth of experience. Similarly, he recognizes not only God as he truly is under the name para Brahman, the supreme Brahman, but also the same being enwrapped in limitations and attributes as apara Brahman, the lower Brahman, who is the world-soul and a personal God. The whole of our lower knowledge, however, our ideas of the world, all our personal experience and our conception of ourselves as distinct personalities—all this is more truly described as ignorance than as knowledge. Liberation comes when a man rises from ignorance to true knowledge. This comes finally by the grace of God, but a man may prepare himself by study of the Veda and by the discipline of the Vedānta. Even after knowledge is attained, the man continues to live; but at death he receives final release: 'Brahman he is and into Brahman he is resolved.'

It is noteworthy that Śaṅkara holds strongly that, while works may prepare the soul for the discipline of knowledge, they can never help the man to reach release, but necessarily bind him ever more firmly to transmigration. Hence, when a man becomes a sannyāsī of the Advaita Vedānta, he gives up sacrifices and the other duties of the ordinary Hindu completely, and seeks knowledge as the only means to release. This renunciation of the regular Hindu life is typified in the act of laying aside the sacred thread, which is part of the ceremony of initiation into the life of the sannyāsī.

§ 196. The striking resemblance which certain features of the teaching of Gauḍapāda and Śaṅkara present to Mahāyāna philosophy led Hindu controversialists to assail it as 'covert Buddhism;'[1] and some modern scholars have been inclined to say that its illusion and its doctrine of double truth have no foundation in the Upanishads and must have been drawn from

[1] e.g. in the *Padma P.*

the rival faith.[1] This contention is strengthened by the fact that there is no doctrine of illusion in the *Vedānta-sūtras.*[2] But scholarly opinion seems now inclined to conclude that, in the early Upanishads, there is unquestionably, along with other ideas, the basis for a doctrine of pure monism, and that we need go no farther afield than the *Śvetāśvatara U.* for the doctrine of *māyā*, but that Gauḍapāda and Śaṅkara were probably influenced in some degree by the two philosophical systems of the Mahāyāna.[3]

§ 197. But there are other characteristics of the Bhāshya which are worthy of attention. Most of them have a basis in the sūtras but they are clearly worked out by Śaṅkara. All the main features of orthodox Hinduism are accepted and buttressed with arguments, e.g. the inspiration of the Purāṇas,[4] the permanent presence of all the traditional gods, even though each is a transient being,[5] the visibility of the gods to ṛishis in ancient time,[6] the eating of the sacrifice by the gods,[7] the assumption by a god of many bodies so as to be present at many sacrifices at one moment,[8] &c. Thus the great philosophy, which began by holding the popular religion in contempt,[9] has now become its willing servant.

It is clear that by Śaṅkara's day the Upanishads, the *Gītā* and the *Vedānta-sūtras* were recognized as the fundamental scriptures of the Vedānta. At a later date they were called the *Prasthānatraya* or Triple Canon. Although the *Gītā* and the Sūtras are but *smṛiti*, they are regarded with almost as much veneration as the Upanishads, which are *śruti*.

Indian scholars frequently speak of Śaṅkara as one of the greatest of the world's independent philosophic thinkers. The

[1] e.g. Walleser, *DAV.* 22 ff.; also Dr. Jhā: see Keith, *JRAS.* 1916, 279 f.

[2] Thibaut, *SBE.* XXXIV. xci-xcvii; Keith, *SS.* 64.

[3] Barnett, *JRAS.* 1910, 1364; Jacobi, *JAOS.* XXXIII. 151 ff.; Poussin, *JRAS.* 1910, 129 ff.; Keith, *JRAS.* 1916, 380.

[4] *Bhāshya* on I. 3, 33; *SBE.* XXXIV. 222-3.

[5] On I. 3, 28: Ib. 202-3.

[6] On I. 3, 34: Ib. 222.

[7] On III. 1, 7: *SBE.* XXXVIII. 110-1.

[8] On I. 3, 27; *SBE.* XXXIV. 199-200.

[9] See § 53.

truth seems to be that he never questioned the truth of the basis of the Vedānta, i.e. those writings which were then recognized as revelation of the first grade, *śruti*. Yet within these theological limits Śaṅkara displays consummate philosophical capacity: he is the Thomas Aquinas of Hinduism.

§ 198. He seems to have been a man of organizing capacity as well as a thinker. Tradition avers that he found the ascetic orders of the Vedānta in disorder and regulated them, dividing them into ten groups, placing each under one of his disciples and naming them after these leaders. Certainly, the sannyāsīs of the Vedānta to-day are in ten groups, and are known as Daśnāmīs, i.e. sannyāsīs of ten names, and they unanimously ascribe their constitution and rule to Śaṅkara.[1] There are also sannyāsinīs. A company of them whom I saw at the Khumbh Mela at Allahabad in 1918 belonged to the Giri order. He also founded four monasteries, to form centres of advaita learning and influence, Śriṅgerī in Mysore, Govardhana in Purī, Śāradā[2] in Dwārkā, and Joshi at Badarināth in the Himalayas. All four have survived to our day, and there are a number of subordinate houses. Śriṅgerī, of which he was himself the head, is the chief monastery, and its ruler is the supreme Pontiff of all advaita sannyāsīs.

§ 199. Śaṅkara made many tours through India, and proved a triumphant controversialist, if we may trust the traditions of

[1] The ten names are: 1. *Tīrtha*, 2. *Āśrama*, 3. *Sarasvatī*, 4. *Bhāratī*, 5. *Vana*, 6. *Araṇya*, 7. *Pārvata*, 8. *Sāgara*, 9. *Giri*, 10. *Purī*. Only the first three are pure, i.e. restricted to twice-born men, or rather to Brāhmans; for Kshatriyas and Vaiśyas are negligible. Half of the Bhāratī order is also said to be pure. The other six are open to the four castes, but to no others. One often hears the phrase *Śaṅkara's Daṇḍīs* also: these are the innermost group of all; for only a Brāhman can receive a *daṇḍa*, i.e. a bamboo rod; and the ceremonial which attaches to it is so troublesome that many prefer to do without it. Many of the Daśnāmīs have discarded clothing, and are called Nāgās (from *Nagna*, 'naked'). There were hundreds of them at the Kumbh Mela of 1918.

[2] The goddess Sarasvatī as patroness of the sciences and speech is called Śāradā, and has five faces and ten arms: Kṛishṇa Śāstrī, *SII.* 187. Tradition runs that to her grace Śaṅkara attributed his powers. To this day the incumbent of Śriṅgerī, whether in the monastery or on tour, publicly worships a large number of idols, Śāradā amongst them towering high above the rest. For this reason some scholars say Śaṅkara was a Śākta.

his school; and, certainly, the extraordinary influence which his teaching had in many parts of India in the following centuries forms the best corroboration of the claim. Thus, it is clear that the whole vast body of Smārta householders in the South and in Gujarāt, and many also throughout the North, became his disciples, and recognized him as their religious head. To this day the superior of the monastery in Śringerī, who always bears the honoured name. Śaṅkara, is Pontiff, not only of all advaita sannyāsīs, but of all the Smārtas of the South and the West as well. Hence the immense influence which the Śaṅkara wields, and the wealth which flows into the monastery. This connexion sheds light on Śaṅkara's acceptance and defence of the main positions of orthodox Hinduism in his *Bhāshya.*

But his teaching produced large results outside the immediate circle of his pledged disciples. The Bhāgavatas [1] in every part of the country, a Ramaite sect,[2] which can be traced in the literature, and which ought in all probability to be located in the South, and, at the other extremity of India, the Śaivas of Kashmir,[3] all fell under the spell of his philosophy, and taught it, in purity or with modifications, for centuries.

§ 200. There are also widespread traditions [4] to the effect that he persecuted the Buddhists and the Jains and destroyed their books, and cleansed the worship of a number of disreputable Hindu sects. To one who for the first time reads the *Bhāshya* these late stories may well seem foolish inventions; nor can any one accept them as they stand; yet his connexions with orthodox householders give a certain plausibility to the statements. He may possibly have originated the Right-hand movement among Śāktas.[5]

[1] See § 210. [2] See § 219. [3] See § 230.

[4] The two *Śaṅkara-vijayas* are clearly far from historical, yet they reflect tradition, portions of which may be in the main true. The work attributed to Mādhava must have been written after that scholar's death; and both seem to have been provoked by the *Maṇimañjari* and the *Madhvavijaya*: Kṛishnasamy Aiyar, 3; and see § 279.

[5] See § 317.

There are some Hindu scholars who say that he originated and enforced the Smārta rule of worshipping the five gods,[1] but there is no evidence in support of the assertion.

§ 201. The next outstanding writer on the Vedānta is Vāchaspati Miśra, who occupies a very noticeable position. He tells us himself that he belonged to Tirhut and that he lived under a king named Nṛiga; and in one of his books, the *Nyāyasūchīnibandha*, he gives A. D. 841 as the year in which it was written.[2] His home and his date are thus known. He was a Smārta Brāhman, and must have been a very capable teacher of philosophy. He left seven books, all expository works, which set forth, in clear and accurate philosophic language, five out of the six orthodox philosophies of Hinduism, the Vaiśeshika being the only one of the six he did not expound. He is thus a very striking figure. Every scholar before his date is a controversialist, upholding his own school against all comers, and fighting the teaching of every other school. Vāchaspati, on the other hand, knows no bias: he is simply an honest expositor of real philosophic grasp and great power of accurate expression. His books have therefore been greatly admired and widely used as text-books since his day. He wrote a commentary, the *Bhāmatī*, on Śaṅkara's *Bhāshya* which has been the most popular and useful of all the innumerable works written to expound that masterpiece, and has been interpreted in turn by many scholiasts.

c. *The Sāṅkhya.*

§ 202. The *Sāṅkhya-kārikā*, which, soon after it was written, was honoured by an attack from the great Vasubandhu, was translated into Chinese in the sixth century by a Buddhist monk.[3] Probably a little later, a scholar named Gauḍapāda (seemingly not the same as Śaṅkara's paramaguru)[4] wrote the *Sāṅkhya-kārikā-bhāshya*, which is of con-

[1] See § 207.
[2] Woods, *Yoga*, xxiii.
[3] Nanjio, 1300. Cf. Takakusu, *BEFEO.* IV. 1.
[4] Jacobi, *JAOS.* XXXIII. 52, *n.* 2; Keith, *JRAS.* 1916, 171; *SS.* 87.

siderable importance in determining the precise meaning of the principles summarized in the stanzas. Then about A.D. 850 Vāchaspati produced his *Sāṅkhya-tattva-kaumudī*, an exposition of the *Kārikā*, which is regarded as one of the most authoritative of Sāṅkhya works, and has been expounded in many super-commentaries.

d. *The Yoga.*

§ 203. There is a similar story to tell of the Yoga. A *Bhāshya* on the *Yoga-sūtra* was written some time after A.D. 650 by an unknown writer, and Vāchaspati wrote the *Tattva-Vaiśāradī*, also an exposition of the *Sūtra*, about A.D. 850. Woods remarks:[1]

> The *Bhāshya* and, still more, the *Tattva-Vaiśāradī* are masterpieces of the philosophical style. They are far from being a loosely collected body of glosses. Their excessively abbreviated and disconnected order of words is intentional.

It is very noticeable that the fresh developments in Yoga theory and practice reflected in the Tantras, Āgamas, and Saṁhitās do not seem to have produced the slightest effect on the ancient school.

e. *The Vaiśeshika.*

§ 204. There is only one Vaiśeshika writer to be mentioned, Praśastapāda, whose date is in the neighbourhood of A.D. 600, and without whose *Bhāshya* the *Vaiśeshika-sūtras* would be almost unintelligible. But another work, the original of which is lost, survives in a translation: in A.D. 648 the pilgrim, Hiouen Tsang, translated the *Daśapadārtha*, said to be by Jñānachandra, into Chinese.

f. *The Nyāya.*

§ 205. The preceding chapter has shown that Vātsyāyana's *Bhāshya*, which lights up the obscurity of the *Nyāya-sūtras*, belongs to the fifth or the beginning of the sixth century. To

[1] *Yoga*, ix.

that we now add Uddyotakara's *Nyāya-vārtika*, on the *Bhāshya*, and Vāchaspati's *Nyāya-vārtika-tātparya-ṭīkā*, the former from about A. D. 650, the latter from about 840.

On these two closely related schools two significant facts require to be chronicled here. First, with Praśastapāda, the atomic school becomes frankly theistic, and about the same time both schools become closely connected with the Pāśupata sect.[1] Secondly, the question has been seriously raised, whether the new doctrine of inference called *vyāpti*, which appears in Indian logical treatises at this time, is not due to the influence of the Aristotelian logic.[2]

The study of logic in early India was greatly enriched by the labours of numerous Buddhist and Jain thinkers. Of all these scholars the most influential by far was the Buddhist Dignāga, who flourished before the middle of the sixth century; but the first Jain logician, Siddhasena Divākara, lived probably a century earlier, and later Jain thinkers did good service.[3]

B. *The Purāṇas.*

§ 206. All the Purāṇas, except the *Bhāgavata*, seem to have been in existence by the end of this period, and probably earlier. It is also probable that there was an authoritative list of the eighteen, in which both the *Śiva* and the *Vāyu* would have a place. But, though the eighteen existed then, all were not in the condition in which they are to-day. Numerous sections, khaṇḍas, saṁhitās, and such like have since then been foisted on the original texts, and large portions of the originals have been lost, either through accident or deliberate sectarian malice.

The *Garuḍa P.* is clearly a manual compiled for the use of Smārta priests; for it contains detailed instructions for the worship of the five gods, and gives information in many other

[1] Keith, *JRAS.* 1914, 1097. [2] Ib. 1096.
[3] Vidyābhūshaṇa, *MSIL.* 22-55; 80.
[4] Chaps. 16; 17; 22-24; 28-40; 42.

subjects which a practising priest would want to have. The *Agni* is also a Smārta document; for it gives detailed instructions about the worship of the five gods;[1] but it may be meant for the use of Bhāgavata priests;[2] for it gives far more attention to Vishṇu than to the other four, it contains a list of Pāñcharātra Saṁhitās,[3] which is possible in a Bhāgavata, but not in a purely Smārta work, and it uses the Bhāgavata mantra at several points.[4] Both Purāṇas show very distinctly the influence of the Śākta teaching given in the Āgamas, Tantras, and Saṁhitās. Of the original character of the *Nārada*, *Varāha*, *Vāmana*, and *Brahmavaivarta* Purāṇas it is hard to speak with certainty, but all seem to have contained Vaishṇava material.[5] The *Śiva*, *Liṅga*, and *Kūrma* Purāṇas are all Śaiva in general character, and all three[6] contain copies of certain parts of the Lakulīśa-Pāśupata material which seems to have appeared first in the *Vāyu*.[7] Of the *Skanda*[8] it is not possible to speak with certainty.

C. *Smārtas and their Literature.*

§ 207. At an early date some organizing genius persuaded the Smārtas to make it a regular practice to worship the five gods, *pañcha deva*, Vishṇu, Śiva, Durgā, Sūrya, Gaṇeśa, in what is called *Pañchāyatana Pūjā*,[9] but the precise time and the name of the organizer are unknown. Many Smārtas say that it was Śaṅkara who imposed the rule; some say Kumārila; while others say the practice is of still earlier origin. But what is clear from the list itself is that the rule was formed at a time when Brahmā had already fallen into the

[1] Chaps. 21; 23; 69; 71; 73; 74.
[2] Bhāgavatas often act as *archakas*.
[3] Chap. 39.
[4] e.g. in chaps. 27 and 48.
[5] See the quotations in Madhva's *Brahma-sūtra-bhāshya*.
[6] *Śiva*, Uttarārdha, IX, ix; *Liṅga*, VII; *Kūrma*, LII.
[7] See § 165.
[8] But see H. P. Śāstrī, I. lii.
[9] That is, 'Five-Shrines Worship'. The methods of the worship as practised to-day explain the name. See § 352. For the word see Jacob, *EAU*. 171.

background, and the five gods were prominent. The evidence contained in this chapter makes it probable that that was true by the opening of the seventh century; but it is impossible to give anything like a definite date. It is also essential to notice that the five are merely a pañchāyat representing all the gods: the orthodox man recognizes the whole pantheon; and, while he worships the five, he may worship as many more as he likes. Towards the end of this period five Upanishads, one on each of the divinities, were put together and called the *Atharvaśiras U.*[1] They are doubtless all founded on sectarian Upanishads.

§ 208. It will be at once recognized that Śaṅkara's philosophical position fits the Smārta conception of the pantheon perfectly. From the point of view of religious practice, the only difference between the advaita Vedānta and the Karma Mīmāṁsā lies in the recognition of the Absolute behind all the gods. Thus it is not at all strange that Śaṅkara won over a large number of Smārtas to the acceptance of his system. To this day, in most parts of South India and Gujarāt, the word Smārta implies allegiance to Śaṅkara as well as to the five gods and to Vedic observance.

§ 209. For the twice-born the most interesting literature published during the period would be the law-books and the works on the Mīmāṁsā. The *Nārada* and the *Bṛihaspati* are the chief legal *smṛitis* produced at this time, but there were many others. The publication of the great works of Prabhākara and Kumārila on the Karma Mīmāṁsā would be of great interest to all Śrautas and Smārtas. Both these writers, and many other notable scholars of the period, Praśastapāda, Vātsyāyana, Udyotakara, and Vāchaspati Miśra were either Śrautas or Smārtas. The *Garuḍa P.*[2] seems to be a manual written for Smārta priests.

[1] Weber, *HIL.* 170; Kennedy, *HM.* 346, &c.
[2] See § 206.

D. *Vaishṇava Literature.*

a. *Bhāgavata Literature.*

§ 210. It seems clear that the Bhāgavatas followed the Smārtas in the two steps we have just dealt with: they accepted the worship of the five gods and the advaita Vedānta. Yet it seems as if their acceptance of the five gods had been less serious than their recognition of Śiva as equivalent to Vishṇu: so much seems to be implied in the practice of the sect to-day. Probably about the end of this period, after the adoption of Śaṅkara's system, some Bhāgavata scholar wrote the *Skanda U.*,[1] to establish the truth of the doctrine of the identity of Vishṇu and Śiva. The philosophy is advaita, and the classical passage in the *Harivaṁśa* on the subject is utilized. A *Bhāgavata S.*[2] is mentioned among the Vaishṇava Saṁhitās, which may be a Bhāgavata document.

§ 211. Many Bhāgavatas are temple ministrants in South India to-day, and there is evidence which tends to suggest that in early times still larger numbers performed that service. The *Agni P.* seems to be a manual prepared for the use of Bhāgavata priests, as is suggested above.[3] In the Tamil country to-day, while in most temples the ritual is conducted in accordance with the rules laid down in the Pāñcharātra Saṁhitās, there are a few temples in which Vaikhānasa Saṁhitās are used. This is true of the shrine of Veṅkaṭeśvara on Tirupati hill, and of the temples in Conjeeveram, and Śrīperumbudur. What the age of these Saṁhitās may be, is not yet known. They differ from the main group first of all in points of ritual. But there is a far more serious distinction: Appaya Dīkshita tells us that Vaikhānasa manuals are consistent with Vedic usage while Pāñcharātra Saṁhitās are unorthodox.[4] Now, it is clear that in the temple of Veṅkaṭeśvara, in which the Vaikhānasa ritual is followed to this day, Śiva and Vishṇu were worshipped as equal until Rāmānuja

[1] Jacob, *EAU.* 15.
[2] No. 105 in Schrader's list, *IPAS.* 8.
[3] § 206.
[4] See the passage quoted by Chanda, *IAR.* 100.

interfered.[1] Thus we can scarcely be wrong in concluding that the Vaikhānasa Saṁhitās have for centuries been used by Bhāgavata *archakas*[2] for the ritual. It also seems clear that there were many more temples in which Vishṇu and Śiva were adored as equal—i. e. Bhāgavata shrines—during this period than there are to-day; for many such temples are mentioned in the hymns of the Āḷvārs[3]; and we know that Rāmānuja sought to substitute Pāñcharātra for Vaikhānasa ritual wherever he went. What is the relation between these manuals and the Vaikhānasa-sūtras?[4]

b. *Pāñcharātra Literature.*

§ 212. The rise of the Vaishṇava, or Pāñcharātra, Saṁhitās[5] is the most notable fact in the Vishṇuite history of the period, but it is not yet possible to state with certainty when or where they were written. They can be traced in Kashmir in the tenth century, in the Tamil country in the eleventh,[6] and at later dates in South Kanara,[7] but clear references at earlier dates are still lacking. The utmost we can say is that their striking similarity to the Śaiva Āgamas and to the early Tāntrik literature, both Hindu and Buddhist, suggests that the earliest of them arose about the same time as these three literatures, i. e. probably between A. D. 600 and 800, and that there is nothing in the general character of the books that is opposed to such a date. More precise evidence may become available any day.[8]

The Saṁhitās are supposed to number 108; but about double that number of names are known. Lists occur in four

[1] Govindāchārya, *R.* 142.
[2] I. e. temple-ministrants.
[3] Kṛishṇa Śāstrī, *SII.* 12.
[4] See § 160.
[5] In this connexion I am much indebted to Dr. Schrader's excellent monograph, *Introduction to the Pāñcharātra and the Ahirbudhnya Saṁhitā*; also to Govindāchārya's art. *JRAS.* 1911, 935 ff.; and to the relevant section in Iyengar's *Outlines.*
[6] Schrader, *IPAS.* 17 f.
[7] In Madhva's *Bhāshya* on the *Vedānta-sūtras.*
[8] A careful survey of Vaishṇava Tamil literature would likely provide some evidence. Śaṅkara's statement about Śāṇḍilya, *Bhāshya*, II. ii. 45, in all probability rests on a Saṁhitā.

Saṁhitās, three containing over 100 names each, the fourth containing only 34. Taking the three long lists first, 52 names are common; taking all four, only 11 are common. The results are thus rather hazy. Further, these books have suffered from interpolation in precisely the same way as the Purāṇas. Hence, it is not strange that the few scholars who have given some time to their study do not agree in their conclusions as to which are the earliest documents.[1]

§ 213. It is probably true that each Saṁhitā, even in its earliest form, represented some sectarian division or some variety of doctrine or worship. Thus one of the Agastya Saṁhitās is a Ramaite work; it is probable that the *Narasiṁha* sprang from the special cult of the Narasiṁha incarnation, which we deal with elsewhere; and the *Dattātreya*, the *Gaṇeśa*, and the *Saura* may reflect the worship of Dattātreya, Gaṇeśa, and the Sun. That later developments are reflected in the Saṁhitā literature is plain. Rāmānuja's stay at Melkote is described in several works; while Mādhva doctrine obtrudes itself distinctly in others. The literature will not be fully intelligible until these sectarian distinctions are realized. Schrader holds that most of the literature was produced in the north, but believes that several of the works belong to the Tamil south, notably *Īśvara*, *Upendra*, and *Bṛihad Brāhma*.[2] He may be right, but, on the other hand, these may be northern works interpolated in the south.

§ 214. The Saṁhitās are historically noteworthy in two ways. They mark first the emergence of Śākta principles in the Vaishṇava sect. But they are also notable as being the first manuals formed to express both the beliefs and the practice of Vaishṇavas. In the matter of practice they are as it were the Kalpasūtras of the Vaishṇavas.[3] Like the

[1] Schrader (*IPAS*. 20) takes the *Paushkara*, *Vārāha*, and *Brāhma* as the earliest of all, while Iyengar (*Outlines*, 175) regards the *Lakshmī* as 'decidedly very old', and says that the *Padma* is 'perhaps the oldest' of all. With this latter judgement my friend, Mr. A. Govindāchārya Svāmin of Mysore city, agrees.

[2] *IPAS*. 16 f.

[3] Govindāchārya, *JRAS*. 1911, 940.

Śaiva Āgamas, the Saṁhitās are said to consist of four sections:

Jñāna pāda: philosophical theology.
Yoga-pāda: the new yoga teaching and practice.
Kriyā-pāda: the building of temples and the making of images.
Charyā-pāda: religious practice.

Only two Saṁhitās, however, are known which are actually divided in this way, the *Padma* and the *Vishṇutattva*. Even those which deal with all the four categories are arranged in other ways; and many deal only with Kriyā and Charyā. Indeed a very large part of all the material of the Saṁhitās deals with practice. This explains why they were so long kept secret.

§ 215. The theology of the chief Saṁhitās is essentially a development of the teaching of the Nārāyaṇīya episode of the Epic with the addition of a considerable Śākta element. The basis of the philosophy is the theistic Yoga. Our brief outline of the teaching is taken from Dr. Schrader's excellent analysis:—In the supreme state Vishṇu and his Śakti[1] are one Paramātman without distinction. It is in creation that they become distinguishable. Primary Creation falls into two stages, and Secondary Creation, which takes place 36,000 times between two Primary Creations, also falls into two.

A. In the first stage of Primary Creation the Śakti awakes as if from sleep in her two aspects, *kriyā*, action, and *bhūti*, becoming, and manifests the six *guṇa*, i.e. attributes, of her Lord, viz. knowledge, unrestricted power, energy, strength, virility, splendour. These six together constitute Vāsudeva, the first vyūha[2], and his śakti Lakshmī. The six fall into pairs, and from them emanate in order Saṁkarshaṇa, Pradyumna, and Aniruddha, the second, third, and fourth vyūhas, and their Śaktis. From the vyūhas proceed twelve

[1] See § 168. [2] See § 106.

sub-vyūhas and twelve Vidyeśvaras. In this stage of creation are produced also the vibhavas, or incarnations of Vishṇu, thirty-nine in number, and Vaikuṇṭha, Highest Heaven, with all its dwellers.

B. In the second stage of Primary Creation the bhūti aspect of the Śakti is manifested in the grosser forms, Kūṭastha Purusha and Māyā Śakti. The Kūṭastha Purusha is the aggregate of individual souls, massed together like bees, while the Māyā is the immaterial source of the universe. From her is produced Niyata, the regulator of all things; from Niyata Kāla, transcendental Time, regarded as a driving force; and from Kāla the Guṇa-body, whence the three Sankhyan guṇas emanate and coalesce into Mūlaprakṛiti, the impalpable source of material things. All these creations remain in existence from the time they are created until the time of Universal Dissolution, Mahāpralaya.

C. The first stage of each Secondary Creation corresponds very closely with the Sankhyan evolution. Yet there are differences; the Vaishṇava system starts not only with the Mūlaprakṛiti and Purusha but with Kāla also, and the Purusha is the one Kūṭastha Purusha instead of an infinite number of souls. The other differences need not detain us.

D. The five gross elements, ether, air, light, water, and earth, having been produced, coalesce into a mass, and the world-egg, with the creator god, Brahmā, the fifth vyūha, in it, is produced, or, according to certain Saṁhitās, innumerable world-eggs; and thereafter there come the details of creation.

Souls are of four classes, the liberated, those fit for liberation, the ever-bound, and those fit for darkness. Predestination is thus clearly taught. A soul reaches knowlege and liberation by the grace of the Lord, and he is not merged in him but joins him in Vaikuṇṭha. A few Saṁhitās are so advaitic in tone as to approach the idea of the absolute identity of the soul and God, but the general teaching clearly recognizes the soul as distinct. The soul is atomic in size, but when liberated is omniscient and in a sense also omnipotent and omnipresent.

The doctrine of the channels and centres of occult force in the human body with its method of Yoga practice and miraculous results, which we describe below [1] as found in the Śākta system, appears in the same form in these Vaishṇava works.[2] The doctrines of mantra and yantra in the Saṁhitās are indistinguishable from the Śākta teaching described below.[3] Magic in all its forms, with innumerable spells and rites and talismans, is carefully described and eagerly commended. The great sectarian mantras, *Oṁ namo Bhāgavate Vāsudevāya* (Bhāgavata), *Oṁ namo Nārāyaṇāya* (Śrī-Vaishṇava), and the famous mantra of Narasiṁha are all adored and studied and expounded in a thousand ways. The sect-mark of the Śrī-Vaishṇavas of South India consists of two white curving lines, like the outline of a vase, and a single red vertical line set in the centre and meeting the white lines at the base. The white lines represent Vishṇu, the red line his śakti, in accordance with the Śākta doctrine of creation. The Saṁhitās ordain that Vaishṇavas shall not only paint the sect-mark on the brow and elsewhere, but shall also brand the symbols of Vishṇu on the body with red-hot irons. The twice-born Vaishṇava is expected to select a guru and receive initiation, *dīkshā*, from him. Initiation consists of five acts, *Tāpa*, branding the symbols on the body, *Puṇḍra*, painting the sect-mark, *Nāma*, taking a name, *Mantra*, reception of the formula of adoration, *Yāga*, worship.[4] There is nothing in Vaishṇavism that corresponds with *chakra-pūjā*,[5] and only vegetarian offerings are allowed in the temples. The strict Vaishṇava uses only vegetarian diet. The Pāñcharātra system is still unorthodox in these manuals,[6] as we found it to be in the Epic.

The religion of the Saṁhitās is open to all four Hindu

[1] See § 232.
[2] Schrader, *IPAS*. 118 ff.
[3] § 232.
[4] Govindāchārya, *JRAS*. 1911, 946.
[5] See § 234.
[6] Schrader, *IPAS*. 97.

castes without distinction, but not to outcastes. The position of the *Gītā*[1] in this matter is retained.

§216. In the Tamil south, alongside of the Pāñcharātra manuals, about a dozen Saṁhitās are found, which are called Vaikhānasa. They are discussed above.[2]

We now deal briefly with the few local groups or sub-sects which can be distinguished at this stage in Vaishṇava history.

1. *Tamil Vaishṇavas.*

§217. We begin with the Tamil country. From the seventh to the tenth century there seems to have been a succession of poet-singers in Tamil-land who wandered about from shrine to shrine, composing hymns and singing in ecstasy before the images of their loved divinity. Many were Śaivas, and many were Vaishṇavas. Of the latter twelve are specially remembered, and honoured under the title of Āḷvārs. Their religion was above all a passionate emotion. Their chief joy was to gaze into the divine eyes of a favourite image, and to pour out their praises in music and song. Often, after a long absence, the poet's feeling was too much for him, and he fell unconscious on the temple-floor before the image, stunned by the flood of his emotions, or, during the night, he would fall sick with longing for the beautiful face which he could not see until the temple-doors were opened in the morning. They taught Outcastes, and some of them are said to have been Outcastes. Apart from local legends and epithets suggested by the temples or the forms of the images, their poems show only the influence of the Epics and early Purāṇas. The Saṁhitās were probably late in penetrating to the Tamil south. Yet these men have been regarded as the teachers of the Śrī-Vaishṇava sect. Their hymns have a great and honoured place in the training of scholars and in public worship, and their images are worshipped in the temples. The following is the list of their

[1] § 88. [2] § 211.

names in the traditional order of their appearance:—1. Poygaiar, 2. Bhutattu, 3. Peyar, 4. Tirumalisai, 5. Śaṭhakopa or Nammāḷvār, 6. Madhurakavi, 7. Kulaśekhar, 8. Periyar, 9. Andal, 10. Tondarippodi, 11. Tiruppanar, 12. Tirumaṅgai. One of these, Andal, was a woman. Tirumaṅgai and Nammāḷvār are the greatest, and Nammāḷvār is the most famous of all. There is no certainty yet as to the chronology of the Āḷvārs. Barnett [1] suggests that Tirumaṅgai and Nammāḷvār belong to the eighth century or thereabouts, but other dates are proposed by other scholars.[2]

There are two Upanishads which probably belong to this period, and which are both devoted to the Nārāyaṇa-mantra, *Oṁ namo Nārāyaṇāya*, namely the *Nārāyaṇa* and the *Ātmabodha* Upanishads.[3] The Śrī-Vaishṇava sect, which took definite shape among Tamil Vaishṇavas during the next period, use this formula as their sect-mantra. Thus the Upanishads are probably connected with the sect.

2. *The Narasiṁha Sect.*

§218. The date of the *Nṛisiṁha-tāpanīya* Upanishads [4] makes it plain that the Nṛisiṁha, or Narasiṁha, sect which worshipped the Man-lion incarnation of Vishṇu, must have been organized, at the latest, quite early in this period. This god is recognized all over India, but traces of his worship are far more abundant in the south than the north; and he is still the family god of many families in the south. Yet we must not assume that the sect was founded in the south. The sectarian mantra is an *anushṭubh* verse, called the royal mantra, *mantrarāja*, of Nṛisiṁha, and it is accompanied by four ancillary mantras. The chief scripture of the sect is the pair of Upanishads already mentioned. The first, called the

[1] *BMCTB.* 7.
[2] K. Aiyaṅgar, *AI.* 220, 377; S. Aiyaṅgar, *TS.* 299.
[3] Deussen, *SUV.* 747 ff.
[4] As they were expounded by Gauḍapāda about A.D. 750 or rather later, they cannot be dated later than the seventh century. See Deussen, *SUV.* 752 ff.

Nṛisiṁha-pūrva-tāpanīya, is in two parts, the first of which glorifies the royal mantra by mystic identifications and interpretations, and also the four Aṅga mantras, while the second gives directions for the making, by means of the royal mantra of Nṛisiṁha and three other famous Vaishṇava mantras, of a diagram, *yantra*, which, worn on the neck, the arm, or in a lock of hair, will prove a potent amulet. The second Upanishad, called the *Nṛisiṁha-uttara-tāpanīya*, also encourages the cult of the royal mantra, but its emphasis falls on the sectarian theology, in which Nṛisiṁha is identified with the supreme Brahman, the Ātman, and the syllable *Om*. Both Upanishads were expounded by Gauḍapāda, and the first at least by Śaṅkara. The use of the famous mantrarāja was not confined to the sect; three chapters are devoted to its exposition in the *Ahirbudhnya S.*[1] The popularity of the Nṛisiṁha Upanishads led to their being imitated in other sects; the most noteworthy of these copies are the *Rāma*, *Gaṇapati*, *Gopāla*, and *Tripurā Tāpanīya* Upanishads.[2] There are two other documents belonging to the sect which in all probability come from this period, the *Nṛisiṁha Upapurāṇa*,[3] and the *Nṛisiṁha S.*[4] The former is mentioned by Alberuni in A.D. 1030,[5] so that it almost certainly belongs to the period, but there is more doubt about the latter, as the earliest known reference to it is in Vedānta Deśika of the fourteenth century.

3. *The Rāma Sect.*

§219. In a late interpolated passage in Vālmīki's *Rāmāyaṇa*,[6] Rāma is hailed as the one eternal God, and his devotees are mentioned, but there is no evidence that an organized Ramaite sect existed in those early days. But there need be no doubt about the existence of such a sect in this period. It is implied in the *Rāma-pūrva-tāpanīya*

[1] Chaps. 54 to 56. See Schrader, *IPAS*. 143.
[2] See § 219; § 239; § 280; § 316.
[3] Eggeling, *SMIO*. 3515.
[4] Schrader, *IPAS*. 8, 18.
[5] Sachau, I. 130.
[6] VI. 119: see § 107.

Upanishad,[1] which sets Rāma forth as an incarnation of Brahman, expounds a royal mantra—*Rāṁ Rāmāya namaḥ*—and describes a mystic diagram which leads to release and other blessings. A secret alphabet is also taught as the vehicle of secret mantras. The *Rāma-uttara-tāpanīya Upanishad*[2] consists mostly of passages taken from earlier Upanishads, and may belong to a later date. One of the Vaishṇava Saṁhitās, the *Agastya-Sutīkshṇa Saṁvāda*,[3] is a Ramaite work, and almost certainly belongs to this period; for it is referred to and quoted in the *Adhyātma Rāmāyaṇa*.[4] Dr. Schrader's assumption that the worship of Rāma is a modern growth, and that a Ramaite Saṁhitā must therefore be a very recent production, is unfounded, for there is plenty of evidence that Rāma has been continuously worshipped from very early times. But until this and other Saṁhitās bearing Ramaite names[5] are carefully examined, the question of their date must remain in doubt.

§ 220. We may also reasonably ask whether there was not a Dattātreya sect. This seems to be implied by what is contained in the *Yādava-giri Māhātmya* in the *Nārada* and *Matsya* Purāṇas, by various references elsewhere to Dattātreya, and by what the Manbhaus say.

E. *Śaiva Literature.*

§ 221. It is not yet possible to say definitely how many Śaiva sects used or produced Āgamas. One is inclined to suggest, very tentatively, a division of mediaeval Śaivas into two groups as under:—

a. Pāśupata Śaivas:
1. Pāśupatas.
2. Lakulīśa-Pāśupatas.
3. Kāpālikas.
4. Nāthas.
5. Gorakshanāthīs.
6. Raseśvaras.

[1] Deussen, *SUV.* 802. [2] Ib. 818. [3] Schrader, *IPAS.* 6, 19.
[4] See § 294. [5] Schrader, *IPAS.* nos. 26, 101, 133 in list, pp. 6 to 9.

b. Āgamic Śaivas
1. Sanskrit School of Śaiva Siddhānta.
2. Tamil Śaivas.
3. Kashmir Śaivas.
4. Vīra Śaivas.

It is clear that the second group were closely allied, and that they accepted the Āgamas. The Tamil and Vīra Śaivas call themselves Maheśvaras to-day and do not call themselves Pāśupatas, although their theology depends on the Pāśupata doctrine of the Epic. Their writers reject the doctrine of the incarnations of Śiva as taught by the Pāśupatas, and tell, instead, stories of his having appeared in numerous theophanies. The first group were also closely connected in several ways, and they do not seem to have recognized the Āgamas; but as only weak remnants of them have survived until our days, it is difficult to get clear information. We now deal with the sects as far as we can trace them.

a. *Pāśupata Śaivas.*

§ 222. There is first the parent sect of Pāśupatas. Praśastapāda, the early commentator on the *Vaiśeshika-sūtra*, was a Śaiva, and almost certainly a Pāśupata, and Bharadvāja, i. e. Uddyotakara, the author of the gloss on the *Nyāya-bhāshya*, is definitely called Pāśupatāchārya. Bāṇa and Hiouen Tsang both refer to the Pāśupatas as one of the prominent sects of the time. Śaṇkara criticizes them in his *Bhāshya*, on the ground that their doctrine of God as the operative but not the material cause of the world stands in opposition to Upanishad doctrine.

1. *The Lakulīśas.*

§ 223. The Lakulīśa system, which seems to be a specialized form of the Pāśupata,[1] arose in Gujarāt, as we have seen, at a very early date, and probably developed a philosophical literature before the opening of the seventh century. Consequently they did not accept the new teaching of the Śaiva

[1] Bhandarkar believes there is but the one system, called indifferently Pāśupata, Lakulīśa, or Lakulīśa-Pāśupata.

Āgamas. During this period the sect spread as far south as Mysore and also into Rajputana. The lists of the incarnations of Śiva, which are copied in the *Liṅga* and *Kūrma* Purāṇas from the *Vāyu*, and which mention Lakulī, are Lakulīśa documents.[1] There is an image of Lakulīśa, which belongs to the seventh century, at Jharapatan in Gujarāt.

2. *The Kāpālikas.*

§ 224. The Kāpālikas, i.e. the skull-men, are another specialization of the Pāśupatas, but it is hard to say whether they were ever a sect. The evidence suggests that they have never been more than an order of ascetics. In doctrine and practice they stand in the closest possible relation to the Left-hand Śāktas. They seem to have been organized about the very beginning of this period. An inscription,[2] dating from the first half of the seventh century, mentions the god Kapāleśvara and his ascetics. In the *Mālatī-Mādhava*, a drama produced early in the eighth century,[3] one of the chief characters is Aghoraghaṇṭa, a Kāpālika ascetic, who acts as priest of the goddess Chāmuṇḍā in a royal city, and is connected with the great Śaiva shrine, Śrī-Śaila, in the Telugu country. Kapāla-Kuṇḍalā, i.e. Skull-earring, is a nun, a devotee of the goddess, and a pupil of Aghoraghaṇṭa. Both practise yoga, and through it have won miraculous powers. The beliefs they hold are full of Śākta ideas, and amongst their practices is human sacrifice. Aghoraghaṇṭa plots to sacrifice the heroine of the play to Chāmuṇḍā, but is finally killed by the hero. The nun wears a necklace of skulls, and carries a heavy rod from which hangs a string of bells.

3. *The Nāthas.*

The Nāthas are extremely hard to get hold of. The Gorakshanāthīs, a special sect derived from them, are Śaivas, while modern Nāthas, e.g. Bhāskararāya of Tanjore, are Śāktas.

[1] See § 227. [2] Bhandarkar, *VS.* 118.
[3] *ERE.* IV. 886; V. A. Smith, *EHI.* 3, 378.

b. *Āgamic Śaivas.*

§ 225. The rise of the Āgamas is the chief literary event in the history of Śaivism during this period. According to tradition there are twenty-eight of these manuals, divided as under[1]:—

i. Śaivic: Kāmika, Yogaja, Chintya, Karaṇa, Ajita, Dīpta, Sūkshma, Sahasra, Aṁsumān, Suprabha (Suprabheda).

ii. Raudric: Vijaya, Niśvāsa, Svāyambhuva, Āgneyaka, Bhadra, Raurava, Makuṭa, Vimala, Chandrahāsa (Chandrajñāna), Mukhayugbimba (Mukhabimba), Udgītā (Prodgītā), Lalita, Siddha, Santāna, Nārasiṁha (Sarvokta or Sarvottara), Parameśvara, Kiraṇa, Para (Vātula).

Each of these Āgamas is then attended by a group of Upāgamas, the total number contained in the list amounting to 198.

The date of the earliest of these manuals is still obscure. The Tamil poets, Tirumūlar, who lived somewhere about A.D. 800, Sundarar, who was either a contemporary of Tirumūlar or came a little later, and Māṇikka Vāchakar, whose date is not far removed from A.D. 900, all refer to the Āgamas, and both Tirumūlar and Māṇikka use much of their phraseology.[2] Mr. J. C. Chatterji tells us[3] that the *Śiva-sūtras* were promulgated in Kashmir by Vasugupta about A.D. 850 with the express purpose of substituting an advaita philosophy for the more or less dualistic teaching of the Āgamas, which were then the foundation of the Śaivism of Kashmir. This statement is supported by references to two Āgamas, the

[1] Ramaṇa's Tr. of Appayadīkshita's Gloss on Śrīkaṇṭha's *Śaiva-bhashya.*

[2] I owe this valuable information about Tirumūlar and Sundarar to my friend, the Rev. Francis Kingsbury of Bangalore. For these poets see § 229.

[3] *KS.* 7–10; 36 (a).

Mataṅga[1] and the Svāyambhuva, in Somānanda of Kashmir,[2] who flourished towards the end of the ninth century, and by numerous quotations in Kshemarāja,[3] another Kashmir writer belonging to the eleventh century. The earliest known MS., a copy of the *Kiraṇa*, is dated A.D. 924.[4] From these facts we may conjecture that the earliest Āgamas, like the Hindu and Buddhist Tantras, are to be assigned to the seventh and eighth centuries, yet, until more definite evidence becomes available, we must not say more. No scholar has as yet ventured an opinion as to which of the Āgamas are oldest.

§ 226. The Āgamas mark the appearance of Śākta ideas among Śaivas, and are also the earliest of their codes of temple-building, image-making, and religious practice. Their contents are supposed to fall into four divisions, like the Saṁhitās. The following sketch of the teaching of the Āgamas is drawn from Iyengar's account,[5] which is based on the *Mṛigendra Ā.*, the first, or knowledge, section of the *Kāmika*, the first Āgama. The whole system is condensed in the first verse of the work: 'Śiva is beginningless, free from defects, the all-knower. He removes from the infinitesimal soul the web of bonds that obscure its nature.' He can create both gradually and suddenly, because creation is of that double character, and he possesses an eternal instrument for the work, the Śakti, who is a conscious being and at the same time the Lord's body. His body is all energy (śakti); it is composed of the five mantras. Being so utterly different from our body, no evils or obstructions can attach themselves to it. Consciousness exists in the ātman at all times and on all sides, perfect in Śiva and in the liberated, but not manifest in the unliberated, because in them obscured.

Śiva-śakti is a category intermediate between Śiva, who is pure consciousness, and Matter, which is unconscious. She is the cause of the bondage of all beings and also of their release.

[1] This is one of the Upāgamas, and is dependent on the *Parameśvara Ā.*

[2] *KS.* 10.

[3] Hall, pp. 197–8.

[4] H. P. Śāstrī, II. xxiv.

[5] *Outlines*, 151 ff.

She is the eternal Word, the subtle link between concept and utterance. To this is attached the whole doctrine of mantras.[1] The theory of the existence of a system of yogic nerves and circles in the body[2] is taught.

Śiva is Paśupati, Lord of flocks. Hence man is called Paśu, the Lord's creature.[3] His body is unconscious; he himself is conscious. The Paśu is, in his own nature, the abode of eternal and omnipresent Chitśakti, mind-energy. But the Paśu is bound by Pāśa, the bond, and it is threefold, *Āṇava*, Ignorance, *Karma*, the result of his action, *Māyā*, the material cause of the world. This last bond, Māyā, does not bear the meaning that it does in Śaṅkara's system. It stands for the beclouding, deceiving, materializing influence of the visible world. Fettered by these bonds, the paśu is a finite, restricted being, bounded by his body. The Śakti is included in these bonds, and through them the Lord's work of obscuration of souls is carried out. The Śakti evolves also into Anugraha, the grace of the Lord, and by the gradual destruction of the bonds leads the soul to liberation. 'It is revealed that *Identity with Śiva* results, when all fetters are removed.'

But while this may stand as an approximation to the teaching of the earliest Āgamas, it is of importance to recognize that they are not a uniform body. Several sects are represented in them, and until these differences are clearly recognized we shall have no accurate conception of Āgamic teaching.

§ 227. The *Liṅga* and *Kūrma Purāṇas* are Śaiva documents comparable with the Vaishṇava *Agni* and *Garuḍa* in general character. It is also probable that, like them, they come from the middle of the period; for they reflect the teaching of the Āgamas and the Tantras and refer to some of these texts. Both Purāṇas[4] repeat with alterations and

[1] See the account of mantras drawn from the *Kiraṇa Āgama* in H. P. Śāstrī, II. xxvi. [2] See § 232. [3] But see § 109.

[4] Liṅga, XXIV. 124–33; Kūrma, I. liii. These texts are quoted by Ramaṇa in his Tr. of Appaya Dīkshita on the *Śaiva Bhāshya*, pp. 13–14. He quotes all the texts, except the original one in the *Vāyu*.

additions the account of the twenty-eight incarnations of Śiva and their disciples from the *Vāyu*.[1] In the *Liṅga* there is a long dissertation on the mystic meaning of the word *Om* and of the letters of the alphabet,[2] in the manner of Śākta treatises,[3] while in the *Kūrma*[4] a number of the Śākta Tantras are referred to, and the worship of the Śaktis is recommended. It is not yet known which Śaiva sects these documents come from, except that the list of incarnations is Lakulīśa.

§ 228. The smearing of the body with ashes was part of the practice of Pāśupata ascetics from the time of the *Atharvaśiras U.*[5] at least; and the sect-mark is now universally made with ashes. In all the sects, these marks seem to date from the first part of this period, when the new manuals taught the power of magic diagrams. The Śaiva sect-mark, the Tripuṇḍra, as it is called, consists of three lines of ash drawn by the fingers horizontally across the brow, and often also on the breast, arms, and other parts of the body as well. It is thus probable that the *Kālāgnirudra U.*,[6] which is a mystic meditation on the Tripuṇḍra, comes from the first half of our period.

1. *Tamil Śaivas.*

§ 229. In the Tamil country the most noteworthy Śaiva personalities during these centuries are poets. There are first of all three who are in every way parallel to the Vaishṇava Āḻvārs, but they are not distinguished by any title. They are called Nayanars, like other religious leaders, but if they are spoken of as a distinct group, they are simply called *The Three*. Their names are Ñānasambandhar, Appar, and Sundaramūrti. The two former belong to the seventh, the last to the eighth or ninth century. Like the Āḻvārs, they were poet-singers, filled with overflowing bhakti towards Śiva. They wandered from temple to temple, singing their hymns and

[1] See § 165.
[2] Muir, *OST.* IV. 329.
[3] See § 232.
[4] Chap. XII.
[5] See § 112.
[6] Deussen, *SUV.* 735.

dancing in rapture before the images of Śiva, the dancing Lord, and his beloved Umā, and drew crowds after them. They show no dependence on the Āgamas, though Sundarar mentions them, but use the Epics and the Purāṇas and express the traditional piety and devotion of the community. Only a few of their hymns have been translated into English.

Tirumūlar[1] (*c.* A.D. 800), in his *Tirumantram*, is the earliest Tamil poet who reflects the theology of the Āgamas. His work is a masterpiece as a poem, and it deals with practical religion.

Rather later there arose a still greater man, Māṇikka-Vāchakar, 'whose utterances are rubies'. He lived about A.D. 900,[2] and left a large number of lyrical poems short and long, which are known as the *Tiru-Vāchakam*, 'The Sacred Utterance'. He was a man of education and position connected with Madura, but a sudden conversion, in which the personal influence of a guru was dominant, led him to give up his position and become a wandering devotee. That he was a cultured man who entered fully into the heritage of the work of those who preceded him is clear from his poems. Contents, style, diction, and mastery of metres all show the accomplished poet. He uses freely the stores of the Epics, the Purāṇas, and the Āgamas, and also the very rich Tamil literature that already lay behind him. He knew also how to find poetry in local customs and homely stories, especially the mass of legends that illustrate Śiva's sacred sports. Over all he threw the glamour of his genius. A considerable amount of the technical theology of the Āgamas appears in his lines, and he frequently speaks of them as revealed by Śiva. We may also note his dislike for the Vedānta, which must mean Śaṅkara's *māyāvāda*.

[1] Barnett, *BMCTB.* 5; Frazer, *ERE.* V. 23.

[2] Barnett (*BMCTB.* 5 *n.*) says between A.D. 800 and 1000; Frazer and others says between A.D. 800 and 900 (*ERE.* V. 23). Cf. S. Aiyangar, *TS.*, App. III.

2. *Kashmir Śaivas.*

§ 230. In Kashmir the Śaiva Āgamas were accepted as revelation and became the basis of all religious thought in the Śaiva community. Then about A.D. 850 the *Śiva-sūtras* were promulgated in a mysterious way as a fresh utterance from Śiva; and under the stimulus of this work a rich philosophical literature continued to spring up for three centuries. The *Śiva-sūtras* and the *Spanda-Kārikās*, which expound them, are rather practical in character, but by about A.D. 900 the *Śiva-dṛishti* of Somānanda provided a more distinctly philosophical groundwork for the system. The ontology is monistic, and release depends upon a discipline which consists in the continuous recognition, *pratyabhijñā*, of man's identity with Śiva. Yet the world is not treated as a mere illusion. It is an *ābhāsa* or manifestation of Śiva through the Śakti, and is present to his consciousness, though not in the form in which it appears to the individual mind. The process of the evolution of the universe keeps in the main to the Sāṅkhya series, but it has several interesting features of its own. The system is called *Trika*, because it deals with three principles, Śiva, Śakti, *aṇu*, or Pati, pāśa, paśu, and also Pratyabhijñā from its law of recognition. An outline of the teaching may be found in Mādhava's *Sarva-darśana-saṅgraha*, or the details may be studied in Chatterji's monograph.[1] The system is distinctly more monistic than the teaching of the Āgamas, with which the new literature struggles to show its full agreement. How are we to account for the change? The activity of the great Śaṅkara falls in the first half of the ninth century, and we may be sure that the traditions are right when they say he visited Kashmir during one of his controversial tours. It is thus most probable that he influenced the Śaiva leaders very deeply and was the source of the stimulus which created the *Śiva-sūtra* and the movement which followed.

[1] *Kashmir Shaivism.*

F. *Śākta Literature.*

a. *The Tantras.*

§ 231. The sect of Durgā is now reorganized with a new theology, a more varied cult, and a fresh literature. It is called the Śākta sect. There is no authoritative canon of the Tantras, the literature of the Śāktas. In several places lists of sixty-four Tantras are found, and one list contains three groups of sixty-four,[1] but these catalogues differ so seriously the one from the other that, as yet at least, they are of little help to the student. Hundreds of Tantras are mentioned in the lists, and, although many are lost for ever, a very large number still survive. In addition there are several Śākta documents scattered about in the Purāṇas, and numerous hymns in praise of the goddess, lineal descendants of those already discussed, are found in various places.

Only a very few of these authorities can be dated with any certainty, but there are a number more whose age can be approximately discerned. It is scarcely possible as yet to classify the texts as belonging to the sub-sects, references to which are found from quite early times.[2] The whole literature awaits the toil of scholarly investigators. What we propose to do is to give brief notices of all the important works whose age is approximately known. In this way an outline of the history will be afforded and a basis of study provided.

A MS. of the *Kubjikāmata T.* in Gupta character proves that that work dates from the seventh century at latest. A MS. of the *Parameśvaramata T.* is dated A.D. 858, and a MS. of the *Mahākaulajñāna Vinirṇaya* is quite as old,[3] the works themselves being probably a good deal older. A careful study of these three Tantras would give a very full account of early Śākta philosophy and worship. From the *Kubjikāmata* we may conclude that a formed Śākta theology and ritual were

[1] Avalon's *Tantrik Texts*, I. ii.; Dutt's *Mahānirvāṇa T.* v.
[2] H. P. Śāstrī, I. lxiv, lxxviii.
[3] Ib. I. lxxvii, lxxviii; II. xxi, xviii.

already in existence about A. D. 600. The *Niśvāsatattva Saṁhitā*, a MS. of which is believed to date from the eighth century,[1] gives detailed regulations for all aspects of Śākta life. It is probable that a few more of the existing Tantras come from this period, but, in the absence of clear evidence, it is better to acknowledge our ignorance.

The *Chaṇḍī-śataka* of Bāṇa belongs to the first half of the seventh century, but it is rather a literary than a religious work, and its value as a source is thus rather limited. The *Mālatī-Mādhava* of Bhavabhūti, a drama produced at Kanouj early in the eighth century, gives in several scenes very vivid pictures of the worship and the magic practices of the Śāktas of that time.

The contents of the Tantras might, like the contents of the Vaishṇava Saṁhitās and the Śaiva Āgamas, quite well be divided into four classes, Theology, Yoga, Construction of temples, images, &c., Religious practices. A very large proportion of the matter falls, as a matter of fact, under the last of the four heads. The Śākta system is fundamentally an unlimited array of magic rites drawn from the practice of the most ignorant and superstitious classes. The following seem to be its more prominent features as represented in the early books.

§ 232. The system[2] sprang from Śaivism, and the main cult gathers round the wife of Śiva, but it is found associated with many other goddesses also. The genetic idea is this that, since the eternal, inconceivable Supreme, Śiva-Brahman, is altogether inactive, while his spouse is pure activity, *śakti*, the creation and recreation of the world and all the work of divine grace and liberation are her functions. She is thus of far more importance than Śiva: without his śakti Śiva is a corpse.[3] From śakti comes the adjective *śākta*, which forms the name of the sect. The dogmatic runs as follows: the Śakti is one with Brahman, but, in so far as she is differentiated, she is the

[1] H. P. Śāstrī, I. lxxvii.
[2] See Avalon, *TGL*. Introd.
[3] *Kubjikā T.*, chap. i.

active aspect and manifests Brahman in all created things and beings. From the point of view of religion she is superior to Brahman. Philosophically, the system, like the sectarian theology of the Purāṇas, follows the theistic Sāṅkhya and uses only a few Vedantic ideas. The Śakti is identified directly or indirectly with Mūla-prakṛiti: the whole world is merely the unfolding of the Śakti.

The mystic and miraculous side of the Yoga system plays a large part in Śaktism. There are two starting-points. The first is dependent on the analysis of the sacred syllable *Om* already carried out in the Yoga Upanishads. *Nāda*, *bindu*, and *bīja* are momenta in creation; the Śakti is *śabda*, sound, the eternal Word. Thus every letter of the alphabet is instinct with the power of the Śakti; and mantras, i.e. words or phrases framed from these letters in accordance with their inner powers, are omnipotent spells, which in Śaktism are at the service of the initiate. Every mantra is thus a divine creation, and the whole body of the mantras is identical with the Śakti. The vast majority of these mantras are nonsense syllables such as Hriṅg, Huṅg, Tha, Aiṅg, Huṁ, Phaṭ, sparks from the blazing furnace of aboriginal superstition whence the system arose, or from the equally superstitious stores laid up in the *Atharva-veda*. On the other hand, within the human frame, the system teaches, there are immense numbers of minute channels or threads of occult force, called *nāḍī*. The most important of all, the Sushumṇā, is in the spinal cord. Connected with these channels there are six great centres, or circles (*chakra*), of occult force situated in the human trunk, the one above the other. Each of these is described as a lotus. Mūlādhāra, the lowest and most important of all, contains Brahman in the form of a liṅga, and the Devī lies asleep, coiled three and a half times[1] round the liṅga like a serpent.[2] In this posture

[1] This probably has reference to the three and a half morae of the syllable *Oṁ*, as taught in the Yoga Upanishads: § 100.

[2] See an image in G. N. Rao, *Hindu Iconography*, I. 328, and Buddhist images in which a snake coils round the Buddha's limbs, Getty, *GNB*. Plate VI.

she is called Kuṇḍalinī, the coiled one. By Śākta yoga she may be waked and induced to ascend to the highest chakra. These channels and centres form the basis of all the miracle-working power which the initiate can achieve. They are mentioned, along with the marvellous results that may be gained through them, in the *Mālatī-Mādhava*.[1]

b. *Mantra*, *Yantra*, *Mudrā*.

§ 233. It is possible to trace in pre-Christian centuries the rise of adoration mantras, brief expressions of the unutterable reverence of the soul for the divine, or human, centre of the faith. In this period the doctrine that the Devī is incarnate in sound led to the conviction that the sectarian mantra is the concentrated essence of all divine truth, and that it is instinct with supernatural power. Hence it was studied in every possible way, worshipped with deepest reverence, and used for the formation of spells and amulets.

Śāktas made large use of mysterious diagrams, *yantra* and *maṇḍala*, often engraved on metal plates, *pātra*, consecrated pots and jars, *ghaṭa*, ritual gestures made with the fingers, *mudrā*, and ritual movements of the hands, called *nyāsa*, for the bringing of the goddess into the body.[2] The belief in the magic power of diagrams led to the use of sect-marks. These are lines, curves, circles, spots, and designs which are painted or smeared on the brow and other parts of the body, in order to place the person under the protection of these powerful instruments and the divinities they represent.[3] The Śākta sect-mark is the Śaiva Tripuṇḍra.[4] All the sect-marks have a phallic significance. They refer to the union of the god with his śakti.

c. *The Cult*.

§ 234. The new Śākta cult is fourfold. There is first the public worship of the goddess in temples. From the very

[1] Act. V. at the beginning. [2] Avalon, *TGL*. xcii, xciv, cv, cvii.

[3] This will be evident at once to any one who will take a look at Moor's table of sects-marks, *Hindu Pantheon*.

[4] See § 228, and cf. Avalon, *TGL*. lxviii.

time when the system was organized, the offerings were vegetarian, animal, and human, and the three forms were practised until the British abolished human sacrifice.[1] Vegetarian offerings are laid before the image, while animals—male goats and buffaloes—are usually sacrificed in the open air at a little distance from it,[2] and there also human sacrifice was carried out. In the first half of the seventh century, during the reign of the emperor Harsha, the greatest of all Chinese pilgrims, Hiouen Tsang, was almost sacrificed to Durgā.[3] In the *Mālatī-Mādhava*[4] the heroine is seized by a priest of Chāmuṇḍā, one of the many forms of the goddess, and carried to her temple to be sacrificed, but is rescued by the hero.

There is, secondly, *Chakra-pūjā*, i.e. circle-worship, which is the characteristic cult. It is now called Vāmāchārī, or Left-hand.[5] An equal number of men and women, who may belong to any caste or castes, and may be near relatives—husband, wife, mother, sister, brother—meet in secret, usually at night, and sit in a circle. The goddess may be represented by an image or a yantra, which is actually a drawing of the pudendum muliebre in the centre of a circle formed of nine pudenda. The liturgy of the cult consists in the repetition of mantras, the ritual in partaking of the *five tattvas*, i.e. elements, viz. wine, meat, fish, parched grain, and sexual intercourse.

The third form of the cult of the goddess is *Sādhanā*, i.e. Yoga practice meant to bring a man to perfection.

The fourth form is sorcery, whether for white or black purposes. Detailed instruction is given in the Tantras. A scene in the *Mālatī-Mādhava*[6] takes us in the twilight to the burning-ground, fetid with the fumes of the funeral pyre, and shows us the hero, Mādhava, his hair ceremonially braided, a sword in one hand and a piece of human flesh in the other.

[1] At both Vindhyachal and Kālighāt the writer was told by the priests that human sacrifice continued at these shrines until it was prohibited by the British. Cf. *ERE.* VI. 850.

[2] The head is usually severed from the body by a sword or big knife.

[3] Watters, I. 360.

[4] Act. V.

[5] See § 317.

[6] Act. V.

He has come to invoke the disembodied spirits that haunt the spot, hoping to barter the human flesh for supernatural power to aid him in winning Mālatī.

§ 235. It is evident on the surface that the major elements in the cult have arisen from gross magic practice; but the goddess is philosophically described as the energy and the manifestation of the supreme Brahman, and the books represent the grossest elements of the *chakra-pūjā* as potent means for reaching release from transmigration.

§ 236. So far as one can discern at present, the earliest worship of the goddess included animal, and probably human, sacrifice, and the ritual use of flesh and wine. Whether it was also stained by erotic practices we do not know. This early cult seems to have persisted unchanged in the temples in most parts of North India until the British put down human sacrifice. When the new Śākta teaching appeared about A.D. 600, the secret circle-worship was added to the old ritual, and also the personal yoga-practice for the awakening of Kuṇḍalinī. It is impossible to tell how widely circle-worship was practised at any particular time in the past, but clearly it had a great vogue for many centuries in Bengal, and it is by no means extinct to-day. Śākta yoga has been practised in all parts of the country down to our own times.

§ 237. Men and women of all castes, and outcastes as well, are welcome to become Śāktas; yet the faith does not interfere in the slightest with the social rules of caste. This freedom was natural in a cult which sprang from the lower orders. Then, when the cult became a regular Hindu sect, it would be retained as necessary in the fight with Buddhism and Jainism, and for the winning of the masses, since such a large proportion of the people of North India at that time must have been outside the castes.

Like the other sects, the Śāktas advised all those who wanted to make real progress in the faith to select a guru and undergo initiation (*dīkshā*).

G. *Saura Literature.*

§ 238. The Saura sect was clearly numerous and powerful during the whole of this period. Numerous Sun-temples existed throughout the north,[1] and many kings were devotees of Sūrya.[2] Of his worship in the south at this period there seems to be no evidence. His priests were called Māgas, Bhojakas, Śākadvīpīya Brāhmans; for the Magians were at an early date accepted as full Brāhmans.[3] By far the most important Saura document belonging to this period is the *Saura Saṁhitā*, a work of the same nature as the Vaishṇava Saṁhitās but devoted to the worship of Sūrya. The only known MS. is in Nepal, and unfortunately has not yet been examined in detail. It is dated A.D. 941, but doubtless the work itself is much earlier.[4] Of considerable interest also is the *Sūrya Śataka* of Mayūra, who seems to have been a rival of Bāṇa at the court of Harsha in the first half of the seventh century. It is a Sanskrit poem of one hundred stanzas in Sragdharā metre and the Gauḍī style, and is rather a literary than a religious work; but, composed by an accomplished poet at the most brilliant court of the time, it naturally exhibits clearly the current theology of the god. The ideas are only a little in advance of those that meet us in the earlier works.[5] Sūrya as the source of Release is the point on which most stress is laid. It is noteworthy that in the *Bhaktāmara Stotra* by the Jain poet, Mānatuṅga, who seems to have been a contemporary, praise is heaped upon Sūrya without stint.[6] The *Sāmba P.*, a Saura document connected with Orissa which tells the story of Sāmba and the Māgas,[7] probably belongs to this period; for it is mentioned by Alberuni in A.D. 1030.

[1] Bhandarkar, *VS.* 154; Vincent Smith, *EHI.* 345, 372.

[2] See especially Chanda, *IAR.* 145, 161.

[3] Chanda, *IAR.* 161; 224; Bhandarkar, *VS.* 154. The *Kubjikā T.*, a very early work, expresses the fear that they will receive such recognition: H. P. Śāstrī, I. lxxx.

[4] H. P. Śāstrī, I. lxxvi. See also no. 203 in Schrader's list, *IPAS.* 11.

[5] Quackenbos, *SPM.*

[6] Ib. p. 266.

[7] Bloch, *ZDMG.* lxiv. 733; Vasu, *Mayūrabhuñja*, iii.

Several chapters in the *Agni P.*,[1] which is a Bhāgavata document, and in the *Garuḍa P.*,[2] which is Smārta, deal with the images and the worship of Sūrya.

H. *Gāṇapatya Literature.*

§ 239. The early development of the god Gaṇeśa or Gaṇapati is traced by Bhandarkar,[3] but our interest in him begins at the point when he became the god of a sect. That probably happened early in this period, but the date remains doubtful. The worship of the god comes before us in the *Yājñavalkya Smṛiti*[4] in the opening lines of the *Mālatī-Mādhava* and in inscriptions of the eighth and ninth centuries, while the theology appears in the Upanishad called indifferently *Varadatāpanīya* or *Gaṇapatitāpanīya*, which probably belongs to this period. Gaṇeśa is proclaimed the eternal Brahman, and a royal mantra in his honour is given and explained in imitation of the *Nṛisiṁha-tāpanīya U.*[5] Another Upanishad belonging to the sect probably lies behind the *Gaṇapati U.* which forms a part of the *Atharvaśiras U.*[6] of the Smārtas. In the lists of Vaishṇava Saṁhitās[7] a *Gaṇeśa Saṁhitā* is mentioned, which probably belongs to the sect. The passages in the *Agni*[8] and *Garuḍa*[9] Purāṇas which give directions for his worship are to be regarded not as belonging to the Gāṇapatya sect but as rules for the cult of the god by Bhāgavatas and Smārtas in Pañchāyatana pūjā.

There is thus the best of evidence that the five gods were widely worshipped during our period, while Brahmā received but little attention.

ii. BUDDHISM.

§ 240. The ancient monastery of Nālandā in Bihar rose about the beginning of the period to the position of a university, and all the schools took part in the teaching, discus-

[1] Chaps. LI, LXXIII, XCIX.
[2] Chaps. VII, XVI, XVII, XXXIX.
[3] *VS.* 147.
[4] Ib. 148.
[5] See § 218.
[6] Vans Kennedy, *HM.* 493. See § 207.
[7] Schrader, *IPAS.* 7.
[8] Chaps. LXXI and CCCXIII.
[9] Chap. XXIV.

sions, and writing that went on there. In China there was great translation activity throughout the period, and two of the most noteworthy of the Chinese pilgrims, Hiouen Tsang and I Tsing, visited India in the seventh century. Japan received Buddhism in A.D. 552, and it was introduced into Cambodia about the same time, and into Tibet about A.D. 640.

A. *The Hīnayāna.*

§ 241. We do not hear of the production of fresh literature by the Indian Hīnayāna sects during this period, and in Ceylon no books of real religious interest seem to have been written. Yet it is clear that a number of the schools were still active. It is noteworthy that the whole Mūlasarvāstivādin Vinaya, and a number of the books of the Vinaya of other Hīnayāna schools,[1] were translated into Chinese, while all the chief works of the Abhidharma of the Sarvāstivādins were reproduced in both Chinese and Tibetan.[2] The Dharmagupta Life of the Buddha, the *Abhinishkramaṇa-sūtra*, was translated into Chinese in A.D. 587, and into Tibetan at a later date.[3] After I Tsing returned to China he spent twelve years in translating texts.[4] Amongst these there is a solid block of thirteen works representing the Mūla-Sarvāstivādin Vinaya, but nearly all the other books of which he produced versions belong to the Mahāyāna school. Chinese Buddhism was essentially Mahāyāna, though it used the Hīnayāna Vinaya and Abhidharma freely, and the old sūtras to some extent.

B. *The Mahāyāna.*

§ 242. In the Mahāyāna literature of the period Sūtras do not play a large part. Two noteworthy books may be mentioned, the *Rāshṭrapāla-paripṛichchhā* and the *Mahākaruṇāpuṇḍarīka*. The former is poor in language and style. It discusses the

[1] Nanjio, 1107, 1127, 1128, 1139, 1142.
[2] Ib. 1263, 1265, 1275, 1277, 1281, 1282, 1296, 1317.
[3] Ib. 680.
[4] Ib. Col. 441.

qualities of the Bodhisattvas, and prophesies the coming fall of Buddhism. The first chapter of the latter work is a discussion between Buddha and the creator Brahmā, in which the former reasons from Buddhist premises to the conclusion that there can be no creator.

§ 243. The ancient monastery of Nālandā in Behar gradually developed, probably in the sixth century, into a great Buddhist university, where thousands of students and numerous teachers of all the schools, both of the Hīnayāna and the Mahāyāna, taught and disputed and wrote. A picture of the buildings, manner of study, teaching, disputation, and worship, may be gathered from the memoirs of Hiouen Tsang and I Tsing. From about A.D. 600 to 850 it is possible to trace the succession of scholars, especially in the Mādhyamaka and Vijñānavādin schools. A continuous series of manuals on each of these philosophies was produced there, and many were translated into Chinese and Tibetan. Here we can notice only the more noteworthy books.

a. *The Mādhyamakas.*

§ 244. The greatest names of the Mādhyamaka school were Chandrakīrti and Śāntideva. Chandrakīrti, who lived in the first half of the seventh century, is famous for his *Prasannapādā*, an excellent commentary on Nāgārjuna's *Kārikā*, and for his *Mādhyamakāvatāra*, which deals with the whole doctrine of the Mahāyāna as well as the Mādhyamaka system. Śāntideva, who lived about the middle of the seventh century, wrote three works, *Śikshāsamuchchhaya*, *Sūtrasamuchchhaya*, and *Bodhicharyāvatāra*, the first and the last of the three being famous. The *Śikshāsamuchchhaya* is a summary of Mahāyāna teaching according to the Mādhyamaka school in twenty-seven verses, kārikās, accompanied by a bulky prose commentary which consists largely of extracts from the literature. The double work forms an excellent manual of the teaching. The *Bodhicharyāvatāra*, i.e. 'Entrance on the Wisdom-life', is a noble poem in praise of the ideal of the Mahāyāna, the life of the Bodhisattva. It is so filled with living devotion, tenderness and passion that M. Barth compares it to the *Imitation.* The root idea is that only by self-sacrifice can the Bodhisattva help to win the world to wisdom and reach enlightenment himself. Therefore must the novice practise charity and compassionate feeling, worship the Buddhas and celestial Bodhisattvas with all the rich accompaniments of the Mahāyāna cult, and prepare himself by careful thought and steady discipline to meet all the difficulties of the long journey and to suffer martyrdom for the sake of others. In both these works Śāntideva seems to go farther than other teachers in this regard. He says the Bodhisattva must not shrink from taking upon himself all the sins and tortures of the damned. The doctrine of vacuity must also be plumbed.

b. *The Vijñānavādins.*

§ 245. Chandragomin was the chief scholar of the Vijñānavādin school. He lived early in the seventh century, and was thus the contemporary and opponent of Chandrakīrti. He is famous as a poet, a learned writer, a logician, and a grammarian. Two of his works have been preserved in Sanskrit, the *Śishyalekhadharma-kāvya*, a romantic poem of the refined classical style, and his grammar,[1] and one, his logic, survives in Tibetan.

C. *The Śākta Movement.*

§ 246. A new movement, which really amounted to a disastrous revolution, arose in Buddhism during this period, the Tāntrik movement. It is in all things parallel with the Tāntrik movement in Hinduism; and, like it, it was repudiated by the best schools of the parent faith. How was such a thing possible in Buddhism?—Because the main conceptions of polytheistic paganism had never been repudiated and condemned.[2] All Buddhists believed in the Hindu gods and

[1] Vidyābhūshaṇa, *JASB.* 1907, no. 2.
[2] Poussin, *Opinions*, 343 ff.

demons, the need of honouring them, the supernatural power of sainthood, the occult potency of yoga-practices, both physical and mental, and the power of magic spells. Although these things were kept in the background in early Buddhism, they were not killed, and in the Mahāyāna they got the opportunity to grow and spread. The numerous Buddhas and celestial Bodhisattvas of the Mahāyāna—above all Avalokiteśvara—conceived like Hindu divinities in heavens of glory and pleasure, and worshipped in like manner, opened the door wide to Hindu superstition.

§ 247. The full system appears in the Tantras. Every Buddha and every Bodhisattva has here a wife, his śakti; a new esoteric cult—in all points the same as the Hindu chakrapūjā—has been formed, in which wine, women, flesh, magic syllables, spells, postures, and diagrams are the most prominent features; eroticism rises in the literature, justified by Gautama's life in the harem before he became an ascetic; hypnotic yoga-practice, with all the Hindu theories of occult centres of power in the body and in the letters of the alphabet, is recommended; the guru, who is identical with Buddha, must be obeyed without question; and a quasi-pantheistic philosophy, based on the Mādhyamaka system of vacuity but closely related to Vedantism, declares that all men are Buddhas.

Tāranātha, the Tibetan historian, says that Buddhist Tantras were first written in the sixth century, and he may well be right. We can trace these books in the first half of the seventh century, but no evidence is yet available to carry them farther back. The *Tathāgata Guhyaka*, a perfect specimen of the class, must belong to the first half of the seventh century; for it is already quoted by Śāntideva in the middle of that century[1]; and the Tantras which Śubhakṛishṇa, Vajrabodhi, and his pupil Amoghavajra translated into Chinese in the second decade of the eighth century,[2] must belong to the latter half of the seventh at latest, for Vajrabodhi died in his seventy-first year in 772, and his name and

[1] Winternitz, II. i. 262. [2] Nanjio, cols. 443-8.

the name of his pupil contain the word *vajra*, which was a distinctive epithet of the new system. This word, which originally meant thunderbolt and diamond, and which had been commonly used in the Mahāyāna in these senses, is used in Tantrism as an esoteric word for *penis*, the ideas of power and preciousness connected with thunderbolt and diamond being carried over with it.

The new system took shape within the Mahāyāna, and was probably for some considerable time scarcely distinguished from it. Even when its nature had become quite clear, and the system as such was frankly repudiated, a good deal of its poison remained in the Mahāyāna.

The aim of the movement is clearly the acquisition of power. Erotic, gruesome, and magic rites are used, in order to secure the help of the most mighty supernatural beings known to the devotee, and hypnotic practices and mighty spells, which are believed to be potent in a thousand ways by themselves, are regularly employed.

§ 248. From the immense mass of Buddhist Tāntrik works the Chinese canon[1] enables us to sever a large number belonging to this period, but most of them are but names to us. Yet a few of the early Tantras are known. The *Tathāgata Guhyaka*, which must date from about A.D. 600,[2] is evidence that the system had been already formed in all its main features by that time. It contains instructions for esoteric worship, meditation, and yoga-practice, has much to say about magic spells, diagrams, and postures, and in obscenity and superstition it is not exceeded by anything later. It may be compared with the Hindu *Kubjikāmata T.*,[3] which probably belongs to the same century. In some points the *Tathāgata Guhyaka* is an extreme work; for it recommends the use of ordure in worship and in food, a feature which comes from the Kāpālikas. The *Mahāvairochana-abhisambodhi*, translated into Chinese in A.D. 724, and preserved also in the Tibetan canon, is one of the most important

[1] Nanjio, cols. 444-8. [2] See § 247. [3] See § 231.

Tantras. The Buddha is here the whole universe. Vajrabodhi and his disciple Amoghavajra, who introduced Tantrism into China, seem to have given the chief Tantras of their school the epithet Vajraśekhara.[1] These also would afford clear evidence of the character of seventh-century Tantrism in India. I Tsing, the Chinese pilgrim, between 700 and 712, translated the *Suvarṇaprabhāsottamarāja*, a Vijñānavādin work, essentially a fuller and later form of the *Suvarṇaprabhāsa*, but showing many Tāntrik features. The *Pañchakrama*, which probably comes from the ninth century, is an elaborate treatise on Tāntrik Yoga, while the *Mahāmeghasūtra*,[2] which belongs to the sixth century, is a manual of magic.

The *Sragdharā-stotra*, an artistic poem in the kāvya style in honour of the Buddhist goddess Tārā, by Sarvajña-mitra of the ninth century, may serve as an example of the best Tāntrik odes.

§ 249. Dhāraṇīs, i.e. magic spells, form a part of the Mahāyāna system, but they found a still wider field in Tantrism. The power of a dhāraṇī may be obtained by pronouncing it once or many times, by writing it over and over again, or by agitating mechanically the paper on which it is written. In Tibet they are twirled in prayer-wheels, or fastened to trees and poles and fluttered by the wind. They are used in worship, in meditation, in hypnotic practice, and in magic. A few of the more potent were incised in stone and set up in temple or monastery. Syllabic spells such as *kruṁ*, *kriṁ*, *phaṭ* are so much more powerful because they are meaningless. The famous mantra of Avalokiteśvara, *Oṁ maṇi padme huṁ*, 'Oṁ, the jewel in the lotus',[3] is the best example of a phrase spell. There are also numerous spells in the form of short or long sūtras. Perhaps the most famous of all is the *Pratyaṅgirā Dhāraṇī*, which is of very

[1] Nanjio, cols. 444-8.

[2] Nanjio, 186, 187, 188, 244, 970; Winternitz, II. i.

[3] Some scholars believe that *Maṇipadme* is a proper name in the vocative: see Thomas, *JRAS*. 1906, 464; Francke, *JRAS*. 1915, 397.

early origin. It is found in all the canons and was incised in stone in many places. The *Mahāmāyūrī* is a collection of spells against snake-bite dating from the seventh century at latest. Such collections were common.

§ 250. Buddhism was introduced into Tibet in 747 by Padmasambhava, and the monastic order was established two years later. The founder was a Tāntrik scholar, but the Buddhism of Tibet may be most fairly described as the Mahāyāna with Tantrism included. The translation of Buddhist books into Tibetan was begun soon after the introduction of the religion. In the middle of the ninth century the king, Ral-pa-Chan, employed a large number of Indian and Tibetan scholars in the work of translation, and the bulk of the existing canon thus came into existence.

iii. JAINISM.

§ 251. One of the most noteworthy features of Jainism at this time is its almost complete immunity from the poison of Śāktism; and this healthy freedom is still characteristic of the religion. Goddesses are praised in hymns and represented in temples, but do not receive worship, and there is no foul ritual. The Śākta Yoga,[1] with its *nāḍīs* and *chakras* in the human frame, is accepted, but it is not very prominent.

A. *Śvetāmbara Literature.*

§ 252. Gujarāt, and especially Valabhi, remained the chief centre of Śvetāmbara activity throughout this period. The sect was now in possession of a formed canon of sacred books. It had been written and published, and copies had been placed in all the chief monasteries. The best Śvetāmbara scholars thus naturally set to work to make these precious documents intelligible to all who cared to read them. The sect also took a very worthy place in the production of popular literature in Prākṛit. A few scholars distinguished themselves in logic.

[1] For some account of Jain Yoga, see Bhandarkar, *R.* 1883-4, 110; Garbe, *SY.* 39; Guérinot, 469.

Amongst the numerous literary men who were attracted to the court of the Emperor Harsha at Kanouj in the first half of the seventh century we find Mānatuṅga, a Śvetāmbara poet, who is remembered on account of his *stotras*, the *Bhaktāmarastotra* and the *Bhayaharastotra*. These stotras are rather sacred odes to be recited by an individual than hymns for congregational singing. Bappabhaṭṭi, who lived in the latter half of the eighth century and won for Jainism King Ama of Kanouj, the son and successor of Yaśovarman, is the author of another famous ode, the *Sarasvatīstotra*. Mallavādin (early ninth century) wrote on logic.

Haribhadra, one of the very greatest of all Jain authors, lived in the latter half of the ninth century. He was born and brought up a Brāhman, and when he became a Jain was able to use his Brāhman culture to help the religion he had chosen. He is famous as a writer on Jain doctrine and conduct, as one of the most brilliant of commentators, and as a competent writer on logic.[1] He also did something for popular Prākṛit literature. Yet he is best known to-day for his *Shaḍdarśanasamuchchhaya*, a treatise dealing with six philosophical systems, the Buddhist, Nyāya, Sāṅkhya, Jain, Vaiśeshika, and Karma Mīmāṁsā. In case some reader should remark that the Nyāya and the Vaiśeshika are practically one, he adds a brief account of the atheistic and materialistic Lokāyata to make the number up to six. Amongst other works he composed several manuals of Jain teaching.[2]

Another famous Śvetāmbara scholar named Śīlāṅka was a contemporary of Haribhadra. These two, wishing to bring the study of the Jain sacred texts into the open scholarly life of India, wrote fresh commentaries on them in Sanskrit, and also translated large parts of the old expository literature into Sanskrit. Haribhadra was a little more conservative than Śīlāṅka; for here and there in translating he left stories and other well-known sections in the old Prākṛit. Of Śīlāṅka's

[1] Vidyābhūshaṇa, *MSIL.* 48 ff. [2] Guérinot, 71; Peterson, III. 34–5.

great body of work a good deal has been lost, but his commentaries on the *Āchārāṅga* and *Sūtrakṛitāṅga* sūtras, and a portion of his work on the *Āvaśyaka* survive. The commentary on the *Āchārāṅga* was finished in A.D. 863. Of Haribhadra's work there remain expositions of the *Prajñāpanā*, *Jambūdvīpaprajñapti*, *Daśavaikālika*, and *Āvaśyaka*. It is noticeable that these brilliant commentators lived just a little later than Śaṅkara and Vāchaspatimiśra.

§ 253. As we have already seen, the Jains took a worthy part in the production of popular literature in Prākṛit. Most of it is lost beyond recall, but a few masterpieces belonging to this period survive and enable us to form some idea of its range and its value. A Jain anthology, consisting of 704 epigrammatic stanzas, well worthy to stand beside Hāla's famous *Sattasaī*, has been preserved. It is named the *Vajjālaggā*, and it was arranged by Jayavallabha. Its date is probably the eighth or ninth century. Haribhadra also wrote a book in Prākṛit, the *Samaraichchhakahā*, which consists of nine romances. As he says himself in the introduction, he wrote the book for the purpose of giving instruction in Jainism, and chose the romantic method in order to attract readers. The book proved very popular, and was later put into Sanskrit. A pupil of Haribhadra's, Siddharshi by name, is the author of an allegorical work in Prākṛit, written in A.D. 906, the *Upamitibhavaprapañchākathā*. It is a view of human life in which the virtues and the vices figure as persons. Jacobi speaks of it as 'a work of rare originality' and says it is worthy of comparison with the *Pilgrim's Progress*. The work was later abbreviated by two Jain authors.[1]

B. *Digambara Literature.*

§ 254. The chief centre of Digambara activity throughout this period was a section of South India, corresponding to the Mysore and the southern part of the Marāṭhā country. The sect enjoyed the favour of the Chalukya kings, who ruled at

[1] Guérinot, pp. 79, 148, 155.

Bādāmī (Vātāpī) from the middle of the sixth to the middle of the eighth century, and received much support and recognition from their successors, the Rāshṭrakūṭas, whose capital at first was Nasik but afterwards Mānyakheṭa farther south.[1] They had also considerable influence in the Tamil country. The literature of the period is extremely rich and varied. Perhaps its most strikingly notable aspects are Jain dogmatics and ethics, legendary literature in the form of Purāṇas, and logic. It is to the Digambara Jains that we owe the rise and early growth of Kanarese literature: they used it for popular literature.

§ 255. Samantabhadra, who came between Umāsvāti and Kumārila, and thus probably flourished about A.D. 600, wrote the *Gandhahastimahābhāshya*, the chief Digambara commentary on Umāsvāti's *Tattvārthādhigama-sūtra*. The introduction, called *Devāgamastotra* or *Āptamīmāṁsā*, a Sanskrit poem of 115 stanzas, is regarded as the best exposition of the Jain method of dialectic, known as Syādvāda, i.e. the 'may-be' doctrine, and of the Jain conception of a Tīrthakara as an omniscient being. Its influence on Jain logic was very great. It contains a review of contemporary schools of philosophy, including the advaita Vedānta. He is also the author of two famous hymns of praise, and of two books on Jain conduct, one of which, the *Ratnakaraṇḍa-Śrāvakāchāra*, is much used.[2] Akalaṅka, a junior contemporary of Kumārila and a senior contemporary of the Rāshṭrakūṭa king Kṛishṇa I, probably lived about A.D. 770. His most famous works were a sacred ode, the *Akalaṅka-stotra*, and a commentary on the *Āptamīmāṁsā* named *Ashṭaśatī*.

In addition to Samantabhadra's famous work, five commentaries on Umāsvāti ought to be mentioned, the first called *Sarvārthasiddhi* by Pūjyapāda, *c.* A.D. 700, the second, *Tattvārthaṭīkāvyākhyālaṁkāra*, which is believed to be by Akalaṅka, the third an anonymous work named *Rājavārtika* also written in the eighth century, the fourth *Ślokavārtika* by

[1] Smith, *EHI*. 427 ff.

[2] The other is *Yuktānuśāsana*.

Vidyānanda *c.* 800, and the fifth a Kanarese work, which seems to have perished, the *Chūḍāmaṇi* by Śrīvarddhadeva, whose date is unknown.

To the ninth century belongs an anonymous work on Jain philosophy called *Jayadhavalā*, which finds a place in the Digambara Secondary Canon.[1] A brief catechism in Sanskrit, *Praśnottaramālā*, dealing with Jain topics, is said to have been written by Amoghavarsha I, the Rāshṭrakūṭa king who reigned from A. D. 815 to 877 and was a munificent patron of the Digambara Jains.

Three famous logicians, Vidyānanda, Māṇikyanandin, and Prabhāchandra, were contemporaries, and may be dated about A. D. 800.

§ 256. We now turn to popular poetry. Ravikīrti, who lived in the first half of the seventh century and wrote in Kanarese, is the author of the *Jinakathe*. He built a temple and inscribed on it a eulogy of Pulikeśin II, which is our chief source of information about him. He was followed by a number of poets who produced Digambara Jain Purāṇas in Sanskrit. The earliest of these was Ravisheṇa, who is the author of the *Padma Purāṇa* and probably lived in the second half of the seventh century. The *Harivaṁśa P.* was written by Jinasena in A. D. 783. During the reign of Amoghavarsha I (A. D. 815–77), who has been already mentioned, there lived Jinasena,[2] pupil of Vīrasena, and his disciple Guṇabhadra, the chief authors of the Digambara Purāṇas. Jinasena wrote the first forty-three chapters of the *Ādi P.* or *Trishashṭilakshaṇamahāpurāṇasaṅgraha*, and is also the author of the *Pārśvābhyudaya*, an imitation of Kālidāsa's *Meghadūta*.

[1] See § 257.

[2] The current identification of the authors of the *Harivaṁśa P.* and the *Ādi P.* rests on the similarity of name only, and is clearly untenable. Not only is there no mention of the *Harivaṁśa* in the Praśasti of the *Uttara P.*, where it could not have been passed over, if it had been Jinasena's work, but the ascription of both works to the same author is chronologically almost impossible: the *Harivaṁśa* was composed in 783; Jinasena, pupil of Vīrasena, was alive in 837, the date of the *Jayadhavalāṭīkā* (*JBBRAS.* 1894, 226), and his pupil Guṇabhadra completed the *Uttara P.* not long before 898. I owe this note to Prof. Keith.

Guṇabhadra completed the Purāṇa left unfinished by his master, and wrote the *Uttara P.* He is also the author of the *Ātmānuśāsana.*

A detailed analysis of the *Harivaṁśa P.* by R. L. Mitra gives a very clear idea of the contents of Jain Purāṇas. It is an imitation of the Hindu *Harivaṁśa.* It contains numerous legends of the Jain Tīrthakaras, mythical histories of the ancient dynasties which we meet in the *Mahābhārata* and Purāṇas, and amongst them the whole story of Kṛishṇa ; but the heroes are represented as Jains and every event speaks in favour of Jainism. Laws of conduct, religious rites, and other ceremonies also bulk large.

The chief monument of Jain literary activity during this period in Tamil is the *Nāladiyār*, an anthology of four hundred quatrains on moral and religious subjects, compiled probably in the eighth century.

§ 257. The Digambaras, as we have seen, acknowledge that they once possessed a Canon, which has been long lost. In place of it they now recognize a sort of Secondary Canon. It might probably be better described as the framework of a Canon ; for, while there are four classes of works recognized, there seems to be no fixed list of books for each, although there are a few works which always find a place in the framework. It seems probable that this Secondary Canon dates from the end of this period, for it bears the mark of the time, as will be readily recognized. We fit into the framework the books which were already in existence before the end of the period. All these are now recognized as belonging to the Canon.

DIGAMBARA SECONDARY CANON.

1. **Prathamānuyoga** (legend and history): *Padma*, *Harivaṁśa*, *Trishashṭilakshaṇamahā* and *Uttara* Purāṇas.

2. **Karaṇānuyoga** (the universe): *Sūryaprajñapti*, *Chandraprajñapti*, and *Jayadhavalā*.

3. **Dravyānuyoga** (philosophy): *Pravachanasāra*, *Samayasāra*, *Niyamasāra*, *Pañchatthiyasaṁgahasutta*, all by Kuṇḍakuṇḍāchārya; Umāsvāti's *Tattvārthādhigama-sūtra* with the following commentaries, a. Samantabhadra, *Gandhahastimahābhāshya*; b. Pūjyapāda, *Sarvārthasiddhi*; c. Akalaṅka, *Tattvārthaṭīkāvyākhyālaṁkāra*; d. *Rājavārtika*; e. Vidyānanda, *Ślokavārtika*; f. Śrīvarddhadeva, *Chūḍāmaṇi*; and the *Āptamīmāṁsā* of Samantabhadra, with the works on dialectic and logic dependent thereon, a. Akalaṅka's *Ashṭaśatī*; b. Vidyānanda's *Ashṭasāhasrī*, and c. *Āptaparīkshā*; d. Māṇikyanandin's *Parīkshāmukha*, and e. Prabhāchandra's *Prameyakamala-mārtaṇḍa*.

4. **Charaṇānuyoga** (practice): Vaṭṭakera's *Mūlāchāra* and *Trivarṇāchāra* and Samantabhadra's *Ratnakaraṇḍaśrāvakāchāra*.

CHAPTER VI

BHAKTI

A. D. 900 TO 1350.

§ 258. The sects which ruled the development of Hinduism during these centuries received their inspiration in large measure from the enthusiastic bhakti of the wandering singers of the Tamil country described in our previous chapter. Much of the peculiar fervour and attractive power of the *Bhāgavata Purāṇa* comes from the devotion of the Āḷvārs, and the introduction of their lyrics into the Śrī-Vaishṇava temples produced great changes and prepared the way for Rāmānuja. So the hymns of the Śaiva singers inspired Māṇikka Väckakar, while their introduction into the temples gave the community a splendid uplift and made possible the creation of the Tamil Śaiva Siddhānta. Rāmānuja's influence, in turn, told powerfully on all the sects. The two greatest books of the period are his *Śrī-bhāshya* and the *Bhāgavata P.* From them come two streams of bhakti characteristic of the period, the one quiet and meditative, the other explosive and emotional. The latter type of devotion can be felt in the atmosphere everywhere from the thirteenth century onward.

The Muhammadan conquest of North India (1193–1203) was an immeasurable disaster to Hinduism as well as to the Hindu people, and it gave Buddhism its death-wound.

i. HINDUISM.

A. *The Philosophies.*

a. *The Karma Mīmāṁsā.*

§ 259. The history of the Mīmāṁsā school during these centuries seems to be a blank until quite the end of the period. Then, probably about A. D. 1300, flourished Pārthasārathi

Miśra,[1] who wrote, among a number of other works on the Karma Mīmāṁsā, the *Śāstra-dīpikā*, which, on account of its popular modern style, soon found readers, and has, since then, been more studied than the ancient manuals. He faithfully follows Kumārila.

But, if we know little about the school itself during the period, we hear a good deal about the system outside. It is very prominent in the *Prabodhachandrodaya*,[2] a drama which was produced about A. D. 1065 and is described below.[3] In the case of most of the theistic sects which rose to the dignity of a presentation of the Vedānta in accord with their own convictions, we find that they held the Karma Mīmāṁsā as well as the Vedānta, and taught that *karma*, action, as well as *jñāna*, knowledge, was necessary for the winning of release.[4] This is true of the Bhāgavatas, Śrī-Vaishṇavas, Mādhvas, and Vishṇusvāmīs, and possibly of others.

b. *The Vedānta.*

§ 260. Quite at the beginning of our period there appears a noteworthy bhāshya on the *Vedānta-sūtras* by a scholar named Bhāskarāchārya, and therefore often called the *Bhāskara-bhāshya*.[5] Its interest lies in this that its standpoint is, not advaita, but bhedābheda ; yet it is not one of the modern sectarian commentaries but definitely of the same type as the lost Vedānta work of Āśmarathya mentioned in the *Sūtras*.[6] Bhāskara does not name Śaṅkara, yet he attacks him all through the commentary, and Bhāskara, in turn, is assailed by Udayana in the *Kusumāñjali*. As Udayana's date is about A.D. 980, Bhāskara must have written between 850 and 980, and

[1] His date is unknown, but as the earliest known reference to the work is in Mādhava's *Nyāyamālāvistara* (§ 338), the above conjecture is not likely to be far from the truth. See Rāmamiśra Śāstrī, *Mīmāṁsā-śloka-vārtika*, Intro., Benares, 1898.

[2] Taylor's *Tr.*, pp. 13, 14, 15, 49, 61, 78 f.

[3] § 270.

[4] See § 285.

[5] Thus Thibaut is mistaken in thinking that Rāmānuja's *Śrībhāshya* is the earliest surviving bhāshya after Śaṅkara.

[6] See *SBE*. XXXIV. xix.

thus probably at some point near the beginning of the period.[1] He attacks the Pāñcharātra Vaishṇavas also. Yādava Prakāśa of Conjeeveram wrote a fresh advaita bhāshya about A.D. 1050, but, at a later date, was won over to Vaishṇavism by his own pupil Rāmānuja. It is not known whether the *Yādava-bhāshya* survives or not. But the main history of the school of the Vedānta during these centuries seems to consist in the continuous study of Śaṅkara's *Bhāshya* with the help of Vāchaspati's *Bhāmatī*. This belief is confirmed by the most outstanding advaita work of the period, the *Vedānta-kalpataru*, which was written by Amalānanda just before A.D. 1260: it is an ample exposition of the *Bhāmatī*.

Two popular advaita works might quite naturally find mention here, the *Prabodhachandrodaya* and the *Yoga-Vasishṭha-Ramāyaṇa*; yet as their connexions are more with householders than sannyāsīs, they are dealt with elsewhere.[2]

§ 261. But the most startling feature of the progress of the Vedānta during the period is the rise of the sectarian bhāshyas. The movement seems to have been created by a single man, Rāmānuja; for the great success of his *Śrī-bhāshya* stirred so much emulation that every sect was impelled to endeavour to produce a bhāshya that would justify its theology. As each of these theistic bhāshyas will be discussed in connexion with the sect which created it, there is no need to deal with them at length here. The dates of a few of them are still uncertain, yet we may with safety conclude that the following appeared during the period: Rāmānuja's *Śrī-bhāshya*, Madhva's *Sūtra-bhāshya*, Vishṇusvāmī's *Brahma-sūtra-bhāshya*, and Śrīnivāsa's *Vedānta-Kaustubha*.[3]

The *Kusumāñjali* of Udayana, which is discussed under the Nyāya philosophy,[4] may be mentioned here as further evidence of the great vogue of theism at this stage of Hindu history. Here also we may mention an extraordinary work, which,

[1] See the Bhūmikā to Vindhyeśvarī Prasād's edition of the *Bhāshya*.
[2] See § 270.
[3] See the table below, § 340.
[4] See § 265.

though it shows a sceptical and destructive spirit, yet maintains the chief positions of the advaita Vedānta, the *Khaṇḍana-khaṇḍakhādya*, i. e. *The Sweets of Refutation*,[1] by Śrīharsha, the date of which is the latter half of the twelfth century.

The chief Upanishad commentator during the period was Śaṅkarānanda, the guru of Mādhava, the advaita Vedantist. He must have flourished in the first half of the fourteenth century. Madhva, the founder of the Mādhva sect, left dvaita commentaries on ten of the chief Upanishads.

c. *The Śāṅkhya.*

§ 262. During these centuries no noticeable manual of the Śāṅkhya philosophy appeared, and the system seems to have undergone very little modification. It is described by Alberuni, the Muhammadan scholar, in his work on India dating from A.D. 1030.

d. *The Yoga.*

§ 263. The Yoga system remained almost stationary also. The only outstanding work belonging to the period is the *Rājamārtaṇḍa*, a commentary on the *Yoga-sūtra*, ascribed to Bhoja, King of Dhārā (1018–60). It is clear and easy but of no great value. Alberuni deals with the Yoga as well as the Śāṅkhya, and Garbe is inclined to believe that he used the *Rājamārtaṇḍa*. If that be so, it must have been written during the earliest years of the king's reign.

The new Yoga of Gorakshanātha, which is described below,[2] found no entrance into the school of Patañjali.

e. *The Vaiśeshika.*

§ 264. In the tenth century two very noteworthy thinkers wrote on the Vaiśeshika system. Udayana, a writer of great clearness and force, left two works on the system. The first is the *Kiraṇāvalī*, or 'Necklace of Rays', which is a commentary on Praśastapāda's *Bhāshya*. The other work, written

[1] See also § 265.

[2] § 302.

in A.D. 984, is called the *Lakshaṇāvalī*, or 'Necklace of Definitions' of Vaiśeshika terms. Śrīdhara, the second writer, who belonged to the south-west of Bengal, is the author of a commentary on Praśastapāda called the *Nyāya-Kandalī*, which has been used as an authoritative manual ever since it was written in A.D. 991.

f. *The Nyāya.*

§ 265. Udayana wrote also on the Nyāya system. His work, which is an exposition of Vāchaspati's *Ṭīkā*, is called the *Nyāya-vārtika-tātparya-pariśuddhi*. But Udayana is most famous for his *Kusumāñjali*, i.e. 'Handfuls of Flowers', a metrical treatise in seventy-two memorial couplets with a paraphrase in prose, the purpose of which is to prove the existence of God. The fact that the work is frequently called the *Nyāya Kusumāñjali*, coupled with the settled theistic teaching of the school, makes it natural we should refer to it here. Cowell, in his text and translation,[1] bespeaks a hearing for the work because,

> though obscure and technical, it professes to grapple, from a Hindu standing-point, with the world-old problem, how the existence of the Supreme Being is to be proved; and perhaps those who are interested in the history of philosophy may turn over some of the pages with curiosity, especially when they occasionally recognize old familiar arguments and objections in their quaint Oriental disguise.

From the eleventh century onwards the Nyāya and Vaiśeshika form practically one combined school. The syncretism commences with Śivāditya's *Sapta-padārtha-nirūpaṇa*,[2] which probably belongs to the eleventh century. It is continued in a twelfth-century work which has been widely used, the *Nyāya Chintāmaṇi* of Gaṅgeśa, in the *Tarka-bhāshā* of Keśava of the thirteenth century, and in Śaṅkara Miśra's *Vaiśeshika-Sūtropaskāra*, written in the fifteenth century. This syncretistic school has been ably described by Suali.[3]

[1] P. v. [2] See Keith on Suali, *JRAS.* 1914, 1089.
[3] *Introduzione allo Studio della Filosofia Indiana.*

From the point of view of logic and dialectic, great interest attaches to that section of the *Khaṇḍanakhaṇḍakhādya*[1] which criticizes logic:

> The object of Harsha is to prove that the logicians with their assumption of the reality of existence were guilty of a complete blunder, and his mode of doing so is the simple one of taking each of the definitions set up by the Nyāya school and proving it to be untenable.[2]

§ 266. During the tenth and eleventh centuries logic was cultivated by Buddhists at Vikramaśīla, but the last name mentioned by Vidyābhūshaṇa is Śaṅkarānanda,[3] whose date is about A.D. 1050. Among the Jains logic was continuously studied, and logical works were produced throughout the period. Devasūri[4] of the twelfth century was the greatest of their writers on logic, but there were many others.

§ 267. Mādhava's *Sarvadarśanasaṅgraha* may be recommended to the student as a most helpful outline of the chief systems current in India towards the end of the period, though its date falls within the limit of the next period.[5]

B. *The Purāṇas.*

§ 268. The emergence of the *Bhāgavata P.* is a fact of signal importance, but it is discussed at another point.[6] If there was already a Canon of eighteen Purāṇas in the ninth century, the rise of the *Bhāgavata* to a position of such authority as to require recognition in the Canon would create a difficulty. The confusion which the lists show to-day may be the direct result of that circumstance.[7]

In the present state of Puranic study, it is very hard to date individual documents occurring in Purāṇas, but the evidence

[1] See § 261. [2] Keith, *JRAS.* 1916, 377.
[3] *MSIL.* 142. [4] Ib. 38. [5] See § 345. [6] See § 272.
[7] If the old Canon stood as follows:—Brahma, Padma, Vishṇu, Vāyu, Śiva, Nārada, Mārkaṇḍeya, Agni, Bhavishya, Brahmavaivārta, Liṅga, Varāha, Skanda, Vāmana, Kūrma, Matsya, Garuḍa, Brahmāṇḍa, the substitution of the *Bhāgavata* for the *Śiva*, followed by various attempts to find a place for the expelled Purāṇa, would account for all the phenomena.

available suggests that the following may belong to the period:

Vaishṇava: *Narasiṁha Upapurāṇa*; part of the Pātāla Khaṇḍa of the *Padma P.*, which praises the *Bhāgavata*; the Uttara Khaṇḍa, which is Śrī-Vaishṇava.

Śaiva: Vāyavīya S. of the *Śiva P.*

Śākta: *Devī Bhāgavata Upapurāṇa.*

Saura: *Brahma P.* xxi–xxviii.

Gāṇapatya: *Gaṇeśa Upapurāṇa.*

C. *Smārta Literature.*

§ 269. The most noticeable piece of Vedic literature produced during this period is Bhaṭṭa Bhāskara Miśra's[1] commentaries on the *Taittirīya Saṁhitā*, *Āraṇyaka*, and *Upanishad* of the *Black Yajus*. He lived in the Telugu country, belonged to the Ātreya Śākhā of the Taittirīya school, and wrote his commentary on the Saṁhitā in A.D. 1188.[2]

Hemādri, a learned Brāhman, held the office of chief minister at the Yādava court in the Marāṭhā country under two kings towards the end of the thirteenth century, and was clearly a man of much influence. He wrote an encyclopaedia of orthodox Hindu observances, the *Chaturvargachintāmaṇi*, a work of large importance to Smārtas.

§ 270. Several pieces of popular literature written from the standpoint of the advaita Vedānta during the period were probably meant for Smārta householders rather than for sannyāsīs, and ought therefore to be mentioned here.

At the court of Kīrtivarman, the Chandel king of Jejākabhukti, about the year 1065 and possibly in the city of

[1] To be carefully distinguished from Bhāskarāchārya who wrote the *Bhāskara Bhāshya*, above, § 260.

[2] The Śloka in the *Bhāshya* on the *Saṁhitā* in the Mysore Text reads *Nishpāvāke śake*, 1410 in the Śaka era, i.e. 1488–9. But the commentary is unquestionably earlier than Sāyaṇa. We must therefore suppose that the śloka ought to be read *nishpāpāke śake*, 1110 Śāka, i.e. A.D. 1188–9. The confusion of *p* and *v* in a South Indian MS. is a very likely error. I owe this note to Prof. Keith. Cf. also Śeshagiri Rao, *SSTM.* 1893–4, p. 3.

Khajuraho, there was produced a Sanskrit drama called *Prabodhachandrodaya*, i.e. The Moonrise of Wisdom. The author was a sannyāsī named Kṛishṇamiśra. The play is an allegory of the deliverance of the human spirit from the temptations and delusions of the world. Vishṇu-bhakti stirs up Discrimination, and, using the Upanishads, Faith, Good Sense, and their numerous allies, inflicts a signal defeat on Delusion, Love, Greed, and their many attendants. The rise (*udaya*) of Wisdom (*prabodha*) naturally follows, and the human spirit realizes its own absolute identity with God, renounces Action, and adopts dispassionate Asceticism as the only right rule of life. The number of abstract conceptions which take part as persons in the play make it rather hard to follow, but it contains abundance of life and movement also. Apart from the fact that Vishṇu-bhakti plays a leading part, there is no aggressive Vaishṇavism in the play. The supreme Brahman is definitely called Vishṇu, and several times his incarnations are referred to, especially Kṛishṇa, but it goes no further. There are no references to Vaishṇava literature, and Lakshmī is mentioned only once. The philosophy is pure Advaitism. The scenes in which followers of Buddhism, Jainism, Materialism, the Karma Mīmāṁsā, the Sāṅkhya, Yoga, and Nyāya philosophies and the Kāpālika form of Śaivism are represented in discussion with one another are amongst the most vivid and interesting in the play. In the great battle the Buddhists, the Jains, and the materialist Lokāyatas, or Chārvākas, range themselves with Kāma and the Vices under their general, Moha, while Vaishṇavas, Śaivas, and Sauras gather round the goddess Sarasvatī, and are aided by all the six orthodox philosophies and by Grammar and the Virtues to inflict a signal defeat on the atheist host. When the question is raised how these ever-hostile Hindu disputants brought themselves to any common action, a sufficient reason is found in hostility to the common foe, and we are told that wise men perceive that the orthodox sects and philosophies are only seemingly opposed to each other, that in truth they all celebrate the one Reality. So far as the writer knows, this is the first time the idea of the inner harmony of the Hindu systems finds expression in Hindu literature.

The *Yoga-Vāsishṭha-Rāmāyaṇa* is one of many Sanskrit poems written in the thirteenth and fourteenth centuries to popularize a philosophy or the theology of a sect. It is scarcely parallel with the *Adhyātma Rāmāyaṇa*; for the story of Rāma here serves merely as a dramatic setting for the exposition of the Vedānta. It is a very long and diffuse poem, running to some 32,000 stanzas. The system taught is the advaita Vedānta, but there already appears in it that admixture of Sāṅkhya ideas which is still more prominent in Mādhava and Vijñāna Bhikshu. The value of yoga is also emphasized. It may date from about A.D. 1300, or earlier.

The Right-hand movement among Śāktas, which is described below,[1] can be traced from the period, and is probably older. As all its connexions are with Vedic Hinduism, it ought to be mentioned here as affecting the religious practice of many Smārtas.

D. *Vaishṇava Literature.*

a. *General.*

§ 271. The only type of general Vaishṇava literature belonging to this period consists of translations or adaptations of the Epics. It is important to realize that vernacular versions of ancient religious books are usually literary rather than religious in their influence. The *Mahābhārata* appeared in Tamil in the tenth century and in Telugu in the eleventh, while the *Rāmāyaṇa* was rendered in Telugu about 1100 and in Tamil in the twelfth century. Jain adaptations of the two Epics were written in Kanarese verse, the *Mahābhārata* in the tenth, the *Rāmāyaṇa* in the eleventh. But all the greatest Vaishṇava literature was produced by the Sects.

[1] § 317.

b. *Bhāgavata Literature.*

1. *The Bhāgavata Purāṇa.*

§ 272. About the beginning of this period the *Bhāgavata P.* seems to have been born from the Bhāgavata community; and during the following centuries a number of new sects sprang from the influence of the Purāṇa. Under this heading we therefore comprehend all the work produced both by the parent body and the dependent sects. Of the two dominating events of this period the earlier is the appearance and the influence of this great Purāṇa. No theory of its date and origin yet advanced has been accepted by scholars as satisfactory. Can sufficient fresh evidence now be produced to bring the problem nearer solution?

§ 273. The work has several characteristic features. While the *Harivaṁśa* and the *Vishṇu P.* each gives some account of Kṛishṇa's youth spent among the gopās and gopīs of Vṛindāvana and its neighbourhood, they deal with the whole life of Kṛishṇa. The *Bhāgavata* scarcely refers to his later life, but spends all its strength over his boyhood and youth. Secondly, the gopīs play a very large part in the work. Rādhā does not appear: she is a later creation. Yet there is a favourite among the gopīs who wanders alone with Kṛishṇa; and the other gopīs remark that she must surely have worshipped Kṛishṇa in a former life with more devotion than the rest, and in that way must have won her favoured position.

The *Bhāgavata* is really a great work. What distinguishes it from all earlier literature is its new theory of *bhakti*; and therein lies its true greatness. Some of its utterances on this subject are worthy of a place in the best literature of mysticism and devotion. A careful study of those passages will convince the student that they are expressions of a living religious experience.[1] We may with absolute certainty conclude that the work arose in some centre where there was a group of

[1] This element may be most conveniently studied in the *Bhaktiratnāvalī*, a collection of bhakti passages from the *Bhāgavata* made by a Mādhva ascetic named Vishṇu Purī.

Vaishṇava ascetics who lived a life of fervent devotion, and that the writer's religious experience was rooted there. In this rich religious element lies the chief source of the power of the *Bhāgavata*. Hence the hold it has had on some of the best Vaishṇava communities and on many of the noble minds of India.

Bhakti in this work is a surging emotion which chokes the speech, makes the tears flow and the hair thrill with pleasureable excitement, and often leads to hysterical laughing and weeping by turns, to sudden fainting fits and to long trances of unconsciousness. We are told that it is produced by gazing at the images of Kṛishṇa, singing his praises, remembering him in meditation, keeping company with his devotees, touching their bodies, serving them lovingly, hearing them tell the mighty deeds of Kṛishṇa, and talking with them about his glory and his love. All this rouses the passionate bhakti which will lead to self-consecration to Kṛishṇa and life-long devotion to his service. Such devotion leads speedily to release. Thus the whole theory and practice of bhakti in this purāṇa is very different from the bhakti of the *Bhagavadgītā* and of Rāmānuja.

But we must also recognize in the *Bhāgavata* the presence of another fresh element of a very different character, a long series of highly erotic passages which go far beyond anything the *Vishṇu P.* and the *Harivaṁśa* contain, and which seem to consort ill with the high devotion to the Lord and the service of his saints which we have been considering. In these passages Kṛishṇa's dalliance with the gopīs is described in sensuous and glowing poetry which captivates the Hindu heart. The tenth book, which contains them, has been translated into all the chief languages of India. Yet the author expects these highly wrought narratives of the passions of the gopīs to stimulate bhakti. The utter self-abandonment of their love for Kṛishṇa has come to be regarded as a symbol of spiritual devotion. Meditation on these scenes is expected to produce that passionate bhakti which is regarded as the highest religious experience. This, the leading religious idea of the *Bhāgavata*, lies at the foundation of the whole series of sects which sprang from it.

Another noticeable feature of the Purāṇa is this, that its philosophic teaching stands nearer to Śaṅkara's system than to the theistic Sāṅkhya which dominates earlier Puranic works.

§ 274. All scholars agree that it is the latest of the eighteen Purāṇas. Old material has been incorporated into it, but as a work it is the latest of all. In the fourth chapter of the first book of the Purāṇa itself there is a passage which implies that it was composed last of all the eighteen; and there is a late section in the *Padma P.* which states that Vyāsa promulgated the *Bhāgavata* last of all as the extracted essence of all the rest.

Hindu estimates of the age of the work vary to an extraordinary extent, some assigning it to the earliest times, others attributing it to Vopadeva, a well-known scholar of the second half of the thirteenth century. Even in the time of Śrīdhara Svāmī, the author of the most famous commentary on it, who probably lived about A.D. 1400, there were Hindus who said it had been written by Vopadeva, a fact which seems to imply that scholarly Hindus of those days suspected that it was a late production. All European scholars have spoken of it as a late work, but, while Colebrooke, Burnouf, and Wilson accept the suggestion that it is the work of Vopadeva, students to-day are inclined to give it a higher date. And the truth is that it is quite impossible to believe that Vopadeva was the author; for Madhva, who regarded it as fully inspired and used it in the creation of his sect, lived at least fifty years earlier than Vopadeva. Vopadeva's name became associated with the Purāṇa because he wrote several books on it. But the belief in its inspiration implies its existence for some considerable time before the days of Madhva's activity; and, fortunately, we possess another piece of evidence which proves clearly that it was already recognized as an authoritative work some two centuries before Madhva wrote. Alberuni, in his work on India, which was completed in A.D. 1030, gives us the list of Purāṇas as it was in the *Vishṇu P.* in his day, and it is precisely the same as the list in our MSS. of to-day. Thus it is absolutely clear that by 1030 the *Bhāgavata* had not only been written but had already gained such acceptance as to have won its present recognized place as the fifth of the Purāṇas. We must, then, acknowledge that it can scarcely have been written later than, say, A.D. 900.

§ 275. Can we discern where it was written? There is a passage in the eleventh book[1] which suggests that it may have been in the Tamil country. The passage runs thus in English:

> Men born in the Kṛita, Tretā, Dvāpara ages wished to take birth in the Kali age, because they knew that in this age would be born great souls devoted to Nārāyaṇa. These souls would be thinly scattered in various places; but in the Drāviḍa land they would be found in some numbers, living by the side of such rivers as the Tāmraparṇī, Kṛitamālā, Payaśvinī, Kāverī the holy.

Then in the *Bhāgavata Māhātmya*, a late appendix to the *Bhāgavata*, there is an episode[2] which bears on the question, but which cannot be understood unless we distinguish carefully between ordinary bhakti and the bhakti of the *Bhāgavata P.* In this episode bhakti, incarnate as a young woman, says, 'I was born in Drāviḍa'. Now to say that the bhakti of the *Śvetāśvatara Upanishad*, *the Gītā*, and the early Purāṇas was born in Drāviḍa would be absurd; but if we realize that, in this appendix to the *Bhāgavata*, bhakti necessarily means the passionate and many-sided devotion of the great Purāṇa, there is no difficulty, and it becomes clear that the work asserts that this bhakti arose in Tamil-land. Now, it was in the Tamil country, by the side of the rivers just mentioned, that those Vaishṇava poet-singers who are known as Āḷvārs composed their hymns and went from shrine to shrine, singing and dancing in fervent devotion before images of Vishṇu and

[1] XI. v. 38–40. It is quoted in another connexion by Govindāchārya, *JRAS.* 1911, 949.
[2] I. 27. Grierson, *JRAS.* 1911, 800.

his Avatāras. Their period is the seventh, eighth, and ninth centuries. No other group of early Vaishṇavas exhibit so much excitement in their bhakti. Further, many of the temples they frequented were dedicated to both Vishṇu and Śiva.[1] We may thus be certain that the ministrants of those temples were Bhāgavatas, and that a considerable section of the people belonged to that community. Now, if in the Tamil-country there was a group of Bhāgavata ascetics who felt the same devotion as the Āḷvārs and expressed it in similar fashion, we should have precisely the 'great souls devoted to Nārāyaṇa' mentioned in the *Bhāgavata*, and in such circumstances the bhakti referred to in the *Bhāgavata Māhātmya* would be born.

§ 276. It thus seems natural to conjecture that the *Bhāgavata* was written about A.D. 900, in the Tamil country, in some community of ascetics belonging to the Bhāgavata sect who felt and gave expression to the bhakti characteristic of the work. If it arose in such a centre, the advaita philosophy would inevitably be one of its characteristics, and it would naturally receive the name *Bhāgavata*.

2. *The Bhāgavatas.*

§ 277. We now turn to the sects. If the Purāṇa arose in the way we suggest, one would expect that it would gradually find acceptance among Bhāgavatas all over the country; and that clearly happened. Whether in the Tamil, Telugu, Kanarese, or Marāṭhā districts, the *Bhāgavata P.* is the chief scripture of the Bhāgavatas.

The *Nārada-bhakti-sūtra* and the *Śāṇḍilya-bhakti-sūtra* are brief compendiums of the bhakti system, probably meant to be committed to memory by ascetics. Both are clearly dependent on the *Bhāgavata P.*, and neither mentions Rādhā. The *Nārada* is simple both in language and thought, and is practical in aim; the *Śāṇḍilya* is sūtra-like and philosophic, its standpoint being *bhedābheda*. The Bhāgavatas of the south

[1] Kṛishṇa Śāstrī, *SII.* 72.

use only the *Nārada*. It is probable that it was produced among the Bhāgavatas at quite an early date. The connexions of the *Śāṇḍilya-sūtra*, which has been much used in the north, are still obscure. It may be a Nimbārkite document.

It seems clear that the *Vāsudeva* and *Gopīchandana* Upanishads[1] are Bhāgavata books; for the Ūrddhvapuṇḍra made with a single line of creamy *gopīchandana*, which these Upanishads praise, is the Bhāgavata sect-mark. As Nārāyaṇa wrote commentaries on them, they belong to this period.

Towards the end of the thirteenth century, Vopadeva, a famous grammarian belonging to the Marāṭhā country, wrote several works on the *Bhāgavata P.*, the chief of which were the *Harilīlā*, which is an abstract of the Purāṇa, and the *Muktāphala*, which sums up its teaching. His name thus became associated with the Purāṇa, and the myth about its authorship arose.

3. *The Bhaktas of the Marāṭhā country.*

§ 278. The Vaishṇavas of the Marāṭhā country are Bhāgavatas, but it is not known when the *Bhāgavata P.* began to be used by them. In the thirteenth century the movement became a popular one, and all their literature is in the vernacular; so that there are marked differences between them and the Bhāgavatas of the Tamil and Kanarese districts. The unbroken tradition of the country is that the Bhakti movement began with a poet named Jñāneśvara, who is popularly called Dnyāndev or Dnyānobā. According to another tradition, which appears in the *Bhakta Mālā*, he was a disciple of Vishṇusvāmī.

Jñāneśvara is the author of a work in Marāṭhī verse on the *Bhagavadgītā* called the *Jñāneśvarī*, which runs to 10,000 couplets. Its date is A.D. 1290. The work is advaitist in tone, but it also lays great stress on yoga, and the author

[1] Jacob, *EAU.* 5 ff.

says he is the disciple of Nivṛittināth, the disciple of Gaṇīnāth, the disciple of Gorakhnāth.[1] He is also the author of the *Haripāṭh*, a collection of 28 *abhangs*, or hymns. His poetry decidedly shows the influence of the *Bhāgavata*, and his note is that of an enthusiastic bhakta. Tradition makes him the greatest of a group of saints. His poems are philosophical in tone and full of reflective thought, and have had a great and lasting influence on the educated classes. There need be no doubt that he was the coryphaeus of the whole bhakti movement of the Marāṭhā country. It is not at all unlikely that he should have also come under the personal influence of Vishṇusvāmī, who was probably his senior by some thirty or forty years at most.[2] That would account for the fact that, while scholarly Marāṭhā Bhāgavatas still use the old Bhāgavata mantra, *Oṁ namo Bhagavate Vāsudevāya*, the mantra in common use is *Rāma-Kṛishṇa Hari*, which is the Vishṇusvāmī Mantra.[3] It ought to be noticed, however, that Jñāneśvara and the other Marāṭhā bhaktas do not, like Vishṇusvāmī, recognize Rādhā. He is also the author of the *Amṛitānubhava*, an advaita Śaiva philosophical work in Marāṭhī verse. He was thus a true Bhāgavata, honouring Śiva as well as Vishṇu, and following Śaṅkara in philosophy.

4. *The Mādhvas.*

§ 279. The first sect directly founded on the *Bhāgavata P.* seems to have been the Mādhvas. They are simply an offshoot from the Bhāgavatas, the sole reason for the schism being the detestation in which the founder held Śaṅkara's Vedānta. Madhva (1199–1278),[4] the founder, was born at Udipi in South Kanara, and organized his sect in the early decades of the thirteenth century. While still quite young, he became a sannyāsī, and received a training in Śaṅkara's system. But in addition to the regular Vedānta treatises, he gave much time to the *Aitareya U.*, the *Mahābhārata*, and

[1] This statement occurs in his *Amṛitānubhava*. [2] See below, § 281.
[3] See § 281. [4] Bhandarkar, *VS.* 58 f.; Grierson, *ERE.* VIII. 232.

the *Bhāgavata P.* This last work clearly dominated his religious life. Before his period of training was over, he broke away from Śaṅkara. Soon after, he began public discussion, and gradually formed a system for himself, based in the main on the *Bhāgavata P.* He was successful in gathering a community of some size and in winning a number of notable converts. The theology which he taught is in many points like Rāmānuja's; but the philosophy is frankly dualistic. He distinguishes very sharply between man and God, and thus stands further away from Śaṅkara than any other exponent of the *Vedānta-sūtras*, except perhaps Vishṇusvāmī. Apart from the theology, his system is very similar to that of the Bhāgavata sect. The centre of the religion is the adoration of Kṛishṇa by bhakti, as taught in the *Bhāgavata*, without recognition of Rādhā; but all the other avatāras are reverenced. Śiva also is worshippped, and the five Gods are recognized.

Madhva's chief works are his *Bhāshya* and *Anuvyākhyāna*, both on the *Vedānta-sūtras.* The *Bhāshya* is a comparatively short prose treatise, which seeks to show by an array of proof-texts that Madhva's explanation of the *Sūtras* is the only right one. The texts are drawn from (*a*) the *Ṛigveda*, (*b*) the Upanishads and the *Gītā*, (*c*) the Purāṇas, the Vaishṇava Saṁhitās, and other late works. The book is thus of very little interest except as an account of the teaching of the sect.[1] His exposition of the *Bhāgavata*, the *Bhāgavata-tātparya-nirṇaya*, and a companion volume on the *Mahābhārata* are also works of considerable importance for the sect. He wrote commentaries on ten Upanishads.

The followers of Śaṅkarāchārya opposed and persecuted Madhva with a good deal of bitterness; so that ever since

[1] It also gives us many quotations from the Purāṇas and Saṁhitās which ought to be useful as revealing in part the condition of these texts in his time. The Saṁhitās quoted are the *Bhāgavata*, *Varāha*, *Nārāyaṇa*, *Purushottama*, *Parama*, *Māyāvaibhava*, which occur in Schrader's list, *IPAS.* 6 ff.: and the *Vyoma*, *Bṛihat*, and *Mahā* besides. The *Bṛihat* is quoted by Mādhava in his exposition of Mādhvism: *SDS.* v.

those days there has been little love lost between the two groups. Madhva believed himself to be an incarnation of Vāyu, and, probably as a result of Śaṅkarite persecution, he taught that Śaṅkara was a reincarnation of an obscure demon named Maṇimat who appears in the *Mahābhārata*.[1]

About half a century after Madhva's death, Jayatīrtha was the head of the sect. His commentaries on the founder's most important works are amongst the chief books of the sect.

5. *Rādhā*.

§ 280. Neither the Bhāgavatas, nor the Mādhvas recognize Rādhā: they do not go beyond what is contained in the *Bhāgavata*. But all the later sects who depend on the great Purāṇa do recognize Rādhā. We must therefore ask whence her story came.

We have seen above that in the *Bhāgavata P.* there is a gopī whom Kṛishṇa favours so much as to wander with her alone, and that the rest of the gopīs surmise that she must have worshipped Kṛishṇa with peculiar devotion in a previous life to have thus won his special favour. This seems to be the source whence Rādhā arose, and it is probable that the name Rādhā comes from the root *rādh* in the sense of conciliating, pleasing. She is thus the pleasing one. In what book she first appeared is not yet known, but an Indian scholar[2] suggests to me that it may have been the *Gopālatāpanī-Upanishad*, which contains an account of Rādhā, and is reverenced by all Rādhā-worshipping sects.

Two early sects recognize Rādhā, the Vishṇusvāmīs and the Nimbārkas, but the chronology and the relationships are

[1] Śaṅkara's demon-origin is mentioned in Madhva's exposition of the *Mahābhārata*. After his death, Paṇḍit Nārāyaṇa, the son of one of his disciples, published two Sanskrit works, the *Maṇimañjarī* and the *Madhvavijaya*, in which the theory of the two incarnations is fully set forth. See Grierson, *ERE.*, VIII. 232. It is possible that the Śaṅkaravijayas were written as a counterblast to these Mādhva works. A long polemic against Mādhvism has also been interpolated into the *Saura Purāṇa*.

[2] Paṇḍita Rādhā Charaṇa Gosvāmī of Brindāban.

still obscure. Tradition sets the leaders in the following order, Madhva, Vishṇusvāmī, Nimbārka; and that order seems to fit in with their teaching; for Madhva does not recognize Rādhā at all, and Vishṇusvāmī's theology is very similar to Madhva's, while Nimbārka strikes out quite a new line for himself. Yet the seemingly natural may not be the historical order. There is one historical fact which necessarily suggests a doubt: it is quite clear that Rādhā was worshipped and praised in song in North India before Madhva's day; for Jayadeva's *Gītāgovinda* belongs to the end of the twelfth century. There is a tradition in Bengal that Jayadeva was a Nimbarkite; but in the *Gītāgovinda* Rādhā is the mistress, not the consort, of Kṛishṇa, as she is in Nimbārka's theology.[1] Sufficient evidence does not seem to be available to settle the question, but we may conjecture that the myth of Rādhā grew up quite spontaneously at Brindāban on the basis of the narrative of the *Bhāgavata P.*, and that her worship was organized there, perhaps about A.D. 1100, and thence spread to Bengal and elsewhere. If that is the history, Jayadeva's poetry, on the one hand, and the rise of the two sects, on the other, are easily explainable; and it is possible that Nimbārka may have developed his Rādhā-theology at Brindāban while Vishṇusvāmī was forming his simpler system in the south.

6. *The Vishṇusvāmīs.*

§ 281. Of Vishṇusvāmī very little is known, but it is believed that he belonged to the South. His system is precisely like the Mādhva system, except that Rādhā is acknowledged. She is simply Kṛishṇa's favourite among the gopīs, his mistress. Vishṇusvāmī, like Madhva, is a dualist, quite as pronounced as Madhva, if not more so. Tradition states that he wrote commentaries on the *Gītā*, the *Vedānta-sūtras*, and the *Bhāgavata P.* His *Bhāgavata-bhāshya* is referred to by

[1] He lived under Laksmaṇa Sena, King of Bengal, who reigned c. 1170–1200 (Smith, *EHI.* 403); and some of his verses appear in the *Saduktikarṇāmṛita*, an anthology by Śrīdhara Dāsa, which dates apparently from A.D. 1205. The chronology is also opposed to his being a Nimbarkite.

Śrīdhara Svāmin in his comment on *Bhāgavata P.* I. 7; and it is said that the work survives, but it has not been seen by any scholar. In Mādhava's *Sarvadarśanasaṅgraha* there is a reference to Vishṇusvāmī's devoted adherent, Śrīkānta Miśra,[1] and to a work by him named *Sākāra-siddhi*, the teaching of which is clearly dualist. The *Bhakta-mālā* says that Vishṇusvāmī was also the teacher of Jñāneśvara, the Marāṭhā bhakta; and the story is probably true.[2] In any case it is clear that the sect was widespread and popular for centuries.[3] The sectarian mantras are said to be *Oṁ Rāma-Kṛishṇāya namaḥ*, and *Oṁ Rāma-Kṛishṇa Hari.* The Vishṇusvāmīs and all other Rādhā-worshipping sects use the *Gopālatāpanīya U.* and the *Gopālasahasranāma.*

The Bhāgavatas, the Mādhvas and the Vishṇusvāmīs, like Rāmānuja,[4] uphold the *Samuchchhaya* doctrine; i.e. they teach that, in seeking release, men should perform their full religious duty as Hindus as well as seek the knowledge of Brahman, while Śaṅkara finds release in knowledge alone.

7. *The Nimbārkas.*

§ 282. Nimbārka was a scholarly Bhāgavata from the Telugu country who settled at Brindāban, accepted the story of Rādhā, and created a sect of his own. The date is uncertain.[5] Nimbārka's philosophic position is *bhedābheda*, dualistic monism.[6] He was considerably influenced by Rāmānuja, and, like him, laid great stress on meditation. He goes far beyond Vishṇusvāmī in his account of Rādhā. She is Kṛishṇa's

[1] Cowell, p. 141. [2] See § 278.

[3] For a suggestion with regard to the *Nārada Pañcharātra*, see § 377.

[4] See § 285. [5] See Bhandarkar, *VS.* 62.

[6] As Nimbārka's original name is said to have been Bhāskara, it has been suggested that he is identical with Bhāskarāchārya, who wrote the *Bhedābheda bhāshya* about A.D. 900: see § 260. But the mere coincidence of name is scarcely sufficient to outweigh the following considerations. It is extremely unlikely that one man should write a pure Vedānta bhāshya and also a sectarian Vṛitti; and, as our knowledge of the literature stands at present, it would seem probable that the name of Rādhā and her worship appeared at Brindāban at a date considerably later than Bhāskarāchārya, say about A.D. 1100.

eternal consort, and lives for ever with him in the Cow-world, Goloka, far above all the other heavens. Like her lord, she became incarnate in Brindāban, and was his wedded wife there. The story of the gopīs remains unchanged. To Nimbārka Kṛishṇa is not a mere incarnation of Vishṇu: he is the eternal Brahman, and from him springs Rādhā, and also uncounted gopās and gopīs, who sport with them in Goloka. Nimbārka thus necessarily centred all his devotion on Kṛishṇa and his consort, to the exclusion of other gods. He thus gave up the Smārta position of the Bhāgavatas, and became fully sectarian. All the later sects owe a great deal to him. He wrote a short commentary, a sort of *Vṛitti*, on the *Vedānta-sūtras* called *Vedānta-parijāta-saurabha*, and a poem of ten stanzas, the *Daśaślokī*, which contains the quintessence of his system; but the Bhāshya of the sect is Śrīnivāsa's *Vedānta-Kaustubha*, a lengthy work of considerable merit. Later leaders also produced scholarly works. Nimbārkas use the *Gautamīya S.*[1] for their ritual; and the Kṛishṇa section of the *Brahma-vaivarta P.* seems to be a Nimbārka document interpolated into the Purāṇa. The *Śāṇḍilya-bhakti-sūtra* may be of Nimbārkite origin.[2]

c. *Pāñcharātra Literature.*

1. *The Śrī-Vaishṇavas.*

§ 283. The Śrī-Vaishṇavas of the Tamil country reached the summit of their history during these centuries, and became the model on which many other sects sought to form their literature and organization. The introduction of the singing of the enthusiastic lyrics of the Āḻvārs[3] into the temple service of the sect is an event of much importance. The use of Tamil in the worship brought the cult nearer the people; and the rich and passionate devotion of the hymns made the bhakti of the sect more vivid and real. The man to whom Vaishṇavas

[1] Schrader, *IPAS.* 7, no. 44. [2] See § 277. [3] See § 217.

owe the change is Nāthamuni.[1] His date has been disputed, but the end of the tenth and the beginning of the eleventh century seems to satisfy the evidence best.[2] He gathered the hymns of Nammāḷvār and of the other Āḷvārs, arranged them in four groups of about a thousand stanzas each, and set them to Dravidian music. The whole collection is called *Nālāyira Prabandham*, or book of four thousand hymns. He also succeeded in arranging for the regular singing of these hymns in the great temple of Śrīraṅgam at Trichinopoly, where he resided. The practice spread to other shrines, and now obtains in most of the more important temples.

But Nāthamuni was also a theologian and teacher. Under him a school of combined Sanskrit and Tamil scholarship arose at Śrīraṅgam,[3] whence he is called the first Āchārya of the sect. The study of the *Nālāyira Prabandham* was one of the chief parts of the curriculum, and a series of commentaries was written on them.

The succession of teachers is Nāthamuni, Puṇḍarīkāksha, Rāmamiśra, Yāmunāchārya. Of the second and third[4] very little is known, but the fourth, who was the grandson of Nāthamuni and lived in the middle of the eleventh century, was a competent scholar and left several significant works. He was a sannyāsī, like the other teachers of the school. His chief books are the *Siddhitraya*, which seeks to establish the reality of the human soul in opposition to the school of Śaṅkara, the *Āgamaprāmāṇya*, on the authority of the Vaishṇava Āgamas or Saṁhitās, and the *Gītārtha-saṅgraha*, an exposition of the *Bhagavadgītā*, all in Sanskrit. In these works is found the earliest statement of the Viśishṭādvaita philosophy, of which Rāmānuja is the classical exponent.

§ 284. Rāmānuja received his early philosophical training

[1] He was the grandfather of Yāmunāchārya, whom Rāmānuja succeeded at Śrīraṅgam.

[2] He was a contemporary of Nambi and of Rājarāja the Great. See § 306.

[3] At quite an early date another school rose in the neighbourhood of Tinnevelly. Govindāchārya, *JRAS*. 1912, 714.

[4] But see Rajagopalachariar, *VRI*.

in Conjeeveram from a teacher belonging to the school of Śaṅkara, named Yādava Prakāśa,[1] but he disagreed with his guru and adhered to the modified monism which was taught at Śrīraṅgam. He was still a young man when Yāmunāchārya died. Although he had not been trained in the school, he was already so prominent as a Vaishṇava scholar that he was invited to succeed him. He accepted the invitation, but did not settle down to teaching until he had learned all he could from former pupils of the school. The appointment gave him control of the temple of Śrīraṅgam as well as of the school, and also a sort of pontifical authority in the sect. He was most successful as a teacher and controversialist. For some twenty years he lectured, held discussions and wrote books. The sect grew steadily in influence. He produced three philosophical works of importance, the *Vedārthasaṅgraha*, which seeks to show that the Upanishads do not teach a strict monism, the *Śrībhāshya*, a commentary on the *Vedānta-sūtras*, and a *Gītābhāshya*. The *Śrībhāshya* is a fine piece of work.

§ 285. The system taught in these works antagonizes Śaṅkara's illusionary monism with great skill and thoroughness, and also opposes the Bhedābheda system of Bhāskarāchārya.[2] Rāmānuja follows a long succession of theistic scholars, the most famous being Bodhāyana, who lived before Śaṅkara and wrote a gloss. *Vṛitti*, on the *Vedānta-sūtras*, now unhappily lost.[3] The following summary of the system is abridged from Thibaut:[4]

> There exists only one all-embracing being called Brahman, who is endowed with all imaginable auspicious qualities. The Lord is all-pervading, all-powerful, all-knowing, all-merciful; his nature is fundamentally antagonistic to all evil. He contains within himself whatever exists—material or immaterial—and is the 'internal ruler' of all. Matter and souls, as forming the body of the Lord, exist in two different, periodically alternating, conditions. During the period of world-rest, matter and souls being apart from bodies, their intelligence is in a state of contraction. The Lord is then said to be in his casual condition. When the period comes to an end, creation takes place owing to an act of volition on the Lord's part. Unevolved matter

[1] See § 260. [2] See § 260. [3] See § 193. [4] *SBE.* XXXIV. xxvii ff.

then, evolving, acquires its sensible characteristics, while souls enter into connexion with bodies, and their intelligence undergoes expansion.

Owing to former actions, souls are implicated in the process of transmigration; and from this Release is possible only through true knowledge of the Lord, which rests on a study of the scripture and consists in constant devotion (bhakti) to him and meditation (upāsana) on him. The released soul enters paradise and enjoys intercourse with the Lord for ever.

The Lord is a personal being. Brahman is but another name for Nārāyaṇa-Vishṇu, the god of the Vaishṇava sect.

Warm-hearted devotion to a god must have been a frequent element in early Hindu religious feeling, and as early as the *Śvetāśvatara U.*, which probably dates from about the fourth century B.C., we find it spoken of as an important part of the highest religion. In the *Gītā* its place is more distinctly affirmed. Here in the school of Rāmānuja it becomes still more prominent, for it is the loftiest and most important factor in the means of deliverance. It remains, however, quiet and meditative, an aspect of man's reaching out towards fuller knowledge of God, and thus very different from the bhakti of the *Bhāgavata P.*

Rāmānuja holds, in opposition to Śaṅkara, that the man who wishes to win release ought to continue to do his duties as a Hindu while he seeks the knowledge of Brahman with a view to final release. Works and knowledge are both necessary for the great end in view. This is called the *Samuchchhaya* or 'combination' doctrine. The serious seeker ought therefore to study the Karma Mīmāṁsā as well as the Vedānta. This theory is then typified in the fact that sannyāsīs of the school of Rāmānuja do not lay aside the sacred thread. They continue the worship of Vishṇu and may even act as ministrants in temples as well as heads of monasteries.[1]

[1] Śrī-Vaishṇava sannyāsīs are quite a distinct order from Śaṅkara's Daśnāmīs. Only Brāhmans are admitted, and they carry a triple *daṇḍa* in contrast with the single *daṇḍa* of Śaṅkara's Brāhman sannyāsīs: see § 198. The two orders are distinguished as Ekadaṇḍīs and Tridaṇḍīs. Rāmānuja's convert, Yādava Prakāśa, wrote the *Yati-dharma-samuchchhaya* on the duties of Tridaṇḍīs: Govindāchārya, *R.*, 73. Non-Brāhman Śrī-Vaishṇava ascetics are called Ekāṅgas.

§ 286. The writing of the *Śrī-bhāshya* was a most important event for the Śrī-Vaishṇavas. It was doubtless meant in the first instance to provide the sect with a clearly expressed philosophy in full accordance with its beliefs and its ancient literature, a matter of great moment for the training of teachers and ascetics. But it was not merely of large practical value. The dignity of the sect was vastly enhanced when it was brought into living connexion with the Vedānta by this illustrious work. It was the first sectarian bhāshya ever written. We may realize how valuable an acquisition it was felt to be from the long array of similar works produced during the following seven centuries.[1] It is also probable that Rāmānuja hoped, by linking the sect to the Vedānta, to get rid, to some extent at least, of the reproach of heterodoxy which had dogged the sect throughout its history.[2] His own punctilious observation of caste rules in the matter of food and intercourse with other castes was doubtless intended to help in the same direction.

§ 287. There were two types of Vaishṇava temples in the south in his day, one class using Pāñcharātra Saṁhitās for their ritual, the other using Vaikhānasa Saṁhitās,[3] the latter class being probably Bhāgavata shrines. Rāmānuja did all he could to unify the sect by substituting Pāñcharātra for Vaikhānasa manuals wherever he could win over the authorities.[4]

§ 288. While he held strictly by the ancient rule that none but the twice-born may read the Upanishads, he was most eager to teach both Śūdras and Outcastes the doctrine of Vishṇu-bhakti. In this he was a faithful disciple of the Āḷvārs. In certain places he arranged that the Outcastes should have the privilege of visiting the temple one day in the year. But there is no reliable evidence for the statement, so often made, that he ate with Outcastes, or that he took any step to alter

[1] See § 340. [2] See § 94 and § 215.
[3] See § 211 and § 384.
[4] Rajagopalachariar, *VRI.* 4; Padmanabhachar, *LTM.* 252; Govindāchārya, *R.* 142.

their social position.[1] He maintained the ancient Hindu restrictions in all their fullness. His position is clearly revealed in the use of the *pavitra*, or thread of purity, with which Śūdra and Outcaste adherents of the sect are invested. It is a low-caste sacred thread. Acknowledgement is thus made that they are capable of receiving spiritual religion, yet they are kept rigorously apart from the twice-born. The Sātānis[2] are a group of people of Śūdra caste whom he taught and connected with the sect, but no suggestion was made that their caste status should be altered.

He took a journey through India for the dissemination of his system, and seemingly with great success. He went south to Rāmeśvaram, up the west coast through Malabar and the Marāṭhā country to Gujarāt, the north-west, and Kashmir, and returned by Benares, Purī, and Tirupati to Śrīrangam. The wide influence of the sect in later times was probably largely due to what he was able to accomplish during this journey.

§ 289. In A.D. 1098 Kulottunga I, the Chola king, started a persecution against the Vaishṇavas, and Rāmānuja was obliged to flee. He withdrew to the Mysore, and there made the acquaintance of the Crown Prince[3] of the Hoysala dynasty. The royal family and a large proportion of the people were Jains, but the prince was won over by Rāmānuja and took a new name to mark his conversion, Vishṇuvardhana. For a long period Rāmānuja resided in Mysore, chiefly at Melkote, teaching and discussing and building, and Vaishṇavism became firmly planted. The Chola persecutor died in 1118, and in 1122 Rāmānuja returned to Śrīrangam, where he died in 1137.[4] He is worshipped as an incarnation in the temples of the sect.

[1] See especially the early Tamil *Life* translated by Govindāchārya, Chap. X, and Rajagopalachariar, *VRI.* 141.

[2] See § 385.

[3] He succeeded to the throne about ten years later and reigned until A.D. 1141. Rice, *JRAS.* 1915, 527 ff.

[4] The chronology of his early life is still doubtful. Tradition places his birth in A.D. 1017, but the whole life becomes more comprehensible if we suppose he was born about 1050 and succeeded Yāmuna about 1080. A record which was recently found in his monastery in Melkote, Mysore, makes it plain that he arrived in Mysore in 1098 and left in 1122: *JRAS.* 1915, 147 ff.

§ 290. There is no lack of early biographical material. Not to speak of contemporary poems and such like, which arose in the school, his early life is dealt with in the *Bhūtapurī Māhātmya* (Bhūtapurī is Śrī Perumbūdūr, where he was born), a section of the *Hārīta Saṁhitā*, while in other Saṁhitās his later activities are dealt with. The *Īśvara Saṁhitā* speaks of Śaṭhakopa, i.e. Nammāḷvār, and Rāmānuja, contains a Māhātmya of Melkote in Mysore, and enjoins the use of the Tamil hymns of the *Nālāyira Prabandham*. The *Bṛihad Brahma Saṁhitā* also refers to Śaṭhakopa and Rāmānuja, and speaks of the Drāviḍa land as the place where Vishṇu's devotees abound. These texts must be old, the sections dealing with Rāmānuja being probably twelfth-century interpolations. Finally, in the thirteenth century, a detailed *Life* was written in Tamil by Pinbaḷagīa-Perumāl-Jīyar.

§ 291. Towards the end of the thirteenth century, or possibly early in the fourteenth, the head of the school of Śrīraṅgam was Piḷḷai Lokāchārya. He wrote a brief treatise in Sanskritized Tamil, the *Artha-pañchaka*, or Pentad of Truths, which is a very excellent summary of Śrī-Vaishṇava doctrine. Sudarśana Bhaṭṭa, who ruled at Śrīraṅgam towards the close of our period, may be mentioned as having written a commentary on the *Bhāgavata P.*, which, though not mentioned by Rāmānuja, had in the interval won itself a place in the sect.

§ 292. The mantra of the sect is the famous early mantra, *Oṁ namo Nārāyaṇāya.*[1] A sect-mark and the branding of symbols on the body are in use, in accordance with the rules of the Saṁhitās. The sect and its system are both called the Śrī-Vaishṇava Sampradāya, i.e. the tradition with regard to Śrī (i.e. Lakshmī) and Vishṇu. No other Hindu sect is more

[1] The old erroneous statement, so often repeated, that the mantra of the sect is *Oṁ Rāmāya namaḥ*, comes from Wilson (*Sects*, 40), and probably arose from the idea that the mantra of Rāmānuja must be the same as Rāmānanda's: see § 387. Śrī-Vaishṇavas use also a secret mantra called the *Dvaya*, or dual mantra, which is clearly phallic, referring to Śrī and Vishṇu: Govindāchārya, *R.* 14, 48, 52.

exclusive in its allegiance; the worship of Śiva or any god other than Vishṇu, his consorts, and his representatives, is forbidden. Rādhā is not acknowledged at all. In matters of food and caste Śrī-Vaishṇavas are extremely strict. The sect ministers to all the four castes, while for many centuries the outcastes were taught Vishṇu-bhakti, and several outcaste names occur in the list of Śrī-Vaishṇava saints. Yet the strength of the sect is in the Brāhman community. Every Śrī-Vaishṇava Brāhman bears one of two names, Āchārya or Aiyaṅgar.

2. *The Manbhaus.*

§ 293. The Mahānubhavas (i.e. men of the great experience) or Manbhaus are a Vaishṇava sect found in the Marāṭhī-speaking area, who claim a high antiquity for their system but acknowledge that their organization dates from the thirteenth century.

Several noteworthy characteristics, which they have in common with the Vīra Śaivas, are probably to be explained as due mainly to racial and local facts, partly to the influence of Rāmānuja. The more noteworthy of these features are these: Both are rather more heterodox than ordinary Vaishṇava and Śaiva sects, so that Hindus frequently deny that Manbhaus are Hindus at all, and some Vīra Śaivas deny that the Vīra Śaiva sect is a Hindu community. They are both strictly sectarian, Vīra Śaivas worshipping Śiva alone, Manbhaus recognizing Kṛishṇa alone. Both sects refuse to worship images, though each worships a symbol of its own god. In each sect all full members may dine together. Both sects are strictly vegetarian, both bury their dead, and in both the ascetics are of far more importance than the temples. Each sect claims to have five founders. Any caste-Hindu is welcomed as a full member in either sect if he is willing to undergo initiation. Round each of the two sects there is a circlet of half-converted groups who do not keep the full law. As the Vīra Śaivas are about a century older than the

Manbhaus, it is possible that the latter may have followed the example of the former sect in some points.

§ 294. The unexplained figure of Dattātreya hovers shadowy and indistinct behind Manbhau history. The sect claims him as the source of its system. If, as is possible, a real historical sannyāsī is concealed in this mist, his connexions were with the Marāṭhā country and with Yādavagiri (i.e. Melkote) in the Mysore.[1] He is usually represented as a sannyāsī with three heads, so that he stands for the trimūrti, and he is accompanied by four dogs and a cow, which stand for the Vedas and the earth; but Manbhaus deny that they worship him in this form. To them he is an incarnation of Kṛishṇa.

Chakradhar, who flourished in the middle of the thirteenth century, seems to be the actual founder of the sect as we know it. He was followed by Nāgadeva Bhaṭṭa, who was a contemporary of Rāmachandra, the Yādava King (1271–1309), and of Jñāneśvara,[2] the author of the *Jñāneśvarī*. He did a great deal to propagate the community. Of their later history very little is yet known. It is clear that they have suffered from orthodox opposition.

Kṛishṇa is to them the Supreme, and they will worship no other god. 'There are many devatās, but only one Parameśvara.' They have, therefore, their own places of worship, and will not enter ordinary temples. Instead of an image, they have in their shrines a quadrangular or circular whitewashed terrace, which they worship in the name of God. The nature of their worship seems to be unknown. They speak of Dattātreya as their founder, and therefore call their system the Dattātreya Sampradāya, the Śrī-Datta Sampradāya, the Muni Mārg (the reference being to Dattātreya), or the Manbhau Panth.

But while they speak of Dattātreya as their original founder, they say they have had a fresh founder in each of the four yugas.

[1] The Manbhaus connect him with the Sahyadri Hills, while the *Yādavagiri Māhātmya* of the *Nārada P.* tells how he visited Yādavagiri in the Mysore. See § 289.

[2] See § 278.

They thus recognize five *pravartakas*, propagators (also called the *Pañchakṛishṇa*),[1] and have a mantra connected with each. When any one wishes to become a Manbhau, he must repeat the five mantras and accept initiation from a Manbhau monk.

§ 295. They fall into two well-marked groups, ascetics and householders, ascetics again falling into two distinctly organized groups, monks and nuns. On the monks rests the sect with its teaching, discipline, and worship. Monks and nuns are carefully kept separate.

Their chief scripture is the *Bhagavadgītā*, but they have a large literature of their own in Marāṭhī. In consequence of the persecution they were subjected to, they adopted a modified Marāṭhī alphabet for their literature, so as to keep it secret. This is one of the reasons why it is still so little known. Amongst their oldest books are the *Līlā Saṁvād*, the *Līlā Charita*, and the *Sūtrapāṭh*. Perhaps we may take these as belonging to this period. The *Dattātreya U.*[2] and the *Dattātreya S.*[3] are probably also connected with the movement.

3. *The Narasiṁha Sect.*

§ 296. Very little is known about the activities of the Narasiṁha sect during this period, but it is clear that the god was still popular. The huge monolithic image at Vijayanagar is proof that the dynasty favoured him. There are still many families in which he is the patron of the family. *The Narasiṁha S.*[4] may belong to this period. The *Narasiṁha Upapurāṇa*, which has been already mentioned,[5] was translated into Telugu about A.D. 1300.

4. *The Rāma Sect.*

§ 297. Serious members of the Ramaite sect, whose early literature has been already noticed,[6] found it hard to reconcile the entirely human words and actions of Rāma and Sītā in Books II–VI of the *Rāmāyaṇa*[7] with their belief that Rāma

[1] *Darśan Prakāś*, 58. [2] No. 112 in the list, p. 364.
[3] No. 61 in Schrader's list, *IPAS*. p. 7. [4] Schrader, *IPAS*. 8.
[5] See § 218. [6] See § 219. [7] See § 48.

is the eternal God. The *Adhyātma Rāmāyaṇa,* or spiritual Rāmāyaṇa, in seven books, bearing the same names as the books of the early Epic, tells the whole story afresh with a view to meeting these difficulties. The theology is *advaita* throughout, but Śākta elements are added, so that Sītā has a place beside the eternal Rāma. In order to shield Sītā from the reproach of having been carried away by Rāvaṇa and kept in his harem, she enters the fire, leaving only an illusory Sītā behind her, before the appearance of the demon; and the real goddess does not return until the fire-ordeal at the end of the story. When Rāma at any point talks as a man, it is explained that his divine consciousness is temporarily clouded by *māyā*. Release is obtainable in Rāma alone; fervent bhakti is the path to release; and a Rāma mantra is taught.[1] The man who wishes to obtain release must give up works altogether; for they only bind the soul to *saṁsāra*. The work is thus opposed to the *Samuchchhaya*[2] doctrine. It contains the *Rāma-hṛidaya*[3] in eight ślokas and the *Rāma-gītā*[4] in fifty-six ślokas, compendia of doctrine meant to be committed to memory for constant repetition and meditation. The work clearly depends not only on the *Rāmāyaṇa* and the advaita Vedānta but also on the *Bhāgavata P.* and the Ramaite *Agastya Saṁhitā*[5] mentioned above.[6] There were already many Rāmāyaṇas[7] in existence when the book was written. Among these there was undoubtedly the *Pampa-Rāmāyaṇa*,[8] a Jain version of the Epic in Kanarese[9]; and possibly the author may have known the *Yoga-Vasishṭha*, the *Adbhuta*, and the *Bhusuṇḍi* Rāmāyaṇas. There existed also an *Adhyātma Nārāyaṇa*, which is several times quoted by Madhva in his *Bhāshya*. The date of the work is probably the thirteenth or fourteenth century: Eknāth, the Marāṭhī poet, who died in A.D. 1608, calls it a modern poem.[10] It was translated into

[1] III. 8, 34. [2] See § 195 and 285. [3] I. i. [4] VII. v.
[5] See III. ii, iii; IV. iv; VI. v. [6] § 219. [7] II. iv. 77.
[8] Some of the episodes in the *Adhyātma* are like episodes in the *Pampa-Rāmāyaṇa*. [9] Rice, *KL*. 30, 33.
[10] Bhandarkar, *VS*. 48.

Malayalim in the seventeenth century. There is also a Kanarese version.[1]

There can thus be no doubt about the existence of an old sect which found release in Rāma alone. Was it in the south or the north? It would be perilous to be dogmatic: but the relations of the literature thus far tend to indicate the south rather than the north. There is no distinct Ramaite sect in the Tamil country to-day, but there are many Rāma-bhaktas, i.e. sādhus, who find salvation in Rāma. These, in all probability, are survivals of the old sect.

E. *Śaiva Literature.*

a. *Pāśupata Śaivas.*

§ 298. A fifteenth-century commentator, Advaitānanda, gives us in his *Brahmavidyābharaṇa* a clear sketch of Pāśupata theology which enables us to realize the essentials of the system. The five categories mentioned by Śaṅkara[2] really give the roots of the system: (*a*) the cause, *Pati*, (*b*) the effect, nature and *Paśu*, (*c*) yoga practices, (*d*) *Vidhi*, requirements, i.e. various necessary practices, (*e*) *Duhkhānta*, release from sorrow. They taught that true knowledge of the cause and effect, constant yoga practice and meditation, and the regular fulfilment of the rules of the order were all necessary for the attainment of the end in view. The rules enjoin bathing and sleeping in ashes, expressing exultation by laughter, dancing, singing or bellowing, and pretending to be asleep, sick, lame, in love, or mad. In release the soul was believed to attain the divine perfections. The chief scripture of the sect seems to have been a sūtra-work called indifferently *Paśupati-sūtra* or *Pāśupata-śāstra*, but it does not seem to have survived.

1. *The Lakulīśas.*

§ 299. Of the Lakulīśas, a branch from the main Pāśupata stem, we have an account by Mādhavāchārya,[3] the fourteenth-

[1] This Kanarese version contains a Mādhva interpolation. Padmanabhachar, *LTM*. 133.

[2] *SBE*. XXXIV. 434 ff.

[3] In *SDS*. See Cowells's tr. 103.

century Vedāntist. The teaching seems to be identical with the Pāśupata theory just sketched. The differences seem to have been confined to the practices enjoined, e.g. bathing and sleeping in sand instead of in ashes. Mādhava quotes a number of books, but in most cases he gives no indication whether the books belong to the main Pāśupata sect or to the Lakulīśa branch, and all the literature seems to have perished. Throughout the period the sect was most active in Gujarāt, Rājputāna, and the Mysore, as is made clear by many inscriptions. They are well summarized by Bhandarkar.[1]

2. *The Kāpālikas.*

§ 300. No Kāpālika literature seems to have survived; so that for this period as well as the previous one we are dependent on scattered notices. The references to them in the *Śaṅkara-digvijaya* imply that they were still active during these centuries. Then, in the *Prabodhachandrodaya*, a drama produced in A.D. 1065 which we have already used,[2] a Kāpālika ascetic and a Kāpālinī are brought on the stage and Kāpālika practice is described and illustrated with great vividness. The evidence of the *Mālatī-Mādhava*[3] is here corroborated. Kāpālika ascetics are practically Śāktas: the characteristic elements of Śākta-worship—human sacrifice, strong drink, and sexual licence—appear, and with them the Śākta jewellery of human bones, the elaborate system of yoga, and the superhuman powers that spring therefrom. The Kāpālika, besides, dwells among the ashes of the dead, and eats and drinks out of a human skull. In this play a Buddhist and a Jain ascetic appear on the stage, and are reduced to a very miserable plight by the Kāpālika and the nun who accompanies him. Rāmānuja's few sentences[4] on the system corroborate the erotic element of this account; for he says the Kāpālika meditates on himself as seated in the pudendum muliebre.[5]

[1] *VS.* 119-20. [2] See § 270. [3] See § 234.
[4] *Śrībhāshya*, *SBE.* XLVIII. 520 f. [5] Cf. § 325.

3. *The Gorakhnāthīs.*

§ 301. The Gorakhnāthīs (*Gorakshanāthīs*) seem to be closely related to the Kāpālikas. They form a sort of inchoate sect; for Gorakhnāth (*Gorakshanātha*) is worshipped in many temples in North India, especially in the Punjab and Nepal; yet the laity does not seem to be organized. The ascetics, who are usually called Kānphaṭa Yogīs, i.e. Split-eared Yogīs, are the strongest part of the sect. It is most probable, but not certain, that the movement sprang from a yogī named Gorakhnāth.

§ 302. Goraksha seems to be a name of Śiva; a great many wonderful tales have gathered round the name of Gorakhnāth, who is said to have founded the sect of Gorakhnāthīs; and both Tāntrik Hinduism and Tāntrik Buddhism glorify the whole company of sainted Nāthas; so that one is tempted to take all the tales as so much mythology. Yet Gorakhnāth is probably a historical character; for the Kānphaṭa Yogīs are a well-defined group of ascetics, and the rise of a new type of Yoga literature, with which his name is associated, is clearly connected with the appearance of the order. It seems most probable that he flourished about the beginning of the thirteenth century; for the earliest historical reference to him yet noted occurs in the *Amṛitānubhava* of Jñāneśvara, the Marāṭhā bhakta, whose *floruit* is A. D. 1290.[1]

Gorakhnāth's name is associated with the rise of a new type of yoga, which has had a considerable vogue in certain circles but has never found its way into the ancient school of yoga. It is called *Haṭha-yoga*, and its most distinctive element is the theory that, by certain ritual purifications of the body and certain prescribed physical exercises, the supreme concentration of mind called *samādhi* in the old yoga can be attained. It therefore deals with a large number of strange bodily postures (*āsana*),[2] purifications of the channels of the body (*śodhana*),

[1] See § 278.

[2] 'The later Yogin relies on *āsana*, the older muni on *upāsana*': Hopkins, *JAOS*. XXII. ii. 334.

modes of breath-regulation (*prāṇāyāma*), and exercises in which posture, breathing, and attention are combined (*mudrā*), and which bring with them miraculous powers. To Haṭha-yoga is usually added in the later books *Rāja-yoga*, a more intellectual discipline to which the physical training is then subordinated. Gorakhnāth is said to be the author of two Sanskrit treatises, *Haṭha-yoga* [1] and *Goraksha-śataka*,[2] and on them depends the later literature, which is dealt with in the next chapter.[3] Several works in Hindī verse exist which are also attributed to the leader; but as their date is said to be the middle of the fourteenth century,[4] clearly they cannot be assigned to him, unless it be found that an earlier date is possible for them. They may have been written by his followers. There thus seems to be sufficient ground for believing that Gorakhnāth was a noted yogī, that he lived and founded his sect somewhere about A.D. 1200, and that early stories connected with the name Goraksha and the Nāthas gathered round his head after his death.

4. *The Raseśvaras.*

§ 303. Another Śaiva school is described by Mādhava,[5] which was called the Raseśvara or Mercury system, but does not seem to have survived. The peculiarity of their teaching was this, that they thought that, without an immortal body, release could not be attained, and that the only way in which an immortal body could be developed was by the use of mercury, *rasa*, which, they declared, was produced by the creative conjunction of Śiva and his spouse. After the acquisition of a divine body, the aspirant, by the practice of yoga, wins an intuition of the Supreme, and is liberated in this life. A number of ancient teachers of the school are named, and several philosophic manuals.

[1] This book does not seem to exist to-day, but see Hall, 17.
[2] Hall, 18; Aufrecht, *Cat. Sansk. MSS. in Bodleian Library*, 236.
[3] See § 423.
[4] *Miśra Bandhu Vinode*, 21.
[5] *SDS.*, ch. ix, Cowell, 137.

b. *Āgamic Śaivas.*

1. *The Sanskrit School of Śaiva Siddhānta.*

§ 304. In his *Sarvadarśanasaṅgraha*[1] Mādhava describes what he calls the Śaiva Darśana, and quotes in illustration of its teaching six of the Āgamas, as many writers, and several anonymous works. All the literature is in Sanskrit, but, apart from the Āgamas, none of it seems to have survived. Several writers, however, belonging to the school lived at dates later than Mādhava ; and these are therefore described in our next chapter. We call it the Sanskrit school of Śaiva Siddhānta.

This school and the teaching of the Tamil Śaivas as contained in the Tamil Śaiva Siddhānta are usually treated as one,[2] but it seems quite clear that they are distinct. The Sanskrit school has in the main a following of Brāhmans, many of them being temple-ministrants, its Vedantic standpoint is Viśishṭādvaita, and its literature is in Sanskrit ; while the following of the Tamil school is almost entirely non-Brāhman, its Vedantic standpoint is Advaita[3] or, according to other writers, Bhedābheda,[4] and all its literature is in Tamil.

2. *Tamil Śaivas.*

§ 305. The literature of the Tamil Śaivas belonging to this period is extremely rich in lyrical poetry, theology, and historical legend. The chronology is still obscure in many points, but the relations of the larger events are fairly clear.

Paṭṭiṇattu Piḷḷai, who probably lived in the tenth century, is the author of some beautiful devotional verse, which, along with the work of several minor authors, found a place in the sacred Canon ;[5] but a number of poems of a highly monotheistic and Puritan character, which belong to a much later date,

[1] Cowell, 112.

[2] e.g. see Cowell's tr. of the Śaiva Darśana in Mādhava's *SDS*.

[3] Nallasvāmī, *SSS*. 63, 67, 68, 88, 244. The standpoint is sometimes called Śivādvaita.

[4] So Umāpati, *Tiru-aruḷ-payan*, lxxv.

[5] In the Eleventh *Tiru-muṟai*.

have been erroneously assigned to this tenth-century poet. They are dealt with below.[1]

§ 306. Nambi-andar-nambi was a contemporary of Nāthamuni the Vaishṇava leader and of Rājarāja the Great, the Chola king (A.D. 985–1018). He gathered the Tamil hymns of The Three into one collection, named it the Tevārām, i.e. DEVĀRĀM, the Divine Garland, and with the help of Rājarāja had them set to Dravidian music. He then arranged to have them sung in the chief shrines. An inscription of Rājarāja's shows that he introduced them into his magnificent temple at Tanjore. Sung by a special choir, quite distinct from the priestly ministrants, they gave the worship a fresh interest and splendour without disturbing the ancient Sanskrit liturgy. Māṇikka Vāchakar's glorious verse was probably too recent to find a place in this collection.

§ 307. Nambi's name is also connected with the formation of a larger body of Tamil scripture, which is called the TIRU MUṞAI, i.e. the Sacred Books. He collected most of the Śaiva hymns then in existence and grouped them in eleven books;[2] and the collection was completed by the addition of a twelfth in the twelfth century. The contents are: (*a*) the *Tevārām*, (*b*) the *Tiruvāchakam*, (*c*) the *Tiru Isaipa*, lyrics by nine authors, (*d*) the *Tirumantram*, (*e*) miscellaneous poems, including Nambi's own works, (*f*) the *Periya Purāṇam*, or Great Legend, a Liber Sanctorum, forming the Twelfth Book. Śekkīrar, the author of the *Periya Purāṇam*, the Great Legend, may be dated in the first half of the twelfth century. It is a poem in seventy-two cantos on the lives of the sixty-three Śaiva saints of the Tamil country, and is founded on a decad of Sundarar's and the *Tondar-tiruv-antādi*, which is one of Nambi's poems. No work is more loved by Śaivas than the *Periya Purāṇam*. To about the same date we may assign a famous translation, the *Skanda P.*, done into Tamil verse and called the *Kanda Purāṇam*, by Kāñchī-Appar of Conjeeveram.

[1] See § 426.

[2] He began the compilation in the reign of Rājarāja and finished it under his son Rājendra I.

§ 308. Thus far the Tamil Śaivas had no formulated theology of their own but were dependent on the Āgamas, which are probably of northern origin and are in Sanskrit. The defect was remedied by a brilliant school of thinkers, who were also Tamil poets, during the thirteenth and fourteenth centuries. Meykaṇḍa Deva, who is regarded as the fountain of the dogmatic, was a Śūdra and lived early in the thirteenth century on the bank of the Penner river to the north of Madras. He translated twelve Sanskrit sūtras from the *Raurava Āgama*[1] into Tamil verse. To this work, which is known as *Śiva-jñāna-bodha*, 'Instruction in Knowledge of Śiva', he added a few notes in Tamil prose, and a series of logical analogies also in prose in support of his reasoning. The system which this work unfolds is called the Śaiva Siddhānta, or 'Reasoned Śaiva system'. He was also a noted teacher and had many pupils. His most famous disciples are Aruḷnandi Deva and Manavāchakam Kaḍandān. The latter is famous for his *Uṇmai Viḷakkam*, a treatise in fifty-four stanzas consisting of questions and answers on the main points of Siddhānta teaching. The former wrote the *Śiva-jñāna-siddhi*, a noted work in two parts, of which the first is a criticism of other Indian schools of thought, including Buddhism and Jainism, while the second is a full statement of Śaiva Siddhānta teaching so put as to form a rich commentary on his teacher's masterpiece, and to meet, if possible, all objections to the Śaiva Siddhānta. Aruḷnandi's disciple was Marai-jñāna-sambandha, a Śūdra and the author of *Śaiva-samaya-neṛi*. A Brāhman named Umāpati from the temple in Chidambaram became a disciple of his, ate the leavings of his food and was in consequence excommunicated. But he became the supreme theologian of the sect, and left numerous works, eight of which are included among the canonical books of the Siddhānta. The following is the list:

[1] See § 225.

THE FOURTEEN SIDDHĀNTA ŚĀSTRAS.

Uyyavandan (A)	1. *Tiruvuntiyār*
Uyyavandan (B)	2. *Tirukkaliṟṟuppaḍiyār*
Meykaṇḍa Deva	3. *Śiva-jñāna-bodha*
Aruḷnandi	4. *Śiva-jñāna-siddhi*
	5. *Irupāvirupathu*
Manavāchakam Kaḍandān	6. *Uṇmai-viḷakkam*
Umāpati Śivāchārya	7. *Śiva-prakāśa*
	8. *Tiru-aruḷ-payan*
	9. *Viñā-veṇbā*
	10. *Poṟṟipakrodai*
	11. *Koḍi-kavi*
	12. *Neñchu-viḍu-tūtu*
	13. *Uṇmai-neṟi-viḷakkam*
	14. *Saṅkalpa-nirākaraṇa*

The four—Meykaṇḍa Deva, Aruḷnandi, Marai-jñāna-sambandha, and Umāpati—who together form a succession of teachers and disciples, are known as *The Four Santāna Āchāryas*, i. e. teachers forming a continuous series. There are two of the writers whose dates are not known with certainty, the two Uyyavandans. They are said to have flourished in the latter half of the twelfth century, but it is possible that they may belong to the school of Meykaṇḍa. It is possible that the development of this dogmatic was influenced in some degree by the literature of Kashmir Śaivism; for the later stands quite near the earlier system; yet Siddhantists do not recognize the Kashmir literature as authoritative; and it is much more probable that the Tamil Siddhānta was influenced by the Sanskrit Siddhānta. The two are quite closely allied.[1] The tradition in the sect is that Meykaṇḍa was directly taught by some one from Kailāsa.

3. *Kashmir Śaivas.*

§ 309. All we know about Śaivism in Kashmir during this period is summed up in the growth of its literature; and it

[1] This stands out in Mādhava's essay, *SDS.* VII.

seems to have been the more philosophic side of the system represented by Somānanda's *Śiva Dṛishṭi* that ruled the development, although the study of the earlier literature was still kept up. The chief followers of Somānanda are his pupil Utpalāchārya, who is the author of the *Īśvara-pratyabhijñā-kārikās*; Abhinavagupta (about A.D. 1000) who expounded Utpala's *Kārikās* in two commentaries, wrote several works on the Śaiva Āgamas and a summary of the Pratyabhijñā doctrine called *Paramārthasāra*; and finally Kshemarāja of the eleventh century, who wrote the *Śiva-sūtra-vimarśinī*. After Kshemarāja the movement died down; yet the literature probably influenced Śaivism in South India during the thirteenth and later centuries.

4. *Vīra Śaivas.*

§ 310. The Vīra Śaivas, also called Liṅgāyats, are a sect which seems to have been founded on the borders of the Karṇāṭak and the Marāṭhā country in the middle of the twelfth century, and soon attained considerable proportions, spreading rapidly towards the south, especially in the Kanarese country. Liṅgāyats believe that the sect is extremely old, and that it was merely reorganized in the twelfth century, but it seems to be rather more probable that, while most of the elements united in the sect are old, the sect itself came into being about A. D. 1160.[1] In the Karṇāṭak for centuries the mass of the people had been either Śaivas or Digambara Jains: the new sect seems to be essentially a fresh formation meant to give Śaivas a more definite theology and a closer organization, and to win over the Jains to the worship of Śiva. Two features of the sect—the great prominence of the monasteries, and the large measure of religious and social equality which full Liṅgāyats enjoy within the sect—are probably in part imitations of Jainism. Racial characteristics may also have played a part in forming the organization;

[1] Bhandarkar believes it came into existence about a century earlier *VS.* 134.

for, as we have already seen,[1] Liṅgāyats and Manbhaus, a Vaishṇava community formed in the Marāṭhā country about a century later, have a large number of common features. Both morality and bhakti are very prominent in Liṅgāyat teaching.

Critical scholars have usually held that the founder of the sect was Basava, the prime minister of Bijjala, the Kalachuri, who became King at Kalyan in A. D. 1156, but Fleet is inclined to believe that Ekāntada Rāmāyya of Ablur, whose career is mentioned in an early inscription, was the real leader, and that Basava came in as a political and military auxiliary. The tradition is that the sect was founded by five ascetics—Ekorāma, Paṇḍitārādhya, Revaṇa, Marula, Viśvārādhya [2]—who are held to have sprung from the five heads of Śiva, incarnate age after age. These are regarded as very ancient, and Basava is said to have been but the reviver of the faith. Yet the early literature shows that the five were all his contemporaries, some older, some younger. But the whole early history is still very obscure; and, until the early literature, Sanskrit, Kanarese, and Telugu, has been carefully read and compared with the inscriptions, this darkness is likely to remain.

§ 311. The organization of the sect is sufficiently noteworthy. Five original monasteries, the first heads of which were the five ascetics, must first be noted:

Monasteries.	*First Mahants.*
1. Kedarnāth, Himalayas.	Ekorāma.
2. Śrī-śaila, near Nandyal.	Paṇḍitārādhya.
3. Balehalli, West Mysore.	Revaṇa.
4. Ujjini, Bellary boundary, Mysore.	Marula.
5. Benares.	Viśvārādhya.

In every Liṅgāyat village there is a monastery, and each is affiliated to one of the five original monasteries. The Jaṅgamas are a caste, and from them come nearly all Liṅgāyat

[1] See § 295.
[2] These five are mentioned in the *Suprabheda Āgama*.

Gurus. *Every Liṅgāyat must belong to a monastery* and *must have a guru*: he need not visit a temple at all.

Liṅgāyats regard Śiva as the Supreme, and must worship him only: that is the meaning of the name of the sect, *Vīra Śaivas*, stalwart Śaivas, worshipping Śiva alone. Then, the modes of their worship of Śiva are two: each Liṅgāyat worships his own Jaṅgama guru; and he worships the small liṅga[1] which he wears in a reliquary hung round his neck, whence the other name of the sect, Liṅgāyat, liṅga-wearers. Image-worship is prohibited.

When a boy is born, the father sends for his guru, and the *ashṭavarṇa*, eight-fold ceremony, which makes the baby a Liṅgāyat is performed: *guru*, *liṅga*, *vibhūti*, *rudrāksha*, *mantra*, *Jaṅgama*, *tīrtha*, *prasāda*. These eight are held to be 'coverings', protections against sin.

When a young Liṅgāyat chooses a guru for himself, a ceremony is held in which five pots, representing the original mahants of the five great monasteries, are used. These are placed precisely as the symbols used by Smārtas in their private worship are placed.[2] Four are so placed as to form a square, while the pot which represents the monastery to which the chosen guru is affiliated is placed in the centre.

A Liṅgāyat worships privately twice a day before meals. He sits down, takes his liṅga from its reliquary, places it in the palm of his left hand, and goes through the prescribed forms of meditation and adoration in that posture. Meditation is in accordance with the six *sthalas*.[3]

When the guru visits the home, an elaborate ceremony, *padodaka*, i.e. the washing of the feet of the guru, is performed, at which all the family, and possibly friends as well, are present.

[1] The liṅga is to the Liṅgāyat what the sacred thread is to the twice-born Hindu. No full Liṅgāyat may wear the sacred thread, even if he be of the best Brāhman blood.

[2] See § 352.

[3] These are six stages of spiritual progress, through which the Liṅgāyat passes in seeking union with Śiva, *bhakti*, *maheśa*, *prasāda*, *prāṇaliṅga*, *śaraṇa*, *aikya*.

The head of the house also worships the guru. The guru sits down in Yoga posture, and the householder, sitting before him, goes through the sixteen operations of Hindu worship, and other elaborate ceremonies.

There are a few Liṅgāyat temples, most of which have been built as memorials to individuals, but they do not form a necessary part of the organization of the sect.

§ 312. The word Jaṅgama is used in two senses, first for a member of the caste, and secondly for a practising Jaṅgama. Only the latter is worshipable. Most Jaṅgamas marry and earn their living. Those who wish to become practising Jaṅgamas must remain celibate They must also be trained in a monastery and receive *dīkshā*, initiation. The whole sect is in the hands of these practising Jaṅgamas. They are of two classes, Gurusthalas and Viraktas.

Gurusthala Jaṅgamas are trained to perform all domestic ceremonies and to act as gurus, and a number of them will be found in every village monastery. These village monasteries, which are the real centres of Liṅgāyat organization and life, and the five original monasteries are called *Gurusthala*[1] monasteries, because they are guru schools and residences.

But there are a few monasteries of another type, in which philosophical and theological instruction is given, and in them Virakta Jaṅgamas are trained. They are usually called *Shaṭsthala* monasteries, because in them the six *sthalas* or stages in the process of reaching union with Śiva are taught. The duty of Viraktas is to teach.

§ 313. The social construction of the community, as it is to-day, is difficult to understand, and the history behind it is still more difficult. Liṅgāyats affirm that Basava did away with all caste distinctions, whether with regard to religious privileges, intermarriage, or interdining, but that at an early date the community fell away from this practice. It would be unpardonable to speak dogmatically about Basava's teaching

[1] Gurusthala monasteries fall into two sub-classes, *Śishyavarga* and *Putravarga*.

until the early literature has been critically examined, but, in the light of other cases in which similar claims have been made, only to be proved untenable when carefully investigated, it is surely wise to reserve judgement. A somewhat similar condition of affairs in the Manbhau sect suggests the idea that the original community in each case may have consisted of a number of social groups among whom caste restrictions were still very elastic. A desire to win over the Jains may have helped to perpetuate the freedom.

In order to understand the present position of affairs, we must distinguish between full Liṅgāyats and semi-Liṅgāyats. Among the latter Liṅgāyat practice is imperfect and caste restrictions are confessedly rigid. Of these semi-Liṅgāyats there are two groups. The first are the Ārādhya-Brāhmans,[1] who are found mainly in the Kanarese and Telugu districts, and are clearly half-converted Smārtas. They wear both the sacred thread and the liṅga. In their private worship they are Liṅgāyat, but they intermarry with Smārta Brāhmans, a Smārta performs the wedding ceremony for them, and they will not dine with other Liṅgāyats. The second group are the Outcaste Liṅgāyats, for whom no Jaṅgama will perform the full ceremonies, and who are not admitted in any sense to Liṅgāyat society.

Amongst full Liṅgāyats caste restrictions in marriage remain rigid, but all are free to dine together. As a matter of fact Jaṅgamas and certain high-class business families do not usually interdine with the rest. When the guru visits a disciple, they dine together.

§ 314. All full Liṅgāyats bury their dead, and no thought of pollution is associated with the place of burial. They are vegetarians and strict abstainers. Child-marriage is condemned, and widow remarriage is allowed, but some sections of the community have fallen back.

Vīra Śaivas are taught that each person may attain Release

[1] In Mysore there is a group known as *Ārādhyas*, who are pure Liṅgāyats and do not wear the sacred thread.

in this life by practising the prescribed meditations and passing through the six stages. Bhakti holds a large place in their practice. Their philosophy[1] shows very clearly the influence of Rāmānuja, and from an early date the teaching and literature of the Tamil Śaivas exercised a considerable influence on them.

§ 315. Liṅgāyat literature is mostly in Kanarese and Sanskrit, but there are also several rather important books in Telugu. Unfortunately, so little critical study has as yet been spent on them that, in many cases, it is impossible to assign dates or to sketch their contents.

One of the very earliest works is the life of Paṇḍitārādhya, the Mahant of Śrī-Śaila. It was written in a mixture of Sanskrit and Telugu by Somanātha, who lived at Pālakūrki near Warangal during the reign of the first Pratāparudra, i.e. in the last decades of the twelfth century. He is also the author of the original *Basava Purāṇa*, which is in Telugu verse. There is another important work in Sanskrit which may be even earlier, the *Śrīkara-bhāshya* on the *Vedānta-sūtras*: its date is discussed in our next chapter.

There are also a number of Liṅgāyat documents in the Āgama literature.[2] The *Sūkshma* is entirely Liṅgāyat, while the *Suprabheda*, *Svāyambhuva*, *Kāmika*, *Parameśvara*, and *Vātula* all contain Liṅgāyat material. It is probable that these sectarian works are of fairly early date.

Of great importance for popular Liṅgayatism are the early Kanarese sermons known as Vachana. Some are attributed to Basava himself, others to later men. The character of the Kanarese in which some of these are written proves that they belong to the thirteenth century at latest.[3]

There are then the Kanarese Purāṇas, which are of various dates. The *Siddharāma* (the legendary life of the first Mahant of Sholapur) for example, by Rāghavāṅka, the pupil of Hari-

[1] See Bhandarkar, *VS.* 134 ff. [2] See p. 193.

[3] My informant is Rao Sahib P. G. Halkatti of Bijapur, who has translated those attributed to Basava into English. Unfortunately they are still unpublished.

hara, is a fourteenth-century work[1]; and several others may belong to the same century.

F. *Śākta Literature.*

a. *The Left-hand School.*

§ 316. A considerable list of Tantras can be formed which seem to date from the tenth or the eleventh century. A MS. of the *Brahma-Yāmala* bears the date A.D. 1052,[2] and a MS. of the *Nityāhnikatilaka*, a work dealing with the daily rites of the Kubjikā sect of Śāktas, is dated 1197[3]; while in the works of two Śaiva scholars belonging to Kashmir, Abhinavagupta, whose *floruit* is A.D. 1000, and his disciple Kshemarāja, there are quotations from the *Devī-Yāmala*, *Kulachūḍāmaṇi*, *Kālottara*, *Kulasāra*, *Amṛiteśa*, and *Mālinī-vijaya Tantras.*[4] Clearly these cannot be dated later than the tenth century. Lakshmīdhara, a scholar who lived at Warangal towards the end of the thirteenth century,[5] quotes from the *Vāmakeśvara T.* a list of sixty-four Tantras, which is almost the same as the list found in MSS. of that Tantra to-day. As the *Vāmakeśvara* was already an authoritative work in his time, it must be a good deal older. The *Kulachūḍāmaṇi T.* also contains a list of sixty-four Tantras, which is very similar to the *Vāmakeśvara* list. In each of these lists there are three groups of Tantras which we may take to be characteristic of the first half of the period, eight Bhairavas, eight Bahurūpas, and eight Yāmalas. These last—the *Brahma*, *Vishṇu*, *Rudra*, *Lakshmī*, *Umā*, *Skanda*, *Gaṇeśa*, and *Graha Yāmalas*—receive their name from *Yamala*, a pair, the reference being to a divinity and his śakti in sexual union. The pose is called *Sambara* in Nepalese Buddhism and *Yab-yum* in Tibetan Buddhism, and images of this character were common.[6] In their character

[1] Rice, *KL.* 43. [2] H. P. Sastri, II. xxii. [3] Ib. I. lxiv.
[4] Hall, 197 f.; Chatterji, *KS.* 38.
[5] See Intro. to *Saundaryalaharī* by A. Mahādeva Śāstrī and Paṇḍitaratnam K. Raṅgāchārya. But see also below, p. 389, n. 1.
[6] H. P. Sāstrī, II. vii.; Getty, *GNB.* 181 and *passim.* There are similar sculptures on some of the temples at Khajuraho.

these Tantras are parallel with the Buddhist Tantras which appear in the Tibetan Canon, and in Chinese translations, in the tenth and eleventh centuries.[1] Some of the names coincide, Śambara, Jāla-Śambara, Kālachakra, Mahākāla.

The *Saundaryalaharī* is a famous ode to the goddess in a hundred stanzas, of which Stanzas 1–41 are frequently published as a separate ode under the name *Ānandalaharī*. The whole is usually ascribed to Śaṅkarāchārya, but serious scholars regard the ascription as a mistake. Lakshmīdhara, the scholar already quoted, who belongs to the end of the thirteenth century, has a valuable commentary on it. As he unhesitatingly accepts the authorship of Śaṅkara, there must be a tradition of some age to that effect behind him. The work thus goes back to a fairly early date, but it is not yet possible to be more definite. Another work often by mistake[2] attributed to Śaṅkara, the *Prapañchasāra T.*, rather a foul book, has been much used and has had many commentaries written upon it. We cannot be mistaken in assigning it to this period. Along with it we may take two books belonging to the Kaulas, who are amongst the extremest of the Śāktas, the *Kaula U.* and the *Paraśurāma-Bhārgava-sūtra*. Of the latter we are told that it is 'a complete exposition of all branches of the Kaula system', and that 'the worship of Devī according to the Kaula marga is generally based on the directions given in this work.'[3] Of the *Kaula U.* we are told that it is a work

> in terse prose, the ethical code of the Kaulas. It is enigmatic, and its directions are vague and indistinct. It hints that the shackles of ritualism cannot lead to liberation, which can be secured only by throwing off the blind restrictions imposed by social conventions.

There are some half a dozen other Śākta Upanishads, all of which probably belong to this period. These are as follows: two *Tripurātāpanīya* Upanishads, modelled on the *Nṛisiṁhatāpanīya* works, the *Tripurā*, *Shaṭchakra*, and *Bhāvanā*

[1] See § 324.
[2] From confusion with a non-Tāntrik work of the same name.
[3] From an anonymous essay in *SJM.* III. (1897).

Upanishads, and finally the *Devī U.*, included in the fivefold *Atharvaśiras U.*,[1] which doubtless rests on an original Śākta Upanishad. The *Tripurā U.*, which consists of sixteen stanzas and claims to belong to the Śākala Śākhā of the *Ṛigveda*, gives a brief outline of the philosophic basis of the Śākta system and describes the various modes of worship in use.

The *Śāradātilaka T.* is a work of very great authority, written by Lakshmaṇa Deśika, a scholar belonging to the eleventh century. The book deals almost exclusively with spells (mantras) and sorcery, and scarcely mentions ritual. It is thus rightly connected with Sarasvatī, who as goddess of speech is called Śāradā. It opens with a philosophy of creation and of human speech. It describes and classifies mantras, gives rules for the preliminary arrangements necessary for the use of mantras, for initiation, and for the use of the sacrificial fire. The body of the work deals with the formation and employment of mantras. A few mudrās are described and many yantras. The last chapter is on Tāntrik Yoga. The *Shaṭchakra U.*, mentioned above, deals, as its name implies, with the six chakras of occult force supposed to lie in the human body. As Nārāyaṇa commented on it, it must belong to this period at latest. The *Bhāvanā U.*, also mentioned above, teaches that the human body may itself be considered a Śrī-chakra.

We may also note two vernacular Śākta works belonging to this period, a Bengali poem on Chaṇḍī belonging to the thirteenth century and a Telugu translation of the *Mārkaṇḍeya P.*, the date of which is about 1300.

b. *The Right-hand School.*

§ 317. There seems to be no evidence in the early literature of the existence of any Devī-worshipping sect which repudiated the coarser elements of the ritual, or of Devī-temples in which animal sacrifice was not permitted. All seem to belong to

[1] See § 207.

what is now called the Left-hand (*Vāmāchārī*) section of the Śākta teaching and cult. But from the thirteenth century, if not earlier, we hear of Śākta scholars who followed the pure path of the Right-hand (*Dakshiṇāchārī*) section, and also of Right-hand literature. In Gujarāt and in South India to-day there are many Devī-temples in which no animal sacrifice is permitted. The individual scholars with their private practice and the temples with their public cult seem to be both connected with the Smārta community, and the cult is in full conformity with Vedic usage. Can it be that these facts point back to a mediaeval reformation? It is curious that, in tradition as well as in the pseudonymous Śaṅkaravijayas, there is said to have been such a movement, and it is attributed to Śaṅkara. For example, in Conjeeveram local tradition says he compelled the goddess Kāmāchīamma, i.e. the Love-eyed Mother, to give up human sacrifice. A very remarkable image of Śaṅkara is worshipped in her temple there,[1] and the ministrants are Nambūtiri Brāhmans, who declare themselves descendants of priests introduced from Malabar by Śaṅkara.[2]

§ 318. The first scholar, so far as we know, who follows the Right-hand path is Lakshmīdhara, who has been already mentioned. His name as an initiate was Vidyānātha. In his commentary on sloka 31 of *Saundaryalaharī* he gives the list of sixty-four Tantras discussed above, and also gives two other lists as follows:

Miśra or Mixed Tantras: (1) Chandrakalā, (2) Jyotisvatī, (3) Kalānidhi, (4) Kulārṇava, (5) Kuleśvarī, (6) Bhuvaneśvarī, (7) Bārhaspatya, (8) Dūrvāsasa.

Samaya or Śubha, i.e. *Pure*, *Tantras*: (1) Vasishṭha, (2) Sanaka, (3) Śuka, (4) Sanandana, (5) Sanatkumāra.

By Mixed Tantras he seems to mean books which give instructions for the worship of the goddess with a view both to earthly blessings and release, while Pure Tantras teach only

[1] See a print from a photograph in my *Primer of Hinduism*, 119.
[2] Maclean, *ERE*. VII. 646.

the way to release. They teach how by meditation and yoga practice the Devī may be raised from the Mūlādhāra, through four other chakras, to Ājñā, and thence to the Sahasrāra.[1] This practice is called *Śrīvidyā*. Unfortunately this last group of five works is not yet known, and no account of them can be given.

c. *The Bhakti School.*

§ 319. There is another form of Right-hand worship among Śāktas which has come from the influence of the *Bhāgavata P.* Release is sought by the path of enthusiastic emotional bhakti towards the goddess. The chief scripture of this discipline is the *Devī Bhāgavata*, which is usually reckoned one of the Upapurāṇas. The devotees of the goddess, however, deny that it is one of the Upapurāṇas and affirm that it is the original work to which the fifth place among the Purāṇas belongs by right, and that the Kṛishṇa *Bhāgavata* was written by Vopadeva about A.D. 1300. A remark which Śrīdhara[2] makes at the beginning of his great commentary on the *Bhāgavata P.* enables us to realize that this claim was already common in his day. It is thus clear that the *Devī Bhāgavata*, being posterior to the *Bhāgavata P.* and prior to Śrīdhara, who lived about A.D. 1400, belongs to this period. It is not yet possible to say anything about the date of the *Agastya-sūtras*,[3] which expound the bhakti of the *Devī Bhāgavata* and are thus parallel to the *Nārada* and *Śāṇḍilya*-sūtras.

G. *Saura Literature.*

§ 320. It is probable that the splendid rise of the chief sects of the Vaishṇavas and Śaivas during our period gradually weakened the cults of the Sun, Gaṇeśa, and other minor gods. The Sauras have an honourable place in the *Prabodhachandrodaya*.[4] There were several great temples built to Sūrya during the early centuries,[5] but towards the end the popularity of the

[1] See Avalon, *TGL.* cxxxii ff.
[2] See § 326.
[3] See the essay in *SJM.* III. (1897).
[4] See § 270.
[5] Notably Mudherā in Gujarāt and Kaṇārak in Orissa.

god waned. There is very little literature to notice. A few chapters [1] in the *Brahma P.* containing the theology of Sūrya and the praise of Orissa and of the temple of the Sun at Kanārak, and the song of the Sun-god in Bengālī recently published by Mr. Dinesh Chandra Sen [2] may belong to this period, and the great inscription at Govindapur in the Gayā district by the poet Gaṅgādhara,[3] which dates from A.D. 1137, is a Saura document.

H. *Gāṇapatya Literature.*

§ 321. The Gāṇapatya sect clearly continued active during the early centuries of this period, even if it decayed towards the close. The usual sectarian mantra seems to have been *Śrī Gaṇeśāya namaḥ*, while the sect-mark was a circlet of red minium on the forehead. The most important document of the sect, apart from the Upanishad described above,[4] is the *Ganeśa Purāṇa*,[5] the bulk of which consists of legends in glorification of Ganeśa, including stories of his having cured leprosy, but also deals with the theology and the worship of the sect and details the thousand names of the god. Gaṇeśa as the supreme Brahman can be known only by mystical contemplation, but he may also be worshipped through his images in the usual Hindu way. The *Mudgala P.* is also a Gāṇapatya work, but seemingly of later origin. The date of the *Śaṅkara Digvijaya* is very doubtful, but it may with safety be regarded as reflecting facts belonging to the latter half of the period. It speaks of the Gāṇapatyas as divided into six sub-sects, according as they worship Mahā-Gaṇapati, Haridrā Gaṇapati, Uchchhishṭa-Gaṇapati, Navanīta-Gaṇapati, Svarṇa-Gaṇapati, and Santāna-Gaṇapati, while one section of the Uchchhishṭa-Gāṇapatyas revered Heramba-Gaṇapati and had very foul

[1] XXI-XXVIII. [2] *VSP.* I. 23-4; 164-71.

[3] *Epigraphia Indica*, II. 338.

[4] See § 239.

[5] The legends are briefly described by Stevenson, *JRAS.* VII. 319. The reference to Moreśvar, noted by him, is probably an interpolation.

rites.[1] Many of these forms of the god occur also in the *Mudgala P.*,[2] and a number of them are still to be seen in images in South India,[3] but the sects have all disappeared.

Yet, as the sect decayed, the position of the god as a minor divinity, the god of obstacles and success, adored by all Hindus, became firmly established. He is praised in this sense in the *Skanda P.*[4] and elsewhere. To this period also belongs a singular document which gives one of the many variant myths about his birth and his elephant head, the Gaṇeśa-Khaṇḍa of the *Brahmavaivarta P.*[5] The story is told to glorify Kṛishṇa as the Supreme, this part of the Purāṇa being probably of Nimbārkite origin.[6]

I. *Dharma Literature.*

§ 322. The gradual decay of Tāntrik Buddhism in Bengal and Orissa left a deep but not altogether healthy deposit in Hinduism. In most cases it was the old sects that received the deposit, but in one case at least there was a fresh growth. The central member of the Buddhist Triratna—Buddha, Dharma, Saṅgha—gave birth to a new Hindu god, Dharma, whose worship spread abroad and produced an important literature in early Bengali, which bears many marks of its Buddhist source. The prime scripture is the *Śūnya Purāṇa*,[7] a lineal descendant of Nāgārjuna's Śūnyavāda, by Rāmāī Paṇḍita, which seems to come from the eleventh century. It deals with both theology and ritual. One of the chief names connected with the cult is Lau Sen, King of Maina in Bengal in the eleventh century, who worshipped Dharma, and from whose heroic feats a famous legend arose. This story forms the basis of a series of Bengali romances known as the Dharma-

[1] They were unclean Śāktas, like the Buddhists who adored Heramba.

[2] This work catalogues thirty-two forms of Gaṇapati, while the *Śāradātikaka T.* speaks of fifty-one forms: Kṛishṇa Śāstrī, *SII.* 173.

[3] Ib. 165–76.

[4] *Skanda P.*, Prabhāsa Māhātmya. See Kennedy, *HM.* 352.

[5] Wilson, *Works*, III. 103 ff.

[6] See § 282.

[7] Sen, *HBLL.*

maṅgal poems, written from the twelfth century onward. The earliest writer was Mayūra Bhaṭṭa.[1]

ii. Buddhism.

A. *The Śāktas.*

§ 323. The Tāntrik University called Vikramaśīla, on the Ganges, founded early in the ninth century, rose to splendour about the opening of this period and showed a great succession of scholars for two centuries. Yet the religion was slowly dying, poisoned by Tantrism and weakened by Hindu violence and criticism. Few books were produced except Tāntrik works and manuals of logic,[2] and even these failed towards the end of the eleventh century. Islam destroyed Buddhism in India in the great conquest of the North just before A.D. 1200.

§ 324. There is a considerable number of Tantras and related works which, from their common features, and from the dates at which they were translated into Chinese and Tibetan, would seem to belong to the tenth century or thereabouts. One of the most distinctive, the *Śrīkālachakra T.*, is said to have been written in A.D. 965. The *Chaṇḍamahāroshaṇa*, *He-vajra*, *Heruka*, *Ḍākinī-jāla-sambara*, *Mañjuśrī-mūla*, and *Bhūta-ḍāmara* Tantras, and the *Mañjuśrī-nāma-saṅgīti*[3] (called also *Paramārtha-nāma-saṅgīti*), in which a long list of the names of Mañjuśrī forms a hymn of praise, belong to the same time and class.

§ 325. In these there appears first an intensification of the erotic features of Tantrism.[3] New Buddhas, each with his śakti, make their appearance, e.g. Heruka and Vajrayoginī, and the high religious value of intercourse with women is more insisted on than ever. It was probably as a result of this

[1] Sen, *HBLL.* 30 ff. [2] Vidyābhūshaṇa, *MSIL.* 135 ff.

[3] Vajrasattva utters the *Chaṇḍamahāroshaṇa T.* from the *pudendum muliebre* of Vajradhātviśvarī. Cf. the Buddhist Tāntrik monk in Act III of *Prabodhachandrodaya* (pp. 34 f. in Taylor's tr.), which was produced about A.D. 1060, and see § 300.

movement that the practice of representing in scripture these Buddhas in sexual union with their spouses arose, a practice which appeared also in Hinduism.[1] In Bengal the erotic Buddhism of this period was called Sahaja.[2] Romantic love for beautiful girls was made the path to release. Very little of the literature of the school remains, but it is reflected later in the poetry of Chaṇḍīdās, the Hindu śākta, and its foul practice long infected Bengal.

§ 326. The second fresh feature of these works is a theistic or pantheistic theology,[3] the final outcome of the Mahāyāna theory of the three bodies of the Buddha[4] and of the idealism of the Vijñānavāda school, especially as expressed in the term *alayavijñāna*.[5] The movement was also powerfully influenced by the Vedānta, by the theism of the Nyāya, and by Śaivism. The universe and all Buddhas come from an eternal being called Ādi-Buddha, i. e. the original Buddha, and Svayambhū, i. e. the self-existent, the process being represented by the triple system of Dhyāni-Buddhas, Dhyāni-Bodhisattvas and Mānushi-Buddhas, as follows:

ĀDI-BUDDHA.

		Dhyāni-Buddhas.		
Vairochana	Akshobya	Ratnasambhava	Amitābha	Amoghasiddha
		Dhyāni-Bodhisattvas.		
Samantabhadra	Vajrapāṇi	Ratnapāṇi	Avalokiteśvara	Viśvapāṇi
		Mānushi-Buddhas.		
Dīpaṅkara	Kanakamuni	Kāśyapa	Gautama	Maitreya

The three grades of being are suggested by the three bodies of the Buddha, while the five beings in each grade come from the original five Buddhas of early Buddhism, the three Former

[1] See § 316.
[2] Kumaraswamy, *The Dance of Śiva*, 103 (New York, 1918); Sen, *HBLL.* 37.
[3] See Poussin, *ERE.* art. 'Ādi-Buddha'.
[4] See § 176.
[5] See § 178.

Buddhas, Gautama, and the coming Buddha, for these are the Mānushi Buddhas of the third grade. The theory was developed alongside Tantrism, which teaches that every Buddha and every Bodhisattva has a wife.

By five acts of his contemplative power (*dhyāna*), the *Ādi-Buddha* creates five *Dhyāni-Buddhas*. The Dhyāni-Buddhas have nothing to do with man or the world, but live in thoughtful peace in nirvāṇa. Each, however, has a son who is a *Dhyāni-bodhisattva* and has never been a man. Through him, in turn, a *Mānushi-Buddha*, i. e. a human Buddha, is brought into being, and a world within which the Mānushi-Buddha plays his part.

In most of the forms of this theology the eternal One is personal, so that the system is distinctly theistic, e. g. the Aiśvārika system of Nepal, but in others, where Vijñānavādin thought is prominent, the idea tends to exclude personality and thus to approach the pantheistic conception of Brahman as held by Śaṅkara and other Māyāvādins. The system is found most often in Tantrik works, such as the *Śrīkālachakra T.*, but it was held by Mahayanists also; for it appears in the *Guṇakāraṇḍavyūha*, which is a new poetic version of the old *Kāraṇḍavyūha*.[1]

B. *Buddhist Lands.*

§ 327. Buddhism lingered on in great weakness in Bengal, where a few pieces of literature may be traced,[2] until the sixteenth century, when the last groups of Tantrik monks and nuns were absorbed by the Chaitanya sect.[3] In Orissa the faith has survived in disguised forms down to the present time.[4]

But if Buddhism died out in India proper, it continued to thrive elsewhere.

§ 328. In Nepal, in the first part of the period, we trace the rise of the Aiśvārika, or Theistic, system explained above, and fresh literature seems to have been written. It is in Nepal

[1] See § 175. [2] Sen, *HBLL.* 15–55. [3] See § 370.
[4] Vasu, *Archaeological Survey of Mayurabhunja*, Chap. II.

that the theistic *Guṇakāraṇḍavyūha*[1] is found. The same theology appears in the *Svayambhū P.*, which is a Māhātmya of Nepal and probably is as late as the twelfth or thirteenth century.[2] The *Daśabhūmīśvara* is a later recension of the Mādhyamaka *Daśabhūmaka-sūtra*,[3] augmented with résumés in Prākṛit verse. It is found in Nepal.

The most interesting fact about Nepalese Buddhism is that its sacred books were in Sanskrit, and the great majority of existing Sanskrit texts, whether Mahāyāna or Tāntrik, have been found there. They can be most conveniently studied in R. L. Mitra's *Nepalese Buddhist Literature*. No traces of a Nepalese Buddhist Canon have been found. The character of the texts found there would naturally lead to the conclusion that the books in use in the middle ages must have been very similar to those of Tibet, i. e. the literature is Mahāyāna with a considerable infusion of Tāntrik works. Further, while there is no real Canon, there is a curious sort of substitute for one: Nine very famous works—eight of them being Mahāyāna sūtras, the ninth, one of the greatest of the early Tantras—are held in special reverence and receive regular divine worship. The following is the list:

THE NINE DHARMAS.

1. *Ashṭasāhasrikā Prajñāpāramitā.*
2. *Gaṇḍavyūha.*
3. *Daśabhūmīśvara.*
4. *Samādhirāja.*
5. *Laṅkāvatāra-sūtra.*
6. *Saddharma-puṇḍarīka.*
7. *Tathāgata-guhyaka.*
8. *Lalita-vistara.*
9. *Suvarṇaprabhāsa.*

[1] See § 326.
[2] This inference rests on a reference to Rādhā (Mitra, 254): See § 280
[3] See § 177.

§ 329. Buddhist literature in Pāli has been written in Ceylon continuously until our times,[1] and also in Burma from the eleventh century downwards.[2]

§ 330. In A.D. 972 the Chinese Canon, as it then was, was printed from wooden blocks. Numerous editions followed; for the blocks were often destroyed by fire or by civil war. But many new translations, especially of Tāntrik works, were added between A.D. 972 and the beginning of the fourteenth century.[3] Since then there has been no change. The full Canon was printed in the fourteenth century, and has since been frequently published.[4]

§ 331. Corea and Japan did not translate the sacred books, but contented themselves with the Chinese Canon. It is important to realize how wide a field the Chinese Canon—a set of rather imperfect translations—has had for its influence. A few years ago, stimulated by the example of the Christian Scriptures in Japanese, one of the Amida sects[5] published Japanese versions of the three Sukhāvatī texts which they regard as supremely valuable, but until then no Japanese could read a Buddhist text in his own tongue.

§ 332. Though the bulk of the Tibetan translations had been made by the end of the ninth century, more were added in the eleventh, and a few as late as the thirteenth century. The following quotation gives some facts about the Canon as published:

> The whole forms a series of over three hundred volumes, each of which with its wooden covers makes a package about 26 in. long, 8 in. broad, 8 in. deep, and weighing about 10 lb. The volumes generally are in the form of xylographs, or prints from carved wooden blocks, as with ancient Chinese books, no movable type having been employed; occasionally MS. sets of the entire canon are to be found.
>
> The sacred texts consist of two great collections: (a) the canon, and (b) the commentaries.

[1] Winternitz, II. i. 174–81.
[2] Mabel Bode, *Pali Literature of Burma*. [3] Nanjio, Cols. 450–8.
[4] Nanjio, *Intro.* xxii. [5] i.e. sects that worship Amitābha.

The canon, or *Ka-gyur* (vulgarly *Kanjur*), 'translated word', forms a series of one hundred, or in some editions, one hundred and eight, volumes, and comprises 1,083 distinct books. It is divided into seven great sections, as compared with the three divisions of the Pali canonical scriptures, or Tripiṭaka.

The commentary *Tan-gyur* (vulgarly *Tanjur*) is a great encyclopaedic library of ancient lore on metaphysics, logic, composition, arts, alchemy, &c., including the commentaries of ancient Indian Buddhist writers, Nāgārjuna and others, and also some texts by Tsong-Kha-pa and other Tibetan saints.[1]

About A.D. 1206 Jenghiz Khan the Mongol conquered Tibet. His grandson Kublai Khan, converted to Buddhism by a Tibetan abbot, gave this abbot and his successors temporal power in Tibet in A.D. 1270, and opened Mongolia to Buddhism. The abbot, with the aid of a staff of scholars, carried out the stupendous task of translating the whole Tibetan Canon into Mongolian. The Mongol script is a modification of Syriac which had been introduced into Central Asia by Nestorian missionaries. Thus Indian Buddhist literature received a sudden expansion of influence, and was carried wherever the Mongols went.[2]

iii. JAINISM.

A. *Śvetāmbara Literature.*

§ 333. Śvetāmbara literature was already very rich and varied at the opening of this period, and during the first three centuries it rose to its utmost splendour and strength, displaying all its variety and brilliance in its chief representative Hemachandra. Then came the Muhammadan conquest of the North, in which Jains were cut to pieces, harried, and persecuted in the same way as Hindus and Buddhists were. The fact that the community survived at all is proof of the strength of its character and organization, but it has never regained its former influence and splendour.

The work of elucidating books of the Canon in the classical

[1] Waddell, *ERE.* VII. 789. [2] *ERE.* VII. 786.

style in Sanskrit, so brilliantly begun by Haribhadra and Śīlāṅka in the ninth century, was carried forward by another pair of writers, Abhayadeva of the eleventh century, who took Śīlāṅka for his model, and Malayagiri of the twelfth century, who followed Haribhadra. There were other scholars—notably Śāntisūri, Devendragaṇi and Tilakāchārya—who did further expository work of real value in Sanskrit. Śrīchandrasūri, a junior contemporary of Hemachandra, left a number of Prākṛit commentaries.

Several works of genuine religious power were written during the period, especially by Hemachandra and Āsaḍa; and Jain apologetic, dogmatic, and philosophy were eagerly cultivated. Criticism of Hindu and Buddhist philosophy was very popular, the writers usually following the example of Haribhadra and calling their works 'Six systems'. A number of famous sacred odes were composed, the most notable writers being Śobhana, his brother Dhanapāla, and Abhayadeva the expositor.

Innumerable romantic tales both in Sanskrit and Prākṛit appeared. Dhanapāla, Devendragaṇi, and Devabhadra wrote in Sanskrit, while Hemachandra's *Vasudeva Hiṇḍa* is in Prākṛit. Closely allied to these is the *prabandha*, a narrative of a semi-historical character consisting of a series of stories about well-known men of the recent past, and also the *charita*, or biography of a Jain saint. Both of these types of books minister to the instinct which seeks to know the facts of men's lives, but they are first of all edifying literature, and for that reason the tales are treated with a good deal of freedom. Hence, while a great many of the stories, especially those of more recent date, contain historical elements, legend plays a large place in them.[1] Most of these books are in Sanskrit, but a few are in Prākṛit, e.g. Guṇachandra's *Mahāvīra-charita*.

§ 334. During the first half of the period the powerful influence of the Vedānta leads to the acceptance among Jains

[1] Bühler, *Hemachandra*, 6; Tawney, *Prabandhachintāmaṇi*, Preface.

of a sort of Brahman, an eternal spirit behind the Tīrthakaras[1]; and the idea survives here and there to this day, but it has never really modified or weakened the essential atheism of the system. This faint reflection of Vedantic thought in Jainism is curiously similar to the far more powerful Ādi-Buddha doctrine in Buddhism.

§ 335. The following seem to be the most outstanding personalities among the writers of the time.

Two brothers belonging to the latter half of the tenth century, Śobhana and Dhanapāla, the latter a protégé of both Muñja and Bhoja, kings of Malwa, distinguished themselves greatly as writers of sacred odes in Sanskrit. Dhanapāla's *Ṛishabhapañchāśikā*, fifty stanzas in praise of Ṛishabha, one of the Tīrthakaras, is well known, while Śobhana's hymns are still more famous. Dhanapāla's *Tilakamañjarī*, a volume of tales in highly artificial Sanskrit, is worthy of comparison with the *Yaśastilaka* by the contemporary Digambara scholar Somadeva.

Abhayadeva is the greatest name among Śvetāmbaras of the eleventh century. Following the example of Śīlāṅka, he wrote Sanskrit commentaries on nine of the chief canonical works, viz. the third to the eleventh Aṅgas inclusive, and many other texts. Of his original works the best known is an ode to Pārśvanātha called *Jayatihuyaṇastotra*, which he is said to have composed, as a plea for release from a disease, while standing in worship before that Tīrthakara's image.

Devabhadra (1086–1169), a famous logician, completely defeated the Digambara scholar Kumudachandra in a controversy on the question of the salvation of women, held at the court of Jayasiṁha at Anhilvāra-pāṭaṇ in Gujarāt in A. D. 1124, and thereby prevented the Digambaras from getting a foothold in the city.

But the greatest of all Śvetāmbara writers is Hemachandra, who lived from 1089 to 1173, and spent most of his life in Anhil-

[1] *IA.* VII. 106; Rice, *Mysore and Coorg from the Inscriptions*, 103; Suali, *GSAI.* IX. 28; Barth, *RI.* 146.

vāra-pāṭaṇ the capital of Gujarāt. He had great influence at court from A. D. 1125 onwards, and still greater after 1159, when he won over king Kumārapāla to Jainism. He was a writer of extraordinary industry, scholarship, and versatility. His chief religious books are the *Yogaśāstra*, a treatise on Jain ethics and asceticism, and the *Vītarāgastuti*, a poem in thirty-two stanzas in praise of the passionless life, both written to establish his royal convert in the faith. His three works in the field of legendary history and biography, already referred to, are the *Trishashṭi-śalākā-purushacharita*, a Jain history of the world, its appendix, the *Pariśishṭaparvan*, which contains the lives of the Jain prophets and teachers, and his biography of Mahāvīra, the *Mahāvīracharita*. His *Vasudeva Hiṇḍa*, a large collection of romantic tales, told in Prākṛit and mostly in prose, may be set beside Haribhadra's *Samarāichchhakahā*. He is also the author of a Jain Rāmāyaṇa, the *Rāmacharita*. But his literary activity was not merely religious but covered almost the whole field of the culture and science of mediaeval India. He wished to give Jains the fullest possible opportunity of becoming educated and capable men. He therefore wrote on logic, grammar, rhetoric, poetics, lexicography, and politics. His Sanskrit and Prākṛit grammars and lexicons are weighty scientific works which have been widely used.

Āsaḍa came of the royal family of Bhilmal in Gujarāt. One of his sons died young, and a Jain teacher did his best to give him religious consolation. The bereaved father wrote in 1191 the *Vivekamañjarī* in memory of his son, working the teacher's words of consolation into beautiful verse. Another of his works, the *Upadeśakandalī*, is praised as being rich food for pilgrims on the road to Release.

Jinadatta's *Vivekavilāsa*, which was written about A. D. 1220, is a sort of summary of religious knowledge, including sketches of systems other than Jain.

Amarachandra, a noteworthy poet of the middle of the thirteenth century, wrote for the Jains the *Bālabhārata*, a sketch of the *Mahābhārata* in some 6,500 Sanskrit verses, and a *Kāvya* on Padmanābha, the Jain Tīrthakara who is expected to appear next. He is also the author of three works on poetics.

Prabhāchandra is the author of the earliest life of Hemachandra, the *Prabhāvakacharita*, which appeared about 1250, while his contemporary Devendrasūri is remembered because he wrote five of the six Karmagranthas.

Merutuṅga (A) flourished early in the fourteenth century, and is most famous for his *Prabandhachintāmaṇi*. The first four chapters of this *prabandha* contain a good deal of valuable history and biography, but the remainder is legend. He also wrote the *Muñjaprabandha* in Prākṛit. Rājaśekhara is the author of *Prabandhakośa* (published in 1349 at Delhi), which is of considerable value, and a collection of tales called *Antarakathāsaṅgraha*.

B. *Digambara Literature.*

§ 336. The Digambara literature of the period is not so rich as the Śvetāmbara, yet it has considerable variety and a large part of it is in Kanarese. Commentaries were written on several of Kuṇḍakuṇḍa's works, and Nemichandra (late tenth century) produced a number of fresh philosophic books of considerable importance. Numerous purāṇas both Sanskrit and Kanarese appeared, and legendary history and biography were not neglected. Amongst the most popular works are Jain versions of the Epics in Kanarese.

At the beginning of the tenth century lived Amṛitachandra, a brilliant commentator. He expounded three of the works of the early Digambara scholar Kuṇḍakuṇḍa, the *Samayasāraprābhṛita*, the *Pañchatthiyasaṅgahasutta*, and the *Pravachanasāra*, and wrote a work on the Digambara categories, the *Tattvārthasāra*, and the *Purushārthasiddhyupāya* on the means whereby man may reach perfection. Bālachandra (*c.* 1100) wrote a commentary on the *Prābhṛitasāra*, another of Kuṇḍakuṇḍa's works.

One of the most famous of Kanarese poets is Pampa, who wrote in 941 his Kanarese adaptation of the *Mahābhārata*, which is known as the *Pampa-Bhārata*, or the *Vikramārjuna Vijaya*. He is also the author of the Kanarese *Ādi Purāṇa*.

We notice next the *Yaśastilaka* of Somadeva, a series of tales told in very artistic Sanskrit, to recommend the Jainism of the Digambara sect. It is technically a *kathā*, i. e. a composition in prose which breaks into verse when the story becomes surcharged with feeling. It is a work of great literary power, which would have held a high place in Sanskrit literature, had it not been Jain. It was written in A. D. 960 under the Rāshṭrakūṭa king Kṛishṇa III.

Chāmuṇḍarāya was chief minister to the Western Gaṅga king Mārasiṁha II and also to his successor Pañchāladeva. They reigned in Mysore. He is noteworthy first as having erected at Śravaṇa Beḷgoḷa a colossal image of Gommateśvara about A. D. 980, and secondly as being the author of the *Chāmuṇḍarāya Purāṇa*, which is the earliest existing work in Kanarese prose and is dated A. D. 978. It gives an account of each of the twenty-four Tīrthakaras.

One of the teachers whom Chāmuṇḍarāya revered was Nemichandra Siddhānta-chakravartī, who is the author of five dogmatic works in Prākṛit verse, which have been much used, *Dravya-saṁgraha*, *Gommatasāra*, *Labdhisāra*, *Kshapaṇasāra*, and *Trilokasāra*. The *Dravyasaṁgraha* and the *Trilokasāra* are always included among the books mentioned under the Secondary Canon. He seems to be the Nemichandra who lived about A. D. 990 and wrote the first Kanarese novel, *Līlāvatī*.

The *Paramātma-prakāśa* is a Sanskrit work in 344 stanzas by Śrī-Yogīndra Āchārya, but the date is not known. The purpose of the work is to oppose theistic teaching, and the method employed is to try to show that the human soul is the truly divine spirit. Numerous Vedantic terms are used.

Āśādhara, a layman and a native of the country by the

Sambhar lake, fled, while still a young man, from his home, at the end of the twelfth century, to escape the violence of the Musulman invaders and took refuge in Dhārā. There he became a learned Jain, and wrote fourteen works, most of them on the Jain faith. The most famous of these is the *Dharmāmṛita*, or Nectar of Religion, which describes the duties of Jain ascetics and laymen. His *Trishashṭismṛiti* is a collection of stories about sixty-three persons drawn from the Jain Purāṇas.

There were a number of notable men among the Kanarese Jain poets. Pampa, Ponna, and Raṇṇa—all tenth-century men—are called the three gems, but Abhinava Pampa also deserves a place beside them. Pampa's *Ādi Purāṇa* is said to be 'unequalled in style among the Kanarese poets'. His Kanarese *Mahābhārata*, called the *Pampa Bhārata*, in which he identifies his own princely patron Arikesari with Arjuna, is also much admired. The fame of Ponna and Raṇṇa rests in each case on a Kanarese Purāṇa. Abhinava Pampa, who flourished about A.D. 1100, is also the author of a Purāṇa, but it is his *Pampa Rāmāyaṇa* that has brought him glory. It is a Jain recast of the ancient story. The whole atmosphere is Jain, and all the heroes are faithful to the Jain faith.

We may also mention the *Jīvaka-Chintāmaṇi*,[1] a Jain Tamil *Kāvya* or romance in verse, written probably in the tenth century.

[1] Barnett, *BMCTB*. 4.

CHAPTER VII

MUSLIM INFLUENCE

A.D. 1350 TO 1800.

§337. The new factor in the religion of India during these centuries is the influence of Islam. That influence seems to be scarcely traceable in the literature before 1400; but we choose 1350 as the opening year of the new period, because it is most probable that further research will succeed in discerning its activities a good deal earlier. Islamic ideas are not so generally diffused as the great elements which have hitherto formed the distinguishing features of our periods, but they seem to be of greater importance than any other force operative during these centuries.

It was, in the first instance, through the teaching of Sūfīs that Islam found entrance to Hindu hearts. They fraternized with Hindu ascetics and gurus; and each learned to respect the other's religious faith and life. But not until the last quarter of the fifteenth century did the movement show any notable force. Kabīr was the man through whom the leading ideas were popularized. From his time the condemnation of idolatry and polytheism became frequent. But large sections of Hinduism show little or no reaction to the influence of Islam.

Perhaps the extraordinary rise of the vernaculars from the fourteenth century onwards may be partly due to the serious weakening of Sanskrit scholarship consequent on the impoverishment of Hinduism and the destruction of Hindu schools and monasteries by the invaders.

Akbar, who had come to the throne in 1542, transformed the character of the empire by his policy of giving Hindus equal rights with Muslims and admitting them to the highest positions in the army and the administration. He thereby not only gave Hinduism freedom once more to raise its head, but greatly changed the feeling of Hindus towards the Empire. He had many Hindu works translated into Persian, and his great-grandson, Dārā Shikoḥ, followed his example.

i. Hinduism.

A. *The Philosophies.*

a. *The Karma Mīmāṁsā.*

§ 338. From the very beginning of this period to the middle of the seventeenth century there was great activity in the Karma Mīmāṁsā school. Three authors produced each a famous treatise and a very large number of ancillary works appeared. The earliest, written during the first decades of our period, is Mādhava's *Jaiminīya-nyāya-mālā-vistara*, a full exposition of the system in verse, accompanied by a commentary in prose. Colebrooke says:

> It follows the order in Jaimini's text; not by way of paraphrase, but as a summary (though the title rather implies amplification) of its purport, and of approved deductions from it; sometimes explaining separately the doctrine of Bhaṭṭa and of Guru, under each head; at other times that of the old scholiast; but more commonly confined to that of Bhaṭṭa alone; yet often furnishing more than one application to the same text, as Bhaṭṭa himself does.[1]

This work has had a great vogue, partly because of its clearness, largely also because the verses could be easily committed to memory. The author and his brother Sāyaṇa were closely connected with the court of Vijayanagara and with Śaṅkara's monastery at Sriṅgerī. They are amongst the most illustrious of Hindu scholars. Āpa Deva[2] wrote, about A.D. 1630, an elementary manual, the *Mīmāṁsā-nyāya-prakāśa*, which is usually called the *Āpadevī* and has been much studied, because it is easy. Then Khaṇḍadeva (died 1665) produced the

[1] *ME.* I. 300.

[2] His son, Ananta Deva, author of the *Smṛiti Kaustubha*, wrote at the command of Baz Bahadur Chandra of Kumaon, who died in 1678. Duff, *CI.* 281.

Bhāṭṭadīpikā, which has won itself an honoured place because of its brilliant logical reasoning. Appaya Dīkshita[1] (1552–1624) has a treatise in verse on the Mīmāṁsā which was much talked of in its day, the *Vidhi-rasāyana*: in it he attacks Kumārila.

The Mīmāṁsā has been atheistic, in the sense of not recognizing the Supreme, throughout its history; yet that has never hindered Smārtas, who almost to the last man recognize the Brahman of the Upanishads, from making full use of the system. Vedānta-Deśika[2] in his *Seśvara Mīmāṁsā* maintains that Kumārila acknowledged the existence of God, and other writers have argued that the acknowledgement of God is quite consistent with its principles.

b. *The Vedānta.*

§ 339. During this period an immense number of treatises were written on the advaita Vedānta, commentaries, super-commentaries, summaries in prose and verse, and partial expositions. Here we note only a few of the more noteworthy manuals. At the beginning of the period there appeared the *Pañchadaśī* by Bhāratītīrtha and Mādhava, an independent exposition in verse of the whole system running to fifteen chapters, as the name implies. It betrays the tendency, which went further later on, to bring into the Vedānta ideas belonging to the other systems, especially the Sāṅkhya. In the fifteenth century, Advaitānanda wrote the *Brahma-vidyābharaṇa*, a prose commentary on Śaṅkara's *Bhāshya* which Colebrooke found useful. His disciple Sadānanda is the author of a brief outline of the Advaita in prose called the *Vedānta-sāra*, which forms a useful introduction to the philosophy; but the student must realize that contamination of the Vedānta from the Sāṅkhya proceeds further in it than in earlier works. Madhusūdana Sarasvatī, a sannyāsī of the Sarasvatī order, flourished before A.D. 1550, and wrote a well-known work on the nature of release in the Advaita, the *Vedānta-kalpalatikā*. He belongs

[1] See § 354. [2] See § 381.

to the group who believe that all the six systems of Hindu philosophy teach essentially the same doctrine.[1] Vijñāna Bhikshu's *Vijñānāmṛita* is a dualist bhāshya, an attempt to prove that the dualism of the Sāṅkhya can be established within the Vedānta.[2]

§ 340. Several fresh sectarian bhāshyas were written during this period. The following table may be found useful:

SECTARIAN BHĀSHYAS.

Approx. date.	*Author.*	*Sect.*	*Name of bhāshya.*	*Philosophic Standpoint.*
1085	Rāmānuja	Śrī-Vaishṇava	*Śrī-bhāshya*	Viśishṭādvaita
1230	Madhva	Mādhva	*Sūtra-bhāshya*	Dvaita
XIII	Vishṇusvāmī	Vishṇusvāmī	*Brahma-sūtra-bhāshya*	Dvaita
XIII	Śrīnivāsa	Nimbārka	*Vedānta-kaustubha*	Bhedābheda
c. 1400	Śrīkaṇṭha	Śaiva	*Śaiva-bhāshya*	Viśishṭādvaita
XVI	Vallabha	Vallabhāchārya	*Anubhāshya*	Śuddhādvaita
?	Śrīpati	Liṅgāyat	*Śrīkara-bhāshya*	Śakti-viśishtādvaita
?	Śuka	Bhāgavata	*Śuka-bhāshya*	Viśishṭādvaita
XVIII	Baladeva	Chaitanya	*Govinda-bhāshya*	Achintya-bhedābheda

§ 341. A scholar named Nārāyaṇa, who, coming later than Śaṅkarānanda, the guru of Mādhava, probably lived early in this period, wrote commentaries on many Upanishads, and gives a list of fifty-two Upanishads which is of considerable historical importance. The *Muktikā U.* contains a list of 108 Upanishads of considerable interest. In the year 1656 Dārā Shikoḥ, one of the sons of the Mugal Emperor Shah Jahan, gathered a number of paṇdits at Delhi and got them to translate fifty Upanishads into Persian. Anquetil Duperron, the French scholar who went to India to study Zoroastrianism in the latter part of the eighteenth century, obtained a copy of

[1] See § 346. [2] His position is explained in § 342.

this work, and when he returned to Europe translated it word for word into Latin. This was the form in which the Vedānta first reached Europe.

c. *The Sāṅkhya.*

§ 342. Throughout this period the *Sāṅkhya Kārikā* continued to be much read; for Mādhavāchārya's summary of Sāṅkhya doctrine in his *Sarva-darśana-saṅgraha,* written about A.D. 1380, is based on it; and several commentaries on it and on Vāchaspati's *Sāṅkhya-tattva-kaumudī* have been written. But there are two other expositions of Sāṅkhya teaching which have also been largely used, the *Sāṅkhya-sūtras* and the *Tattva-samāsa.* The date and the author in each case are quite unknown. Max Müller thought that the *Tattva-samāsa* was older than the *Kārikā*; but scholars of to-day do not follow him. Clearly, it is much more likely that these two are comparatively late works; for there is no clear reference to either before the fifteenth century. The *Tattva-samāsa* represents a form of arrangement of the Sāṅkhya principles considerably different from the form exhibited in the *Kārikā.* The *Sāṅkhya-sūtra* gives a good deal of space to criticism of the other philosophical systems, including the Vedānta; yet it makes a very great advance towards the Vedantic conception of God. Keith says[1]:

> The work makes remarkable efforts to prove that its views are in full accord with scripture, to which it attributes conclusive value, and endeavours to show as accordant with the Sāṁkhya itself *the statements in scripture regarding the personality of God,* the unity of the absolute, the joy which is asserted to be part of the nature of the absolute, and the heavenly bliss acknowledged in the Vedānta as a step on the way to final release. Indeed the text goes so far as to hold that obedience to the traditional rules of action has a good effect towards securing final release, and to talk of the attainment of the nature of the absolute.

The Sūtra thus approaches the doctrine, which became very popular during this period, that all the six Hindu systems can

[1] *SS.* 94.

be shown to be in harmony with each other. There are other developments of doctrine of less interest.[1] In the middle of the sixteenth century there lived in the vicinity of Benares a Sāṅkhya sannyāsī named Vijñāna Bhikshu who carried this movement a little farther. His fundamental conceptions seem to havebeen those of the ancient theistic system called *Sāṅkhya-yoga*. In any case he was a Sāṅkhya dualist, and yet a theist, conceiving God not as the universal spirit, but as a special soul, perfect and ever free. He wrote a bhāshya on the *Sāṅkhya Sūtra*, the *Sāṅkhya-pravachana-bhāshya*. In it he gives expression to the conviction that all the six systems are authoritative, in spite of their differences.

Sāṅkhya sannyāsīs are now so rare that it is of interest to know that, as late as 1912, a learned Sāṅkhya yati named Svāmī Hariharānanda was alive and teaching in Calcutta.[2]

d. *The Yoga.*

§ 343. Three useful works on Yoga produced during this period may be mentioned. Mādhava's chapter on the subject in his *Sarvadarśanasaṅgraha* (*c*. A.D. 1380), Vijñāna Bhikshu's *Yogasārasaṅgraha* (mid. sixteenth century), and Rāmānanda Sarasvatī's commentary on the *Yoga-sūtra*, called *Maṇiprabhā*, written about A.D. 1600.

Yogīs of this great old school have become very rare. I have never had the good fortune to meet one.

e. *The Vaiśeshika and the Nyāya.*

§ 344. The work of the combined school of Vaiśeshika and Nyāya was vigorously pursued by Annam Bhaṭṭa and Viśvanātha Pañchānana, who were Vaiśeshikas, and by Jagadīśa and Laugākshi Bhāskara, who were Naiyāyikas. All four lived somewhere about 1600. The Bengālī school of New Logic started with Vāsudeva Sārvabhauma,[3] who taught at Nuddea from 1470 to 1480, but was brought to full intellectual free-

[1] See the fine analysis in Keith, *SS*. 92 ff. [2] Chatterji, *HR*. xiv.

[3] Sen, *CC*. 80 ff. Sārvabhauma became an enthusiastic follower of Chaitanya.

dom by his pupil, Raghunātha Śiromaṇi. There was a long succession of teachers thereafter down to the end of the seventeenth century.[1]

§ 345. The most famous of the numerous critical summaries of philosophical systems written in India saw the light about A.D. 1380, the *Sarvadarśanasaṅgraha* of Mādhava. Sixteen systems are sketched, arranged so as to form a gradually ascending series. First come the materialistic Chārvākas, the Buddhists and the Jains, then six of the sectarian theologies, and finally the Hindu philosophies,[2] the whole series culminating in the Vedānta.[3]

B. *Reconciliation of Systems.*

§ 346. We noticed above[4] the statement made in the *Prabodhachandrodaya* that the six systems of Hindu philosophy are not mutually exclusive systems but that they all celebrate from various points of view the same glorious and uncreated God. Vijñāna Bhikshu,[5] the sixteenth-century Sāṅkhya sannyāsī, who is a theist, acknowledges that the Sāṅkhya system and the Karma Mīmāṁsā are atheistic, yet he holds that all the systems are authoritative, and reconciles them by distinguishing between essential and practical truths, the latter being false or imperfect theories inculcated with a view to some practical end, and therefore to be neglected in a general survey. Similarly, Madhusūdana Sarasvatī[6] wrote rather later:

> The ultimate scope of all the Munis, authors of these different systems, is to support the theory of illusion, and their only design

[1] See a full statement by Manamohan Chakravarti in *JASB.* Sept. 1915, pp. 259 ff.

[2] These are seven instead of six, because Pāṇini's grammatical teaching is included, on account of his theory of the eternity of sound.

[3] In the vulgate text of the work there is no essay on the Vedānta, the explanation probably being that readers were expected to turn to the *Pañchadaśī.* Recently, however, a text was published in Poona on the basis of a manuscript discovered in Tanjore, in which an essay on the Vedānta completes the work. Is this essay genuine?

[4] In § 270.

[5] See § 342.

[6] *Prasthānabheda*: Muir, *OST.* IV. 102.

is to establish the existence of one Supreme God, the sole essence; for these Munis could not be mistaken since they were omniscient. But as they saw that men, addicted to the pursuit of external objects, could not all at once penetrate into the highest truths, they held out to them a variety of theories, in order that they might not fall into atheism. Misunderstanding the object which the Munis thus had in view, and representing that they even designed to propound doctrines contrary to the Vedas, men have come to regard the specific doctrines of these several schools with preference, and thus become adherents of a variety of systems.

§ 347. Most modern Hindu scholars occupy a similar standpoint. Mr. J. C. Chatterji's statement [1] may be taken as representative. The Nyāya, Vaiśeshika, and Karma Mīmāṁsā systems are all realistic; the Sāṅkhya and the Yoga are dualistic; the Vedānta monistic. From this he proceeds:

Thus, in reality, there are only three metaphysical systems of the Hindus. These systems again are not considered as mutually contradictory. They are regarded as forming a graduated series in which the three systems form, as it were, three great standards, suited to different types or grades of minds—different intellectual (and only intellectual) capacities and temperaments.

§ 348. The position of Kabīr,[2] and all his school, seems at the first glance to be still wider; for in him there is a reconciliation of Islam and Hinduism; but the truth in it is far simpler, surer, and more practical. For the reconciliation is between one school of Islam and one school of Hinduism, the latter already seriously modified by the laying aside of idolatry.

§ 349. But the boldest of all is Akbar's Divine Faith, the *Dīn Ilāhī*,[3] which was meant to sum up all religions, a creation which died with its own imperial creator. A little later, Hindu paṇḍits at the court of Aurungzebe suggested to Bernier [4] the idea that there might be many true religions, all proceeding from the one God.

§ 350. Early in the eighteenth century, Prāṇnāth taught, at

[1] *HR*. 5.
[2] See § 396.
[3] V. A. Smith, *Akbar*, 209 ff.
[4] *Travels*, 328.

Panna in Bandelkhand, that all the religions of India were reconciled in his own person, since he was at once the Christian Messiah, the Mohammedan Mahdi, and the *Nishkalaṅkāvatāra*, 'the stainless incarnation', of the Hindus, and expressed the dogma in his *Kulljama Saheb*.[1]

C. *The Hindu People.*

§ 351. The Hindu people are still roughly divisible into the three old groups. There is first the mass of the common people, caste or outcaste, who belong to no sect, but acknowledge all the gods and worship whichever they think is likely to help at the moment. There come next the orthodox twice-born men, who acknowledge all the gods and worship them with Vedic rites, and in addition hold some religious philosophy, either monistic or theistic. The third group are the Sectarians. Each sect holds a theistic theology, worships its own god as the personal Supreme, and identifies him with the Brahman of the Upanishads. Groups of the uncultured common people may be found here and there, especially in the south, who cling intelligently to a sectarian theology and cult.

As will be evident from our survey, Hinduism produced a long series of great sects from the twelfth to the sixteenth century. From about 1550, however, the effort rapidly weakened and died away. One of the most noteworthy facts in the history of the religion since 1700 is the steady persistent decay of the sects[2] all over North India and also in wide regions farther south. Multitudes have drifted back to undifferenced polytheism, carrying with them the merest shreds of the old thought. Uneducated *pūjārīs*[3] with their numerous images and mongrel ritual strengthen the reactionary movement. This fact makes fruitful research exceedingly difficult over wide areas.

[1] Wilson, 315 f.; Griswold, *Forman Christian College Magazine*, July and Nov. 1905; Growse, *M.* 230 ff.; *JASB.* XLVIII. 171: Russell, *TCCP.* 216 ff. Mirza Ghulam Ahmad Khan of Qadian is an exact modern parallel: see Walter's *Ahmadiya Movement*, Calcutta, 1918.

[2] See Chanda's statement, *IAR.* 143 ff. [3] I.e. temple-ministrants.

D. *Smārta Literature.*

§ 352. The orthodox twice-born fall into two groups. The first, the *Śrautas*, who still perform some of the ancient Śrauta sacrifices, are so few in most parts of India that they are seldom distinguished from the much larger group, the *Smārtas*, who content themselves with the worship of the five gods and the observance of the Sandhyā, i. e. the daily prayers. In South India and in Gujarāt the word Smārta connotes, in addition, allegiance to Śaṅkara's Vedānta; but in North India the Smārta is free in philosophy. He may follow Śaṅkara; he may accept the Nyāya system; or he may find satisfaction in an attempt to blend Rāmānuja's theism with the strength and simplicity of Śaṅkara's thought. The worship of the five gods in *Pañchāyatana Pūjā* is observed at home.[1] Images, or stone and metal symbols,[2] or diagrams, or earthenware pots, may be used to represent the divinities. The image or symbol of the god whom the worshipper prefers is placed in the centre, and the other four are so set as to form a square around the central figure.[3]

§ 353. Hindu temples are supposed to fall into two classes, Smārta and Sectarian. In a Smārta temple, whether it is dedicated to Śiva, Vishṇu, Devī, Sūrya, Gaṇeśa, or some other god, the ritual and liturgy ought to be Vedic, and the five gods ought to be worshipped. In sectarian temples, the ritual and liturgy ought to be Tantric (i. e. based on the Saṁhitās in a Vishṇava temple, on the Āgamas in a Śaiva temple, and on

[1] In Gujarāt and in the Tamil country Smārtas may be found who no longer worship the five: they worship Śiva and reverence the others.

[2] The more usual symbols are: Vishṇu, the *Śālagrāma* pebble; Śiva, the *Narmadeśvara* pebble; the Devī, a piece of metal, or the *Svarṇarekhā* stone found in a river in South India; Sūrya, a round piece of *Sūryakānta*, i. e. sun-stone, or of *sphaṭika*, i. e. crystal; Gaṇeśa, the *Svarṇabhadra*, a red slab from a stream near Arrah.

[3] A Smārta Brāhman one day invited me to have a look at his domestic chapel. It was a very small room. The sacred place was about two and a half feet square, and was sunk some six inches below the main level. In the centre of this little quadrangle stood the liṅga, while an image stood in each of the corners, Vishṇu, Devī, Sūrya, and Gaṇeśa.

the Tantras in a Śākta temple), and the chief deity ought to be some form of the god of the sect, even if other divinities are also recognized. As a matter of fact, in the north, comparatively few pure Smārta temples are to be found [1]; and, while in the south and west sectarian temples are managed with a good deal of strictness, in the north laxity is widespread. Pūjārīs are usually men of little education, and they very naturally tend to introduce images of popular gods in addition to the divinity of the temple, and to follow their own whims in matters of ritual.

In most Śaiva temples in North India a Smārta Brahman can go forward to the liṅga and perform his own worship in accordance with the directions of the Gṛihya-sūtra of his own *charaṇa*. The pūjārī of the temple conducts the pūjā of sixteen operations (*shoḍaśa upachāra*) at certain fixed times, but the Smārta Brāhman's worship is quite independent. In South India this personal worship in the temple is not permitted. In many Śaiva temples in the north, all worshippers, including women, are allowed to approach the liṅga, place a few *bilva* leaves upon it, and pour some Ganges water over it, while they mutter their mantras or prayers.

Most Smārtas give their preference to Śiva, but others are Vaishṇava or Śākta in their leanings, and in earlier times, doubtless, many, like Rāja Bīrbal,[2] were Sauras.

§ 354. The first fifty years of the period are memorable for the brilliant Vedic and philosophic work done by the brothers, Mādhava and Sāyaṇa. Mādhava's three books, the *Nyāya-*

[1] A temple may be found here and there in which the five gods are arranged according to rule. Thus in the Vallabhāchārya temple in Udaipur the main temple is the shrine of Kṛishṇa, while Śiva has a small shrine in the NE. corner, Durgā in the NW., Sūrya in the SW., and Gaṇeśa in the SE. In Śaiva temples in Gujarāt one frequently finds, in addition to the liṅga, images of the Devī and of Gaṇeśa, while Vishṇu is represented by a tortoise, and Sūrya is not pictured, because he is visible in the sky. There is usually an image of Hanumān also. Frequently there is no separate image of the Devī: she is represented by a snake coiled round the lower half of the liṅga. This is the concept of Kuṇḍalinī from Śākta Yoga: see § 232, and cf. Kṛishṇa Śāstrī, *SII.* 185, *n.* 1.

[2] V. A. Smith, *Akbar*, 165.

mālā-vistara on the Mīmāṁsā, the *Pañchadaśī* on the Vedānta, and the *Sarvadarśanasaṅgraha*, a review of philosophic systems, have been dealt with above under the philosophies; but the style as well as the subject would inevitably make each a work of very great interest to thinking Smārtas. The works of Sāyaṇa (died 1387), on the other hand, deal directly with the literature on which the orthodox twice-born depend. A series of valuable commentaries on the *Ṛigveda*, the *Aitareya Brāhmaṇa* and *Āraṇyaka*, and on the *Taittirīya Saṁhitā*, *Brāhmaṇa*, and *Āraṇyaka* of the *Black Yajurveda* were written in whole or in part by Sāyaṇa. They have been of large service to Hindu scholars ever since, and European scholarship owes them a great debt. The *Prasthānabheda* of Madhusūdana Sarasvatī, who has been already mentioned, is interesting as showing the orthodox method of regarding the various philosophies and sectarian systems with their literature. The title of the work means 'Varieties of the Ways', i.e. to God.

In Bengal Raghunandana Bhaṭṭāchārya (*c.* A.D. 1500) dealt fully with the detailed religious duty of the Hindu in his *Ashṭāviṁśati Tattva*, a work greatly treasured by the orthodox.

Appaya Dīkshita, 1552–1624, one of the most famous Smārta scholars of the time, produced a large number of books on very varied subjects. Amongst his religious works is the *Śivārkamaṇidīpikā*, a Sanskrit commentary on Śrīkaṇṭha's *Śaiva-bhāshya*, which has been much used.[1] In his later years he followed the right-hand practice of Śāktism.[2]

One very practical type of Smārta literature consists of manuals, usually called *prakaraṇa-granthas*, written for the purpose of applying Mīmāṁsā principles to the ceremonies enjoined in *smṛiti* books, and forming an offshoot from the Mīmāṁsā proper. One of the earliest and chief of these is the *Smṛiti-Kaustubha*, written by Ananta-deva, son of the author

[1] See § 424. [2] See § 270 and § 317.

of the *Āpadevī*.[1] They may be found in local forms in all parts of the country.

Mukundarāj is the author of an exposition of the Vedānta in Marāṭhī verse called the *Vivekasindhu*, which is much admired. It has been referred to the reign of Jaitrapāl, King of Devagiri in the Marāṭhā country at the end of the twelfth century, and has therefore been called the earliest piece of Marāṭhī literature, but the character of the language scarcely bears out the claim. It does not seem to be nearly so ancient as the language of the *Jñāneśvarī*.[2] Further, Mahīpati, who wrote lives of many of the Marāṭhī poets, makes him a contemporary of Tukārām. His date is thus quite uncertain.

The *Yoga-Vasishṭha-Rāmāyaṇa*, discussed above,[3] was widely used. It is mentioned and quoted by Bhāratītīrtha and Mādhava in the *Pañchadaśī*; and the *Jñāna-Vasishṭham*, an adaptation in Tamil verse by Alavantar Madavappattar, appeared about A.D. 1600.

E. *Vaishṇava Literature.*

a. *General.*

§ 355. The most prominent type of general Vaishṇava literature produced during the period consists of free renderings and adaptations of the Epics and the Purāṇas in the vernaculars. The *Mahābhārata* appeared in a Bengālī dress in the fourteenth century and often afterwards, in Tamil in the fifteenth, in Kanarese about 1500, and in Hindī in the nineteenth century. The *Rāmāyaṇa* was produced in Bengālī in the fourteenth century and often afterwards, in Malayalim in the fifteenth, in Kanarese in the sixteenth, in Hindī in the seventeenth, and in Oṛiya at a later date. Three Vaishṇava Purāṇas, the *Vishṇu*, *Varāha*, and *Padma*, were translated into Telugu in the fifteenth century. It would be unwise to lay much religious stress on these versions. The bulk of serious Vaishṇava literature arose in the sub-sects.

[1] See § 338. [2] See § 278. [3] § 270.

b. *Bhāgavata.*

1. *The Bhāgavata Community.*

§ 356. Probably about A.D. 1400, Śrīdhara Svāmī, Mahant of the Śaṅkarite monastery, Govardhana, in Purī, wrote a commentary on the *Bhāgavata P.*, the *Bhāgavata Bhāvārtha Dīpikā*, which is by far the most famous exposition of the work. He was clearly an excellent scholar, and he must have had access to a very trustworthy tradition. He begins his commentary with the distinct statement that the great Purāṇa was not written by Vopadeva. The fact that this theory was already current proves that Śrīdhara wrote at a time considerably later than A.D. 1300, when Vopadeva flourished. As the commentary was well known everywhere by the end of the fifteenth century, Śrīdhara's *floruit* may reasonably be placed about A.D. 1400. His interpretation of the Purāṇa is advaitist, since he was a follower of Śaṅkara; and since the *Bhāgavata* itself tends to be monist, his *Dīpikā* is usually regarded as most authoritative.

The Purāṇa was translated into many languages, either completely or partially, during the period. It appeared in Telugu and Bengālī in the fifteenth century, in Braj and Persian in the sixteenth, in Marāṭhī and Kanarese about A.D. 1600, in Gujarātī and Malayalim in the seventeenth century, and in Hindī in the nineteenth.

A sectarian bhāshya on the *Vedānta-sūtras*, which is called the *Śuka Bhāshya*, and which purports to be a Bhāgavata work, seems to have been written late in this period. Its standpoint is Viśishṭādvaita, and the texts used to establish the teaching of the bhāshya are drawn from the *Bhāgavata P.*, Upanishad texts being cited only as subsidiary evidence. The author is called Śukāchārya, and is said to have been the founder of the Bhāgavata monastery at Talkad in Mysore, but the work is probably pseudonymous. It is a suspicious circumstance that a Bhāgavata bhāshya should be not advaita but viśishṭādvaita. Further, no Śukāchārya appears in the *guruparampara* of Talkad, nor yet among the gurus of the *Maṭha* of Mulubazil, the only other Bhāgavata monastery in Mysore, while the authorities of both monasteries refuse to recognize the *Śuka Bhāshya* as a Bhāgavata work.[1]

The Bhāgavatas, being both Smārtas and devotees of Vishṇu, occupied from the first rather an unstable position between the orthodox and the sects, and their acceptance of the *Bhāgavata P.* deepened the difficulty for them. The results are visible in their history. In the Mysore and the Tamil south they are a scattered community possessing very few temples of their own and only a few monasteries. They worship in Śrī-Vaishṇava temples but distinguish themselves from Śrī-Vaishṇavas by wearing the ancient sect-mark, a single upright line of cream-coloured gopīchandana,[2] and by using the Bhāgavata mantra.[3] Occasionally individual Bhāgavatas pass over to the Śrī-Vaishṇava community. In the Kanarese country on the western coast they still maintain themselves, although greatly outnumbered by Mādhvas, and have a number of temples. Throughout these wide areas they still venerate Śiva as well as Vishṇu, observe Vedic rites, and are recognized as Smārtas. They recognize no commentary on the *Bhāgavata* except Śrīdhara's. All the other sects dependent on the *Bhāgavata P.* have experienced the same difficulty of maintaining the Vedic position, and most are in consequence now frankly sectarian.

2. *Marāṭhā Bhaktas.*

§ 357. There seems to have been an interval of quite a century after Jñāneśvara before another star of any magnitude arose among the Marāṭhā Bhāgavatas. The next notable singer is Nāmdeva. There is a local tradition to the effect

[1] I am deeply indebted to Mr. R. Narasimhachar, Director of Archaeological Research in Mysore, who, at my request, wrote to Talkad for information with regard to the age of the *bhāshya*, and elicited the facts stated in this sentence.

[2] See § 277.

[3] See § 161.

that he and Jñāneśvara met at least once, while in the *Bhaktamālā* they are regarded as master and disciple. In consequence of this Nāmdeva has usually been placed at the end of the thirteenth, and the beginning of the fourteenth, century; but his Marāṭhī is of such a character that Sir Rāmakṛishṇa Bhandarkar is inclined to date him a century later.[1] Now, a number of his hymns occur in the Sikh *Granth*, and he is regarded as one of a few bhaktas who, coming just before Rāmānanda, prepared the way for him. There seems to be sufficient evidence to show that Rāmānanda flourished in the second and third quarters of the fifteenth century; so that Nāmdeva's *floruit* would be somewhere about 1400 to 1430. Mr. Baleśvar Prasād, who is a most careful student of Hindī literature, gives[2] A.D. 1423 as his *floruit*, which agrees perfectly with the above reasoning and with Sir Rāmakṛishṇa's conjecture. This chronology is finally established by one of Nāmdeva's own *abhaṅgs*, 'Gone are the saints',[3] which makes it absolutely clear that Jñāneśvara and his saintly companions lived long before him. He was a tailor, *shimpi*, by birth and occupation, but he spent his life propagating bhakti in the Marāṭhā country and in the Punjab. In his verse the influence of Islam first appears in the Marāṭhā country. He and those who followed him criticized idolatry with some severity but continued the use of idols. A large body of Marāṭhī hymns are attributed to him, and a considerable number of Hindī hymns appear under his name in the *Granth*, the whole forming a mass of verse of very high quality. A careful comparison of the two groups would probably throw further light on the man and his life. He was influential in the Punjab as well as in the Marāṭhā country, as is proved by his hymns in the *Granth* and by a shrine dedicated to his memory and still in use at Ghuman in the Gurdaspur district.[4] Another Marāṭhā singer, Trilochan

[1] *VS*. 92.
[2] *SBS*. II. 26.
[3] Macnicol, *PMS*. 41.
[4] Macauliffe, VI. 39.

by name, seems to have been a contemporary of Nāmdeva, but very little is known about him. Three of his Hindī hymns appear in the *Granth*, but his Marāṭhī hymns, and even his memory, seem to be lost in his native land.

The next leader of eminence among the Marāṭhā bhaktas is Eknāth (died 1608), who was a Brāhman and lived at Paithan. He is said to have spoken and acted in opposition to caste, and to have suffered for his zeal. But he has been most influential through his Marāṭhī verse translations from the *Bhāgavata P.*[1] He left also a collection of twenty-six abhangs called *Haripāṭh.* In philosophy he was a monist, like Mukundarāj and Jñāneśvara.

Tukārām (1608–49) was a petty shopkeeper. He is passionately devoted to Viṭhobā, and his personal religious life is reflected with great vividness in his moving lines—his longing for God, his humility, his sense of unworthiness, his boundless need, his trust in God, and his appeals and prayers for help. It is his own religious life that occupies his soul; as in most forms of Hinduism, there are but few traces of the passion for winning others. His worship centres in the image of his god. He is conscious of Viṭhobā's omnipresence, and his spirituality, and yet somehow the invisible God is identified with the adored image before which the worshipper bends. His hymns are of a very high order, and are probably the largest religious influence in the Marāṭhā country. There is scarcely a theological or philosophical system to be found in his writings, but so far as philosophical thinking may be traced, he tends to be a monist. Śivajī, the man who welded the Marāṭhā race into a strong people, rose to prominence in the last few years of Tukārām's life, and he sent some of his councillors to beg him to come to court, but Tukārām sent him a few stanzas instead.

Nārāyaṇa (1608–81), who later took the name of Rām Dās, probably under the influence of the Rāmānandī movement, was also a poet, but his verse has not laid hold of the

[1] Parts of these are sung in Sankīrtan in the temple at Paṇḍharpur.

people in the same way as Tukārām's. Yet he exerted great personal influence over Śivajī from 1650 onwards. His poem, *Dasabodha*, contains much shrewd wisdom, but it is philosophical rather than religious. A small sect, the Rām-dāsīs, still perpetuate his name, wear a sect-mark, and use a secret mantra of their own. The head-quarters are at Sajjangarh, near Satāra, where there is the Samādh of Rām Dās, a temple to Rām Chandra, and a Rām-dāsī monastery. There are many sādhus belonging to the sect.

A Brāhman poet, named Śrīdhara, rose to great fame and popularity during the first quarter of the eighteenth century. His leading works present in stirring Marāṭhī verse the great stories of the *Rāmāyaṇa* and the *Mahābhārata*. His influence is not directly religious, except in so far as the stories he reproduces have a religious character.

Mahīpati, who flourished later in the same century, gave his strength to writing the lives of devotees and saints.

§ 358. The Bhāgavatas of the Marāṭhā country to-day form a popular bhakti movement, the literature of which, apart from the *Bhāgavata P.* itself and Śrīdhara's commentary, is all in the vernacular. The god is Viṭṭhal or Viṭhobā; both these names are merely local variations of Vishṇu. The chief centres are Paṇḍharpur, Alandi, and Dehu, but there are numerous shrines throughout the country. In the chief temple of Paṇḍharpur Viṭṭhal wears a curious sort of crown, which the priests say is Śiva's *liṅga*; so that the image, standing for both gods, is truly Bhāgavata. Viṭṭhal has several consorts installed near him, each in a separate shrine, Rakmabai (i.e. Rukmiṇī), Rādhā, Satyabhāmā, and Lakshmī; but it is noteworthy that Rādhā takes no place in Marāṭhī literature. Mahādeva, Gaṇapati, and Sūrya are also installed; so that, taking Lakshmī as devī, the five gods are still worshipped there. No Outcaste is admitted to Bhāgavata temples in Mahārāshtra. Nāmdeva's head, represented in brass, is placed on the lowest step of the stair which leads up to the gate of the temple; and the shrine of an Outcaste named

Chokamela[1] is on the opposite side of the street. Monthly and annual pilgrimages are made to the chief sacred places. The pilgrims are called Warkaris. Those who have made the pilgrimage a number of times are allowed to carry a red banner. As they march along, they shout 'Dynanobā, Tukārām', and sing Abhangs. There are also hired singers called Haridāsīs, who sing Marāṭhī Abhangs and portions of Eknāth's translations from the *Bhāgavata* in the temple of Paṇḍharpur.

One of the best institutions of the movement is called *Harikathā*, a sort of sermon in song which the leader opens by shouting aloud several times, *Jai Rāma-Kṛishṇa Hari.* He then sings a number of hymns and other texts in verse, expounding each in prose. This method of mingled song and exhortation is found in the south also, where the singer is called Bhāgavata and the musical sermon is called *Kālakshepam.*

§ 359. The bhakti movement in Gujarāt remains Smārta in general character to the present day. The two chief temples are dedicated to Raṇachor Rai, i.e. the king who left the fight, an allusion to the occasion on which, according to the mythology, Kṛishṇa left Mathurā and came to Dwārkā. These two great shrines are at Dwārkā and at Daker near Ahmadabad. In both the ritual is still conducted in accordance with Vedic rules.

3. *The Mādhvas.*

§ 360. The history of the Mādhva sect during this period is not yet known; so that all we can do is to give some account of the literature, so far as scholars have dealt with it.

A Mādhva ascetic named Vishṇu Purī, who belonged to Tirhut and probably lived in the second half of the fourteenth century, made a selection of the finest utterances on bhakti in the *Bhāgavata*, and arranged them according to subject in thirteen groups. He called each of these collections a string of gems, and named the whole *Bhaktiratnāvalī*, or 'Necklace

[1] He was a Mahār. His poetry survives, and parts of it are very fine.

of Bhakti Gems', the best introduction to Bhāgavata bhakti. It was translated into Bengali by Lauriya Kṛishṇa Dāsa early in the fifteenth century.

It was a later Mādhva ascetic, Īśvara Purī, who won Chaitanya[1] to the faith. The new leader amply repaid the Mādhva community for this service. During his southern tour, 1509–11, he stimulated Mādhvas by his preaching and his enthusiastic singing. It is probable, indeed, that it was he that started Saṅkīrtan and Nagarkīrtan in the sect; for there seems to have been little emotional singing before his day. In any case the first great outburst of Kanarese hymn-writing among Mādhvas came shortly after his visit. The chief singer was Puraṁdar Dās, but there were many others. One of the most noted Mādhva scholars, Śrī Vyāsa Rāja, was a contemporary of Chaitanya. He lived in the south and wrote a number of works which are still much used.

In the eighteenth century another group of enthusiastic bhaktas produced Kanarese hymns in praise of Kṛishṇa. The chief writers were Timmappa Dās and Madhva Dās. About the same time lived Chidānanda whose Kanarese work *Haribhakti-rasāyana*, the 'Sweets of Devotion to Kṛishṇa', is well known. The *Harikathāsāra*, a clear account of Mādhva doctrine in Kanarese prose, the date of which I do not know, is a very popular book.

There are also many Kanarese translations of Sanskrit works. They are almost without exception Vaishṇava, and many of them are probably the work of Mādhvas, but they are rather entertaining poems than religious books. Yet they must have helped the Mādhva cause. Between 1508 and 1530 the *Mahābhārata* was rendered into Kanarese by a number of writers, and about 1590 the *Rāmāyaṇa* was translated by a poet who called himself the younger Vālmīki, Kumāra Vālmīki. The *Bhāgavata P.* was translated about the same time, and rather later a special translation of the tenth book, known as *Kṛishṇa Līlābhyudaya*, was written by

[1] See § 364.

a Mādhva named Veṅkāya Ārya. The *Jaimini Bhārata* by Lakshmīśa Devapura, the date of which is 1760, is a description of the wanderings of the horse for Yuddhishthira's horse-sacrifice, but the aim in view is the praise of Kṛishṇa.

Mādhva ascetics are sannyāsīs belonging to Śaṅkara's Daśnāmīs. Madhva himself and his chief disciples belonged to the Tīrtha order, but in the later history many were Purīs or Bhāratīs.

4. *The Vishṇusvāmīs.*

§ 361. The history of the Vishṇusvāmī sect is very obscure throughout this period. Since the seventeenth century they have been very weak; and the absence of a strong tradition is sufficient to account for the lack of information.

Bilvamaṅgala, a Vishṇusvāmī ascetic, is remembered because of his *Kṛishṇakarṇāmṛita*, a Sanskrit poem on Kṛishṇa and Rādhā which has been much admired. There are stories which connect him with Calicut and with the foundation of the temple of Padmanābha at Trivandram, Travancore. He probably lived early in the fifteenth century. Another scholar belonging to the sect, Varadarāja by name, wrote a *ṭīkā* on the *Bhāgavata P.* A manuscript of it, about 200 years old, lies in the library of the Sanskrit College, Benares, but it has not been examined. The date of the writer is unknown.

The rise of the Chaitanya and Vallabha[1] sects at the beginning of the sixteenth century bore very heavily upon the Vishṇusvāmīs and the Nimbārkas; and the Vishṇusvāmīs were in the long run almost completely absorbed by the Vallabhas. The sect is now extremely small. At the Kumbh Mela at Allahabad in February, 1918, I met some half a dozen Vishṇusvāmī ascetics. They wore the old sect-mark on their foreheads, and talked freely about the sect. Two monasteries, they averred, still survive, one at Kaṅkraoli near Udaipur in Rajputana and one at Kamban near Bhurtpore in

[1] See § 364 and § 372.

the U. P. They also say that Vishṇusvāmī's *Bhāgavata-bhāshya* still survives, and that a copy lies in each monastery. They use two books, the *Vishṇu-rahasya* and the *Tattvatraya*, which they ascribe to Vishṇusvāmī.

5. *The Nimbārkas.*

§ 362. The history of the Nimbārkas from 1350 to 1500 is unknown, but a reorganization of the sect appears to have been carried out about A.D. 1500, whereby the householders of the community were placed under one pontiff and the sannyāsīs under another. The succession in each case seems to have been faithfully kept up until to-day. The first pair of leaders, Keśava Kashmīri, the head of the lay division, and his brother-in-law, Harivyāsa Muni, head of the ascetics, were contemporaries of Chaitanya and Vallabha. Keśava Kashmīri was a well-known scholar and commentator. His *Krama-dīpikā*, a manual of the ritual, consists in the main of extracts from the *Gautamīya S.* The Nimbārkas practise a very quiet type of Saṅkīrtan, the hymns for which were written by Harivyāsa Muni and Śrī Bhaṭṭ, who lived about the same time. It is probable that the Saṅkīrtan was suggested by the practice of the Chaitanyas.[1]

The two chief centres of the Nimbārka sect to-day are Salīmabad, south of Ajmere, and Brindāban. The succession of the pontiffs in each case has been preserved,[2] but not much is known about the history. They have suffered from the competition of the Chaitanyas and the Vallabhas, like the Vishṇusvāmīs, but not to the same extent. They still possess a number of temples at Brindāban and elsewhere.

6. *Rādhā-Kṛishṇa Literary Verse.*

§ 363. During the fourteenth and fifteenth centuries a great deal of Rādhā-Kṛishṇa literature was written in North India. Chaṇḍī-Dās, who belonged to Jayadeva's district of Bengal and

[1] I owe many of these facts about the Nimbārka sect to Mr. Rādhā Charaṇa Goswāmī, Honorary Magistrate, Brindāban.
[2] Growse, *M.* 147 ; Bhandarkar, *VS.* 62.

flourished about 1380 to 1420, though a Śākta,[1] wrote Rādhā-Kṛishṇa hymns of great power in Bengālī; and Vidyāpati, who belonged to Tirhut, and used Maithilī, the dialect of that part of India, produced in the middle of the fifteenth century Rādhā-Kṛishṇa lyrics which not only pleased his own people, but captured the heart of Bengal when re-expressed in Bengālī. It seems most likely that Umāpati Dhara also, whose Krishnaite songs in Maithilī and Bengālī have recently been made known, belonged to Tirhut and was a contemporary of Vidyāpati. Narsiṅg Mehtā, a Brāhman belonging to Junāgaḍh in Kathiawar and a famous Gujarātī poet, wrote many Rādhā-Kṛishṇa lyrics which are very popular, but are also rather erotic. His flowering time may be placed at 1450–80. Mīrā Bāī, a princess of the house of Merta in Jodhpur, became the wife of the heir-apparent to the Mewar throne, but he died before the assassination of his father, the great Kumbha Rāṇā, in 1469.[2] Left a widow, and rather ungraciously treated by her brother-in-law, who had succeeded to the throne, she left Chittore and became a disciple of Rai Dās,[3] the Rāmānandī, and then a devotee of Kṛishṇa. Her Rādhā-Kṛishṇa lyrics in Braj are very famous but rather disappointing. There are also numerous songs in Gujarātī attributed to her, some of them containing an erotic element. The two groups require to be critically examined together. It is not known whether any of these poets belonged to the Vishṇusvāmī or the Nimbārka sect. As Chaṇḍī Dās was a Śākta, the others also may have written Krishnaite verse without belonging to any Krishnaite community. Yet this rich literature proves the vogue of the teaching of the two sects.

[1] Hence his name, Servant of Chaṇḍī, the goddess.

[2] My information comes from the palace records of the Mewār family. I am greatly indebted to my friend the Rev. Dr. James Shepherd of Udaipur for ascertaining the actual facts. Much legend has gathered round Mīrā Bāī's name.

[3] She mentions him in three of her lyrics. See § 393.

7. *The Chaitanya Sect.*

§ 364. Two new sects were founded at the opening of the sixteenth century, the Chaitanyas and the Vallabhas. Vallabha was probably the earlier of the two, but we take Chaitanya first because his teaching and practice stand in closer relation to the earlier sects.

Viśvambhara Miśra (1485–1533) was born in Nuddea, in Bengal, and made himself a name as a student and teacher of logic and grammar while still young. In A. D. 1507 he was won to a serious life and the practice of the passionate bhakti of the *Bhāgavata P.* by Īśvara Purī, a Mādhva sannyāsī. He at once began to preach, and disciples and supporters gathered round him, notably Advaitāchārya, an old and revered Vaishṇava scholar, and Nityānanda, who for many years had been a Mādhva. But he came also under the influence of the Nimbārkas and the Vishṇusvāmīs, and used with great delight the songs of Jayadeva, Chaṇḍī Dās, and Vidyāpati. He thus went beyond his Mādhva teachers, and gave Rādhā a very prominent place in his thought and his worship. He spent a great deal of time singing Rādhā-Kṛishṇa hymns with his followers, rousing them to devotional excitement (*saṅkīrtana*). Frequently he led them out through the city in procession, dancing and singing with such fervour and contagious emotion as to carry the people away in devotional raptures (*nagarkīrtana*). These new methods were destined to prove very fruitful.

In 1509 he became initiated as a Bhāratī sannyāsī by a Mādhva, Keśava Bhāratī, and took the name Kṛishṇa Chaitanya. He then went to Purī in Orissa to the temple of Kṛishṇa (here called Jagannāth, Lord of the World), but for some years he spent most of his time in long journeys in the south and in the north. He was already believed to be an avatāra of Kṛishṇa by the people of Nuddea. and his cult had begun. From about 1516 he lived at Purī. His adherents increased rapidly from the time he became a sannyāsī, notably

Sārvabhauma, the greatest authority on logic of the day, Pratāpa Rudra, the King of Orissa, and Rāmānanda Rai, Pratāpa Rudra's Brāhman minister. Rather later, he won two scholars who were destined to become the theologians of the faith. He gave them new names, Rūpa and Sanātana, and sent them to Brindāban to seek out the old sacred sites (then lying desolate through Muslim fury) and produce a Sanskrit literature for the sect. Several of his disciples became accomplished hymn-writers, especially Narahari Sarkar, Vāsudeva Ghosh, and Vaṁśīvadana. They wrote not only Rādhā-Kṛishṇa hymns but songs in praise of Chaitanya, called *Gaur Chandrikā*; for his beauty and fair complexion had brought him the name Gaur Chandra. He passed away in 1533.

Chaitanya was neither an organizer nor a writer. He left the organization of the sect to Nityānanda, while Rūpa and Sanātana took up the task of expressing the theology. Nor can we be sure that he had a settled system in his mind; though it was probably he that decided that the philosophic position of the sect should be the Bhedābheda of Nimbārka rather than the Dvaita of Madhva. His chief reading seems to have been the *Bhāgavata P.* with Śrīdhara's commentary, the lyrics of Jayadeva, Vidyāpati, and Chaṇḍī Dās, the *Brahma Saṁhitā* and the *Kṛishṇakarṇāmṛita*.[1] His power over men came from the reality of his religious experience, from the overpowering emotions which he exhibited when gazing on a divine image or discoursing on Kṛishṇa and his love, and from the sincerity and contagious passion of his new modes of praise. He made the Rādhā-Kṛishṇa myth the basis of his teaching and worship, because, as he tells us himself, the Hindus had nothing else that could touch the hearts of men so powerfully.[2] In his hands the unpleasing tale was unquestionably used in masterly fashion for noble ends.

[1] He brought manuscripts of the two last-mentioned works back with him from the south.

[2] Sen, *HBLL.* 536.

The historian of Bengālī literature describes the Vaishṇava community in Bengal as utterly stunned and crushed by the passing of Chaitanya :

> From 1533 to 1590[1] the Vaiṣṇava community of Bengal lay enervated by an overpowering feeling of forlornness. The saṅkīrtana parties lost all heart, and their great music which had taken the country by surprise and flooded it with poetry, broke in the midst of their enthusiastic performances, and sounded no more on the banks of the Ganges. The companions of Chaitanya, mute and stricken with a sense of their great loss, one by one departed from the world ; and the history of this period shows no striking feature of the Vaiṣṇava movement and no activity of any noteworthy nature.[2]

But, though literature failed and music died away, the sect lived on. Nityānanda continued to organize the community and give it rules of conduct ; and his son Vīrachandra carried on the work after his father's death, receiving as many as 2,500 Buddhist monks and nuns into the new ascetic orders in one day.[3]

§ 365. Rūpa and Sanātana and some others had been settled in Brindāban for some years before the death of Chaitanya, and the little community continued to grow. The leaders, six of the companions of the Master—Rūpa, Sanātana, with their nephew Jīva, Raghunātha Dās, Gopāla Bhaṭṭa, and Raghunātha Bhaṭṭa—were known as the six Gosvāmīs, a word which had come to mean authoritative religious leaders. These men preached, taught, and won converts, but their chief task was to form the theology and the ritual of the sect and to express both in dignified Sanskrit literature. They wrote on bhakti, philosophy, and ritual, and produced commentaries, dramas, and lyrics, each work having a bearing on the faith, worship, or everyday life of the community. No Bhāshya on the *Vedānta-sūtras* was produced at this time, but Jīva's *Satsandarbha*, a philosophical and theological work of large compass, more than made up for the lack. The *Hari-bhakti-vilāsa* on the ritual was composed by Sanātana, but was attributed to Gopāla

[1] Probably a slip for 1570. [2] Sen, *VLMB.* 68. [3] Ib. 164.

Bhaṭṭa. They sought out all the ancient sacred spots in and around Mathurā and Brindāban, and described them in the *Mathurā = māhātmya*, now a portion of the *Varāha P.*, and in the *Braj-bhakti-vilāsa.* It was they that established the pilgrimage round the sacred places of Mathurā and Brindāban called the *Ban-jātrā.* They also arranged and started the annual festival, the *Rās = līlā.*

§ 366. An awakening in Bengal about 1570 led to the writing of five distinct works on Chaitanya's life within a very few years. Two of these were in Sanskrit, the others in Bengālī. One of these was Kavikarṇapūra's Sanskrit drama, the *Chaitanyachandrodaya*, the title suggested by the *Prabodhachandrodaya*, the scenes taken from Chaitanya's life. Another was Vṛindāvana Dāsa's *Chaitanya Bhāgavata*, a beautiful life in Bengālī verse. But much though the Gosvāmīs of Brindāban admired the *Chaitanya Bhāgavata*, they desiderated a fuller and completer work. Accordingly, at their request, Kṛishṇadāsa Kavirāja, in seven years of unremitting labour, produced the *Chaitanya-charitāmṛita* (1582), which is now the standard life of the leader. Mr. D. C. Sen calls it 'the most erudite and instructive work in Bengali about Chaitanya and his followers.' It is on the whole historical, yet there is a considerable admixture of legend. Many members of the sect commit the whole long poem to memory.

§ 367. It was a fortunate circumstance for the Gosvāmīs that the great Akbar mounted the Mogul throne during the earlier years of their residence at Brindāban; for through his religious tolerance, they were able not only to continue their religious and literary work without molestation but also to erect a series of magnificent temples in Brindāban. They received the large sums of money necessary for these beautiful works of art from certain Rajput princes and other wealthy men whose favour they had won.

§ 368. During the first forty years of the seventeenth century the Chaitanya movement produced in Bengālī a group of brilliant hymn-writers. The greatest of the choir was Govinda Dās, but Jñāna Dās, Balarāma Dās, Jadunandana Dās, and Rāja Vīra Hamvīra produced work of striking excellence also.

At the beginning of the eighteenth century Baladeva wrote for the sect a bhāshya on the *Vedānta-sūtras*, calling it the *Govinda-bhāshya* and giving its philosophic point of view the distinctive name *achintya-bhedābheda*, thus confessing that the relation between God and the soul is in the last analysis inconceivable.

§ 369. Among the Chaitanyas, as in certain other sects, the rules of caste were relaxed in the matter of religious privileges. Any person could become a member of the community, share its worship, and read its books. There were a few of the ascetics who were ready to eat with faithful bhaktas, no matter what their caste was; but there does not seem to be any evidence that Chaitanya ever broke his caste. Then, most of these breaches of caste-law soon passed away; and the rules of marriage and of the priestly function of the Brāhman were never disturbed. Only lineal descendants of the personal companions of Chaitanya[1] are recognized as Gosvāmīs. These rule the monasteries and control most of the temples.

§ 370. Chaitanya was a sannyāsī of the Bhāratī order of Śaṅkara's Daśnāmīs, and a few of his companions also accepted sannyāsa, but Nityānanda and Vīrachandra introduced the easier discipline of the modern *sādhu*, calling the ascetics Vairāgīs and Vairāginīs, precisely as Rāmānanda did. These orders were soon flooded with thousands of converts from the degraded Śākta Buddhist orders, then passing through the last stage of decay in Bengal. The consequence was that great impurity prevailed, despite the fact that marriage was permitted. To this day these ascetic orders have a very bad reputation even among members of the sect.

[1] There are a few exceptions to this rule, especially in Orissa.

§ 371. In the temples of the sect the chief images are Kṛishṇa and Rādhā, but Chaitanya with Advaita and Nityānanda are also installed in each temple. There are also a number of temples dedicated to Chaitanya himself. Saṅkīrtana plays an important part in the worship. As in the sects of Tamil India, this vernacular psalmody is an extra which does not interfere with the ritual of the Sanskrit liturgy. The Kīrtanīya or head-singer and his choir sit in the *jagamohana*, the section of the temple in front of the main shrine, and sing to the accompaniment of cymbals and drums; and now and then there is dancing as well. It is the rule to sing one or more *Gaur Chandrikā* as a sort of interpretative preparation for the Rādhā-Kṛishṇa hymns, a series of which is sung on each occasion. Saṅkīrtan parties are now and then held in private houses also, and are kept up for many hours, hymns illustrative of many forms of religious emotion being rendered.

A number of sects of rather doubtful teaching and morals claim some connexion with Chaitanya. The Kartabhajas, the Darbesh, and the Shains show the influence of Islam and are more or less respectable, but the Bauls and the Kishoribhajas are no better than the left-hand Śāktas.

8. *The Vallabhāchāryas.*[1]

§ 372. Vallabha, or Vallabhāchārya (1479–1531), a Brāhman belonging to the Telugu country and a contemporary of Chaitanya,[2] was born in Benares, the son of a member of the Vishṇusvāmī sect. He received a Sanskrit education and wandered about for several years meeting scholars in disputation. Mention is specially made of his vanquishing Smārta scholars at the court of Kṛishṇadeva of Vijayanagar (1509–29). The details of his life are by no

[1] I have received much help in the understanding of this community from Paṇḍit Magan Lāl Śāstrī of Broach and Poona, who is a sincere Vallabha and also a competent scholar.

[2] But he was not his father-in-law: the two men had the same name, but that is all the basis the story has.

means clear nor yet the influences that went to the making of his sect. His relation to the Vishṇusvāmī sect especially requires to be cleared up. There need be no doubt, however, about the teaching of the sect; for there is abundance of literature; but it waits to be studied.

Vallabha called himself an incarnation of the god Agni. He acknowledged no human teacher but said he learnt his system direct from Kṛishṇa. Yet it seems absolutely clear that he took over from Nimbārka the theory of Kṛishṇa as the eternal Brahman, of Rādhā as his eternal spouse and of the highest heaven where they sport.

He calls his philosophic system Śuddhādvaita, i. e. *pure monism*, but his monism is certainly not so rigid as Śaṅkara's. It is called pure monism in contrast with the 'impure' monism of Śaṅkara, whose system includes the doctrine of māyā and does not lay stress on bhakti. Vallabha acknowledges that men of knowledge may rise to release by means of knowledge, but his way is the way of bhakti. Bhakti is the means, but it is also the end; for bhakti is higher than knowledge; and the true bhakta will live and sport for ever with Kṛishṇa. According to Vallabha, bhakti is given by God: it comes by his grace. The word for grace in the system is *pushṭi*. This use of the word is founded on a passage in the *Bhāgavata P.*[1] I am assured that the word pushṭi is never used in the literature as a name for Vallabha practice.

§ 373. The following is an outline of the theology of the sect. Kṛishṇa, who is Brahman—reality, intelligence, joy—alone exists. From him there go out, as sparks from fire, the material world, souls, and the antaryāmin, or indwelling, god. In souls, which are atomic and identical with Brahman, the balance of the three guṇas being upset, the attribute of joy is concealed; so that they are seen to possess only reality and intelligence as attributes. Released souls rise to Kṛishṇa's heaven, which is far above the heavens of Vishṇu, Śiva, and Brahmā, and there, by the favour of

[1] II. x. 4. The *līlā* in Book VI is called Poshaṇa.

Kṛishṇa-Brahman, they attain to the pure condition of his divine nature.

Kṛishṇa's heaven is called Vyāpi-Vaikuṇṭha, and in it is a heavenly Vṛindāvana and glorious forests. From Kṛishṇa's side springs Rādhā, and from the pores of the skin of Kṛishṇa and Rādhā come millions of gopās and gopīs and also cattle and all the denizens of the woods. Kṛishṇa and Rādhā sport eternally in the celestial Vṛindāvana with their devotees. The loftiest aspiration of a Vallabha is to become a gopī and sport with Kṛishṇa in his heaven.

The cult is called *seva*, service of Kṛishṇa. There are eight times of worship daily in each temple.[1] The mantra of the sect is *Śrī Kṛishṇa śaraṇam mama.*

§ 374. One extraordinary peculiarity of this sect is the position held in it by Vallabha's son Viṭṭhalnātha and his descendants. No one can become a guru of the sect, or own one of the temples of the sect, except a descendant of Viṭṭhalnātha in the male line. The pūjārīs in the temples are paid servants of the guru to whom the temple belongs. Along with this there goes the old Hindu doctrine that the guru is god. Since the faithful Vallabha who is devoted to Kṛishṇa ought to dedicate everything to Kṛishṇa, and since the guru is Kṛishṇa, the highest teaching of the sect leads the faithful bhakta to shower his wealth on his guru. This is the more significant since a large percentage of the rich business class of Western India belong to the sect. Originally, the title given to gurus was āchāryas, teachers, but when they became wealthy, they began to live as princes; and since then they have been called Mahārājas.

Each Mahārāja lives in a house which is also a temple, and in it he has a reception-room next the room in which Kṛishṇa is worshipped. Since the guru is Kṛishṇa, he must be worshipped as Kṛishṇa. This worship is performed in the reception-room, and in many cases the worship of the guru is more elaborate and passionate than the worship of

[1] Wilson, *Works*, I. 126 ff.

the god. The ritual and the liturgy remind the worshippers of the story of the gopīs; and, whether they be men or women, they look forward to becoming gopīs and sporting with Kṛishṇa in Goloka. In worshipping the Mahārāja, women shower their devotion upon him as being actually Kṛishṇa, the darling of the gopīs. Hence, when the Mahārāja is a vicious man, they are in the utmost danger. There has been a great deal of immorality in certain cases. According to my informant, these abuses arose in the eighteenth century. He assures me that there is no basis for them in the literature.

§ 375. In certain cities societies have been formed among Vallabhas which meet from time to time in the *Rās-maṇḍalī*, or circle of holy sport. An equal number of men and women meet and take a meal together, after which there is promiscuous intercourse. The circle gets its name from Kṛishṇa's dalliance (*rās-līlā*) with the gopīs, but its methods are copied from the *chakra-pūjā* of the left-hand Śāktas.

The facts about the Mahārājas and the *Rās-maṇḍalī* were made public in a suit for libel which was heard in Bombay in 1862. A full account of it is given in *The Sect of the Mahārājahs.*

Another very remarkable fact in the history of the Vallabhas is the absorption of the Vishṇusvāmī sect. There is no close connexion in doctrine. Vishṇusvāmī's philosophy is dualistic, and he regards Rādhā as a woman, Kṛishṇa's mistress at Brindāban. Vallabha's philosophy is monistic, and he holds Rādhā to be the eternal spouse of Kṛishṇa. Yet for a long time there has been a saying common in North India to the effect that the Vishṇusvāmīs and the Vallabhas are the same, which is true only in the sense that, since most Vishṇusvāmīs have entered the Vallabha fold, there is now no difference between them. The idea that the two sects are one can be traced back to the middle of the seventeenth century, and was probably one of many means employed by the Vallabhas in the process of absorbing the sect. It is usually said that Vallabhas reckon themselves as belonging to the Rudra

Sampradāya along with the Vishṇusvāmīs, but that is a mistake.

§ 376. Vallabha wrote a number of scholarly books in Sanskrit, both commentaries and original works, in exposition of his system. There are first three fundamental works:—the *Vedānta-sūtra-anubhāshya*, the *Subodhinī*, which is a commentary on the *Bhāgavata P.*, and a manual of his doctrine in verse, the *Tattva-dīpa-nibandha*, which is accompanied by a gloss in prose called *Prakāśa*; and then seventeen short poems. The chief of these is the *Siddhānta Rahasya*, in which he tells how Kṛishṇa gave him his revelation. He left nothing in Hindī. Giridharajī and Bālakrishna Bhaṭṭa are two early leaders whose *Śuddhādvaitamārtaṇḍa* and *Prameyaratnārṇava* are systematic Sanskrit works of considerable value. Of more recent scholars Gosvāmī Śrī Purushottamajī seems to be the most noteworthy.

The *Nārada Pañcharātra*, the text of which was published in Calcutta a good many years ago, has thus far proved an enigma, and it will remain such until it is carefully read in the light of the history of the sects. From a superficial glance one might conjecture that it is an old Vaishṇava Saṁhitā interpolated or partly re-written, first by Vishṇusvāmīs and then by Vallabhas.

Vallabha had four noteworthy disciples, and his son Viṭṭhalnātha, who succeeded him, had also four; and all the eight lived in the Braj district, i. e. Mathurā and Brindāban and the country round, and wrote religious poetry. They were called the *Ashṭa Chhāp*, literally the Eight Seals, or die-stamps, producing genuine poetic coin. They used the local dialect of Hindī, which is called Braj.[1] Hence, since their time all vernacular Krishnaite poetry has been written in Braj. Many other Vallabha singers followed them. By far the greatest of these lyric poets was Sūr Dās, the blind poet of Agra, who flourished seemingly in the latter half of the sixteenth century. He was a singer of wonderful power. Besides writing Rādhā-

[1] Grierson, *LH.* 20.

Kṛishṇa songs, he reproduced in beautiful verse a large number of episodes and passages from the *Bhāgavata P.*

There was also a far less admirable Vallabha literature in Braj which laid a good deal of stress on the erotic side of the Kṛishṇa myths. Perhaps the most prominent are Gokul Nath's *Chaurāsī Bārtā* (1551), i.e. eighty-four tales, and the *Braj Vilāsa* (1743) by Braj Bāsī Dās, which is the popular authority for Rādhā's life and loves. A long list of these books is given by Growse. Dayārām (1762–1852), one of the greatest of Gujarātī poets, was a Vallabha. Much of his verse is erotic.

9. *The Bhakta-mālā.*

§ 377. One of the most important modern bhakti books is the *Bhakta-mālā*,[1] or Garland of Vaishṇava Saints. It is not a sectarian work but a most catholic effort to commemorate the greatest figures in many sects. We deal with the work here because the author, Nābhājī, though not a Vallabha himself but a Rāmānandī, was a disciple of the Vallabha poet Agra Dās, and was asked by him to write the Garland. Priyā Dās, who wrote the gloss, was a follower of Chaitanya. In those days some of the Vaishṇava bhaktas of the north did not make much of these sectarian distinctions. Nābhājī flourished when Giridharajī was head of the Vallabhas and Tulsī Dās was still alive, i.e. between 1585 and 1623.[2] The *Bhakta-mālā* is a poem in old Western Hindī and mainly in the Chappai metre. It is an extremely compressed work, and, like a sūtra, is scarcely comprehensible apart from its commentary, which is a most valuable exposition of the text, though written about a century later. The Garland is a most useful work, though parts of its contents are legendary. It has been imitated and adapted in several of the vernaculars.

[1] See Sir G. Grierson's articles, *JRAS.* 1909, 607; 1910, 87, 269.

[2] For this information I am indebted to Mr. Śyāma Bihārī Miśra of Allahabad, one of the authors of *MBV.*

10. *The Rādhā-Vallabhīs.*

§ 378. Hari Vaṁśa, also called Hit Jī, was much indebted to both the Mādhvas and the Nimbārkas, but he founded a new sect in Brindāban about 1585, the Rādhā-Vallabhīs. The chief temple of the sect still stands there, dedicated to Rādhā-Vallabha, Rādhā's darling, Kṛishṇa. The founder left three works, the first *Rādhā-sudhā-nidhi*, 170 couplets in Sanskrit, the others, *Chaurāsī Pada* and *Sphuṭ-pada*, both in Hindī. Many works were written by his followers. They are Śāktas, placing Rādhā above Kṛishṇa. A member of the sect said to me in Brindāban, in December 1917: 'Kṛishṇa is the servant of Rādhā. He may do the coolie-work of building the world, but Rādhā sits as Queen. He is at best but her Secretary of State. We win the favour of Kṛishṇa by worshipping Rādhā.'

11. *The Hari-Dāsīs.*

§ 379. Svāmī Hari Dās, who lived at the end of the sixteenth and the beginning of the seventeenth century, founded the Hari Dāsīs, and appears to stand close to Chaitanya in his teaching and sympathies. He left two poems in Hindī, the *Sādhāran Siddhānt* and the *Raske Pada*. The sect still owns a fine temple in Brindāban.

12. *The Svāmī-Nārāyaṇīs.*

§ 380. In Gujarāt there is an active reforming sect called Svāmī-Nārāyaṇīs who worship Kṛishṇa and Rādhā. The founder, Sahajānanda, or Svāmī-Nārāyaṇa, disgusted with the gross immorality of the Vallabhas, began shortly after 1804 to denounce them and to teach a purer system. He soon gathered a large company of followers and a sect was formed. Jetalpur, twelve miles south of Ahmadabad, is the head-quarters, but there are temples elsewhere also. In worship they frequently use pictures instead of images. Besides the householders, who form the body of the sect, there are two orders of ascetics.

Their philosophy is the Viśishṭādvaita of Rāmānuja, but in their theology they follow Vallabha. They conform strictly to Hindu law, keeping the rules of caste with great care; they worship the five gods and they are vegetarian in diet. They retain the Vallabha mantra. They have produced a good deal of Gujarātī poetry.

c. *Pāñcharātra.*

1. *The Śri-Vaishṇavas.*

§ 381. Among the Śrī-Vaishṇavas, Vedānta-deśika was head of the school in Srī-raṅgam just after the middle of the fourteenth century,[1] and proved a prolific writer as well as a stimulating teacher. A poet of some power as well as an exact scholar, he wrote numerous books in both Sanskrit and Tamil, commentaries, dogmatic manuals, controversial works, and poems. One of his most famous works is an allegorical drama, the *Saṅkalpasūryodaya*, and another is the *Śatadūshaṇī*, a controversial work against Śaṅkara's system.

§ 382. He had a number of active theological opponents, who wrote and spoke against him freely, and the outcome of the controversy was the formation of two schools within the community, which finally led to a serious schism. He is recognized as the leader of the northern school, the Vaḍa-galai. Rāmya-jāmātṛi-muni (1370–1443), also called Manavāla-mahāmuni, is recognized as the leader of the southern school, the Teṅgalai. He taught at Śrī-raṅgam rather later than Vedānta-deśika. His commentaries are scholarly works and have been much used, but his original writings are of little importance. Since the days of the two leaders the gulf between the subsects has become deeper. They differ in doctrine on a number of minor points,[2] but, unfortunately, the schism which has resulted from the difference of opinion is much more serious than the doctrinal differences. Each sect has seized as many

[1] He was a contemporary and friend of Mādhava, and is quoted in *SDS.*, Cowell, 76.

[2] Govindāchārya, *JRAS.* 1910, 1103; 1912, 714.

of the temples as possible and numerous law-suits have resulted. So deep is the division that it prevents intermarriage.

The northern school stands in general nearer the central Vaishṇava doctrine, and in questions concerning Śrī stands nearer the Śākta theology, while the southern school represents more fully the special theology of the Śrī-Vaishṇava sect. While both schools use both Sanskrit and Tamil, the southern uses both the Tamil language and the hymns of the *Nālāyira Prabandham* more than the northern does. In consequence of the division, two forms of the sect-mark have been evolved, the southern having a slight prolongation down the nose. Widows belonging to the southern school do not undergo tonsure. The northern pontiff has his seat at Trivallur, while his southern rival resides at the Ahobila Monastery at Nanganur, near Tinnevelley.

§ 383. Appaya Dīkshita (1552–1624), though a Smārta Śaiva, commented on several Śrī-Vaishṇava books, especially the works of Vedānta-deśika. The *Yatīndramatadīpikā*, i.e. Light on Rāmānuja's Opinions, a useful summary of Śrī-Vaishṇava doctrine, contains a good many new ideas not found in the Saṁhitās. It is by Śrīnivāsa of the first half of the seventeenth century. Raṅgarāmānuja, who lived in the eighteenth century, wrote a series of Viśishṭādvaita commentaries on the Upanishads for the sect.

The bulk of the Uttara Khaṇḍa of the *Padma P.* will probably be found to be a Śrī-Vaishṇava document belonging to the beginning of this period.

§ 384. The ritual in almost all Śrī-Vaishṇava temples is *Pāñcharātra*, each temple using one particular Saṁhitā, but there are still a few which use Vaikhānasa Saṁhitās, e.g. Conjeeveram, Śrīperumbūdūr, and Veṅkaṭeśvara on Tirupati hill. It seems clear that these Saṁhitās are Bhāgavata in origin and have been used by Bhāgavata ministrants for many centuries.[1] Rāmānuja, in his eagerness to extend Pāñcharātra influence, sought to oust them and to introduce

[1] See § 211 and § 287.

Pāñcharātra Saṁhitās and ritual instead; but he did not succeed in all places. About a dozen Vaikhānasa Saṁhitās are known.[1]

2. *Sātānis.*

§ 385. The Sātānis are a group of people who are attached to the Śrī-Vaishṇava sect, and who, though they have only the status of Śūdras, exercise certain priestly functions. The name is said to be a corruption of the word *Sattadaval*, 'non-wearers': they do not wear the tuft of hair on the crown of the head nor the sacred thread. The explanation of their position seems to be this, that they came under the influence of Rāmānuja, and that he allowed them to continue certain sacerdotal usages which they had practised from time immemorial. They are found in the Mysore and in certain Telugu districts as well as in the Tamil country. They act as priests in certain temples, usually those dedicated to Hanumān. These temples bear the Śrī-Vaishṇava sect-mark, and Śūdras worship in them freely, while Brāhmans also visit them, but merely to do *darśana*, i. e. to look at the images, not to make offerings. When about to begin the rites of worship, Sātānis shout 'Rāmānuja, Rāmānuja'. They are also appointed to certain functions in the regular Śrī-Vaishṇava temples, the chief of which is to bear processional images; and they are employed by Brāhmans to brand Outcastes with the *discus* and *conch* of Vishṇu. Some Sātānis of earlier times receive honours in the temple of Śrīraṅgam at Trichinopoly. It is sometimes stated that they claim to be Brāhmans and to know the Vedas. These claims they probably do make; for they are priests, and know and use the hymns of the *Nālāyira Prabandham*, which is called the Tamil Veda.

[1] Śeshagiri Śāstri, *SSTM.* 1893–4, p. 6. The Adyar Library possesses a few manuscripts.

3. *The Manbhaus.*

§ 386. The only feature of Manbhau history during this period which is clear is the enmity which separates the community from the more orthodox sects. The hatred which Marāṭhā bhaktas have always had towards Manbhaus comes out very distinctly in the poems of Eknāth, Giridhar, and others, and is active to-day in the prohibition which keeps them away from Paṇḍharpur and the other shrines. A similar rule operates in Gujarāt. Smārta Brāhmans show as severe an attitude. In 1782 Madho Rao Peshwa promulgated a degree to the following effect:

> The Manbhaus are entirely to be condemned. They are to be entirely outcasted. They have no connexion with the four castes nor with the six Darśanas. No caste should listen to their teaching. If they do, then they are to be put out of caste.

What the real cause of this hate may have been is not yet known. The orthodox have always charged the Manbhaus not only with heterodoxy but also with gross crimes, especially seduction. They are also often spoken of as if they were Outcastes. There are to-day persistent tales to the effect that they procure little girls to be brought up as Devadāsīs, but how much truth there is in them is not clear.

The Manbhaus are found scattered about wherever Marāṭhī is spoken, but they are not a numerous body. They wear dark grey robes, and beads and ear-rings of tulsī-wood.

Their own Marāṭhī literature is gradually being made known by Marāṭhī scholars. Only when it has been carefully investigated, and when kindly intercourse with the community has enabled scholars to learn about their life, will it be possible to sketch their teaching and their history, and to settle the question of the charges so frequently brought against them.

The chief mahant has his monastery at Ridhpur, Karanjhar, Berar, but they have a number of monasteries and shrines elsewhere.

4. *The Rāmānandīs.*

§ 387. We now turn to a noteworthy development in North India, the rise of the Ramaite movement. Several Vishnuite bhaktas preceded Rāmānanda, the real leader of the movement, notably Nāmdeva and Trilochan[1] from the Marāṭhā country, and Sadana and Beni[2] who belonged to the north. Rāmānanda is one of the most important names in modern Hinduism, yet we know very little about him with certainty. Widely divergent dates have been suggested for his activity, but it now seems possible to fix his *floruit* within narrow limits. His royal disciple Pīpā was born in A.D. 1425,[3] while another disciple, Kabīr, seems to have lived from 1440 to 1518.[4] It is clear that he was not Rāmānanda's latest disciple.[5] Hence we shall not be far wrong if we suppose that Rāmānanda lived approximately from 1400 to 1470.[6] We may be ten years wrong either way, but scarcely more. He was an ascetic, and seems to have spent most of his life in Benares.

All tradition agrees that he belonged to the sect of Rāmānuja; and, as his followers to-day use a modification of the Śrī-Vaishṇava sect-mark, we may be certain that he had at least some connexion with it; but no more definite statement seems possible. The Śrī-Vaishṇavas have from the earliest days acknowledged all the incarnations of Vishṇu and their consorts; and although Kṛishṇa has always been most prominent, Rāma has been continuously revered and also Narasiṁha. It is therefore very noteworthy that Rāmānanda worshipped Rāma and Sitā and their attendants alone: the common practice of his disciples makes it impossible to escape from this conclusion. To him and his followers is due the practice of using the name Rām for the Supreme which is

[1] See § 357.
[2] Macauliffe, VI. 84; 88.
[3] Ib. VI. 111.
[4] See § 396.
[5] See a hymn by Dhana in Macauliffe, VI. 109.
[6] The above date places Rāmānanda 350 years after Rāmānuja. The guru-paramparā in two forms given by Grierson (*Ind. Ant.* XXII. 266) would agree well with this interval.

so common in the north. Further, the mantra is not the Śrī-Vaishṇava mantra[1] but *Oṁ Rāmāya namaḥ*; the *tilak*, as we have seen, is not the same; there is a difficulty about the name of the Sampradāya[2]; Rāmānanda was not a Tridaṇḍī[3] sannyāsī, as he would have been, had he belonged to the Śrī-Vaishṇava sect; and he was not nearly so strict in matters of food as the Śrī-Vaishṇavas are. How are we to account for the divergences?[4]

§ 388. We have already seen that a sect which found release in Rāma alone had been long in existence, and that the literature tends to indicate the south rather than the north as its home. If now we suppose that this Ramaite community lived in the Tamil country among the Śrī-Vaishṇavas and that Rāmānanda belonged to it, the puzzle is completely solved. Rāmānanda would then come to the north with his doctrine of salvation in Rāma alone, and with his Rāma-mantra.[5] The very similar but not identical sect-mark is then comprehensible, and also the different attitude to certain caste-rules. Further, Rāmānanda would bring with him to the north the *Adhyātma Rāmāyaṇa* and the *Agastya-Sutīkshṇa Saṁvāda*. Now, we cannot prove that he actually carried these books with him, but it is clear that the *Adhyātma Rāmāyaṇa* was much used by his followers; for it is one of the chief sources of Tulsī Dās's great work, and all Rāmānandīs know it and use it to-day; and the *Agastya-Sutīkshṇa Saṁvāda* is also used by Rāmānandīs to-day; for it is published with Rāmānanda's biography included in it.[6]

§ 389. We therefore believe that Rāmānanda was an ascetic belonging to the Ramaite sect which produced the *Adhyātma Rāmāyaṇa*, that he came to the north about 1430 and had so much success that he decided to stay, and took up his

[1] See § 292. [2] See § 393. [3] See § 285.
[4] Clearly, the story told in *ERE*. X. 569 does not explain the facts.
[5] See § 297.
[6] Bhandarkar, *VS*. 67, n. 2. I have not seen this edition of the work, but I have received a letter from Sir Rāmakṛishṇa, saying that it is the *Agastya-Sutīkshṇa Saṁvāda*.

residence in Benares. It is probable that he was accustomed to use Rāmānuja's *Śrī-bhāshya*; for, though it is written from the Śrī-Vaishṇava standpoint, its clear and moderate doctrine of theism made it a most attractive work to all the theistic sects. This would explain its use by his followers to-day and also the fact that no Rāmānandī bhāshya has ever appeared. Its continued use would also help to blur the original distinction between the two groups, while during the early decades of the movement the newly fledged bhaktas of the north would be glad to link themselves with the illustrious scholar of the south.

§ 390. The greater freedom which Rāmānanda's movement enjoyed in certain caste matters requires closer definition. The master's complete neglect of all caste distinctions in the acceptance of disciples is scarcely a novelty; for the theistic sects had already recognized that men of all classes could by means of bhakti press on to spiritual religion and Release; but Rāmānanda seems to have gone a little farther. Among his personal disciples we find not only a Śūdra, a Jāt, and an Outcaste, but a Muhammadan and at least one woman. In this extended freedom we see evidence of Muslim influence. Certain Hindu and Musulman teachers in the fifteenth century were ready to receive both Hindus and Musulmans as disciples, and there was a tendency to recognize both religions as in some sense legitimate. But there is no evidence that he relaxed the rule that restricts priestly functions to the Brāhman; and he made no attempt to overturn caste as a social institution: it was only certain of the religious restrictions of caste that were relaxed. Those who follow Rāmānanda are still strictly orthodox in all caste matters. Not until Christian criticism was brought to bear at the beginning of the nineteenth century was there any definite attempt made to show that caste as a social system is cruel, inhuman, and immoral. Much confusion has been caused by careless statements to the effect that Rāmānanda gave up caste-distinctions altogether. Rāmānanda did, however, use greater freedom in matters of food than is the custom among Śrī-Vaishṇavas.

In harmony with his great care for the common people stands the almost unbroken custom among Rāmānandīs and the related sects of using the vernaculars for their literature. It had long been customary in the chief sects to use the vernacular as well as Sanskrit; but the Marāṭhā bhaktas and Rāmānanda practically gave up the use of Sanskrit altogether. Rāmānanda does not seem to have been a distinguished writer: one single hymn of his survives, not among his own followers but in the Sikh *Granth*.[1]

§ 391. It has been frequently assumed that Rāmānanda taught the Viśishṭādvaita system of Rāmānuja. This is one of the many points with regard to the leader on which no direct evidence is available; but the indirect evidence which does exist scarcely points to that conclusion. One of the characteristics of the whole movement that springs from him is a constant use of advaita phrases, a clinging to advaita concepts while holding hard by the personality of Rāma. The teaching is usually a sort of compromise between theism and strict monism.[2] That certainly seems to be true of Kabīr, Tulsī Dās, Nānak, and others who owe their inspiration to Rāmānanda. Naturally, the suspicion arises that they may owe the common teaching to their common master; and we remember the advaita theology of the *Adhyātma Rāmāyaṇa*.[3] Yet it is quite likely that he used Rāmānuja's *Śrī-bhāshya*: in these vernacular movements there is very little strictness about the philosophical standpoint of the sect.

§ 392. Like the Marāṭhā bhaktas, Rāmānanda may have criticized idols severely, but there is not the slightest sign that he or his immediate followers gave up Hindu worship. It was Kabīr who initiated the practice of eschewing all idolatry as wrong. What is to be recognized in Rāmānanda and all his

[1] But see Grierson, *LH.* 7.

[2] In the few cases in which a clearly conceived theology actually appears, as in Kabīr, the approach is to the *Bhedābheda* doctrine rather than to the *Viśishṭādvaita* of Rāmānuja.

[3] See § 297.

followers is their vivid faith in the reality of the one personal God, spiritual and invisible, whom they called Rām. Yet, in spite of this vivid faith, no break was made with idolatry, the Brāhman priest, the Hindu pantheon, or the old mythology. There is a compromise between a living theism and an idolatrous and mythological polytheism. Kabīr was the first to preach a theism so real and consistent that it would tolerate neither gods, nor idols, nor myths.

§ 393. About A.D. 1500, if we may hazard a conjecture, the theory of the four Sampradāyas took shape in the north, as follows:

1. Śrī Sampradāya: the Rāmānandīs.
2. Brahmā Sampradāya: the Mādhvas.
3. Rudra Sampradāya: the Vishṇusvāmīs.
4. Sanakādi Sampradāya: the Nimbārkas.

This theory must have had its origin in the north, where these four sects were dominant and the famous old Bhāgavata Sampradāya, the Śrī-Vaishṇava Sampradāya, and the Dattātreya Sampradāya were little heard of, and before the rise of the sects of Chaitanya and Vallabha. The names are taken to mean the 'tradition handed down from Śrī', i.e. Lakshmī. It has been generally held that the Śrī Sampradāya covers the Śrī-Vaishṇavas of the south, but their phrase is the Śrī-Vaishṇava Sampradāya, so that it cannot be accurately applied to them. Similarly, it has been said that the Rudra Sampradāya covers the Vallabhāchāryas, but they altogether repudiate the title.

Rāmānanda's influence has been so widespread that the student needs to be careful to recognize the whole. In the most direct line of descent stands the order of ascetics who bear his name, the Rāmānandī *Vairāgīs*, i.e. those without passion, also called *Avadhūtas*, i.e. liberated ones. They are sāḍhus, and live under a less rigid discipline than Śaṅkara's sannyāsīs. They have many monasteries in Benares, Ayodhyā, and elsewhere. They are very numerous: at the Kumbh Mela at Allahabad in 1918 they alone could be compared in numbers with Śaṅkara's Daśnāmīs. Rāmānanda's influence upon the Hindu laity of Hindustan has been very great, but it is diffused and irregular. The ordinary Hindu householder who worships Rām and Sītā belongs to no sect or sub-sect; yet his thought and his practice are saturated with the ideas of Rāmānanda, borne down to him by the teaching of his disciples, and above all by a disciple who came several generations later, Tulsī Dās. Rāmānanda does not seem to have wished to found a sect; and certainly no community named after him exists to-day, although two or three petty groups founded by his followers may still be traced. Of his immediate disciples who did not found sects but left at least a few hymns two deserve mention, Dhanna and Pīpā. There seem to have been a number of organized sects formed by the disciples of Rāmānanda, but most of them have passed away. These sects of direct Rāmānandī origin (i. e. which acknowledge Sītā as well as Rām and use images) seem to have suffered severely from that process of sectarian decay which we have already mentioned, probably because there is little reason for their existence: the ordinary householder who belongs to no sect feels Rāmānanda's influence quite as strongly as the sectarian. The following are the only clear cases:

Name.	*Founder.*	*Approx. Date.*	*Centre.*
1. Rai Dāsīs[1]	Rai Dās[2]	1470	
2. Senā Panthīs	Senā	1470	Rewa
3. Malūk Dāsīs	Malūk Dās	1630	Kara Manikpur

Their literature will be found in the Bibliography.

§ 394. But Tulsī Dās (1532–1623) is the Rāmānandī who above all others has influenced the beliefs and the feelings of the multitudes of the Hindu people. He was a Smārta Brāhman, born in the Banda district to the south of the Jumna. He married, and a son was born to him but he died, and the mother thereafter left Tulsī Dās and returned to her

[1] The sect has still a large following in the Punjab.
[2] Mīrā Bāī was his disciple: see § 363.

parents in order to devote herself altogether to the worship of Rāma. Tulsī went to her and begged her to return but she refused, and in turn urged him to give himself to the religious life. Inspired by her words and her devotion, he decided to do as she suggested. He began the new life by becoming a Vairāgī, his guru being Narahari, the sixth in preceptorial descent from Rāmānanda. From Ayodhyā as head-quarters, he wandered far and wide, preaching the faith of Rāma. But a command which, as he believed, he had received from Rāma in a dream decided him to write a Rāmāyaṇa in the language of the common people. He began the work at Ayodhyā in 1574, writing in the Hindī dialect used in that district, which is called Eastern Hindī or Baiswārī; and since that time that dialect has been recognized as the Ramaite speech, just as Braj[1] is recognized as the Krishnaite vehicle. At a rather later date he left Ayodhyā and settled at Asi Ghat, Benares, where his room and his idols may still be seen. The great poem, the title of which is the *Rāma-charit-mānas*, the Lake of Rāma's deeds, was finished in Benares about 1584. He wrote a number of other works, but the first work is his masterpiece. Indeed it is one of the greatest books of modern Hinduism, and has probably influenced a far larger number of Hindus these last three centuries than any other work.

The poem is based primarily on the old *Rāmāyaṇa*, and, in imitation of it, is divided into seven books with the same titles. But the faith of Rāmānanda was in the main the outgrowth of the Vaishṇava life and literature of the centuries immediately preceding his time. The mediaeval Rāmāyaṇas, above all the *Adhyātma*, but also the *Yoga-Vaśishṭha*, the *Adbhuta*, and the *Bhusuṇḍi*, and other works such as the *Hanumān Nāṭaka*, were much read and studied by the bhaktas. Hence the main story of Tulsī Dās's work is the same as Vālmīki's, but the religion is that of the mediaeval poems, and many of the incidents reflect them also. Tulsī Dās had been a Smārta Brāhman who worshipped the five gods. At many points in

[1] See § 376.

his poem his great reverence for Śiva is clearly expressed, indeed takes such shapes as are scarcely reconcilable with a true theism. Thus, in one place, Rāma says 'Without prayer to Śiva no one can attain to the faith that I require.' The teaching of the poem also contains many advaitic elements which strike one as very strange beside the personality of the god of love whom Tulsī adores. He accepts all the mythology of Hinduism and also a great many grotesque modern stories. The Hindu system is carefully preserved, the duty of observing caste and upholding the old institutions being emphatically taught. Men are saved by dying in Ayodhyā or Benares as truly as through faith in Rāma. Yet, in spite of all this, Tulsī Dās's faith in Rāma uplifts him and enables him to present a very noble conception of God. His tender love for the humblest as well as the greatest of his devotees, his condescension in becoming incarnate for their sakes, his sympathy and endurance of suffering for those who are devoted to him, and his readiness to forgive are expressed with great dignity and power. Many of Tulsī's ideas come very near Christian thought indeed; and there is not an impure image or word in the book from beginning to end. The Tulsī Dās *Rāmāyaṇa* is thus the vernacular *Gītā*: it is a noble poem, which teaches theism, divine incarnation and the love of God, although it is burdened with the whole vast weight of Hindu orthodoxy and mythology. Tulsī Dās deserves the splendid renown which his great work has brought him. He lived for the people and loved them, and taught the very best he knew, in the language of the people, and in poetry which reaches the heart even in a translation.

d. *Reformed.*

1. *Kabīr and his Influence.*

§ 395. Sects of indirect Rāmānandī origin show far more vitality than those which sprang from the master's direct influence. All these groups arose from the teaching of Rāmānanda's disciple Kabīr, the earliest being the church of his own followers, the Kabīrpanthīs. All the others are clearly the outcome of his influence; yet no single one of the founders was an immediate disciple.

§ 396. Rāmānanda's movement provided the Hindu influence which went to the making of Kabīr (1440–1518), but Islam also contributed largely. It is possible, but it is not certain, that he was brought up by Muhammadans. It is plain, however, that the mystic Islam of the Sūfīs laid hold of him, whether he ever lived the Muhammadan life or not.

Sūfī mysticism has its roots in Muhammad's experience and teaching, but the leading elements of the system came from two external sources. The first was Neoplatonism, which flowed into Islam through Greek philosophy, Gnosticism, Christian teaching, and Christian asceticism. The other source was Indian thought, but whether it reached the Sūfīs through Buddhism at a very early date, or through Vedantism later, is not yet clear. The Sūfī conception of God tends to be immanental rather than transcendental. He works everywhere but especially in the human heart. It is possible for the humble soul which turns away from the things of sense to find Him, and see Him, and know Him. Many Sūfīs go so far as to identify self with God, like the thinkers of the Vedānta; and the state of bliss into which they hope to enter after death, called *fana*, lies very near Hindu thought. It is not quite absorption in God, for it is accompanied by everlasting life in God; yet individuality passes away. In order to reach illumination (*gnosis*) and union with God (called *al-haqq*, the Real, the True, *sat*), it is necessary to walk the path (*tariqat*), a way of life usually divided into stages. The spirit of this rule of life is to some extent ascetic, and many Sūfīs have been fakirs, but the great majority have been householders and have earned their bread by labour. The teacher, whether called Shaikh, Pir, or Murshid, has to be obeyed implicitly. The details of Sūfī practice are not unlike the methods of Yoga, the purpose being to escape from one's own individuality and, through illumination, to realize that God is the only reality. This temper of thought goes so far in many Sūfīs as to induce the idea that revelation and every organized religion belong to unreality. Hence all religions are of equal value, and a Sūfī is no longer an orthodox Muslim.

Kabīr, then, came into close touch with this system, but it does not seem possible to tell who the teachers were whom he met or which books he read. When the story of Islam in India is written in detail, it may be possible to realize more clearly the influences that went to form him. It seems probable that he lived from A.D. 1440 to 1518. He was a weaver and lived in Benares, and was probably brought up as a Muhammadan. But he became a disciple of Rāmānanda, and Hindu ideas poured into his mind. There can be no doubt of his relationship to the great leader; for he says in one of his poems, 'Rāmānanda illumined me'.[1] He also mentions Rai Dās, the Chamār, as a contemporary. He was brought before the Emperor Sikandar Lodi, who reigned from 1489 to 1517. The student can thus feel here that he is on the firm ground of history. The Emperor banished him from Benares, and he thereafter lived a wandering life, and died at Maghār near Gorakhpur.

§ 397. In the life of Kabīr the two religions mingled. The strongest elements of each laid hold of him and formed his thought, the Sūfī conviction that all ordinary religions are but forms dictating his general attitude to the two faiths. Hence he was persecuted from both sides, and the Emperor banished him from the centre of Hinduism in the interests of peace. The groundwork of his system of beliefs is Hindu; for he accepts transmigration and karma, and thus stands within the circle of Indian rather than Islamic thought. A further catalogue of Hindu ideas might be compiled—Brahman, māyā, līlā, release, detachment, cessation from work, 'He is I', the *bhedābheda* relation, &c.—but most of these coincide or almost coincide with Sūfī conceptions; so that a number of them may

[1] Tagore, *One Hundred Poems of Kabir*, 36.

be regarded as common ground. On the other hand, he denounces idolatry as foolish, false, and wrong, declares divine incarnation impossible and laughs at the forms of asceticism as silly practices: here Islam rules. Sir George Grierson believes that Christian influence also may be traced in his teaching.[1]

He was a strict theist, calling God Rām, but recognizing no consort, incarnation, or other divine attendant. He sees God both in nature and in man, and realizes the close relationship between God and man, declaring that man is the same as God and yet distinct from him. His verses refer to God in many shining phrases which touch both the heart and the spirit. The love of God for man finds clear and strong expression in his lines, and he constantly speaks of the rest and peace there is for the man who realizes that love, and the detachment from the things of the world which it brings.

398. Kabīr's poetry is in Hindī,[2] and is blunt, unpolished, sometimes even coarse. There is little attempt made to reach literary form. He does not care whether his words are Hindī, Persian, or barbarous, nor whether his sentences are grammatical or not, so long as they strike home. Tagore's beautiful renderings scarcely reflect the style of the original, though they are not unfaithful as translations. But he was a mystic of great penetration and a poet of considerable power. His best utterances are probably the loftiest work in the Hindī language; and hundreds of his couplets have laid hold of the common heart of Hindustan.

Large masses of poetry are ascribed to him, but until the whole has been examined critically, it is impossible to tell how much is genuine. About the year 1570 the *Bījak*, a collection of short poems and utterances, was compiled by one of his followers. Some thirty years later a large number of his hymns and sayings were included in the Sikh *Granth*.

[1] *JRAS*. 1918, 156.

[2] The dialect is 'old Awadhi, the language spoken in West Mirzapur, Allahabad and Audh', Sir George Grierson, *JRAS*. 1918, 152.

Besides these, innumerable couplets and witty sayings are currently ascribed to him, and the Kabīrpanthīs have a considerable literature, much of which they say came from the master, but which, in the main, is clearly of later date.

§ 399. The following is a list of the chief sects which have sprung from his teaching and influence:

Name of Sect.	*Founder.*	*Approx. Date.*	*Centre.*
1. Kabīrpanthīs	Kabīr	1470	Benares
2. Sikhs	Nānak	1500	Punjab
3. Dādūpanthīs	Dādū	1575	Rajputana
4. Lāl Dāsīs	Lāl Dās	1600	Alwar
5. Satnāmīs		1600	Narnol, south of Delhi
6. Bābā Lālīs	Bābā Lāl	1625	Dehanpur, nr. Sirhind
7. Sādhs	Birbhan	1658	Near Delhi
8. Charan Dāsīs	Charan Dās	1730	Delhi
9. Śiva Nārāyaṇīs	Śiva Nārāyaṇa	1734	Chandrawār, Ghāzīpur
10. Garīb Dāsīs	Garīb Dās	1740	Chudani, Rohtak
11. Rām Sanehīs	Rām Charan	1750	Shahapur, Rajputana

A number of common features are traceable in all these groups at the time of their foundation, but the Hinduism which surrounds them presses heavily on them and finds entrance at many points, so that most of the distinctive features tend to become progressively weaker. Four characteristics seem to have been common to them all:

1. God alone is worshipped and idolatry is strictly prohibited; so that Hindu worship is completely abandoned; and men of any caste may exercise religious functions.
2. The sect is open to all Hindus and to Muslims also.
3. Great stress is laid on the value of the guru.
4. The literature is in vernacular verse.

There were many other ideas which were accepted by all or nearly all at first, but they were not so rigidly held, e.g. the value of the repetition of the name, *Rām*, the denial of the doctrine of divine incarnation, the rejection of asceticism and begging, and the prohibition of the use of flesh as food, of intoxicating drink and of tobacco. In a few cases infanticide and widow-burning were prohibited. The drift towards Hinduism, however, soon brings in the doctrine of divine incarnation, the worship of gurus, and the formation of an order of Sādhus, who become the divine gurus of the sect; the rules against flesh, wine, and tobacco are gradually relaxed; the sect tends to become restricted to the clean castes; Hindu mythology, especially the story of Rādhā, creeps in; and finally idols reappear. In one case obscene rites find an entrance at an early date.

2. *The Kabīrpanthīs.*

§400. Kabīr formed a community, which is known as the Kabīrpanth (*panth*, representing the Sūfī *tariqat*), but how much of its present character and organization comes from him it scarcely seems possible to say. Since he was altogether opposed to idolatry, he must have made fresh arrangements for the worship of God, but how far he went we do not know. We can hardly believe that he instituted an ascetic order. He would be certain to give the guru a prominent place in the sect, yet he would by no word or act lead men to believe that he or any other teacher was an incarnation of God. Since his day Hindu influence in various forms has found its way into the community. There is an order of monks and also a few nuns. The monks are the teachers and leaders of the community, and they are ruled by two chief mahants or abbots. The earliest centre seems to have been the Kabīr-chaurā monastery in Benares, with which is associated the monastery at Maghār where Kabīr died. The rival mahant has his seat at Chattisgarh in the Central Provinces. There are many monasteries subordinate to each. The Benares mahants trace their descent from Surat Gopāl, while the Chattisgarh mahants look back to Dharm Dās. Each sub-sect has its own literature. The worship, which consists of prayers, ritual, and exhortation, is conducted in the monasteries. The various acts of worship are described by the Bishop of Lucknow in his manual.[1] There is an initiation ceremony comparable with baptism, and a rite called Jot Prasād, which has analogies with the Lord's Supper. But a considerable place is taken by the worship of the mahant, and in the monastery in Benares a large picture of Kabīr is used in such a way as to indicate a return to idolatry. Although Kabīr denounced divine incarnation, the books teach that he is an incarnation of the Supreme. Indeed the practice of the sect as a whole is saturated in Hinduism. The sect-mark, the rosary, the mantra, and many other details are conspicuous.

3. *The Sikhs.*

§ 401. Nānak (1469–1538), the founder of the religion of the Sikhs, i. e. the disciples, was a Punjābī, born in Talwandi in the Lahore district. His life is told in numerous *Janamsākhīs*, i. e. Birth-witnesses, but there is not much that is yet known with certainty about him. He belonged to the movement which produced Kabīr, and was unquestionably influenced by him, but there is no evidence that they ever met. Nānak associated with numerous teachers, both Hindu and Muslim.[2] Knowing both Persian and Hindī, besides Punjābī, he read Sūfī writings as well as the hymns of the Hindī-speaking saints. He wandered all over North India, giving utterance to his teaching in hymns and brief sayings in a mixture of Punjābī and Hindī which would be understood far and wide. His disciple Mardana went with him and played the rebeck while Nānak sang. He gathered large numbers of followers, and arranged for them the *Japjī*, a collection of pieces of verse, most of them in praise of God, put together for daily prayer. As a poet he is not comparable with Kabīr; yet his verse is clear, simple, and pithy, an excellent vehicle for his teaching. Two Sanskrit works on philosophy are also ascribed to him, the *Nirākāra Mīmāṁsā* and the *Adbhuta Gītā*.[3]

[1] Westcott, *Kabīr*. [2] See for example Macauliffe, VI. 356–414.
[3] Barnett, *Hinduism*, 39, n. 1.

His religious convictions are in the main the same as Kabīr's. God is one, eternal, spiritual, and he must be worshipped from the heart, and not with images. Hinduism and Islam are two paths, but there is but one God. Men of all castes and races can know and love God. The life of home is praised rather than asceticism, and the moral side of religion is strongly emphasized. In Nānak many fragments of the monistic Vedānta appear along with numerous phrases which imply the personality of God. Karma and transmigration are retained, the conception of *māyā* as a delusive, deceptive force, and also the conviction of the importance of the guru. Release brings union with God, or rather absorption, in which individuality is lost. Nānak was a humble man who confessed his own sinfulness freely, and did not dream of calling himself an incarnation of God. Yet he stands nearer Hinduism than Kabīr; for the whole Hindu pantheon is retained in his poems.

§ 402. Nānak was followed by nine other gurus. The first, Guru Aṅgad, invented for Nānak's hymns a new alphabet, which is known as Gurumukhi, and is now used for the vernacular of the Punjab. He left a few utterances in verse. Gurus Amar Dās and Rām Dās each wrote a considerable number of hymns. Guru Arjan, with whom the succession became hereditary, was a notable figure, a poet, and a man of affairs. His leadership covered the last twenty-four years of the reign of Akbar, and he took full advantage of the opportunity which the Emperor's toleration afforded him. He built the central Sikh shrine, known as the Golden Temple, at Amṛitsār. But his chief service to the community was the formation of its sacred book.

It is possible that the collection of Kabīr's poems in the *Bījak*, which took place about the time when Arjan became guru, suggested the idea to his mind. In any case he gathered together the hymns of Nānak and the other gurus, and added to them his own hymns and a considerable body of poetry by Kabīr and other singers.[1] He placed the *Japjī* first, then the *So-Daru*, which is used by the Sikhs for even-song, and then two other sets of verses, which are used as a prayer before retiring to rest. Thereafter the whole body of hymns is divided into groups according to the Rāg,[2] i.e. the type of music, to which they are sung.[3] The *Granth Sahib*, or Noble Book, has proved of very large value to the Sikhs. It is their manual of instruction and theology as well as their hymnal and prayer-book. As is evident from Arjan's own compositions, Hindu ideas and practices were finding their way into Sikhism in his days. The gūru was already worshipped as the Supreme Being.

While Akbar honoured Arjan, his son Jahangir was suspicious of the *Granth*, and subjected him to tortures to which he succumbed. His death did a great deal to rouse the martyr-spirit in the community. His son Har Gobind, the next guru, formed a bodyguard for himself. The ninth guru, Teg Bahadur, who was an old man when he accepted the head-ship of the community, wrote a number of hymns and stanzas. The intolerant Emperor Aurunzebe imprisoned him and finally put him to death, but not before the guru, according to Sikh tradition, had prophesied that Europeans would come to India and destroy his empire. This prophecy has done a great deal to bind the Sikhs to British rule. A poetical work of some importance was produced by Bhai Gur Dās, a contemporary of the fourth, fifth, and sixth gurus. It is an outline of the Sikh faith, and is partly translated by Macauliffe.[4] It is called *Bhai Gur Dās Ki Wār*.

§403. Gobind Singh, the son of Teg Bahadur, saw that the Sikhs must fight the Mogul empire. He therefore formed and trained an army which became a formidable force. In

[1] These hymns by others than Sikhs were altered here and there by the editors.

[2] For the Rāgs see Macauliffe, V. 333. For an exposition of the Indian Rāg see Fox Strangways, *Music of Hindustan*.

[3] For the prosody of the hymns see Trumpp, *Ādi Granth*, cxxviii ff.

[4] IV. 241.

order to give his warriors the fullest support from religion, he summoned them to accept from his hands the Khanda-di-Pahul, or Baptism of the Sword, and to take a series of solemn vows. These vows bound them to wear five articles the names of which begin with the letter K,[1] to worship God regularly, to share a common meal, and to eschew idolatry, pilgrimage, satī, infanticide, tobacco, and intoxicants. Each man adopted the surname Siṅgh, Lion. They thus became a new community within which Caste disappeared. It was called the *Khālsā*, a title derived from a word meaning pure. He refused to appoint another guru, declaring that the *Granth*, to which he added his father's hymns and a single couplet of his own, must henceforward be their guru; and no other guru has been appointed. Doubtless he realized from what he saw in Sikhism and elsewhere the grave danger of guru-worship.

With him Hindu influence came into the community still more freely than before. Before organizing the Khālsā, he seems to have worshipped the goddess Durgā,[2] and he certainly had translations made by his court poets of the episode of Chaṇḍī in the *Mārkaṇḍeya P.*[3] These and other Hindu narratives were used to fire the valour of his men. He left also a number of other writings, mostly in Hindī,[4] but some in Persian.[5] After his death his works, along with certain translations and compositions by men employed by him, were gathered together in one volume by Bhai Maṇi Siṅgh. Later it was called the *Granth of the Tenth Guru*, but it has never been received as authoritative. It is used by the followers of Gobind Singh for worldly ends, e. g. the promotion of valour, while the *Ādi* or Original *Granth* is used for religious ends. Parts of it are translated by Macauliffe.

[1] *Keś*, hair (never cut); *Kach*, drawers; *Kirpan*, dagger; *Kartha*, bangle (of iron); *Kaṅga*, comb.

[2] According to one account he offered her human sacrifices: Trumpp, xi. But see Macauliffe, V, Chap. VIII. He may have been moved by Sivajī's example.

[3] Macauliffe, V. 80. See above, § 168.

[4] One of these is a set of prayers called the *Jap Saheb*.

[5] Macauliffe, V. 1, 22, 67, 68, 83, 201, 260 ff.

§ 404. The transformation of the church into an army did not prove altogether healthy; for preaching practically ceased among them, and Hinduism continued to press into the community. The *Granth*, now recognized as the Guru, began to receive divine honours. Idols reappeared in Sikh houses and even in Sikh shrines. Many Sikhs drifted back to Hinduism. The formation of the Khālsā necessarily divided the Sikh community into two parts and within these certain subdivisions have appeared. Yet all worship together. The following list shows the subdivisions:

A. SAHIJDHĀRĪS.[1]

Name.	*Approx. Date.*	*Founder.*
1. Sikhs, Nānakpanthīs[2]	1500	
2. Udāsīs[3] (ascetics)	1538	Śrī Chand, Nānak's son
3. Handalīs[4]	1570	Handal
4. Minas[5]	1581	Prithī Chand, son of Guru Rām Dās
5. Rām Rañjas[6]	1656	Rām Rāi, son of Guru Har Rāi
6. Sewapanthīs[7]	1700	Kanaiya, a water-carrier

B. SIṄGHS.

Name.	*Approx. Date.*	*Founder.*
1. The Khālsā	1690	Guru Gobind Siṅgh
2. Nirmalas[8] (ascetics)	1690	Bīr Siṅgh
3. Akālīs[9] (soldier ascetics)	1690	Mān Siṅgh

§ 405. Public worship is conducted in the *gurudvāras* of the sect. There are several of these that are buildings of some size, but the majority are unpretentious little houses, and a great many villages have none. The worship ought to consist merely of the recitation of the regular portions of the *Granth* appointed for the purpose and the singing of hymns;

[1] i. e. easy-goers. [2] Barnett, *Hinduism*, 38; *ERE*. II. 49 f.
[3] Macauliffe, I. 79 f.; Oman, *Ascetics*, 194 ff.
[4] Macauliffe, I. 80 f. These have a *Granth* and a *Janamsākhī* of their own.
[5] Macauliffe, I. 80.
[6] Macauliffe, I. lii. They have a temple at Dehra Dun.
[7] Macauliffe, V. 174.
[8] Oman, ib. 196 ff.; Macauliffe, I. lii; *ERE*. IX. 375.
[9] Also called *Nihaṅgs*, Macauliffe, I. 52; Oman, ib. 198 f.; *ERE*. I. 268.

but the adoration of the sacred book itself is now a very prominent part of Sikh observance, as any one may see in the Golden Temple of Amṛitsār. In one place at least it is worshipped by fire-sacrifice.[1] How great the fascination of Hindu worship is may be realized from the fact that Sikh ascetics frequently go on pilgrimage and visit Hindu temples to gaze on the idols. The Prayer Book in common use is called the *Pañjgranthī*. It contains (*a*) the *Japjī*, (*b*) the *Rahras*, (*c*) the *Kīrtan Sohila*, (*d*) the *Sukhāmaṇi*, (*e*) the *Āsa-ki-wār*. The first three of the five have to be recited daily by Khālsā Sikhs.

4. *The Dādūpanthīs*.

§ 406. Dādū (1544–1603) was a Brāhman who belonged to Ahmadabad, but he spent most of his life in Rajputana, and there the bulk of his followers are still found. He expressed his teaching in *Bānī*, i.e. poetic utterances. His work contains 5,000 verses, arranged in 37 chapters, which deal with the leading religious questions. Hymns also are included. He had fifty-two disciples, each of which set up at least one *Dādū-dvāra*, or place of worship. Apart from Dādū's *Bānī*, the sect has a large literature in Hindī, produced by two of his sons and a number of his followers. Sundar Dās the younger is a famous Hindī poet. Nischal Dās was a Vedantist, and through his influence some members of the sect have accepted the *advaita* doctrine. Only twice-born Hindus are allowed to read the *Bānī*, but Śūdras may learn the 24 *gurumantra* and the 24 *śabda*. The sect has no dealings with Outcastes.[2]

§ 407. The followers of Dādū are either householders or celibate ascetics. Householders are called *Sevaks*, i.e. servitors, while the title *Dādūpanthī* is reserved for ascetics. The latter are divided into five orders:

a. *Khālsās*, the pure. Their head-quarters are in Naraina,

[1] In the Sikh monastery at Conjeeveram.

[2] These and other particulars I learned from Dādūpanthīs at Allahabad at the Kumbh Mela in Feb. 1918.

forty miles from Jaipur, where Dādū died. Learned Khālsās lead in worship, study, and teach.

b. *Nāgās* (a corruption of the Sanskrit Nagna, naked) are an order of celibate mercenaries founded by Sundar Dās, the elder. In nine camps on the Jaipur border there are some 20,000 of them, paid by the Jaipur government for the defence of the state.

c. *Utrādīs,* an order founded in the Punjab by Banwāri Dās. Many of them are learned men and teach ascetics. Others are doctors.

Members of these three orders may take up any profession.

d. *Viraktas*, the passionless. These must not practise any profession nor touch money. They live a wandering life, and devote themselves to study and literature.

e. *Khākīs*, 'ash-covered' ascetics, who lay stress on austerities.

§ 408. The cult, which is carried on in the Dādū-dvāras, consists in the worship of a manuscript copy of Dādū's *Bānī* with all the operations of Hindu idolatry, such as the offering of flowers, perfume, and food and the waving of lights. *Bānī* are also recited and hymns are sung. The pūjā is conducted by an ascetic; so that wherever there is an ascetic and a manuscript of the sacred book, there may be a Dādū-dvāra. At Naraina Dādū's sandals and clothes are preserved and receive worship.

5. *The Lāl Dāsīs.*

§ 409. Lāl Dās (died 1648), the chief saint of Alwar, came of the Meos, originally a predatory tribe. His teaching and hymns are gathered in a collection called *Bānī.* The Lāl Dāsī teachers, like their master, are married men. The worship of the sect consists of the repetition of Rām's name and the singing of hymns to rude music.

6. *The Satnāmīs.*

§ 410. The origin of the Satnāmī sect seems to be altogether lost; so that the date suggested in the table (p. 334), A.D. 1600, is quite conjectural. The name of the sect, 'True-name', means that they worship the one Reality (*Sat, al Haqq*) and proves that they belong to the sphere of Kabīr's influence. They appear in history for the first time in 1672, at Narnol, 75 miles south-west of Delhi, where a trivial quarrel led to a wild rising of Satnāmī ascetics against the government of Aurungzebe. It was finally crushed in a battle fought in March 1673, when thousands of Satnāmīs were killed. No book of their own belonging to this date is extant, but a contemporary Hindu historian, Īśwar Dās Nāgar, tells us of their immorality and filthy habits. Clearly their original doctrine had been seriously tainted by some outside influence.

The sect seems to have been reorganized, about A.D. 1750, by Jagjīvan Dās, at Kotwa between Lucknow and Ayodhya. Throughout its history, since this time, the members of the sect have been mostly Outcastes. Jagjīvan was a poet and left his teaching in Hindī verse. One of his disciples Dūlan Dās, who spent his life near Rai Bareilly, was also a poet. The sect is said to be strictly vegetarian and to abstain from liquor. Bhaṭṭāchārya avers that the sect practises the rite known as Gāyatrī Kriyā, the drinking of a mixture of human excreta.

A further development occurred under Ghāzī Dās, a Chamār belonging to Chattisgarh in the Central Provinces, between 1820 and 1830. He introduced it among the Chamārs[1] of the district, mainly with a view to the social betterment of the race, and he did not acknowledge his indebtedness to Jagjīvan and his people. He taught his people to worship the one God, formless and eternal, who is the sole Reality. He forbade the use of flesh and also of certain vegetables which look like flesh or blood, and the worship of idols. These Chamār Satnāmīs used to compel young wives to undergo a rite of promiscuity, but it is gradually passing out of use. One group has reverted to idols.

[1] Outcastes who work in leather.

From the condition of the Satnāmīs to-day one would be inclined to infer that from the beginning their propaganda has had its chief success among Outcastes, and that the unclean practices which have dogged their history are probably ancient customs long practised in Outcaste tribes, which it has not been possible to eradicate.

7. *The Bābā Lālīs.*

§411. Bābā Lāl, the founder of the petty sect, the Bābā Lālīs, attracted the attention of Prince Dārā Shikoḥ, the son of Shah Jahan, in 1649, and had seven interviews with him. The teaching he then gave was written in Persian by two Hindus belonging to the court under the title *Nadiru'n-nikat.*[1] The sect still possesses a religious house at Lāl Bābā Ka Śaila near Baroda.

8. *The Sādhs.*

§412. The Sādhs[2] are found chiefly between the two rivers from Delhi southwards. The sect was founded in 1658 by Birbhan. He expressed his teaching, like Kabīr, in verses and couplets which are gathered in a volume called *Ādi Upadeśa*, the Original Teaching. One element in the book is a set of twelve commandments, which prove the sect to have been more distinctly Puritan than any of the others, and show Christian influence in one point at least, viz. in the strict injunction of monogamy. They hold a meeting at the full moon.

9. *The Charan Dāsīs.*

§413. The Charan Dāsīs are a sect founded at Delhi about 1730 by Charan Dās. He left a considerable literature in Hindī verse, and two women who were his disciples have also left books. The basis of his system is the same as Kabīr's, the name of the eternal God, the Word of God, the practice of bhakti, the need of the guru, and the avoidance of idolatry; but the influx of Hinduism is plainly visible in the divine

[1] Wilson, *Sects*, 347; *ERE.* II. 308.

[2] Wilson, *Sects*, 352.

claims he makes for the guru and in his use of the *Bhāgavata P.* Naturally the sect has gone farther. They have images in their temples, and recognize God in the form of Rādhā and Kṛishṇa.[1]

10. *The Śiva Nārāyaṇīs.*

§ 414. The Śiva Nārāyaṇī sect[2] was founded by a Rajput named Śiva Nārāyaṇa at Bhelsari near Ghāzīpur in 1734, and their four monasteries called Dhāms are all in the Ghāzīpur district. People of any religion or class are admitted. Most of the members to-day are people of the lower classes including Outcastes, but in earlier times Brāhmans and Rājputs joined in appreciable numbers. Muhammad Shah, Emperor of Delhi, 1719–48, became a member of the sect and gave his royal seal to the founder. They believe in the formless Brahman, and venerate Śiva Nārāyaṇa as an incarnation. The founder left sixteen volumes of Hindī verse.

11. *The Garīb Dāsīs.*

§ 415. Garīb Dās (1717–82)[3] lived at Churani in the Rohtak district. His *Guru Granth Sahib* contains 24,000 lines. The sect still exists, but they have only one monastery, and have no lay followers. Only twice-born men are accepted as Sādhus. I met a few Garīb Dāsīs at the Kumbh Mela at Allahabad, in February 1918.

12. *The Rām Sanehīs.*

§ 416. The Rām Sanehīs, or Lovers of Rām, are a sect founded by Rām Charan about the middle of the eighteenth century. Rām Charan left a body of *Bānī*, and of hymns. The third guru, Dulhā Rām, left about 10,000 verses and

[1] Grierson, *ERE.* III. 365.
[2] Wilson, *Sects*, 358; Gait, *Census Report*, 1901, I. 115; Grierson, *JRAS.* 1918, 114.
[3] Prasād, *SBS.* I. 181; II. 195.

4,000 couplets.[1] Their prayer-houses are called Rāmdvāra, and are found mostly in Rajputana; and the worship consists of singing and teaching. Their head-quarters are at Shahpur, but they are represented also at Jaipur, Udaipur, and elsewhere. They have no settled following among laymen, so that the sect has decayed, and is now merely an order of sādhus.

§417. Several other leaders founded schools and expressed their teaching in Hindī verse, from the end of the seventeenth to the beginning of the nineteenth century. Their names and literature will be found in Prasād's volumes.

§418. The tragedy in the history of these sects which, under the influence of Islam, gave up Hindu worship, is that they have been unable to find a satisfactory substitute for it. The mere reading of pieces of vernacular poetry and the singing of hymns does not grip the common people. Those sects which restrict themselves to that tend to lose their hold on the laity, while the rest revert to Hindu guru-worship, as the Kabīrpanthīs have done, or fall to bibliolatry, as is the case with the Sikhs and the Dādūpanthīs.

F. *Śaiva Literature.*

a. *General.*

§419. A good deal of unsectarian Śaiva literature arose during the period, and some of it is well worthy of notice. The Śaiva movement in Bengal produced a literature of its own in Bengālī, which is described by Mr. Sen, the most prominent book being Rāmakṛishṇa's *Śivāyana*, which dates from about 1750. In Gujarāt, Śivānand, who lived towards the middle of the eighteenth century, produced lyrics which are much used. In the Telugu country we trace the activity of Śaivas in the translation of three Śaiva Purāṇas, the *Skanda* (fifteenth century), the *Kūrma* (*c.* A.D. 1500), and the *Matsya* (*c.* A.D. 1550); and also in the famous gnomic verses of Vemana, a prince belonging to the family of the

[1] Bhaṭṭāchārya, *HCS.* 447-8; Grierson, *LH.* 87.

Vema Reddis, who ruled in the Kistna, Guntur, and Nellore districts for a century. Vemana flourished early in the fifteenth century. In Travancore, in the seventeenth century, the *Śiva P.* and the *Brahmāṇḍa* were done into Malayalim. So, in Tamil, in the fifteenth century Aruṇa-giri-nāthar wrote the *Tiru-puhal*, a series of lyrics on the god *Subrahmaṇya*. The famous Liṅgāyat work in Kanarese, *Prabhu-liṅga-līlā*, was translated into Tamil verse by Śiva Prakāśa Svāmī in the seventeenth century, and is used by all Śaivas. Two translations from the Sanskrit may be mentioned: the *Liṅga P.* was done in Tamil verse by Varatuṅga Pāṇḍya, a fifteenth-century prince of the ancient house, and the *Kūrma P.* by his brother, Ativīrarāma Pāṇḍya. Two collections of local religious legends, the *Tiru-viḷaiy-āḍat-purāṇam*, composed by Parañjoti early in the seventeenth century, and the *Kāñchī-purāṇam*, by Kāñchī Appar and his teacher, Śiva-jñāna-yogī the Siddhantist, in the latter half of the eighteenth century, the former dealing with Madura, the latter with Conjeeveram, are extremely popular.

b. *Pāśupata Śaivas.*

§ 420. The ancient Pāśupata sects have almost completely disappeared. A very few Aghorīs may be met: they are the old Kāpālikas; and a few Aughars, who are Kāpālikas reformed under the influence of Kabīr, may also be seen.

1. *The Gorakhnāthīs.*

§ 421. But there are plenty of Gorakhnāthīs to be found. Their temples are Śaiva temples, but Gorakhnāth is worshipped in them as a form of Śiva, and animals are sacrificed. In the temples of the sect in Nepal buffaloes as well as goats are sacrificed. In the monastery at Gorakhpur, where he is said to have died, there is a shrine to his memory in which pūjā is done three times a day. It contains his *charaṇa*, i.e. his footprints in stone, but no image. Outside the shrine, to the right, is a fence of trisul of various sizes, and behind it the place where goats are sacrificed.[1]

§ 422. Kānphaṭa Yogīs have a great slit cut in the central hollow of each ear[2] so as to admit a big circular ear-ring of glass, wood, or horn.[3] They usually wear several necklaces, and from one of them there hangs a slender silver whistle called *Siṅginād*, which they blow before worship and before meals. Amongst the necklaces will usually be seen one consisting of small whitish stone beads, which is worn as a badge indicating that the wearer has visited the famous Vāmāchārī Śākta temple of Hiṅglāj in Baluchistan; for they are accustomed to visit Śākta as well as Śaiva temples. Their mantra is *Śiva Goraksha.* They worship Gorakhnāth and claim a high antiquity for him. He and the other Nāthas are believed to live in the Himalayas. They do not do very much in the way of yoga-practice; for modern ascetics tend to degenerate to a common rudimentary type. Yogīs whom I met at the Kumbh Mela at Allahabad and at Benares gave me a long list of books which they say Gorakhnāthīs use.

§ 423. On the *Haṭha-yoga* and the *Goraksha-Śataka,* which are mentioned above as works attributed to Gorakhnāth, three more modern works depend, the *Haṭha-yoga-pradīpikā* by Svātmārāma Yogīndra, the disciple of Śrīnāth, the *Gheraṇḍa S.*, and the *Śiva S.* The first is the earliest of the three. The *Pradīpikā* and the *Gheraṇḍa S.* deal with the same subjects, but only part of the *Śiva S.* is devoted to Haṭha Yoga; the rest of it is more like a treatise on Śākta Yoga.

[1] I owe this information to Mr. D. W. P. Hill of Benares, who visited the monastery in December 1917.

[2] At the Kumbh Mela at Allahabad in February 1918 I saw a yogī who had just been initiated. He was wearing a pair of huge ear-rings, and his ears were very painful.

[3] When asked what the meaning of the wearing of ear-rings is, they merely say that Gorakhnāth ordered it. We may note that Śiva wears large circular ear-rings in many of his images, and Rāmānuja tells us that the ear-ring was one of the *mudrās*, seals, worn by Kāpālikas: *SBE.* XLVIII. 521.

c. *Āgamic Śaivas.*

1. *Sanskrit School of Śaiva Siddhānta.*

§424. In the Tamil country there are no sectarian distinctions in the Śaiva temples. They are sacred to Śiva; they are open to all caste Hindus, whether Smārtas, ordinary Śaivas, Siddhāntists, or Liṅgāyats, and the ministrants are all Brāhmans, except in the case of a few of the smaller temples where Pandarams, i.e. non-Brāhman Śaivas, act as *archakas.* These Brāhman ministrants form the chief constituency of the Sanskrit school of Śaiva Siddhānta, but numerous Smārtas who are not *archakas* doubtless belong to it also. The earliest surviving document representing the school is, as we have already seen, the essay in Mādhava's *Sarvadarśana-saṅgraha* called the *Śaiva Darśana.* The literature of this school is all in Sanskrit; it recognizes the Āgamas, and its philosophical standpoint is Viśishṭādvaita. It is thus very clearly marked off from the Tamil school; for the literature of the latter is all in Tamil, its standpoint is advaita, and most of its people are non-Brāhmans.

The next noteworthy book belonging to the school is Śrīkaṇṭha Śivāchārya's *Śaiva-bhāshya* on the Vedānta-sūtras. The date of the work has never been settled. Tradition runs that he was a friend of Govinda, the guru of the great Śaṅkara, that, after writing the *bhāshya*, he had a philosophical disputation with Śaṅkara and defeated him; but against this there stands the blank silence of several centuries in all schools, and also his manifest dependence on Rāmānuja. The great success of the *Śrī-bhāshya*, which vindicates the Vedantic orthodoxy of the Vaishṇava position, founded on the Nārāyaṇīya section of the Epic and the Vaishṇava Saṁhitās, seems to have roused Śrīkaṇṭha to do a similar service for his own Śaiva school, which recognizes the Pāśupata theology and the Śaiva Āgamas. His philosophic position is the same as Rāmānuja's and he uses the same epithet for it, Viśishtādvaita[1]; at many points his reasoning follows the *Śrī-bhāshya* implicitly; and I am told that sentences occur in the *bhāshya* which are verbally the same as sentences in the *Vedānta-sāra* attributed to Rāmānuja. There need thus be no doubt that he is later than Rāmānuja. But, if the *bhāshya* had been in existence when Mādhava wrote the *Sarvadarśanasaṅgraha*, he would have almost certainly referred to it; so that his silence would lead us to think of a later date. Now, the earliest known reference to the work is in the *Śaṅkaravijaya* attributed to Mādhava, which is clearly pseudonymous, and therefore subsequent to Mādhava. Thus, if we suppose the *bhāshya* was written about A.D. 1400, there would seem to be no evidence in existence which conflicts with that date. Yet it would be unwise to speak dogmatically until the work has been carefully examined and the quotations contained in it have been identified. The *bhāshya* is used by all Āgamic Śaivas in South India.

The earliest existing commentary on the *bhāshya* is Appaya Dīkshita's *Śivārkamaṇidīpikā*, dating from about A.D. 1600.

Śambhudeva's *Śaiva-siddhānta-dīpikā*, which belongs to the sixteenth century, is the most noteworthy dogmatic work after the *bhāshya*; but Nīlakaṇṭha's *Kriyāsāra*, which contains a synopsis of the *bhāshya*, is also much used. There is an account of the school and its theology in the Vāyavīya S. of the *Śiva P.*

2. *Tamil Śaivas.*

§ 425. There is, strictly speaking, no organized sect connected with the Tamil Śaiva Siddhānta. A sort of incomplete sectarian organization has grown up around the literature and the monasteries. These are schools of theology and literature in which monks are trained and priests learn a little. The Mahants keep touch also with their initiated disciples all over the country. A majority of the monasteries are under non-Brāhmans, the remainder under Brāhmans. Indeed com-

[1] On II. i. 22.

paratively few Brāhman families are connected with the movement, the mass of Tamil Brāhmans being either Smārtas or Vaishṇavas. Siddhantists recognize the Vedas, but in practice they usually restrict themselves to the Upanishads and the Śaiva portions of the *Yajurveda*, especially the eleven Rudra Hymns.[1] The *Gītā* they do not use at all[2]: it is too distinctively Vaishṇava. The books on which their religious life is really nourished are their own Tamil literature: the Āgamas remain in the background, and even the *Śaiva Bhāshya* is read by only a few. No serious theological change is visible in the theology during this period, but a number of valuable pieces of literature appeared. Kaṇṇudaiya Vaḷḷalār is the author of *Oḷivil-Oḍukkam*, a theological work in Tamil verse belonging to the fifteenth century, while Ḳumāraguruparasvāmī wrote many short religious poems in the seventeenth. The most noted scholar of the time, Śiva-jñāna-yogī, who died in A.D. 1785, wrote two famous Tamil commentaries, one lengthy, the *Drāviḍa Bhāshya*, the other short, the *Laghu Ṭīkā*, on the foundation scripture of the Siddhānta, *Śiva-jñāna-bodha*, and also produced the *Kāñchī-purāṇam* in collaboration with his disciple, as has been already stated.[3] But unquestionably the greatest Śaiva production of the period is Tāyumānavar's volume of lyrics, which are equally famous for religious feeling, beauty of language, and sweetness of rhythm. He also belongs to the eighteenth century.

The philosophic standpoint of the school is called Śivādvaita,[4] and they are thus distinguished from the Sanskrit Siddhānta school; but no attempt will be made here to describe the theology, for it differs in important details from the other schools, and thus requires to be expounded with fuller knowledge than the writer possesses.

[1] *Taittirīya Saṁhitā*, IV. v.
[2] Pope's dictum, *Tiruvāśagam*, xxxvi, is erroneous.
[3] See § 419.
[4] Others give Bhedābheda as the standpoint.

3. *Sittars.*

§ 426. There was a Śaiva school in Tamil-land, which held a monotheistic and Puritan creed, and roundly condemned idolatry. They are usually called the Chittars, or Sittars, i.e. *Siddhas*, Sages, but their history is not known. They seem to have been most active in the sixteenth and seventeenth centuries.

Ahappey and Pambatti are believed to have been their chief singers. Many of the hymns of the Sittars are collected in the *Śiva-vākyam*, Śiva's utterance, but orthodox lyrics have also crept in beside the pure material. On the other hand, a number of beautiful lyrics which show the Sittar spirit are mistakenly attributed to Paṭṭinattu Piḷḷai, the tenth-century poet.[1] Tattuva Rayar, who wrote in the seventeenth century a work against idolatry, *Adaṅgan-Muṟai*, was probably another leader. This movement may be an outcome of Muslim influence, like similar anti-idol movements in the north, or Muslim and Christian teaching may have both had something to do with it.

4. *Kashmir Śaivās.*

§ 427. Kashmir Śaivism still exists, but it shows very little vitality. Yet scholarly paṇḍits are not wanting: their work, clothed in English, may be seen in Chatterji's *Kashmir Shaivism*. Sir George Grierson refers to 'a wise old woman known as Lal Ded' who lived in Kashmir in the fourteenth century, 'whose apophthegms in short verses are still freely quoted in the happy valley', and he quotes and translates one of her stanzas. Mr. Chatterji names only a single writer belonging to this period, Śivopādhyāya of the eighteenth century, who wrote a commentary on the *Vijñāna Bhairava Tantra*.

[1] See § 305.

5. *Vīra Śaivas.*

§ 428. It is not yet possible to sketch Liṅgāyat history during those centuries. All that can be done is to give a brief account of the literature produced by the sect in Kanarese. Purāṇas bulk most largely, the *Basava*, translated in 1369 from the Telugu by Bhīma Chandra Kavi, the *Padmarāja*, the story of Kereya Padmarasa, written about 1385 by Padmanāṅka, the *Mahābasava* by Siṅgi Rāja of rather uncertain date, and the *Channa Basava*, which tells of Basava's nephew, written by Virūpāksha Paṇḍit in 1585. The *Prabhuliṅgalīlā*, which is not called a Purāṇa, is at once a legendary history and a book of dogmatics. It is founded on the life of Allāma Prabhu, an associate of Basava. It was written by Chāmarasa about 1460, and was translated into Tamil at the end of the seventeenth century.[1] About the middle of the seventeenth century lived Śivaguṇayogī, whose *Vivekachintāmaṇi*[2] is a sort of cyclopaedia of Śaiva lore in *champū*, i.e. in mingled prose and verse. The *Kriyāsāra* is a Śaiva manual in Sanskrit by Nīlakaṇṭha,[3] much used by Liṅgāyats. Chapters I–IV are a synopsis in Kārikās of the *Śaiva-bhāshya*.

The *Śrīkara Bhāshya* on the *Vedānta-sūtras* is attributed to Śrīpati Paṇḍitārādhya[4] of the twelfth century; but it seems to have been unknown until quite recently; so that its date is very doubtful. Its standpoint is called Śakti-viśishṭādvaita.

G. *Śākta Literature.*

a. *The Left-hand School.*

§ 429. Our account of the large Śākta literature produced during this period must be very fragmentary, partly because our knowledge of the chronology is still slight, but even more because we know so little about the sub-sects.

[1] See § 419. [2] Rice, *KL.* 68. [3] § 424. [4] § 311.

§ 430. Bengal, including Assam, seems to have produced far more Śākta literature than any other part of India during these centuries. The most famous Śākta temple in Bengal is Kāmākhya near Gauhati in the upper basin of the Brahmaputra in Assam. It is noticeable that the ancient name for Assam is Kāmarūpa. The temple of Kālighāt close by Calcutta comes next in importance. Human sacrifices were offered in these shrines until British authority put them down.

The *Kālikā Purāṇa* or *Tantra*, which has long been well known, is clearly a manual of the Śāktism of Bengal, and probably comes from a date near the beginning of the period. The Blood Chapter gives directions for the offering of animal and human sacrifices to Chaṇḍikā. The list of sacrificial animals is most formidable: birds, tortoises, alligators, fish, nine species of wild animals, buffaloes, bulls, he-goats, ichneumons, wild boars, rhinoceros, antelopes, iguanas, reindeer, lions, tigers. Human sacrifice is of more avail than anything else. Blood drawn from one's own body may also be offered. The *Yoginī T.* probably belongs to the sixteenth century; for it refers to Vishṇusiṅha, a king who ruled in Kooch Behar shortly after A.D. 1500. It is in two parts, the first dealing with all the chief Tāntrik subjects, the second being really a Māhātmya of Kāmākhya. It is one of the foulest Tantras. The *Viśvasāra T.* probably belongs to the same time; for it has a reference to the Bengālī Vaishṇava leader, Chaitanya (1485-1533). In it is found the *Durgāśatanāma Stotra.* It contains a list of 64 Tantras, which appears also in the *Āgama Tattva-vilāsa.*[1] A large number of the works mentioned are clearly modern, and several were produced in Bengal, but their dates are not known.

§ 431. There is another group of Tantras produced in Bengal the dates of which are known, but they are much later. The *Mahānirvāṇa*, though a Left-hand Tantra, is a noble work, but a mystery hangs over its origin. It is not mentioned in early literature, and the earliest attempt at a commentary

[1] Dutta, *MT.*, p. v.

that exists is the set of notes by Hariharānanda Bhāratī, Ram Mohan Ray's paṇḍit. Ram Mohan was born in 1772 and died in 1833; so that the Bhāratī lived at the very earliest at the close of the eighteenth century. Some scholars believe that he was the author of the book, others doubt the conjecture. In any case the book is probably a product of the eighteenth century. It is in two parts but only the first has been published and translated. The translator writes:

> This Tantra is, further, one which is well known and esteemed, though perhaps more highly so amongst that portion of the Indian public which favours 'reformed' Hinduism than amongst some Tantrikas, to whom, as I have been told, certain of its provisions appear to display unnecessary timidity. The former admire it on account of its noble exposition of the worship of the Supreme Brahman, and in the belief that certain of its passages absolutely discountenance the orthodox ritual. Nothing can be more mistaken than such a belief .... This any one will discover who reads the text............................... The section of Tantrikas to whom I have referred are, I believe, also in error. For the design of this Tantra appears to be, whilst conserving commonly-recognized Tantrik principles, to secure that, as has sometimes proved to be the case, they are not abused. Pārvvatī says (Chap. I, verse 67): 'I fear, O Lord! that even that which Thou hast ordained for the good of men will, through them, turn out for evil'.[1]

The first and second chapters are introductory; the third is a discourse on the worship of the Supreme Brahman. The remaining chapters form a very full manual not only of worship and its accompaniments but also of conduct, and of family and funeral rites; and chakra-pūjā and the five Ms are not omitted. The *Tantrasāra* is a compilation which dates from 1812. There is very little of the Left-hand element about it, and it contains several fine hymns. A number of yantras, chakras, and maṇḍalas are reproduced in its pages. It is much used in Bengal. It would be most interesting to discover what the influence was which led to the production in Bengal, where Tāntrik literature had been so impure, of

[1] Avalon, *TGL.* XI ff.

two Left-hand works of such a character as the *Mahānirvāṇa T.* and the *Tantrasāra* are.

The *Prāṇatoshiṇī* was written by Rāmatoshiṇī Śarma in 1821 [1] and the *Mahāsiddhasāra* seems to be still later. It contains a catalogue of 192 names,[2] distributed in three lists of 64 each, and labelled *Vishṇukrānta*, *Rathakrānta*, and *Aśvakrānta*; but the list seems to be quite recent; for it contains the *Mahānirvāṇa T.*, and of all the 192 names only 10 correspond with names in the *Vāmakeśvara* list.

A large number of odes to the goddess are scattered through this group of Tantras.

§432. From the end of the fourteenth century, when the great poet Chaṇḍī Dās wrote his hymns, a stream of Śākta poetry in Bengālī flowed almost without a break. Numerous translations of the episode of Chaṇḍī in the *Mārkaṇḍeya P.* were made from the fifteenth century downward. An artistic Bengālī epic on the same subject was written by Mukundarāma in 1589. Manasā, one of the local forms of the goddess, was much worshipped, and many poems in her honour were produced. Finally, in the eighteenth century, two of the greatest of Bengālī poets, Rāma Prasād Sen and Bhārata Chandra Rai, exerted their powers to the utmost in praising the goddess in song.

Śākta feeling also expressed itself in the vernacular in Gujarāt, in translations of the Chaṇḍī episode by Bhālaṇ, about A.D. 1500, and by Raṇchhoḍjī Diwān at the beginning of the nineteenth century, and in numberless popular songs called Garbās, which are sung by companies of men or of women. Vallabha Bhaṭṭ, who flourished about 1700, is the most notable of the writers of the Garbās. In the Marāṭhā country the Gondhal is a dance performed in honour of Ambā Bhawānī, in connexion with which songs are sung in her honour. The worship of the goddess took a great hold of the country in the seventeenth century, when under Śivajī patriotic

[1] *Catalogus Catalogorum*, s.v. *Prāṇatoshiṇī T.*
[2] Avalon, *TT.* I. ii ff.

feeling stirred the people to the depths. The *Mārkaṇḍeya P.* was translated into Telugu in the sixteenth century; and the *Devī Māhātmya* from the *Mārkaṇḍeya* exists in Malayalim, but its date is unknown.

The *Mantramahodadhi* is a manual of ritual prepared by Mahīdhara in 1589, and is much used by both Śāktas and Śaivas throughout Hindustan and the west.

Śākta sannyāsīs may be met here and there. A small group with whom I talked one morning at Vindhyachal belonged to the Purī order of Śaṅkara's Daśnāmīs.[1] So Totā Purī, the guru of Rāmakṛishṇa Paramahaṁsa of Dakshiṇeśvara, Rāmakṛishṇa himself, and also Vivekānanda and the other svāmīs of the mission, were Śākta sannyāsīs and belonged to the Purī order.[2]

b. *The Right-hand School.*

§ 433. In the ordinary Right-hand worship by Smārtas in their houses the goddess is represented by a *yantra* or by a garlanded pot, and the ritual includes the throwing of Kuṅkuma powder on the *yantra* and the presentation of vegetarian offerings. But the most important part of the service is the liturgy, which consists in the recitation of the Chaṇḍī episode, preceded and followed by other sacred texts, the *Kīlaka*, the *Kavacha*, the *Argalāstotra*, &c., drawn from the *Mārkaṇḍeya* and *Varāha* Purāṇas. In other circles in South India, Lalitā, a beautiful goddess of dazzling appearance, takes the place of Chaṇḍī.[3] The ritual is the same, but the texts recited are the *Lalitopākhyāna*, in which the goddess kills Bhaṇḍāsura and other demons, with the *Lalitātriśatī* and the *Lalitāsahasranāma*, litanies of three hundred and a thousand names, all three drawn from the *Brahmāṇḍa P.* The temple-cult is practically the same as the domestic worship,

[1] See above, § 198.
[2] P. 191 of my *Modern Religious Movements in India* requires to be corrected in this sense.
[3] H. Krishna Sastri, *SII.* 220.

only the goddess may be represented by an image with a large metal yantra on the ground at the feet of the image.

§434. The man who wishes to practice the famous Right-hand *Śrīvidyā* and through it to seek release, has to receive initiation (*dīkshā*)[1] from his guru, to take severe vows and live a life of strictest purity, both physical and mental, for a period of several days. Starting from the ordinary cult, which we have just described, he passes on to the meditations and practices prescribed in the Śrīvidyā.[2]

§435. Appaya Dīkshita (1552–1624) belonged to a Smārta Śaiva family of the Tanjore district. Three stages may be traced in his religious life: he cultivated first the Karma Mīmāṁsā, then Śaṅkara's Vedānta, and lastly the Śrīvidyā. When he was a Mimamsist, he did not merely study the system, but received initiation (whence his title *Dīkshita*) as a Vedic priest and performed many sacrifices. But he ended his life as a devotee of the goddess, and individual members of his family to this day follow his example. They are then called Vīra Śaivas, stalwart Śaivas, who dare to undertake the very trying discipline of the Śrīvidyā.

§436. Three later scholars may be mentioned who belonged to the same part of India and are famous for their devotion to the goddess. They form a short *guruparamparā* of three—Nṛisiṁhānandanātha, Bhāskarānandanātha, and Umānanda-nātha. These names proclaim them initiates of the school to which Lakshmīdhara Vidyānātha belonged. The second, who is usually called Bhāskararāya, is the greatest of the three. He was court paṇḍit at Tanjore in the early decades of the eighteenth century. He is the author of a learned exposition of the Śākta system in Ārya metre, called *Varivasyārahasya*, and of an elaborate commentary on the same. He also wrote commentaries on the following Śākta works, the *Vāmakeśvara T.*, the *Tripurā*, *Kaula*, and *Bhāvanā* Upanishads, and the *Lalitāsahasranāma*, and on the *Mahā* and *Jabāla* Upanishads and the *Īśvara Gītā*. His disciple,

[1] Avalon, *TGL.* lxxiii. [2] See § 318.

Umānandanātha, wrote a practical commentary on the *Paraśurāma-Bhārgava-sūtra.*

c. *The Bhakti School.*

§437. We have seen in our previous chapter that the *Agastya-sūtra* and the *Devī Bhāgavata* sprang from a special school of Śāktas who sought release by bhakti, deep devotional feeling, centred on the Devī.[1] Bhaṭṭa Nīlakaṇṭha is the author of a well-known commentary, the *Tilaka*, on the *Devī Bhāgavata*, in which he urges the claim, already referred to, that this is the real Purāṇa, and that the Vaishṇava *Bhāgavata* is by Vopadeva. He calls himself a disciple of Śrīdhara, the author of the chief commentary on the Vaishṇava work. As Śrīdhara flourished about A.D. 1400,[2] Nīlakaṇṭha may belong to the fifteenth or the sixteenth century.

ii. Jainism.

The spontaneous energy of the Jain community visibly declines during this period, if literature is a trustworthy index.

A. *Śvetāmbara Literature.*

§438. In the fifteenth century, at Ahmadabad, where Muhammadan influence was very powerful, a few Śvetāmbaras became convinced of the folly of image-worship and noted that there is no mention of idols in the earliest Jain books. They therefore formed a new sect called the Loṅkā or Lumpāka, which gave up the temple-cult altogether. A stricter body called the Sthānakavāsīs arose in the seventeenth century and absorbed the Loṅkās.[3] They are a fine people but have produced no noteworthy literature.

§439. Śvetāmbara literature is in the main commentaries, but a few dogmatic works were written, and several authors produced *charitas*, *prabandhas*, and tales. The following are the most interesting men.

[1] See § 319. [2] See § 356. [3] Mrs. Stevenson, *HJ.* 19; 88.

Merutuṅga (B) who was born in 1347, wrote commentaries and abstracts of older works, but dared also to compose a kāvya named *Meghadūta*, thus challenging comparison with the great Kālidāsa. Jñānasāgara (born 1349) and Somasundara (born 1384) were commentators, the former dealing with canonical works, the latter writing simple expositions of popular religious works for children. Guṇaratna (*c.* 1400) wrote a useful comment on Haribhadra's *Shaḍdarśanasamuchchhaya*. Jinamaṇḍana (*c.* 1436), Jinakīrti (1437), Śubhaśīla (1464) produced tales and biographies, while Ratnaśekhara (1401–61) wrote commentaries. Dharmasāgara, of the middle of the sixteenth century, wrote an interesting polemic, the *Kupakshakauśikāditya*, against ten Jain heretical sects. Samayasundara, one of whose books is dated A.D. 1630, published several anthologies of sacred verse, a catechism, and a commentary, called *Kalpalatā*, on the *Kalpa-sūtra*.

A popular literature in Gujarātī accompanied the learned literature in Sanskrit, but it has not been described in detail. The chief type is the *Rāsās*, interesting tales told to enforce religion and morals.[1]

B. *Digambara Literature.*

§ 440. The Digambara literature of this period consists in the main of commentaries, Purāṇas, tales, and biographies. The two most prominent authors are Sakalakīrti and Śubhachandra.

Sakalakīrti, whose *floruit* is A.D. 1464, wrote many books. His chief work, the *Tattvārthasāradīpikā*, which, despite its title, seems to be an independent work, deals with the seven categories of the Digambara system, but gives also the list of the books of the original Digambara canon. His other works are a catechism, a Purāṇa, and biographies. Śrutasāgara wrote, at the end of the fifteenth century, a commentary on Kuṇḍakuṇḍa's *Shaṭprābhṛita*, the *Tattvārthadīpikā* on the Digambara categories, and the *Jinasaṁhitā* on Digambara worship.

[1] Jhaveri, *MGL.* 18, 139, 167.

Nemidatta, who flourished about 1530, wrote biographies of Tīrthakaras and saints, a volume of tales, and a manual of rules for the conduct of the laity, the *Śrāvakāchāra*. Śubhachandra, who lived in the sixteenth century, was a voluminous writer. He has six works on worship, biographies of three of the Tīrthakaras, several volumes of tales, and a Purāṇa, the *Pāṇḍava P.* Ratnachandra (*c.* 1626) wrote lives of two of the Tīrthakaras, while Banārasī Dāsa, who lived under Shah Jahan (1628–58) wrote in Hindī verse on dogmatic subjects.

BIBLIOGRAPHY

I. HISTORIES OF THE LITERATURES

A. SANSKRIT: Macdonell; Winternitz; Bloomfield, *ERE.* viii. 106 ff. Also Müller, *ASL.*; Weber, *HIL.*; Schroeder, *ILK.*

B. PĀLI: Winternitz, II. i; Macdonell, *ERE.* viii. 85 ff.

C. PRĀKṚIT: No history has yet been written; but see Pischel, *GPS.* 10; Konow and Lanman, *Rājaśekhara's Karpūra-mañjarī*, 191, Harvard, 1901; Guérinot.

D. VERNACULAR LITERATURES: See the Introductions in Grierson's *Linguistic Survey of India*, Calcutta, 1904, &c.; also Art., Grierson, *BSOSL.* 1918, p. 47.

E. ASSAMESE: *IA.* xxv. 57.

F. BENGĀLĪ: Sen, *HBLL.*; *VSP.*; *VLMB.*; *CC.*

G. GUJARĀTĪ: Jhaveri, *MGL.* Also, Tripathi, *The Classical Poets of Gujarāt*, Bombay, 1894; Scott, *Gujarātī Poetry*, Surat, 1911; Dāhyābhai P. Derāsari, *Shāṭhīna Sāhityanuñ Digdarśanam*, Ahmadabad, 1911.

H. HINDĪ: *Miśra Bandhu Vinode*; Prasad, *SBS.*; Grierson, *LH.*; Lyall, *EB.* xiii. 483 ff.; Tripāṭhī, *Kavitā Kaumudī*, Allahabad, 1918.

I. KANARESE: Rice, *KL.* Earlier sketches: *British Museum Catalogue of Kannada Books*, London, 1910; Kittel, *Nāgavarma's Canarese Prosody*, Mangalore, 1875; R. Narasiṁhachar, *Karṇāṭaka Kavi Charite*, vol. i, Mysore City, 1907.

J. MALAYALIM: Sketch: *Travancore State Manual*, ii, Ch. x, Trivandrum, 1906.

K. MARĀṬHĪ: Brief sketch in Acworth, *BM.*

L. OṚIYA: Brief sketch, Chatterji, *JASB.*, vol. 66, i. 317; vol. 67, i. 332. Cf. *IA.* i. 79. Hunter, *Orissa*, ii. 199 ff., London, 1872.

M. SINGALESE: *IA.* xii. 53. Geiger, *Literatur und Sprache der Singhalesen*, Grundriss, 1900.

N. TAMIL: Brief sketches: *BMCTB.*; Rost, in *EB.* xxvi. 390 ff. Also Aiyangar, *TS.*; Purnalingam Pillai, *A Primer of Tamil Literature*, Madras, 1904 (uncritical).

O. TELUGU: Vireśaliṅgam Pantulu, *Andra Kavula Charitra*, Rajamundry; *British Museum Cat. of Telugu Books*, London, 1912. Early sketch: Brown, *Madras Journal of Literature and Science*, x.

II. HINDU LITERATURE.

i. The Vedas.

A. THE ṚIGVEDA: **Gen. Intro.**: Macdonell, 40–170; Winternitz, i. 47–103; Macdonell and Keith, *Vedic Index*, London, 1912. **Religion**: Oldenberg, *RV.*; also in French, Henry, Paris, 1903; Bloomfield, *RV.*; Kaegi, *The*

Ṛigveda, Boston, 1898. **Mythology:** Macdonell, *Vedic Mythology*, Grundriss, 1897; Hillebrandt, *Vedische Mythologie*, Breslau, 1891-1902; Oldenberg, *RV*. 39-301; Keith, *Indian Mythology*, Boston, 1917. **Philosophy:** Deussen, *AGP*. I. i. 72-158; Bloomfield, *RV*. **Ritual:** Oldenberg, *RV*. 302; Hillebrandt, *RL*. 1-17. **Translations:** ETr. Griffith, *RV*.; GTr. (verse) Grassmann, Leipzig, 1876-7; GTr. (prose) Ludwig, Prag, 1876-88. **Partial translations:** *SBE*. xxxii, xlvi; GTr. hymns illustrating the religion, Hillebrandt, Göttingen, 1913. Deussen, GTr. of philosophic hymns, *AGP*. I. i. 93-158; Ninth book: FTr. Regnaud, Paris, 1900.

B. THE SĀMAVEDA: **Gen. Intro.:** Macdonell; Winternitz; Oldenberg, *ZDMG*. xxxviii. 439, 469; Caland, *Die Jaiminīya S., mit einer Einleitung über die Sāmavedaliteratur*, Breslau, 1907. **Translations:** Benfey, Text and GTr., Leipzig, 1848; Griffith, ETr., Benares, 1893. **Ritual:** Hillebrandt, *RL*. 99-105.

C. THE YAJURVEDA: **Gen. Intro.:** Macdonell; Winternitz; Keith, *TS*. **Religion:** Oldenberg, *RV*.; Schroeder, *ILK*. vii-xii. **Ritual:** Hillebrandt, *RL*. 97-166. **Translations:** *White Yajus*: Griffith, Benares, 1899. *Taittirīya S.*: Keith, *TS*.

D. THE ATHARVAVEDA: **Gen. Intro.:** Bloomfield, *AV*.; Whitney and Lanman, *AV*.; Macdonell; Winternitz. **Religion, Magic, and Ritual:** Oldenberg, *RV*.; Hillebrandt, *RL*., 167-86. **Philosophy:** Deussen, *AGP*. I. i. 209-336. **Translations:** ETr. Whitney and Lanman, *AV*.; ETr. Griffith, Benares, 1897. **Partial Trs.:** Eng.: Bloomfield, *SBE*. xlii. French: Henry, Paris, 1891-6; German: Weber, *Indische Studien*; Grill, Stuttgart, 1888; Deussen, *AGP*. I. i. 210-83 (philosophic hymns).

E. THE BRĀHMAṆAS: **Gen. Intro.:** Müller, *ASL*. 313-455; Macdonell, 202-18; Winternitz, i. 171-96. **Culture and Philosophy:** Deussen, *AGP*. I. i. 159-336. **Analyses** of *Aitareya, Kaushītaki, Pañchaviṁśa, Shaḍviṁśa, Chhāndogya, Taittirīya, Śatapatha*, Deussen, *SUV*. **Translations, &c.:** *Aitareya*: Text, Intro., ETr., Haug, Bombay, 1863. *Aitareya* and *Kaushītaki*: ETr. Keith, vol. xxv, *HOS*., in the press. *Shaḍviṁśa*: Text and GTr. Klemm, Gütersloh, 1894. *Adbhuta*: Text and GTr. Weber, *Zwei vedische Texte über Omina und Portenta*, Berlin, 1859. *Talavakāra*: Text and ETr. Oertel, *JAOS*. xiv, xv, xvi, xviii. *Ārsheya, Devatādhyāya, Vaṁśa, Saṁhitopanishad*, Brāhmaṇas: Texts with Intro. Burnell, Mangalore, 1873; 1876; 1877. *Sāmavidhāna*: Intro., Text, Comm., Burnell, London, 1873; GTr. Konow, Halle, 1893. *Śatapatha*: Intro. and ETr. Eggeling, *SBE*. xii, xxvi, xli, xliii, xliv. *Gopatha*: Intro. and Analysis, Bloomfield. *AV*.

F. THE ĀRAṆYAKAS: **Gen. Intro.:** Macdonell, 34; Winternitz, i. 199; 202, n. 1. Deussen, *PU*. 2 ff.; *SV*. 8; Oldenberg, *Die Hymnen des Ṛigveda*, Berlin, 1888, 291; Keith, *AĀ*. 15, 257. **Translations, &c.:** *Aitareya*: Text, Intro., ETr., Comm., Keith, *AĀ*. *Śāṅkhāyana*; ETr. Keith, London, 1908; see also *JRAS*. 1908, 363. *Taittirīya*, Analysis, Deussen, *SUV*. 213. *Bṛihat* = *Śatapatha Br*. xiv. 1-3. ETr., Eggeling, *SBE*. xliv. 441-510.

G. THE UPANISHADS: **Gen. Intro.:** Deussen, *PU*.; *SUV*.; Oldenberg, *LU*. Brief Introductions: Macdonell, 218-43; Winternitz, i. 196-

228; Barnett, *Brahma-Knowledge*, London, 1911; Jacob, *Concordance to the Principal Upanishads*, Bombay, 1891.

List of chief Upanishads: RIK: **1.** *Aitareya*; **2.** *Kaushītaki.* SĀMAN: **3.** *Chhāndogya*; **4.** *Kena.* BLACK YAJUS: **5.** *Taittirīya*; **6.** *Mahānārāyaṇa*; **7.** *Kāṭhaka* or *Kaṭha*; **8.** *Śvetāśvatara*; **9.** *Maitrāyaṇa.* WHITE YAJUS: **10.** *Bṛihadāraṇyaka*; **11.** *Īśā.* ATHARVAN: **12.** *Muṇḍaka*; **13.** *Praśna*; **14.** *Māṇḍūkya*; **15.** *Garbha*; **16.** *Prāṇāgnihotra*; **17.** *Piṇḍa*; **18.** *Ātma*; **19.** *Sarva-Upanishat-sāra*; **20.** *Gāruḍa*; **21.** *Brahmavidyā*; **22.** *Kshurikā*; **23.** *Chūlikā*; **24.** *Nādabindu*; **25.** *Brahmabindu*; **26.** *Amṛitabindu*; **27.** *Dhyānabindu*; **28.** *Tejobindu*; **29.** *Yogaśikhā*; **30.** *Yogatattva*; **31.** *Haṁsa*; **32.** *Brahma*; **33.** *Sannyāsa*; **34.** *Āruṇeya*; **35.** *Kaṇṭhaśruti* or *Kaṭhaśruti*; **36.** *Paramahaṁsa*; **37.** *Jābāla*; **38.** *Āśrama*; **39.** *Atharvaśiras A.*; **40.** *Atharvaśikhā*; **41.** *Nīlarudra*; **42.** *Kālāgnirudra*; **43.** *Kaivalya*; **44.** *Mahā*; **45.** *Nārāyaṇa*; **46.** *Ātmabodha*; **47.** *Nṛisiṁhapūrvatāpanīya*; **48.** *Nṛisiṁhottaratāpanīya*; **49.** *Rāmapūrvatāpanīya*; **50.** *Rāmottaratāpanīya*; **51.** *Kaula*; **52.** *Amṛitanāda*; **53.** *Bṛihajjābāla*; **54.** *Maitreya*; **55.** *Subālā*; **56.** *Mantrikā*; **57.** *Nirālamba*; **58.** *Śukarahasya*; **59.** *Vajrasūchī*; **60.** *Nāradaparivrājaka*; **61.** *Triśikhibrāhmaṇa*; **62.** *Sītā*; **63.** *Yogachūḍāmaṇi*; **64.** *Nirvāṇa*; **65.** *Maṇḍalabrāhmaṇa*; **66.** *Dakshiṇāmūrti*; **67.** *Śarabha*; **68.** *Skanda*; **69.** *Tripādvibhūtimahānārāyaṇa*; **70.** *Advayatāraka*; **71.** *Rāmarahasya*; **72.** *Vāsudeva*; **73.** *Mudgala*; **74.** *Śāṇḍilya*; **75.** *Paiṅgala*; **76.** *Bhikshuka*; **77.** *Śārīraka*; **78.** *Turiyātītāvadhūta*; **79.** *Paramahaṁsaparivrājaka*; **80.** *Akshamālikā*; **81.** *Avyakta*; **82.** *Ekākshara*; **83.** *Annapūrṇā*; **84.** *Sūrya*; **85.** *Akshi*; **86.** *Adhyātma*; **87.** *Kuṇḍikā*; **88.** *Sāvitrī*; **89.** *Pāśupatabrahma*; **90.** *Parabrahma*; **91.** *Avadhūta*; **92.** *Tripurātāpanīya*; **93.** *Devī*; **94.** *Tripurā*; **95.** *Kaṭharudra*; **96.** *Bhāvanā*; **97.** *Rudrahṛidaya*; **98.** *Yogakuṇḍalī*; **99.** *Bhasmajābāla*; **100.** *Rudrākshajābāla*; **101.** *Gaṇapati*; **102.** *Darśana*; **103.** *Tārasāra*; **104.** *Mahāvākya*; **105.** *Pañchabrahma*; **106.** *Gopālatāpanīya*; **107.** *Krishṇa*; **108.** *Yājñavalkya*; **109.** *Varāha*; **110.** *Śāṭyāyana*; **111.** *Hayagrīva*; **112.** *Dattātreya*; **113.** *Kalisaṁtaraṇa*; **114.** *Jābāli*; **115.** *Saubhāgyalakshmī*; **116.** *Sarasvatīrahasya*; **117.** *Bahvṛicha*; **118.** *Muktikā*; **119.** *Gopīchandana*; **120.** *Varadatāpanīya*; **121.** *Varadottaratāpanīya*; **122.** *Shaṭchakra*; **123.** *Atharvaśiras B.*

Groups: Nos. 1–14 are the Classical Upanishads. Nos. 1–50 with the addition of nine pieces from Dārā Shikoh's Persian collection and the *Praṇava U.* (a portion of the *Gopatha B.*), form Deussen's sixty Upanishads (2nd ed.): *SUV.* For the lists of Nārāyaṇa, Dārā Shikoh, and Colebrooke, see Deussen, *SUV.* 535–7. The 108 Upanishads given in the list in the *Muktikā U.* correspond to the above list, with the omission of Nos. 6, 17, 25, 34, 35, 38, 41, 51, 119–23, the *Chūlikā*, No. 23 above, being the *Mantrikā*, No. 32 in the *Muktikā* list, and the pairs of Upanishads, Nos. 47–8 and 49–50 above, being each taken as one, Nos. 27 and 55 in the *Muktikā* list. Bare text of the Upanishads of this list: W. L. Sastri Pansikar, Bombay, 1917.

Commentaries:

8th c. Gauḍapāda, Nos. 14, 47, 48.

Early 9th. Śaṅkara, Nos. 1, 3, 4, 5, 7, 8, 10, 11, 12, 13, 14, 39, 40, 47: Deussen, *SV.* 37.

13th c. Madhva, Nos. 1, 3, 4, 5, 7, 10, 11, 12, 13, 14. ETrs. of all, except Nos. 1 and 5, *SBH.* i, iii, xiv.

c. 1350. Śaṅkarānanda, Nos. 2, 4, 8, 9, 12, 15, 16, 17–19, 21–34, 36, 37, 39–41, 43, 45, 49, 50, 106.

Nārāyaṇa, Nos. 4–8, 12–20, 23, 25, 27–32, 34, 36, 37, 40–50, 72, 106, 107, 119–21, and others: Deussen, *SUV.* 538; Jacob, *EAU.*, Preface.

16th c. Rāmatīrtha, No. 9.

Raṅgarāmānuja, a Śrī-Vaishṇava: Rājagopalāchārya, *VRI.* 34.

18th c. Bhāskararāya, Nos. 4, 7, 12, 37, 44, 94, 96, 122.

Translations and Introductions: ETrs. of 1–5 and 7–13, Max Müller, *SBE.* I. xv; ETrs. of 3, 4, 7, 10, 11, 12, 13, 14, with Madhva's comms., S. C. Vasu, *SBH.* I. III. xiv; ETrs. of the five Upanishads included in *Atharvaśiras B.*, No. 123, Kennedy, *HM.* 346, 442, 443, 491, 493; ETrs. of 72, 119, Jacob, *IA.*, 1887, 84, 89. Introductions and GTrs. of 1–50, Deussen, *SUV.*; ETrs. of selections, Barnett, *Brahma-Knowledge*, London, 1911. Introductions to 20, 38, 42, 44, 45, 46, 68, 72, 107, 119, 120, Jacob, *EAU.*

ii. The Kalpa Sūtras, &c.

Gen. Intro.: Macdonell, 244–64; Winternitz, i. 232–40: also Müller, *ASL.* ch. i.

A. Śrauta Sūtras: **Chief Texts**: (Ṛik) **1.** *Śāṅkhāyana*; **2.** *Āśvalāyana.* (Sāman) **3.** *Maśaka*; **4.** *Lāṭyāyana*; **5.** *Drāhyāyaṇa*; **6.** *Jaimini.* (W. Yajus) **7.** *Kātyāyana.* (B. Yajus) **8.** *Āpastamba*; **9.** *Hiraṇyakeśin*; **10.** *Baudhāyana*; **11.** *Bhāradvāja*; **12.** *Mānava.* (Atharvan) **13.** *Vaitāna.* **Ritual**: Hillebrandt, *RL.* 18–36; 97–166. **Translations**: GTrs. *Vaitāna*, Garbe, Strassburg, 1878; Caland, Amsterdam, 1910.

B. Gṛihya Sūtras: **Chief Texts**: (Ṛik) **1.** *Śāṅkhāyana*; **2.** *Śāmbavya*; **3.** *Āśvalāyana.* (Sāman) **4.** *Gobhila*; **5.** *Khādira*; **6.** *Jaimini.* (W. Yajus) **7.** *Pāraskara.* (B. Yajus) **8.** *Āpastamba*; **9.** *Hiraṇyakeśin*; **10.** *Baudhāyana*; **11.** *Bhāradvāja*; **12.** *Mānava*; **13.** *Vaikhānasa.* (Atharvan) **14.** *Kauśika.* **Ritual**: Hillebrandt, *RL.* 18–36; 41–97. **Translations**: ETrs. of 1, 3, 4, 5, 6, 7, 8, Oldenberg, *SBE.* xxix, xxx. GTrs. of 1 (Oldenberg, *Indische Studien*, xv), of 3 and 7 (Stenzler, Leipzig, 1864, 1876), of 6 (Caland, Amsterdam, 1906), of 4 (Knauer, Dorpat, 1886). On 13, see Bloch, *Ueber das Gṛihya und Dharmasūtra der Vaikhānasa*, Leipzig, 1896. On 14, see Bloomfield, *JAOS.* xiv. 1.

C. Dharma Sūtras: **Intro.**: Jolly, *RS.* 1–13; Bühler, intros. to *SBE.* ii and xiv. **Vedic school manuals**: (B. Yajus) **1.** *Āpastamba*; **2.** *Hiraṇyakeśin*; **3.** *Baudhāyana.* **Manuals for all**: **4.** *Gautama*; **5.** *Vāsishṭha.* **Translations**: ETrs. of 1, 3, 4, 5, Bühler, *SBE.* ii and xiv. For later Dharma-sūtras, see Law Literature.

D. Śulva Sūtras: **Intro.**: Thibaut, *JASB.* xliv, Calcutta, 1875; **1.** *Baudhāyana Śulva Sūtra*, Text and ETr. Thibaut, *Paṇḍit*, ix; **2.** *Āpastamba Śulva Sūtra*, Text and GTr., Bürk, *ZDMG.* lv and lvi.

E. The Vedāṅgas: **Intro.**: Müller, *ASL.* 108 ff.; Macdonell, 264–75.

F. TEXTS ON MAGIC: **Gen. Intro.**: Bloomfield, *AV.* 15–17, 57; Rose, *ERE.* viii. 292; Henry, *La Magie dans l'Inde antique*, Paris, 1909; Caland, *Altindisches Zauberritual*, Amsterdam, 1900; Winternitz, i. 147, 239. **1.** *Ṛigvidhāna*: Macdonell, 251, 274. For the *Sāmavidhāna*, *Abdhuta*, and *Gopatha* Brāhmaṇas, see above, under the Brāhmaṇas.

iii. Law Literature.

Gen. Intro.: Jolly, *RS.*

A. DHARMA-SŪTRAS: see above, p. 365.

B. LAW IN THE MAHĀBHĀRATA: Jolly, *RS.* 29–31; Bühler, *SBE.* xxv, Intro.; Hopkins, *GE.* 17–23; Winternitz, i. 364.

C. SECONDARY DHARMA-SŪTRAS: **Intro.**: Jolly, *RS.* 7–13. Chief texts: **1.** *Vishṇusmṛiti*: Intro. and ETr. Jolly, *SBE.* vii; **2.** *Vaikhānasa*: Jolly, *RS.* 9–10; Bloch, *Ueber das Grihya und Dharmasūtra der Vaikhānasa*, Leipzig, 1896; **3.** *Hārīta*, Jolly, *RS.* 8–9.

D. THE DHARMAŚĀSTRAS: **Intro.**: Jolly, *RS.* 13–29; Bühler, *SBE.* xxx, Intro. Chief texts: **1.** *Mānava Dharmaśāstra*, or lawbook of Manu: Intro. Jolly, *RS.* 13–19; Intro. and ETr. Bühler, *SBE.* xxv; **2.** *Yājñavalkya*: Intro. Jolly, *RS.* 19–21; Max Müller, *ASL.* 301 n. Text and GTr. Stenzler, Berlin, 1849; **3.** *Nārada*: Intro. Jolly, *RS.* 21–3; Intro. and ETr. Jolly, *SBE.* xxxiii; **4.** *Bṛihaspati*, Jolly, *RS.* 21; Intro. and ETr. Jolly, *SBE.* xxxiii. There is a large number of later Dharmaśāstras: Intro. Jolly, *RS.* 23–9; text and ETrs. M. N. Dutt, Calcutta, 1908.

iv. The Epics.

A. MAHĀBHĀRATA: **Gen. Intro.**: Holtzmann, *MBH.*; Hopkins, *GE.*; *ERE.* viii. 325; Macdonell, 281; Winternitz, i. 259. **Analysis**: Monier Williams, *Indian Epic Poetry*, London, 1863; Jacobi, *Das Mahābhārat* Bonn, 1903. **Religion**: Hopkins, *RI.* chs. xiv–xv. **Philosophy**: Hopkins, *GE.* ch. iii; Deussen, *AGP.* I. iii. 8; *Die Sāṁkhya Philosophie nach dem Mahābhārata*, Dahlmann, 1902.

Vernac. versions: Kanarese (Jain), 10th c.; Telugu, 11th to 13th c.; Tamil, 15th c.; Kanarese, 16th c.; Bengālī, 17th c. (earlier versions from 14th c.); Malayalim, 17th c.; Hindī, 19th c.

Translations: ETrs. P. C. Roy, Calcutta, 1884–96; Dutt, Calcutta, 1895. Partial FTrs. Fauche, Paris, 1863–70; Foucaux, Paris, 1862. Partial ITr. Pavolini, 1902. GTr. of the four philosophical sections, Deussen und Strauss, Leipzig, 1906; ETr. of the *Gītā*, the *Sanatsujātīya*, and the *Anugītā*, Telang, *SBE.* viii.

Bhagavadgītā: **Gen. Intro.**: Barnett, *Bhagavadgītā*, London, 1905; Garbe, *ERE.* ii. 535; Winternitz, i. 365 ff.; Farquhar, *Gītā and Gospel*, Madras, 1906; Jacob, *Concordance to the Principal Upanishads and Bhagavadgītā*, Bombay, 1891. **Origin and date**: Garbe, *Die Bhagavadgītā*, Leipzig, 1905; Hopkins, *JRAS.*, 1905, 384; Keith, *JRAS.*, 1915, 548. **Translations**: ETrs. Davies, London, 1894; Telang, *SBE.* viii; Barnett, London, 1905; Annie Besant, Madras; GTrs. Garbe, Leipzig, 1905; Deussen, *Der Gesang des Heiligen*, Leipzig, 1911.

B. RĀMĀYAṆA: **Gen. Intro.**: Macdonell, *ERE*. x. 574; Jacobi, *R.*; Macdonell, 302; Winternitz, i. 423; Hopkins, *GE.* ch. ii. **Analysis**: Monier Williams, *Indian Epic Poetry*, London, 1863; Jacobi, *R.* 126. **Vernac. versions**: Kanareṣe (Jain), 10th c.; Tamil, 1100; Telugu, 1300; Bengālī, 14th c.; Malayalim, 15th c.; Hindī, 1584; Kanarese, 1590. **Trs.**: ETr. (prose), Dutt, Calcutta, 1892; ETr. (verse), Griffith, Benares, 1870–4; FTr. Fauche, Paris, 1858; ITr. Gorresio, Parigi, 1843–70.

v. Philosophical Literature.

Gen. Intro.: Deussen, *AGP.* Also Colebrooke, *Essays*; Hall; Müller, *SS.*; Garbe, *Philosophy of Ancient India*, Chicago, 1897.

A. KARMA MĪMĀṂSĀ.

Intro.: Jhā, *PSPM.*; Garbe, *ERE.* viii. 648. Also Colebrooke, *Essays*, i. 295; Müller, *SS.* v; Mādhava, *SDS.* xii: Cowell, 178.

4th or 5th. Jaimini; **1.** *Pūrva-mīmāṁsā-sūtras*: ETr. Jhā, *SBH.* x.

c. 500. Śabara Svāmin; **2.** *Bhāshya*, on No. 1.

7th c. Prabhākara; **3.** *Bṛihatī*, on No. 2: full intro., Jhā, *PSPM.*

c. 700. Śālikanātha, disciple of Prabhākara; **4.** *Ṛijuvimalā*, on 1: Jhā, *PSPM.* 1, 2, 18; Hall, 195; **5.** *Prakaraṇapañchikā*, a sketch of Prabhākara's system: Jhā, *PSPM.* 1, 4, 18. Text, Benares, 1904.

Early 8th. Kumārila; **6.** *Mīmāṁsā-śloka-vārttika*, on No. 2: ETr. in *BI.*; **7.** *Tantra-vārttika*, on No. 2: ETr. in *BI.*; **8.** *Tupṭīkā*, on No. 2.

c. 850. Maṇḍanamiśra; **9.** *Vidhiviveka*: Woods, *Yoga*, xxii, 357; Jhā, *PSPM.* 8.

c. 850. Vāchaspatimiśra; **10.** *Nyāyakaṇikā*, on 9: Woods, *Yoga*, xxi; 357. Nos. 9 and 10 published together, Benares, 1907.

c. 1300. Pārthasārathimiśra; **11.** *Śāstradīpikā*, on 1: Hall, 173; Colebrooke, *ME.* i. 299; **12.** *Tantra-ratna*, on 1; **13.** *Nyāya-ratnākara*, on 6: Jhā, *PSPM.* 18; **14.** *Nyāya-ratna-mālā*, on 7: Hall, 172.

c. 1350. Vedānta-deśika; **15.** *Seśvara-mīmāṁsā*, on 1; Rajagopalachariar, *VRI.* 107.

c. 1380. Mādhava; **16.** *Jaiminīyanyāyamālāvistara*, on 1: Hall, 186; **17.** *Sarvadarśanasaṅgraha*, ch. xii: Cowell, 178.

c. 1400. Someśvara; **18.** *Nyāya-sudhā*, or *Rāṇaka*, on 7: Hall, 170; Jhā, *PSPM.* 8.

c. 1525. Vallabhāchārya; **19.** *Jaiminīya-sūtra-bhāshya*: Hall, 208.

c. 1543. Rāmakṛishṇa; **20.** *Siddhānta-chandrikā*, on 11: Hall, 173.

c. 1580. Nārāyaṇa; **21.** *Śāstradīpikā-vyākhyā*, on 11: Hall, 178.

c. 1600. Bhaṭṭa Dinakara; **22.** *Bhāṭṭa-dinakara*, on 11: Hall, 175.

Early 17th. Appaya Dīkshita; **23.** *Vidhi-rasāyana*: Hall, 194.

Early 17th. Āpadeva; **24.** *Mīmāṁsā-nyāya-prakāśa* or *Āpadevī*: Hall, 185. ETr., Jhā, Benares.

Early 17th. Laugākshi Bhāskara; **25.** *Arthasaṅgraha*: Macdonell, 451. Text, Intro., and ETr., Thibaut, Benares, 1882.

d. 1665. Khaṇḍadeva; **26.** *Bhāṭṭa Dīpikā*, on 1: Hall, 179.

Mid 17th. Anantadeva; **27.** *Smṛiti Kaustubha*: Hall, 185.

Sucharitamiśra; **28.** *Kaśikā*, on 6: Jhā, *PSPM.* 18.

B. VEDĀNTA.

Intro.: Colebrooke, *Essays*, i. 325; Müller, *SS.* ch. iv; Deussen, *SV.*; Thibaut, Intro. *SBE.* xxxiv.

4th or 5th. Bādarāyaṇa ; **1.** *Vedānta-sūtras* : Intro. and ETr. Thibaut, *SBE.* xxxiv, xxxviii.

Mid 8th. Gauḍapāda ; **2.** *Māṇḍūkya-Kārikā*, on *Māṇḍūkya U.* : Intro. and GTr. Deussen, *SUV.* 573. ETr. Dvivedī, Bombay, 1909; ETr. *SBH.* i.

788–c. 850. Śaṅkara ; **3.** *Vedānta-sūtra-bhāshya*, on No. 1 : Intro. and ETr. Thibaut, *SBE.* xxxiv, xxxviii. GTr. Deussen, Leipzig, 1887. Life, works, and system, Deussen, *SV.* Sketch of system, Deussen, *Outline of the Vedānta*, London, 1907.

c. 850. Maṇḍanamiśra, or Sureśvarāchārya ; **4.** *Naishkarmya-siddhi*, a polemic against the Mīmāṁsā : Hall, 159.

c. 850. Padmapāda ; **5.** *Pañchapādikā*, on No. 3 : Hall, 88. ETr. Venis, Benares.

c. 850. Vāchaspatimiśra ; **6.** *Bhāmatī*, on No. 3 : Woods, *Yoga*, xxi–xxiii ; Hall, 87.

c. 900. Bhāskarāchārya ; **7.** *Brahma-sūtra-bhāshya*, on No. 1 : Colebrooke, *Essays*, i. 334.

c. 1050. Yādava Prakāśa ; **8.** *Yādava-bhāshya*, on No. 1.

c. 1250. Amalānanda ; **9.** *Vedānta-kalpataru*, on No. 6 : Colebrooke, *Essays*, i. 333 ; Hall, 87 ; Jacob, *JRAS.*, 1916, 853.

c. 1350. Bhāratītīrtha and Mādhava ; **10.** *Pañchadaśī* : Winternitz and Keith, *Bodleian Catal.* ii. 190. ETr. Nanda Lal Dhole, Calcutta, 1899.

15th c. Advaitānanda ; **11.** *Brahmavidyābharaṇa*, on No. 3 : Colebrooke, *Essays*, i. 333 ; Hall, 89.

End 15th. Sadānanda ; **12.** *Vedānta-sāra* : Intro., ETr., and notes, Jacob, *Manual of Hindu Pantheism*, London, 1891 ; Intro. and GTr., Deussen, *AGP.* I. iii. 615. See Keith, *SS.* 102.

Bhavadevamiśra ; **13.** *Vedānta-sūtra-vyākhyā-chandrikā*, on 1 : Colebrooke, *Essays*, i. 334.

Before 1550. Madhusūdana Sarasvatī ; **14.** *Vedānta-kalpalatikā* : Hall, 132 ; **15.** *Advaita-siddhi*, a refutation of the Nyāya : ETr., Jhā, Allahabad.

Mid 16th. Vijñāna Bhikshu ; **16.** *Vijñānāmṛita*, on 1.

End 16th. Rāmānanda Sarasvatī ; **17.** *Brahmāmṛita-varshiṇī*, on No. 1 : Colebrooke, *Essays*, i. 334 ; Hall, 89, 93.

c. 1600. Appaya Dīkshita ; **18.** *Vedānta-kalpataru-parimalā*, on No. 9 : Hall, 88 ; **19.** *Siddhānta-leśa* : criticism of other forms of the Vedānta, &c. : Hall, 153 : ETr. Venis, Benares.

Prakāśānanda ; **20.** *Vedānta-siddhānta-muktāvalī* ; Macdonell, 451 : Hall, 99. ETr. Venis, Benares, 1890.

C. SĀṄKHYA.

Gen. Intro. : Keith, *SS.* Earlier works, Colebrooke, *Essays*, i. 227 ; Müller, *SS.* ch. vi ; Garbe, *Die Sāṅkhya Philosophie*, Leipzig, 1894 ; Garbe, *SY.* ; Dahlmann, *Die Sāṁkhya Philosophie nach dem Mahābhārata*, Berlin, 1902.

1st or 2nd. Vārshagaṇya ; **1.** *Shashṭitantra* : Keith, *SS.* ch. v ; Schrader, *ZDMG.* 1914, 101 ; *IPAS.* 110.

c. 300. Īśvara Krishṇa ; **2.** *Sāṅkhya Kārikā* : Keith, *SS.* ch. viii. ETr. Davies, London, 1881 ; ETr. Colebrooke, London, 1837 ; ETr. Siṅha, *SBH.* xi.

7th c. Gauḍapāda; **3.** *Bhāshya*, on 2: Hall, 5. ETr. Wilson, London, 1837.

c. 850. Vāchaspatimiśra; **4.** *Sāṅkhya-tattva-kaumudī*, on 2: Woods, *Yoga*, xxi; Keith, *SS.* 70. ETr. Jha, Bombay, 1896.

Early 14th. Bhāratī Yati; **5.** *Tattva-kaumudī-vyākhyā*, on 4.

c. 1380. Mādhava; **6.** *Sarvadarśanasaṅgraha*, xiv: ETr. Cowell, 221; Keith, *SS.* 91.

7. *Tattva-samāsa*: Keith, *SS.* 89–91. ETr. Siṅha, *SBH.* xi.

8. *Sāṅkhya-pravachana-sūtra*: Keith, *SS.* 91. ETr. Hall, *BI.*, 1865; ETr. Ballantyne, London, 1885; ETr. Siṅha, *SBH.* xi.

c. 1500. Aniruddha; **9.** *Sāṅkhya-sūtra-vṛitti* or *Aniruddha-vṛitti*, on 8: Keith, *SS.* 92. ETr. Garbe, *BI.* 1892; ETr. Siṅha, *SBH.* xi.

Mid 16th. Vijñāna Bhikshu; **10.** *Sāṅkhya-pravachana-bhāshya*, on No. 8: GTr. Garbe, Leipzig, 1889: ETr. Siṅha, *SBH.* xi; **11.** *Sāṅkhya-sāra*, Intro. and Text, Hall, *BI.* 1862.

Late 16th. Bhāvā Gaṇeśa Dīkshita; **12.** *Sāṅkhya-sāra*, a summary of Sāṅkhya doctrine; **13.** *Tattva-yāthārtha-dīpana*, on 7: Hall, 4.

Late 17th. Mahādeva Vedāntin; **14.** *Sāṅkhya-vṛitti-sāra*, on 9: ETr. in Garbe, *Aniruddha's Commentary*, Calcutta, 1892; ETr. Siṅha, *SBH.* xi.

Early 18th. Nāgeśa Bhaṭṭa; **15.** *Laghu-sāṅkhya-sūtra-vṛitti*, on 10.

D. YOGA

Gen. Intro.: Garbe, *SY.*; Müller, *SS.* ch. vii.

Early 4th. Patañjali; **1.** *Yoga-sūtras*: Intro. and ETr. Woods, *Yoga*. ETr., with No. 4, Mitra, *BI.* 1883; ETr. Rāma Prasād, *SBH.* iv.

7th or 8th. Veda-vyāsa; **2.** *Yoga-bhāshya*, on No. 1: Intro. and ETr. Woods, *Yoga*; ETr. Rāma Prasād, *SBH.* iv.

c. 850. Vāchaspatimiśra; **3.** *Tattva-vaiśāradī*, on. No. 2; Intro. and ETr. Woods, *Yoga*; ETr. Rāma Prasād, *SBH.* iv.

Early 11th. Bhoja; **4.** *Rāja-mārtaṇḍa*, on 1: Hall, 10; Garbe, *SY.* 41; Woods, *Yoga*, xiii; ETr. Mitra, *BI.* 1883.

c. 1380. Mādhava; **5.** *Sarvadarśanasaṅgraha*, xv: Cowell, 231.

Mid 16th. Vijñāna Bhikshu; **6.** *Yoga-vārttika*, on No. 2; **7.** *Yoga-sārasaṅgraha*: Hall, 12; ETr., Jhā, Bombay, 1894.

End 16th. Rāmānanda Sarasvatī[1]; **8.** *Maṇiprabhā*, on No. 1: Hall, 12. ETr. Woods, *JAOS.* 1914, 1.

E. VAIŚESHIKA

Gen. Intro.: *ERE.* ii. 199 ff.; Chatterji, *The Hindu Realism*, Allahabad, 1912; Colebrooke, *Essays*, i. 261; Müller, *SS.* ch. ix; Suali, *Introduzione*; H. Ui, *The Vaiśeshika Philosophy acc. to the Daśapadārthaśāstra*, London, 1917; Faddegon, *The Vaiśeshika System*, Amsterdam, 1918; Keith, *Logic and Atomism; a Study of the Nyāya and Vaiśeshika Systems of Indian Philosophy*, in the Press, Oxford.

4th or 5th. Kaṇāda Kāśyapa; **1.** *Vaiśeshika-sūtra*: ETr. Gough, Benares, 1873; ETr. Siṅha, *SBH.* vi; GTr. Roer, *ZDMG.* xxi. 309–420; xxii. 383–422.

[1] Disciple of Govindānanda Sarasvatī: Hall, 89. Another disciple, named Nārāyaṇa Sarasvatī, wrote a work in 1592. Woods, *JAOS.* 1914, p. 1.

Late 6th. Praśastapāda; **2.** *Padārtha-dharma-saṅgraha*, on 1: Hall, 64. ETr., with No. 6, Jhā, Benares.

c. 600. Jñānachandra; **3.** *Daśapadārtha*: CTr. by Hiouen Tsang, A.D. 648: Nanjio, 1295. ETr. of this Chinese version, H. Ui, op. cit.

Fl. 984. Udayana: Keith, *JRAS.* 1908, 524; **4.** *Kiraṇāvalī*, on No. 2: Hall, 65; Chatterji, *HR.* ix; **5.** *Lakshaṇāvalī*, definitions of Vaiśeshika terms: Chatterji, *HR.* ix.

Fl. 991. Śrīdhara: Chanda, *IAR.* 197; **6.** *Nyāya-Kandalī* on No. 2. Keith, *JRAS.* 1908, 523; Chatterji, *HR.* ix. ETr.: see No. 2, above.

11th c. Śivāditya; **7.** *Saptapadārthī*: Hall, 74.

12th c. Vallabha Nyāyāchārya; **8.** *Nyāya-līlāvatī*: Hall, 71.

12th c. Vardhamāna Upādhyāya[1]; **9.** *Kiraṇāvalī-prakāśa* on 4: Hall, 65.

c. 1380. Mādhava; **10.** *Sarvadarśanasaṅgraha*, ch. x: ETr. Cowell, 145.

Late 15th. Śaṅkara Miśra; **11.** *Vaiśeshika-sūtropaskāra*, on No. 1: Chatterji, *HR.* x; Hall, 68. ETr. Siṅha, *SBH.* vi.

End 16th. Annam Bhaṭṭa; **12.** *Tarka Saṅgraha*: Hall, 68. ETr. Ballantyne, Allahabad, 1852. Numerous comms.: see Hall, 69–71.

Early 17th. Viśvanātha Pañchānana; **13.** *Bhāshā-parichchheda*: elementary, in verse: Hall, 73. ETr. Roer, *BI.* 1850; **14.** *Siddhānta-muktāvalī*: Comm. on No. 13. ETr. Roer, *BI.* 1850.

Early 17th. Laugākshi Bhāskara; **15.** *Tarka-kaumudī*: Text, Intro., and notes, Dvivedī, Bombay, 1886.

F. NYĀYA.

Gen. Intro.: Colebrooke, *Essays*, i. 261; Müller, *SS.* viii; Vidyābhūshaṇa, *MSIL.*; Jacobi, *Gött. Nach.* 1901, 460; *ERE.* ii. 198; ix. 422; M. Chakravarti, *JASB.* 1915, 260; Suali, *Introduzione*: Keith, *JRAS.* 1914, 1089; Keith, *Logic and Atomism*, in the Press, Oxford.

4th or 5th. Akshapāda Gotama; **1.** *Nyāya-sūtras*, ETr. with Nos. 2 and 3, Jhā, Allahabad, 1915: see Keith, *JRAS.* 1916, 613; ETr. Vidyābhūshaṇa, *SBH.* viii.

c. 500. Vātsyāyana; **2.** *Nyāya-bhāshya*, on No. 1: *JASB.* 1910, 307. ETr., see No. 1.

Fl. 630–50. Uddyotakara; **3.** *Nyāya-vārttika*, on No. 2: Vidyābhūshaṇa, *JRAS.* 1914, 603; Keith, *JRAS.* 1914, 1091. ETr., see No. 1.

A.D. 841. Vāchaspatimiśra; **4.** *Nyāya-vārttika-tātparya-ṭīkā*, on 3; **5.** *Nyāya-sūchī-nibandha*, appendix to 4: date: Woods, *Yoga*, xxi.

c. 900. Jayanta; **6.** *Nyāya-mañjarī*, an encyclopaedia of the system.

c. 980. Udayana; **7.** *Nyāya-vārttika-tātparya-pariśuddhi*, on 4; **8.** *Kusumāñjali*: ETr. Cowell, *BI.* 1864.

Śrīkaṇṭha; **9.** *Nyāyālaṁkāra*: Vidyābhūshaṇa, *MSIL.* xvii; 53.

Bhā-sarvajña; **10.** *Nyāya-sāra*, with 18 commentaries: Vidyābhūshaṇa, *MSIL.* 53; Mādhava, *SDS.*: Cowell, 165; 170.

Abhayatilaka; **11.** *Nyāya-vṛitti*: Vidyābhūshaṇa, *MSIL.* xvii; 53.

Early 12th. Gaṅgeśa; **12.** *Tattva-chintāmaṇi*: Vidyābhūshaṇa, *MSIL.* xviii; Hall, 28.

12th c. Vardhamāna[1]; **13.** *Nyāya-nibandha-prakāśa*, on 7: Hall, 21.

[1] Son of Gaṅgeśa, author of the famous Nyāya work, *Tattva-chintāmaṇi*.

Early 13th. Jayadevamiśra; **14.** *Tattva-āloka*, on 12: Vidyābhūshaṇa, *MSIL.* xviii.

13th c. Keśava Miśra; **15.** *Tarka-bhāshā*: Keith, *JRAS.* 1914, 1089; Hall, 22. ETr. Jhā, Allahabad.

c. 1380. Mādhava; **16.** *Sarvadarśanasaṅgraha*, xi: ETr. Cowell, 161.

c. 1475. Vāsudeva Sārvabhauma; **17.** *Tattva-chintāmaṇi-vyākhyā*, on 12: Hall, 30; **18.** *Sārvabhauma-nirukti*, Sen, *CC.* 81.

c. 1500. Raghunātha Śiromaṇi; **19.** *Tattva-dīdhiti*, on 12: Hall, 31.

End 16th. Mathurānātha; **20.** *Tattva-āloka-rahasya* or *Mathurānāthī*, on 12: Hall, 29.

c. 1600. Jagadīśa Tarkālaṁkāra; **21.** *Tattva-dīdhiti-ṭippaṇī*, on 19: Hall, 35.

Early 17th. Viśvanātha Pañchānana; **22.** *Nyāya-sūtra-vṛitti*, on 1. ETr. Ballantyne, Calcutta.

Early 17th. Laugākshi Bhāskara; **23.** *Padārtha-mālā*: Hall, 26.

G. THE MATERIALISTIC SCHOOL.

They are called Lokāyatikas, Chārvākas or Bārhaspatyas.

Gen. Intro.: Poussin, *ERE.* viii. 493; Garbe, *ERE.* viii. 138; Pizzagalli, *Nāstika, Chārvāka e Lokāyatika*, Pisa, 1907; Müller, *SS.* 86; 94; Hopkins, *GE.* 86; Haribhadra, *Shaḍdarśanasamuchchhaya*: FTr. Suali, *Le Muséon*, ix. 277; Mādhava, *SDS.* ch. 1: ETr. Cowell, 2.

H. COMPARATIVE AND CRITICAL PHILOSOPHICAL LITERATURE.

c. 600. Samantabhadra, a Dig. Jain; **1.** *Āptamīmāṁsā*: Guérinot, 63; Vidyābhūshaṇa, *MSIL.* 23: contains a review of the various philosophic schools.

c. 600. Bhāvaviveka, a Mādhyamaka Buddhist; **2.** *Tarkajvālā*: criticism of the Mīmāṁsā, Sāṅkhya, Vaiśeshika, and Vedānta. Walleser, *DAV.* 7; *AMG.* ii. 367.

c. 800. Vidyānanda, a Dig. Jain; **3.** *Ashṭasāhasrī.* In this work he criticizes the six Hindu systems, except the Nyāya, and also Buddhism: Vidyābhūshaṇa, *MSIL.* 26.

Late 9th. Haribhadra, a Śvet. Jain; **4.** *Shaḍdarśanasamuchchhaya*, a review of six schools.

1065. Kṛishṇamiśra, a Vedantist; **5.** *Prabodhachandrodaya*, a drama.

12th c. Śrīharsha, a Vedantist: Macdonell, 330; **6.** *Khaṇḍanakhaṇḍakhādya*, a criticism of the Nyāya and other schools. ETr. Jhā, Allahabad, 1913: see Keith, *JRAS.* 1916, 377. H. P. Śāstrī, I. xlvi.

1304. Merutuṅga, a Śvet. Jain; **7.** *Shaḍdarśanavichāra*: Guérinot, 393.

1380. Mādhava, a Vedāntist; **8.** *Sarvardarśanasaṅgraha*, a review of sixteen schools: Macdonell, 406. ETr. Cowell, London, 1908.

vi. The Purāṇas.

Gen. Intro.: **Origin and date**: Hopkins, *GE.* 47–54: Pargiter, *JRAS.* 1912, 254; Fleet, *JRAS.* 1912, 1046; Keith, *JRAS.* 1914, 740; V. Smith, *EHI.* 21. **The Dynastic Lists**: Pargiter, *PTDKA*; V. Smith,

EHI. 22; Keith, *JRAS.* 1914, 1021. **Analyses**: Wilson, *Works*, iii. 1–155; *VP.* I. i–cxvii; Winternitz, i. 450. **Contents**: Pargiter, *ERE.* x. 447.

Harivaṁśa: **Intro. and analysis**: Winternitz, i. 378. Date: Jackson, *JRAS.* 1907, 408, 681; 1908, 529; Keith, *JRAS.* 1908, 173; Hopkins, *GE.* 9. FTr. Langlois, Paris, 1834; ETr. Dutt, Calcutta, 1897.

1. *Brahma*: Wilson, *Works*, iii. 8.

2. *Padma*: Wilson, *Works*, iii. 21. Telugu Tr., 1420. Analysis of the *Kriyāyogasāra* (an Appendix), Fonseca, Jahrbericht, *DMG.* 1846, 153.

3. *Vishṇu*: **Intro. and analysis**: Wilson, *VP.* I. cxii; *Works*, iii. 120; Winternitz, i. 455. Trs.: Kanarese, 12th and 17th cents.; Telugu, 1450; ETr. Wilson, *VP.*; ETr. Dutt, Calcutta, 1894.

4. *Vāyu*: **Analysis**: Wilson, *VP.* I. xxxv; *Works*, iii. 140. Date: Hopkins, *GE.* 68; Bāṇa, *Harshacharita*, Cowell's ETr. 72; Winternitz, i. 403.

5. *Bhāgavata*: Wilson, *VP.* I. xxxix. Trs.: Telugu, 1435; Gujarātī, 1484; Kanarese, 1600; Malayalim, 17th c.; Gujarātī, 1725; Partial Trs.: Bengālī, 1480; Braj, Sūr Dās, 16th c.; Marāṭhī, Eknāth, 1580; Kanarese, 1600; Gujarātī, 1690. Intro. and FTr. Burnouf, Paris, 1840 ff.; ETr. Dutt, Calcutta; ETr. (only 3 books) Kṛishṇāchārya, Madras, 1916. For the *Bhāgavata Māhātmya*, see *JRAS.* 1911, 800; 1912, 481.

6. *Nārada*: Wilson, *VP.* I. ii.

7. *Mārkaṇḍeya*: Intro. and ETr. Pargiter, Calcutta, 1904; ETr. Dutt, Calcutta, 1897. ETr. of *Chaṇḍīmāhātmya*, Wortham, *JRAS.* xiii. 355. Telugu Tr., 13th c.

8. *Agni*: Wilson, *VP.* I. lviii; *Works*, iii. 82. ETr. Dutt, Calcutta, 1903.

9. *Bhavishya*: Wilson, *VP.* I. lxii.

10. *Brahmavaivarta*: Wilson, *Works*, iii. 91.

11. *Liṅga*: Wilson, *VP.* I. lxvii. Tamil Tr., 16th c.

12. *Varāha*: Wilson, *VP.* I. lxx. Telugu Tr., 1470.

13. *Skanda*: Wilson, *VP.* I. lxxii; H. P. Sāstrī, I. lii. Partial Telugu Tr., 1450.

14. *Vāmana*: Wilson, *VP.* I. lxxiv.

15. *Kūrma*: Wilson, *VP.* I. lxxiv. Trs.: Telugu, 1500, Tamil, 16th c. Contains the *Īśvara Gītā*: see Mitra, *Notices*, vi. 115, i. 257. ETr. Kennedy, *HM.* 444.

16. *Matsya*: Wilson, *VP.* I. lxxx. Telugu Tr., 1550; ETr. of chaps. 1–128, *SBH.* 1916.

17. *Garuḍa*: Wilson, *VP.* I. lxxxiii. ETr. Dutt, Calcutta, 1908. ETr. of *Garuḍa P. Sāroddhāra*, *SBH.* 1911.

18. *Brahmāṇḍa*: Wilson, *VP.* I. lxxxiv. Malayalim Tr., 17th c. Includes the *Adhyātma-Rāmāyaṇa* and the *Lalitopākhyāna*.

Śiva: Wilson, *VP.* I. lxxxviii. Trs.: Malayalim, 17th c.; Partial ETr., *Siddhānta-Dīpikā*.

UPAPURĀṆAS: Madhusūdana Sarasvatī, *Prasthāna-bheda*; Wilson, *VP.* I. lxxxvi.

1. *Kālikā*: a Śākta work.

2. *Narasiṁha*: a Vaishṇava work.

3. *Sāmba*: a Saura work.

4. *Saura*: Intro. and full analysis, Jahn, *Das Saurapurāṇam.*

5. *Devī Bhāgavata*: a Śākta work.
6. *Āditya*: Alberuni, Sachau, i. 130; quotations in Madhva, *Bhāshya* on *Vedānta-sūtras*.
7. *Bhārgava*: Śeshagiri Śāstrī, *STMSS*. 1896–7, p. 151.

vii. Smārta Literature.

Note. The mass of books which are used by Smārtas are Vedic literature, and are dealt with elsewhere. Here only a few special works which spring from the Smārta position are mentioned. Books in Sanskrit, unless otherwise described.

1. *Baudhāyana Gṛihyasūtra Pariśishṭas*: Bühler, *SBE*. XIV. xxx ff.
2. The fivefold *Atharvaśiras U.*: Weber, *HIL*. 170. ETr. Kennedy, *HM*. 346, 442, 443, 491, 493.
3. *Garuḍa P.*: see § 206.
c. 1065. Kṛishṇamiśra: Smith, *EHI*. 392; 4. *Prabodhachandrodaya*: ETr. Taylor, Bombay, 1893; GTr. anon. (Th. Goldstücker), Königsberg, 1842; Hindī paraphrase, Keśava Dāsa Miśra, *Vijñāna Gītā*: Grierson, *LH*. 58; *JRAS*. 1908, 1136.
Prob. 13th c.; 5. *Yoga-Vasishṭha-Rāmāyaṇa*: ETr. Vihari Lal Mitra, Calcutta, 1891.
c. 1300. Hemādri; 6. *Chaturvarga Chintāmaṇi*: Bhandarkar, *EHD*. 88.
Late 14th. Vīreśvara; 7. *Vīreśvara Paddhati*, a manual of conduct, Tirhut: Sen. *HBLL*. 140.
c. 1500. Raghunandana; 8. *Ashṭāviṁśati Tattva*, a manual of conduct, Bengal: Sen. *HBLL*. 74; 421.
Mukundarāj; 9. *Vivekasindhu* (Marāṭhī): Acworth, *BM*. xxiii; Mackichan, *Indian Interpreter*, Jan. 1913, 166 f.
Before 1550. Madhusūdana Sarasvatī; 10. *Prasthāna-bheda*: GTr. Deussen, *AGP*. I. i. 44.
c. 1600. Alavantar Madavappattar; 11. *Jñāna-Vasishṭham*, a Tamil adaptation of No. 5.
c. 1660. Ananta Deva[1]; 12. *Smṛiti Kaustubha*, a manual of conduct, North India: Hall, 185.

viii. Vaishṇava Literature.

A. General.

1. *Purusha Sūkta*: *Ṛigveda*, x. 90.
2. *Mahānārāyaṇa Upanishad*, No. 6, p. 364, above.
3. *Mahābhārata*, and vernacular versions.
4. *Rāmāyaṇa*, and vernacular versions.
5. *Bhagavadgītā*.

B. Bhāgavata Literature.

I. THE BHĀGAVATA SAMPRADĀYA.

Note. Bhāgavatas are interested in all the books used by Smārtas and in general Vaishṇava literature as well. Here only works springing from the community are mentioned. All books in Sanskrit.

[1] Son of Āpadeva, author of the *Āpadevī*, above, p. 367.

4th or 5th. **1.** *Harivaṁśa*, or at least the passages on Vishṇu and Śiva. See § 161.

2. Vaikhānasa Saṁhitās: Appaya Dīkshita, quoted in Chanda, *IAR.* 100; Schrader, *IPAS.* 55; Śeshagiri Rao, *STMSS.* 1893–6, p. 6.

7th or 8th. **3.** *Agni P.*: see § 206.

4. *Skanda U.*, No. 68, p. 364, above; Jacob, *EAU.* 15.

c. 900. **5.** *Bhāgavata P.*: see § 272.

6. *Nārada-bhakti-sūtra*: Text and ETr. Siṅha, *SBH.*; ETr. Sturdy, London (Watkins), 1904.

7. *Śāṇḍilya-bhakti-sūtra*: ETr. Cowell, Calcutta, 1878; Text and ETr. with Svapneśvara's comm., Paul, *SBH.* 1911. Comms. also by Muralīdāsa, a Marāṭhā Vallabha, and Nārāyaṇatīrtha of the 17th c.; Hall, 143.

8. *Vāsudeva*, and **9.** *Gopīchandana* Upanishads, Nos. 72 and 119, p. 364, above: Jacob, *EAU.* 5–7; ETr. *IA.* 1887.

c. 1300. Vopadeva; **10.** *Muktāphala* and **11.** *Harilīlā*, both on the *Bhāgavata P.*: Bhandarkar, *EHD.* 89; *IOM.* 3542; 3533.

c. 1400. Śrīdhara; **12.** *Bhāgavata-bhāvārtha-dīpikā*, comm. on 5.

Śrī-Śukāchārya; **13.** *Śuka-bhāshya* on *Vedānta-sūtras*; text in Telugu characters, T. Veṅkaṭāchārya, Bangalore, 1892.

2. LITERATURE OF MARĀṬHĀ BHAKTAS.

Gen. Intro.: Bhandarkar, *VS.* 87 ff.; Acworth, *BM.* Intro.; Macnicol, 'The Indian Poetry of Devotion,' *Hibbert Journal*, 1917; Macnicol, *Psalms of Marāṭhā Saints*, an anthology in ETrs., Calcutta, 1919. All literature in Marāṭhī.

c. 1290. Jñāneśvara; **1.** *Jñānesvarī*; **2.** *Svātmānubhava*; **3.** *Haripāṭh*; **4.** *Amṛitānubhava*; **5.** *Chāṅgdeva Pāsashti* (possibly spurious). ETrs. of a few hymns and a few selections from the *Jñāneśvarī* in Macnicol, *PMS.*

c. 1300. Muktabai; **6.** *Abhaṅgs*: ETrs. Macnicol, *PMS.*

c. 1425. Nāmdev; **7.** *Abhaṅgs*: ETrs. of Marāṭhī Abhaṅgs: Bhandarkar, *VS.* 90 ff.; Macnicol, *PMS.*; Patwardhan, *Indian Interpreter*, April, 1913. Hindī hymns, *MBV.* i. 254: ETr. Macauliffe, vi. 40.

c. 1425. Trilochan; **8.** Hindī hymns: ETr. Macauliffe, vi. 78.

c. 1540. Bhānu Dās; **9.** *Abhaṅgs*. He was the grandfather of Eknāth.

d. 1608. Eknāth; **10.** *Eknāthī Bhāgwat*: ETrs. of passages: Macnicol, *Indian Theism*, 270; *PMS.*; **11.** *Chatuślokī Bhāgwat*; **12.** *Bhāvārtha Rāmāyaṇa*; **13.** *Haripāṭh*.

1608–49. Tukārām; **14.** *Abhaṅgs*: complete ETr., Fraser and Marathe, Madras, 1909, &c.; select ETrs. Bhandarkar, *VS.* 94–9; Macnicol, *PMS.*; Barnett, *HI.* 60; Rawlinson, *Shivaji*, Oxford, 1915, 114–16.

1608–81. Rām Dās; **15.** *Daśabodha*: Rawlinson, op. cit., 116–22, including a few translations.

1679–1728. Śrīdhara; **16.** *Rāma Vijaya*, &c.; ETrs. in Bell, *Some Translations from the Marathi Poets*, Bombay, 1913, pp. 3–25, 167–209.

18th c. Mahīpati; **17.** *Santa Līlāmṛita* (1757); **18.** *Bhakta Vijaya* (1762); **19.** *Kathā Sārāmṛita* (1765); **20.** *Bhakta Līlāmṛita* (1774); **21.** *Santa Vijaya*: ETr. Bell, op. cit., 27–42.

3. MADHVA LITERATURE.

Gen. Intro.: Padmanabhachar, *LTM*; Krishnaswami Iyer, *Śrī Madhvāchārya*, Madras; Grierson, *ERE*. viii. 232; Bhandarkar, *VS*. 57; Mādhava, *SDS*. v: Cowell, 87. Books in Sanskrit, unless otherwise described.

1199-1278. Madhva: for his works, see Padmanabhachar, 196; Bhandarkar, *R*. 1882-3, 207; **1.** *Sūtra-bhāshya*, on *Vedānta-sūtras*: ETr. S. Subba Rau, Madras, 1904; **2.** *Anuvyākhyāna* (verse), on *Vedānta-sūtras*; **3.** *Gītā-bhāshya*; **4.** *Bhāgavata-tātparya-nirṇaya*; **5.** *Mahābhārata-tātparya-nirṇaya*; **6.** Bhāshyas on ten Upanishads: see above, p. 365; **7.** Ten Prakaraṇas, or special treatises, including *Tantra-sāra* on the ritual.

Late 13th. Trivikrama; **8.** *Tattva-pradīpikā*, on 1.

Late 13th. Padmanābhatīrtha; **9.** *Sanyāya-ratnāvalī*, on 2.

c. 1340. Jayatīrtha; **10.** *Tattva-prakāśikā*, on 1; **11.** *Nyāya-sudhā*, on 2.

c. 1360. Nārāyaṇa; **12.** *Maṇimañjarī*; and **13.** *Madhvavijaya*, polemical works: summary, Krishnaswami Iyer, op. cit.; Grierson, *ERE*. viii. 232.

c. 1380. Mādhava; **14.** *Sarvadarśanasaṅgraha*, ch. v: Cowell, 87.

c. 1400. Vishṇu Purī; **15.** *Bhatiratnāvalī*: Text and ETr., *SBH*. vii.

16. *Adhyātma Rāmāyaṇa*, in Kan.: contains a Mādhva interpolation: Padmanabhachar, *LTM*. 133.

16th c. Vyāsa-rāja-svāmī; **17.** *Chandrikā*, on No. 10; **18.** *Nyāyāmṛita*, a criticism of Śaṅkara's Vedānta; **19.** *Tarka-tāṇḍava*, a criticism of the Nyāya.

16th c. Puraṁdara Dās, Kanaka Dās, Viṭṭhala Dās, Veṅkaṭa Dās, Vijaya Dās, Kṛishṇa Dās: writers of Kan. hymns: Rice, *KL*. 59. ETrs. Gover, *FSSI*. 17 ff.

18th c. Varāha Timmappa Dās, Madhva Dās: writers of Kan. hymns: Rice, *KL*. 59. ETrs. Gover, *FSSI*.

20. *Harikathāmṛitasāra*: popular Kan. book on doctrine.

18th c. Chidānanda; **21.** *Hari-bhakti-rasāyana*: Kan. work on devotion: Rice, *KL*. 60.

4. EARLY RĀDHĀ LITERATURE.

1. *Gopālatāpanīya* and *Kṛishṇa* Upanishads, above, p. 364, Nos. 106, 107.

2. *Gopālasahasranāma*: the thousand names of Kṛishṇa. *IOM*. No. 2536.

3. *Nārada Pañcharātra*: an old Vaishṇava Saṁhitā, seemingly used and interpolated by Vishṇusvāmīs and Vallabhāchāryas; Schrader, *IPAS*. No. 71, p. 8; Bhandarkar, *VS*. 40, 86.

5. VISHṆUSVĀMĪ LITERATURE.

13th c. Vishṇusvāmī; **1.** *Gītā-bhāshya*; **2.** *Vedānta-sūtra-bhāshya*; **3.** *Bhāgavata-bhāshya*; **4.** *Vishṇu-rahasya*; **5.** *Tattvatraya*.

c. 1300. Śrīkāntamiśra; **6.** *Sākāra-siddhi*: Mādhava, *SDS*.: Cowell, 141; 142.

c. 1400. Bilvamaṅgala or Līlāśuka; **7.** *Kṛishṇakarṇāmṛita*.

Varadarāja; **8.** *Bhāgavata-laghu-ṭīkā*: MS. in Library of Sanskrit College, Benares.

6. NIMBĀRKA LITERATURE.

Gen. Intro.: Bhandarkar, *VS.* 62; Growse, *Mathurā*, 147, 148, 189, 194, 200; Wilson, *Sects*, 150. All books in Sansk. unless otherwise described.

1. *Gautamīya S.*: early work used by Nimbārkas for ritual: Schrader, *IPAS.* 7; *IOM.* iv. 865.

13th c. Nimbārka; **2.** *Vedānta-pārijāta-saurabha*, a vṛitti on the *Vedānta-sūtras*; **3.** *Daśaślokī*, or *Vedānta-ratna*, or *Siddhānta-ratna*: Hall, 114. ETr. Bhandarkar, *VS.* 63.

13th c. Śrīnivāsa; **4.** *Vedānta-Kaustubha*, a bhāshya on the *Vedānta-sūtras*.

Purushottama; **5**. *Vedānta-ratna-mañjūshā*, on 3: Hall, 114.
Devāchārya; **6.** *Siddhānta-jāhnavī*.
Sundara Bhaṭṭa; **7.** *Dvaitādvaita-siddhānta-setuka*, on 6.

Early 16th. Keśava Kashmīri; **8.** *Vedānta-kaustubha-prabhā*, on 4; **9.** *Gītā-tattva-prakāśikā*: Hall, 118; **10.** *Kramadīpikā*, selections from No. 1.

Early 16th. Harivyāsa Deva; **11.** *Daśaślokī-bhāshya*, on 3: Hall, 115.

Early 16th. Harivyāsa Deva and Śrī Bhaṭṭ; **12.** *Pada*, Hindī hymns for saṅkīrtan.

13. *Kṛishṇa-janma-khaṇḍa* of *Brahma-vaivarta P.*

7. CHAITANYA LITERATURE.

Gen. Intro.: Wilson, *Sects*, 152; Sen, *HBLL.*; *CC.*; *VLMB.*; Sarkar, *CPT.*; Bhandarkar, *VS.* 82. For the temples in Brindāban, see Growse, *M.*, and Sen, *VLMB.* 51. Estimates of the movement, Kennedy, *Young Men of India*, July, 1918; Underwood, *Calcutta Review*, 1919, p. 37. Lit. in Bengālī, unless otherwise described.

1509-11. Govinda Dās; **1.** *Kaḍchā*, i.e. note-book, of very dubious authenticity: Sen, *CC.* 232; Bhāgavata Kumāra Gosvāmī Śāstrī, art., 'Vaishṇava Dharma o Śrī-Chaitanya Yuga,' in *Sāhitya Saṁhitā*, 1309 (i.e. A.D. 1903).

1514. Murāri Gupta; **2.** Kaḍchā (Sansk.): Sen, *CC.* 109.

c. 1518. Sārvabhauma; **3.** *Gaurāṅgāshṭaka* (Sansk.): Sen, *CC.* 88.

Early 16th. Narahari Sarkar; **4.** Hymns: Sen, *CC.* 100.

Early 16th. Vaṁśīvadana; **5.** Hymns: Sen, *CC.* 104.

c. 1540. Vāsudeva Ghosh; **6.** Hymns: Sen, *CC.* 107.

d. 1591. Rūpa (works in Sansk.): Sen, *VLMB.* 26; **7.** *Vidagdha-mādhava*; **8.** *Lalita-mādhava*; and **9.** *Dānakeli-kaumudī*, dramas; **10.** *Padmāvalī*; and **11.** *Stavamālā*, hymns; **12.** *Gaṇadveśadīpikā*: Chaitanya's companions are gopīs incarnate; **13.** *Bhaktiratnāmṛitasindhu*; and **14.** *Ujjvalanīlamaṇi*, on bhakti and love; **15.** *Mathurā-māhātmya* of the *Varāha P.*: Growse, *M.* 78, 89, 142, 198; Sen, *VLMB.* 36.

d. 1591. Sanātana (works in Sansk.): Sen, *VLMB.* 36, 38; **16.** *Haribhaktivilāsa*, a ritual code; **17.** *Vaishṇavatoshiṇī*, comm. on *Bhāgavata P.*

d. 1572. Murāri Gupta; **18.** *Chaitanyacharita* (Sansk.): Sen, *VLMB.* 70, 73.

d. 1572. Kavikarṇapūra; **19.** *Chaitanyachandrodaya* (Sansk. drama): Sen, *VLMB.* 71.

c. 1570. Vṛindāvana Dās; **20.** *Chaitanyabhāgavata*, A.D. 1573, Sen, *VLMB.* 74; *HBLL.* 464; **21.** *Nityānanda-vaṁśa-vistara*, Sen, *VLMB.* 164.

c. 1575. Lochana Dās; **22.** *Chaitanyamaṅgal*, Sen, *VLMB.* 80.

c. 1575. Jayānanda; **23.** *Chaitanyamaṅgal*, Sen, *VLMB.* 80; *HBLL.* 471.

1581. Kṛishṇa Dās Kavirāj; **24.** *Chaitanyacharitāmṛita*, Sen, *HBLL.* 477; *VLMB.* 58. ETr. of middle section, Sarkar, *CPT.*

Fl. 1580–1610. Jīva (works in Sansk.); **25.** *Satsandarbha*, Theology; **26.** *Kṛishṇārchanadīpikā*, Ritual; **27.** *Kramasandarbha*, comm. on *Bhāgavata P.*; **28.** Comm. on *Brahma S.*; and many other works: Sen, *VLMB.* 40.

Fl. 1610–40. Govinda Dās, Jñāna Dās, Balarāma Dās, and other hymn-writers: Sen, *VLMB.* 183; 197.

c. 1625. Nityānanda Dās; **29.** *Premavilāsa*, history of sect in verse: Sen, *VLMB.* 169.

1704. Viśvanātha Chakravartī; **30.** Comm. on *Bhāgavata P.*: Sen, *VLMB.* 177.

Early 18th. Narahari Chakravartī; **31.** *Bhaktiratnākara*, history of sect: Sen, *VLMB.* 177.

Early 18th. Vaishṇava Dās; **32.** *Padakalpataru*, anthology of the hymns: Sen, *HBLL.* 563.

Early 18th. Baladeva; **33.** *Govinda-bhāshya* (Sansk.), on *Vedānta-sūtras*: ETr. S. C. Vasu, *SBH.* v.

8. VALLABHĀCHĀRYA LITERATURE.

Gen. Intro.: Wilson, *Sects*, 119; Bhandarkar, *VS.* 76; *History of the Sect of Mahārājas, or Vallabhāchāryas, in Western India*, London, 1865; Growse, *M.* 283; 295; Hall, 145–6. For Vallabha lit. in Braj, see Growse, *M.* 295; Grierson, *LH.*, pp. 20 ff. Lit. in Sansk., unless otherwise described.

1479–1531. Vallabha; **1.** *Brahma-sūtra-anubhāshya*, on the *Vedānta-sūtras*; **2.** *Tattva-dīpa-nibandha*, a manual of his system; **3.** *Prakāśa*, comm. on 2, by Vallabha, with **4.** *Āvaraṇa-bhaṅgavyākhyā*, a super-comm. on 3, by Pītambara. Nos. 2, 3, and 4 together form the *Vidyā-vaijayantī*; **5.** *Śrī-subodhinī*, on the *Bhāgavata P.*; **6.** *Gāyatrī-bhāshya*; **7.** *Jaiminīya-sūtra-bhāshya*: Hall, 208; **8.** *Siddhānta Rahasya*: Text and ETr. Growse, *M.* 285; **9.** *Kṛishṇa-prema-amṛita*, with gloss by Viṭṭhalnāth.

c. 1540. Viṭṭhalnāth; **10.** *Ratna-vivaraṇa*: Growse, *M.* 295; Grierson, *LH.* 20.

c. 1550. Kṛishṇa Dās; **11.** *Prem-ras-ras* (Braj): Grierson, *LH.* 21.

1551. Gokulnāth; **12.** *Chaurāsī Bārtā* (Braj): Lyall, *EB.* xiii. 487; Wilson, *Sects*, 132; Growse, *M.* 296.

Late 16th. Sūr Dās: Grierson, *LH.* 21; Prasād, *SBS.* ii. 55; *MBV.* i. 269. **13.** *Sūr Sāgar*, Trs. in Braj from *Bhāgavata P.*; **14.** *Sūrsārāvalī*, an anthology from the *Sūr Sāgar*.

c. 1600. Giridharajī; **15.** *Śuddhādvaita-mārtaṇḍa*.

Bālakṛishṇa Bhaṭṭa; **16.** *Prameyaratnārṇava*.

c. 1743. Braj Bāsī Dās; **17.** *Braj Bilās*, Braj poem on Rādhā: Grierson, *LH.* 97; Growse, *M.* 75 n.

1767-1852. Dayārām; **18.** Many works in Braj, Gujarātī, &c.: Jhaveri, *MGL.* 216.

9. RĀDHĀ-VALLABHĪ LITERATURE.

Gen. Intro.: Growse, *M.* 199; Grierson, *LH.* 28; *ERE.* x. 559. Lit. in Hindī, unless otherwise described.

c. 1580. Hari Vaṁśa; **1.** Rādhā-sudhā-nidhi (Sansk.): Text and ETr. of 26 stanzas, Growse, *M.* 204; **2.** *Chaurāsī Pada*: or *Hit Chaurāsī Dhām*: Text and ETr. of 12 stanzas, Growse, *M.* 208; **3.** *Sphuṭ Pada*, hymns.

Early 17th. Dhruva Dās; **4.** *Jīv-dasā*, and many other works: Growse, *M.* 216.

Dāmodar Dās; **5.** *Sevak-bānī*, and other works, Growse, *M.* 100, 216; Wilson, *Sects*, 177.

10. HARI DĀSĪ LITERATURE.

Gen. Intro.: Growse, *M.* 217; Grierson, *LH.* 59. Lit. in Hindī.

c. 1600. Hari Dās. Life and Selections, Prasād, *SBS.* ii. 67; **1.** *Sādhāran Siddhānt*: Text and ETr. Growse, *M.* 223 ff.; **2.** *Ras ke pada*, hymns; **3.** *Bharatharī-vairāgya.*

c. 1650. Bihāriṇī Dās; **4.** *Pada*, hymns; one hymn in Text and ETr. Growse, *M.* 222. There were several other writers.

11. SVĀMĪ NĀRĀYAṆĪ LITERATURE.

Gen. Intro: Monier Williams, *BH.* 148; Russell and Hira Lal, i. 326 ff. *The Svāmī-Nārāyaṇī Sect*, Education Society's Press, Bombay, 1887.

Early 19th. Svāmī Nārāyaṇa; **1.** *Śikshā-pātrī*: a Sanskrit code of 212 precepts, accompanied by a long commentary: Monier Williams, *BH.* 148.

Much Gujarātī verse by Premānand, Brahmānand, Muktānand, Niskulānand, and other ascetics: Jhaveri, *MGL.* 181; 199 ff.

12. RĀDHĀ-KṚISHṆA POETRY, LITERARY AND UNSECTARIAN.

Late 12th. Jayadeva; **1.** *Gītāgovinda* (Sansk.): Macdonell, 344. ETr. Arnold, London, 1881; GTr. Rückert, Leipzig; FTr. Gourtillier, Paris, 1904; **2.** Rādhā-Kṛishṇa songs in Bengālī attributed to him: Sen, *HBLL.*

c. 1400. Chaṇḍī Dās; **3.** Songs in Bengālī: Sen, *HBLL.* 115. ETr. of two songs, Beames, *IA.* 1873, 187.

15th c. Vidyāpati; **4.** Songs in Maithilī: Sen, *HBLL.* 135 ff. Text and ETr. Grierson, *Introduction to the Maithilī Language*, Calcutta, 1882; *LH.* 9. ETr. of over 100 songs from the Bengālī text, Coomaraswamy, *Vidyāpati, Baṅgīya Padābalī*, London, 1915.

15th c. Umāpati; **5.** Songs in Bengālī and in Maithilī: Sen, *VLMB.* 1-9,[1] where the text of three of the songs is given. Grierson, *LH.* 11.

[1] Mr. Sen identifies this Umāpati with the Sanskrit poet Umāpati Dhara referred to by Jayadeva at the beginning of the *Gītāgovinda*, but the evidence tends to the conclusion that the author of the Bengālī poems was a contemporary of Vidyāpati. See *Miśra Bandhu Vinode*, i. 250.

Late 15th. Narsiṅgh Mehtā; **6.** Songs in Gujarātī and Hindī: Jhaveri, *MGL.* 35 ff.; text of two Hindī songs in Prasād, *SBS.* ii. 78 (date erroneous).

Late 15th. Mīrā Bāī; **7.** Songs in Braj and Gujarātī: a few Braj songs in Prasād, *SBS.* ii. 68. One Braj song in ETr., Macauliffe, vi. 342. Gujarātī songs: see Jhaveri, *MGL.* 29. Date erroneous in all three works. See also *MBV.* i. 297.

16th and 17th. Numerous Maithilī poets. Sen, *VLMB.* 7.

1650. Bihārī Lāl Chaube; **8.** *Sat Saī*: 700 couplets in Hindī in praise of Kṛishṇa: Grierson, *LH.* 75.

9. Malayalim songs: Gover, *FSSI.* 248; 255.

C. Pāñcharātra Literature.

1. GENERAL.

1. Pāñcharātra sections in *MBH.*: see above, § 105.

2. Vishṇu and other Purāṇas.

3. *Mahā*, *Nārāyaṇa*, *Ātmabodha*, and *Subālā* Upanishads, Nos. 44, 45, 46, and 55, p. 364, above.

4. The Saṁhitās: Schrader, *IPAS*; Govindāchārya, *JRAS.* 1911, 935; Iyengar, *Outlines*, 174.

2. ŚRĪ-VAISHṆAVA LITERATURE.

Lit. in Sanskrit, unless otherwise described.

7th to 9th. The Āḷvārs; **1.** Hymns in Tamil: Govindāchārya, *The Holy Lives of the Azhvars*, Mysore (uncritical but useful); K. Aiyangar, *AI.* chs. vii, xv, xviii, xix; S. Aiyangar, *TS.* chs. viii, xi; Barnett, *BMCTB.* vi. Nammāḷvār's works are held to represent the Vedas (K. Aiyangar, *AI.* 398), thus:

a. *Tiruviruttam*: Ṛik.
b. *Tiruvoymoḷi*: Sāman.
c. *Tiruvaśiriyam*: Yajus.
d. *Periyatiruvandādi*: Atharvan.
} Drāviḍa Veda.

c. 1000. Nāthamuni: Govindāchārya, *R.* ch. i; Rajagopalachariar, *VRI.* 1–11; 26; **2.** *Nālāyira Prabandham*, the hymns of the Āḷvārs (Tam.) edited for study and singing; **3.** *Nyāya-tattva*; **4.** *Yoga-rahasya*: Hall, 17.

c. 1050. Yāmuna, or Āḷavandār: Govindāchārya, *R.* ch. iii; Rajagopalachariar, *VRI.* 26–49; **5.** *Siddhi-traya*; Text, Benares; **6.** *Āgama-pramāṇya*: Text, Benares; **7.** *Gītārtha-saṅgraha*; **8.** *Alamandāra stotra*; **9.** *Ratnastotra*: a few verses in ETr. Barnett, *HI.* 42.

c. 1080. Yādava Prakāśa or Govinda-jīya (Rāmānuja's former guru); **10.** *Yati-dharma-samuchchhaya*, a work on Śrī-Vaishṇava sannyāsīs: see Govindāchārya, *R.* 74.

c. 1050–1137. Rāmānuja: Keith, *ERE.* x. 572. **Life**: Tamil life by Pinbalagīa-Perumal-Jīya: ETr. Govindāchārya, Madras, 1906; brief life, Rajagopalachariar, *VRI.* 50–77; a life called *Āchāryaparicharya*, Rāma Miśra Śāstrī, Benares. **System**: Thibaut, *SBE.* xxxiv. Intro.; Sukhtaṅkar, *TVR.*; Bhandarkar, *VS.* 50ff.; **11.** *Vedārtha-saṅgraha*: Hall, 116; **12.** *Śrī-bhāshya*, on the *Vedānta-sūtras*: ETr. Thibaut, *SBE.* xlviii; ETr. Raṅgāchārya and Aiyaṅgar, Madras, 1899; **13.** *Gītā-bhāshya*: ETr. Govindāchārya, Madras, 1898; **14.** *Vedānta-sāra*: see

Thibaut, *SBE.* XXXIV. xvi. Two other works, *Vedānta-dīpa* and *Vedānta-tattva-sāra*, are attributed to him, but are of doubtful authenticity: Sukhtaṅkar, op. cit., 3.

15. *Bhagavad-vishayam*, anonymous Tam. comm. on Nammāḷvār's *Tiruvoymoḷi*: Partial ETr., A. Govindāchārya, *Divine Wisdom of Drāviḍa Saints*, Madras, 1902.

13th c. Pinbaḷagīa-Perumal-Jīya; **16.** Tamil life of Rāmānuja: ETr. A. Govindāchārya, Madras, 1906.

End 13th. Piḷḷai Lokāchārya; **17.** *Artha-pañchaka* (Tam.): ETr. A. Govindāchārya, *JRAS*, 1910, 565; **18.** *Tattva-traya* (Tam.): ETr. Pārthasārathi Yogī; **19.** *Śrī-vachana-bhūshaṇa* (Tam.): ETr. Pārthasārathi Yogī.

c. 1350. Sudarśana Bhaṭṭa; **20.** *Śukapakshīya*, comm. on *Bhāgavata P.*, Rajagopalachariar, *VRI.* 99 f.

c. 1380. Mādhava; **21.** *Sarvadarśanasaṅgraha*, ch. iv. Cowell, 64.

c. 1380. Vedānta Deśika, or Veṅkaṭa-nātha: Rajagopalachariar, *VRI.* 91 ff.; Raṅgāchārī, *Brahmavādin*, Oct.–Nov. 1912, 597; Govindāchārya, *YMD.* 171; **22.** *Śatadūshaṇī*: against Śaṅkara's Vedānta; **23.** *Nyāya-siddhāñjana*: Viśishṭādvaita philosophy; **24.** *Seśvara-mīmāṁsā*: on the Mīmāṁsā; **25.** *Rahasya-traya-sāra*: a manual of the system in Tamil; **26.** *Saṅkalpa-sūryodaya*, an allegorical drama: Text and ETr. by K. Nārāyaṇāchārya, Madras, 1917; **27.** *Pāñcharātrarakshā*, on the Vaishṇava Saṁhitās: Schrader, *IPAS.* 4, 18.

Early 15th. Rāmya-jāmātṛi-muni: Rajagopalachariar, *VRI.* 132 ff.; Gopālasvāmī Iyengar, *Brahmavādin*, Oct.–Nov. 1912, 610; Govindāchārya, *YMD.* 171; **28.** *Tattva-nirūpaṇa*; **29.** *Upadeśaratnamālā* (Tam.).

c. 1600. Appaya-dīkshita; many comms.: Govindāchārya, *YMD.*, Preface.

c. 1600. Chaṇḍa-māruta Mahāchārya; **30.** *Chaṇḍa-māruta*, a comm. on No. 22: Govindāchārya, *YMD.* iv; 172.

c. 1650. Śrīnivāsa; **31.** *Yatīndra-mata-dīpikā*: Intro. and ETr. Govindāchārya, Madras, 1912; Schrader, *IPAS.* 176.

3. MANBHAU LITERATURE.

Gen. Intro.: *Bombay Gazetteer*, xviii. 181; xix. 120; Crooke, *ERE.* ii. 504; Monograph 131, *Bombay Ethnographic Survey*; Chandorkar and Rajwade in *Proceedings of Bhārata Itihāsika Saṁśodhaka Maṇḍala*, 1915, 1916; Yādavagiri Māhātmya of the *Nārada Purāṇa*.

1. *Dattātreya U.*: No. 112, p. 364.

2. *Dattātreya S.*: Schrader, *IPAS.* 7.

3. Manbhau books in Marāṭhī: *Līlā Saṁvād*, *Līlā Charit*, *Sūtra-pāṭh*, *Darśan Prakāś*, *Chakradhar Charit*, *Chāṅgdev Charitra*, *Tīrthāvalī.*

4. *Kaivadya Dīpikā* (Sansk.).

4. LITERATURE OF NARASIṀHA SECT.

Gen. Intro.: Deussen, *SUV.* 752; Krishṇa Śāstrī, *SII.* 24.

1. *Nṛisiṁha-pūrva-tāpanīya U.*; and **2.** *Nṛisiṁha-uttara-tāpanīya U.* Intro. and GTr. Deussen, *SUV.* 752. Cf. also Weber, *HIL.* 167; Schrader, *IPAS.* 143.

3. *Nṛisiṁha Upapurāṇa*: Alberuni, Sachau, i. 130. Tel. Tr., A.D. 1300.

4. *Nṛisiṁha Saṁhitā*: Schrader, *IPAS.* 8, 18.

5. RAMAITE LITERATURE.

A. Early Sanskrit Works.

1. *Rāmāyaṇa*, vi. 119.

2. *Saṁkshepa Rāmāyaṇa*: 100 ślokas from the first book of the *Rāmāyaṇa*, for children.

3. *Rāma-pūrva-tāpanīya U.*; and **4.** *Rāma-uttara-tāpanīya U.* Intro. and GTr. Deussen, *SUV.* 802. Cf. also Weber, *HIL.* 168; Schrader, *IPAS.* 121.

5. *Agastya-Sutīkshṇa-saṁvāda*: Schrader, *IPAS.* 6; referred to in *Adhyātma-Rāmāyaṇa*, III. ii. 26; IV. iv. 30–1; VI. v. 9.

11th c. Dāmodaramiśra; **6.** *Hanumān Nāṭaka*, a drama, ETr. Wilson, *TH.* ii. 363.

c. 1300. **7.** *Adhyātma Rāmāyaṇa*: ETr. Lāla Baij Nāth, *SBH.* 1913.

8. *Adbhuta Rāmāyaṇa*: Text, Śrīveṅkaṭeśvara Press, Bombay.

9. *Bhusuṇḍi Rāmāyaṇa*: Grierson, *JRAS.* 1912, 797.

B. Early Hindī Hymns.

Early 15th. Sadana; **1.** Hymns: Prasād, *SBS.* ii. 36. ETr. Macauliffe, vi. 84.

Early 15th. Beni; **2.** Hymns: ETr. Macauliffe, vi. 88.

c. 1425. Nāmdeva: see above, under Marāṭhā Bhaktas; **3.** Hymns: Prasād, *SBS.* ii. 28; ETr. Macauliffe, vi. 17; 40.

c. 1425. Trilochana; **4.** Hymns: ETr. Macauliffe, vi. 76; 78.

C. The Rāmānandīs.

c. 1400–70. Rāmānanda: art. *JRAS.*, Jan. 1920; **1.** Hymns; Wilson, *Sects*, 46; Grierson, *LH.* 7; *ERE.* x. 569. ETr. Macauliffe, vi. 105.

Born 1425. Pīpā; **2.** Hymns: Prasād, *SBS.* ii. 28. ETr. Macauliffe, VI. 111.

Late 15th. Rai Dās; **3.** Hymns: Prasād, *SBS.* i. 35; ii. 32; Bhandarkar, *VS.* 74; Grierson, *ERE.* x. 560. ETr. Macauliffe, vi. 316.

Late 15th. Senā; **4.** Hymns: Bhandarkar, *VS.* 74. ETr. Macauliffe, vi. 120.

1532–1623. Tulsī Dās: Grierson, *LH.* 42; *JRAS.* 1903, 447 ff. Theology, Thibaut, *SBE.* xxxiv, p. cxxvii; Carpenter, *Theology of Tulsī Dās*, Madras, 1918; **5.** *Rāma-charit-mānas*: Grierson, *JRAS.* 1912, 794; 1913, 133; 1914, 416. ETr. Growse, Allahabad, 1897; **6.** *Gītābalī*: the story of Rām in songs: *JRAS.* 1903, 452; **7.** *Kabittābalī*: the story of Rām in songs: *JRAS.* 1903, 453; **8.** *Binay Pattrikā*: hymns to Rām: *JRAS.* 1903, 454. Other works: Grierson, *LH.* 45 f. Selections: Prasād, *SBS.* i. 71; 239; ii. 79. ETr. of extracts: Bhandarkar, *VS.* 75 f.

c. 1600. Nābhājī, **9.** *Bhakta-mālā*: Grierson, *JRAS.* 1909, 607; 1910, 87; 269.

1574–1682.[1] Malūk Dās; **10.** Poems: Growse, *M.* 230; Prasād, *SBS.* i. 99; ii. 102; Wilson, *Sects*, 100; Grierson, *ERE.* viii. 374.

1712. Priyā Dās. **11.** Gloss on *Bhakta Mālā*: Grierson, *LH.* 86; *MBV.* i. 390; ii. 607.

12. *Agastya S.*, including Rāmānanda's life: text and Hindī Tr., Rāma Nārāyaṇa Dās, 1904: Bhandarkar, *VS.* 67 n. 2: this is the *Agastya-Sutīkshṇa-saṁvāda*, No. 5, above.

[1] These dates come from his living descendants: Prasād, *SBS.* i. 99.

D. Reformed Literature.

A. Kabīr and the Kabīrpanth.

1440–1518. Kabīr; **1.** Poems: Westcott, *Kabīr*: Burn, *ERE*. vii. 632; Shah, *Bījak of Kabīr*, Hamirpur, U. P., 1917; Wilson, *Sects*, 68. His mysticism: Evelyn Underhill in Tagore, *One Hundred Poems of Kabir*, London, 1913. ETr. of *Bījak*, Shah, op. cit. ETrs. of selections: Tagore, op. cit.; Wilson, op. cit. 79; Westcott, op. cit.; Bhandarkar, *VS*. 70; Macauliffe, vi. 122.

2. *Guṭkā*, the Prayer Book of the Kabīrpanth: Powlett, *Ulwur*, 60–9, including fragments in ETr.

3. *Puno Granth*, the Service Book of the Kabīrpanth: Westcott, 128.

Dhanī Dharm Dās; **4.** Poems: Prasād, *SBS*. ii. 37; Shah, *Bījak*, 17; *MBV*. i. 256; 356.

1729. **5.** *Sukh Nidhān*: analysis, Westcott, 141.

6. *Amar Mūl*: analysis, Westcott, 148.

B. The Sikhs.

Gen. Intro.: Macauliffe; Trumpp, *Ādi Granth*, London, 1870; Dorothy Field, *The Religion of the Sikhs*, London, 1914.

1469–1538. Nānak; **1.** Hymns; **2.** *Nirākāra Mīmāṁsā*; **3.** *Adbhuta Gītā*.

d. 1574. Amar Dās; **4.** Hymns.

d. 1581. Rām Dās; **5.** Hymns.

d. 1606. Arjan; **6.** Hymns; **7.** *Ādi Granth*: ETr. Macauliffe; partial ETr. Trumpp; a few pieces in ETr. Dorothy Field.

Late 16th. Gur Dās; **8.** *Bhai Gur Dās ki Wār*: partial ETr. Macauliffe, IV. 241.

d. 1708. Gobind Siṅgh; **9.** *Granth of the Tenth Guru*; **10.** *Pañjgranthī*, the Prayer Book.

C. The Dādūpanth.

Gen. Intro.: Traill, *ERE*. iv. 385.

1544–1603. Dādū; **1.** Bānī: Prasād, *SBS*. i. 235; ii. 90. ETr. of two chapters, Siddons, *JASB*. vi. 484; reproduced, Wilson, *Sects*, 106.

Fl. 1600. Rajjab Dās; **2.** *Bānī*.

1598–1689. Sundar Dās; **3.** *Bānī*; **4.** *Gyān-Samudra*; **5.** *Sundar Vilās*. Selections: Purohita Harinārāyaṇa, *Sundarsār*, Benares, 1918; Prasād, *SBS*. i. 106; ii. 107.

Nischal Dās; **6.** *Vichārasāgara*: Text, Bombay, 1900; **7.** *Vṛitti Prabhākara*.

c. 1740. Giridhar Kabraya; **8.** *Kuṇḍaliyā*.

D. Lāl Dāsīs.

Gen. Intro.: Powlett, *Ulwur*, 53, including a few pieces in ETr.

E. Satnāmīs.

Gen. Intro.: Sarkar, *Mod. Rev.* 1916, 383; Wilson, *Sects*, 356; Bhaṭṭāchārya, *HCS*. 491; Russell and Hira Lal, 307.

c. 1750. Jagjīvan Dās; **1.** *Gyān Prakāś*; **2.** *Mahāpralay*; **3.** *Pratham Granth*: Prasād, *SBS*. i. 117; ii. 130; Grierson, *LH*. 87.

c. 1770. Dūlan Dās; **4.** Poems: Prasād, *SBS*. i. 133; ii. 157.

F. Charan Dāsīs.

Gen. Intro.: Grierson, *ERE*. iii. 365.

1703-82. Charan Dās; **1.** Works: Grierson, *ERE*. iii. 368; Prasād, *SBS*. i. 142, 247; ii. 179; Wilson, *Sects*, 178.

c. 1750. Sahajo Bāī; **2.** Poems: Prasād, *SBS*. i. 154; ii. 191.

c. 1750. Dayā Bāī; **3.** Poems: Prasād, *SBS*. i. 167; ii. 194.

ix. Śaiva Literature.

A. General Śaiva Literature.

I. Sanskrit: used everywhere.

1. *Śatarudrīya*, a hymn in the *Black Yajurveda*, *Taittirīya S.*, IV. v; Keith, *TS*. ii. 353; also *White Yajus*, xvi: Griffith, 140. Recited in Śaiva temples every morning.

2. *Śvetāśvatara U.*: No. 8, p. 364, above.

3. Śaiva sections in *MHB*., especially *Śivasahasranāma*. See § 109.

4. Śaiva Upanishads: see § 112.

5 Śaiva Puranic documents: see §§ 159; 206; 226.

6. *Mahimnastava*: Text and ETr. Arthur Avalon, Calcutta, 1917.

7. *Śivānandalaharī*, a poem for children.

II. Vernacular, and therefore Local, but not Sectarian.

a. Tamil:

5th or 6th. Nakkīra Deva; **1.** *Tirumuruhattuppadai*: Barnett, *BMCTB*. iii; Fraser, *ERE*. v. 23.

15th c. Aruṇa-giri; **2.** *Tiru-puhal*.

16th c. Varatuṅga Pāṇḍya; **3.** *Liṅga Purāṇa*.

16th c. Ativīrarāma Pāṇḍya; **4.** *Kūrma Purāṇa*.

17th c. Parañjoti; **5.** *Tiru-Viḷaiy-āḍar-purāṇam*: Pope, *TV*., pp. xvii, xxxvii; *BMCTB*. vi.

Mid 17th. Śiva-guṇa-yogī; **6.** *Viveka-chintāmaṇi*, a Śaiva cyclopaedia.

17th c. Śiva Prakāśa Svāmī; **7.** Tamil Tr. of *Prabhu = liṅga = līlā* (No. 16, p. 387, below): Rice, *KL*. 49; **8.** Tam. Tr. of *Siddhānta = śikhāmaṇi*, No. 6, p. 387, below.

17th c. Kumāraguruparasvāmī; **9.** Religious poems.

1785. Śiva-jñāna-yogī; **10.** *Kāñchī-purāṇa*.

b. Telugu:

c. 1400. Vemana: Life, *Vemana*, Rāmakṛishṇa Rau, Madras. **1**. *Padyamulu*, Verses: ETr. Brown, *The Verses of Vemana*, republished, Madras, 1911; Partial ETr. Gover, *FSSI*. 269 ff. ETr. of a few verses, Barnett, *HI*. 109.

c. 1420. Śrīnath and others: **2.** portions of *Skanda P*.

c. 1500. Rājaliṅga; **3.** *Kūrma P*.

c. 1550. Haribhadra; **4.** *Matsya P*.

c. Bengālī:

Not a large literature: Sen, *HBLL*. 235 ff.

c. 1750. Rāmeśvara; **1.** *Śivāyana*: Sen, *HBLL*. 249.

d. Gujarātī:

Mid 18th. Śivānand; **1.** Lyrics: Jhaveri, *MGL.* 161.

e. Malayalim:

17th c. **1.** *Śiva P.*; and **2.** *Brahmāṇḍa P.*

f. Marāṭhī:

13th c. Jñānadeva; **1.** *Amritānubhava.*
Mukundarāj; **2.** *Mūlasthambha.*

g. Kanarese:

17th c. Sahajānanda; **1.** *Bhaktirasāyana*: Rice, *KL.* 60 n. 1.

B. Literature of Pāśupata Śaivas.

1. LAKULĪŚA-PĀŚUPATAS.

Gen. Intro.: R. D. Bhandarkar, *JBBRAS.* 1908, 151; *ARAD.* 1906-7, 179; Bhandarkar, *VS.* 116 ff.

1. *Vāyu P.*, chs. xi. xiv, xv, xxiii; *Liṅga P.*, ch. vii; *Kūrma P.*, pt. i, ch. liii; *Śiva P.*, Vāyavīya S., pt. ii, chs. ix-x.

2. Early philosophical texts, sūtras, bhāshyas, kārikās, now lost: Mādhava, *SDS.* vi: Cowell, 103; Bhandarkar, *VS.* 120-1.

c. 1380. Mādhava; **3.** *Lakulīśa-Pāśupata*, *SDS.* vi: Cowell, 103.

2. KĀPĀLIKAS.

Intro.: Bhandarkar, *VS.* 118, 127.

3. GORAKSHANĀTHĪS.

Gen. Intro.: Wilson, *Sects*, 213; Grierson, *ERE.* vi. 328; Garbe, *SY.* 42: Richard Schmidt, *Fakire und Fakirtum*, Berlin, 1908. Books in Sanskrit, unless otherwise described.

c. 1200. Gorakshanātha; **1.** *Haṭha-yoga*: Hall, 15; **2.** *Goraksha-śataka*: Hall, 18; **3.** *Jñānāmrita*: Hall, 15; **4.** *Goraksha-kalpa*: Wilson, *Sects*, 216; **5.** *Goraksha-sahasranāma*: Wilson, ib.; **6.** Hindī works in verse attributed to him: *MBV.* I. 241.

Svātmārāma; **7.** *Haṭha-yoga-pradīpikā*, on 1: Hall, 15. Text and ETr. in *SBH.*

8. *Gheraṇḍa Saṁhitā*: Text and ETr. in *SBH.* GTr. in Richard Schmidt, op. cit.

9. *Śiva Saṁhitā*: Hall, 14; 17. Text and ETr., S. C. Vasu in *SBH.*

10. *Haṭha-saṅketa-chandrikā*: Hall, 17.

Madīdhara; **11.** *Goraksha-paddhati*: a Hindī Tr. of No. 4, with a *bhāshya.*

The following works are used by Kānphaṭā Yogīs to-day, and some of them are attributed to Goraksha: *Viśvānanda T.*; *Siddha-siddhānta-paddhati* (see Hall, 15); *Nirañjana P.*; *Yoga-mañjarī*; *Goraksha-kaumudī*; *Goraksha-gītā*; *Goraksha-pañchaya.*

C. Literature of Āgamic Śaivas.

1. GENERAL.

THE ŚAIVA ĀGAMAS: See Ramaṇa Śāstrī's ETr. of Appaya Dīkshita's *Śivārkamaṇidīpikā*, No. 7, p. 385; Chatterji, *KS.* 7; Schomerus, *SS.* 7-23 (chronology erroneous). ETr. of parts of the *Mrigendra Ā.* (the first section of the *Kāmika Ā.*) in the *Siddhānta Dīpikā*, iv ff.

2. SANSKRIT SCHOOL OF ŚAIVA SIDDHĀNTA.

All books in Sanskrit.

1. Early writers, otherwise unknown, mentioned by Mādhava, *SDS*, vii.

c. 1380. Mādhava; **2.** *Śaiva Darśana*, *SDS*. vii: ETr. Cowell, 112.

c. 1400. Śrīkaṇṭha Śivāchārya; **3.** *Śaiva Bhāshya* on *Vedānta-sūtras*: Partial ETr. in the *Siddhānta Dīpikā*, i ff.

16th c. Śambhudeva; **4.** *Śaiva-siddhānta-dīpikā*: Bhandarkar, *VS*. 126–7. Tamil Tr., No. 31, p.386, below. **5.** *Śambhu-paddhati*: dogmatic and ritual.,

6. *Śiva P.*, Vāyavīya S.: Bhandarkar, *VS*. 127, 160.

c. 1600. Appaya Dīkshita; **7.** *Śivārkamaṇidīpikā*, a comm. on 3. Partial ETr. V. V. Ramaṇa Śāstrī, Madras.

c. 1650. Nīlakaṇṭha; **8.** *Kriyāsāra*, containing a synopsis of 3.

9. *Soma-Śambhu-paddhati-vṛitti*: comm. on No. 5.

3. TAMIL SCHOOL OF ŚAIVA SIDDHĀNTA.

Intro.: No history exists; but see, Frazer, *ERE*. v. 23 ff.; Schomerus, *SS*.; Nallasvāmī Pillai, *SSS*. the file of the *Siddhānta Dīpikā*, where numerous Trs. from the Tamil may be read; and Sundaram Pillai, *Some Mile-stones in Tamil Lit.* The System: Hoisington's Tr. of *Śiva-prakāśa*, No. 18, below, is the best exposition in English; the work of Schomerus in German is more recent. All books in Tamil.

7th c. Ñāna-sambandhar; **1.** Hymns. ETrs. Kingsbury and Phillips.

7th c. Appar: Nallasvāmī Pillai, *Saint Appar*, Madras, 1910. **2.** Hymns: ETrs. Kingsbury and Phillips.

8th or 9th. Sundara-mūrti; **3.** Hymns. ETrs. Kingsbury and Phillips. For the chronology of THE THREE, see *BMCTB*. v; art., in *Tamilian Antiquary*, 1909; Frazer, *ERE*. v. 23.

c. 800. Tirumūlar; **4.** *Tirumantram*: ETrs. *Siddhānta Dīpikā*, i ff.

c. 900. Māṇikka Vāchaka. Date: *BMCTB*. v; S. Aiyangar, *TS*. 401; Frazer, *ERE*. v. 23; **5.** *Tiru-vāchakam*: Text, Intro., ETr., and Comm., Pope, *Tiruvāśagam*, Oxford, 1900; ETrs. Kingsbury and Phillips; two ETrs. Arunachalam, *STT*. 7; ETr. of one hymn, Barnett, *HI*. 83; **6.** *Tirukkovaiyar*.

10th c. Paṭṭiṇattu Piḷḷai; **7.** Hymns: Frazer, *ERE*. v. 23; *BMCTB*. vi.

c. 1000. Nambiy-āṇḍār-nambi: S. Aiyangar, *TS*. 220; **8.** *Toṇḍar-tiruvantādi* and other poems.

Early 12th. Śekkirār; **9.** *Periya Purāṇam*: Frazer, *ERE*. v. 23; Pope, *TV*. xciv; *BMCTB*. vi.

12th c. Kāñchī Appar; **10.** *Kanda Purāṇam*, Tr. of the *Skanda Purāṇa*.

12th c. Uyyavandan; **11.** *Tiruvuntiyār*: 45 triplets. ETr. *Siddhānta Dīpikā*, xiv.

12th c. Uyyavandan; **12.** *Tirukkaliṛṛuppaḍiyār*: 100 quatrains.

c. 1223. Meykaṇḍa; **13.** *Śiva-jñāna-bodha*: 12 sūtras: ETr. Barnett, *HI*. 77. ETr. Nallasvāmī Piḷḷai, *SJB*.

c. 1250. Aruḷnandi Śivāchārya; **14.** *Śiva-jñāna-siddhi*, on No. 13. ETr. Nallasvāmī Piḷḷai, Madras, 1913; partial GTr. in Schomerus, *SS*.; **15.** *Irupāvirupathu* (mainly on *Pāśa*): 20 stanzas. ETr. *Siddhānta Dīpikā*, xiii.

c. 1250. Manavāchakam Kaḍandān; **16.** *Uṇmai-viḷakka*, the Light of Reality: 54 quatrains: ETr. Nallasvāmī Piḷḷai, *SSS*. 5.

c. 1280. Marai Jñāna-sambandha; **17.** *Saiva-samaya-neṛi*. ETr. *Siddhānta Dīpikā*, vi.

c. 1313. Umāpati Śivāchārya: Pope, *TV*. xciii; **18.** *Śiva-prakāśa*: 100 quatrains: ETr. Hoisington, *JAOS*. 1854; **19.** *Tiru-aruḷ-payan*: 100 couplets on divine grace: ETr. Pope, *TV*. xxxix ff.; **20.** *Viñā-veṇba*: 13 quatrains; ETr. *Siddhānta Dīpikā*, xiv. **21.** *Poṛṛipakrodai*: 190 lines; **22.** *Koḍi-Kavi*: 4 quatrains: ETr. *Siddhānta Dīpikā*, xiv. **23.** *Neñchu-viḍu-tūtu*: 258 lines; **24.** *Uṇmai-neṛi-viḷakka*: 6 quatrains; **25.** *Saṅkalpa-nirākaraṇa*: 20 stanzas; **26.** *Koyil Purāṇam*.

15th c. Kaṇṇuḍaiya Vaḷḷalār; **27.** *Oḷivil-oḍukkam*: theological treatise in verse.

Early 18th. Tāyumānavar; **28.** Hymns: a few ETrs. in *Siddhānta Dīpikā*, i ff.; in Arunachalam, *STT*. 28; in *Prabuddha Bhārata* during 1913; and one ETr. Barnett, *HI*. 85.

Died 1785. Śiva-jñāna-yogī: *BMCTB*. vi; **29.** *Drāviḍa-mahā-bhāshya*, on No. 13: ETr. Nallasvāmī Piḷḷai, *SJB*.;, **30.** *Laghu Ṭīkā* on No. 13; **31.** *Siddhānta-dīpam*: Tamil Tr. of the *Saiva-siddhānta-dīpikā*, No. 4, p. 385; **32.** *Tattuva Pirakāśa* (i.e. Tattva-prakāśa); **33.** *Tattuva Kattalei*, a summary of No. 32: ETr. by Hoisington, *JAOS*. 1854.

4. KASHMIR ŚAIVISM.

Intro.: Chatterji, *KS*. Literature in Sanskrit.

Early 9th. Vasugupta; **1.** *Śiva-sūtras*: *KS*. 8, 37.

Late 9th. Kallaṭa; **2.** *Spanda-kārikās*: *KS*. 15, 37.

End 9th. Somānanda; **3.** *Śiva-dṛishṭi*: *KS*. 17, 37.

Early 10th. Utpalāchārya; **4.** *Pratyabhijñā-kārikās*, with a comm.: a summary of the teaching of 3: *KS*. 19, 38.

Mid 10th. Rāmakaṇṭha; **5.** *Spanda-vivṛiti*, on 2: *KS*. 16, 28, 38.

Late 10th. Utpala Vaishṇava; **6.** *Spanda-pradīpikā*, on 2: *KS*. 16, 38.

c. 1000. Abhinava Gupta; **7.** *Pratyabhijñā-vimarśinī*, on 4; **8.** *Pratyabhijñā-vivṛiti-vimarśinī*, on 4: *KS*. 20, 38; **9.** *Tantrāloka*: deals with Śaivism in all its aspects: *KS*. 21; **10.** *Paramārthasāra*: a sketch of Kashmir Saivism in 105 verses. Text and ETr. Barnett, *JRAS*. 1910, 707; 1338. Based on the *Ādhāra-kārikās*, about which there is a dispute: *JRAS*. 1912, 257, 474; Chatterji, *KS*. 11, n. 3.

11th c. Bhāskara; **11.** *Śiva-sūtra-vārttika*, on 1: *KS*. 9, 39.

11th c. Kshemarāja; **12.** *Śiva-sūtra-vimarśinī*, on 1: *KS*. 9, 35, 39. ETr. P. T. Śrīnivāsa Iyengar, Allahabad, 1912: see Barnett, *JRAS*. 1912, 1107; **13.** *Spanda-sandoha*: is on the first sūtra of 2, but explains the teaching of the whole work: *KS*. 16.

11th c. Yogarāja; **14.** Comm. on 10. ETr. Barnett, *JRAS*. 1910, 718.

Late 12th. Jayaratha; **15.** Comm. on 9: *KS*. 39.

14th c. Lal Ded; **16.** Kashmīri verses: Grierson, *JRAS*. 1918, 157.

1380. Mādhava; **17.** Essay in *SDS*. viii: Cowell, 128.

18th c. Śivopādhyāya; **18.** Comm. on *Vijñāna Bhairava Tantra*: Chatterji, *KS*. 39.

5. VĪRA ŚAIVISM.

Gen. Intro.: Enthoven, *ERE*. vii. 71; Bhandarkar, *VS*. 131; Rice, *KL*. chs. iv and v. Books in Sanskrit, unless otherwise described.

1. Vīra Śaiva documents in the Āgamas.

c. 1200. Somanātha of Pālakūrki; 2. *Basava P.*, Tel.; 3. *Life of Paṇḍitārādhya* in mixed Sansk. and Tel. verse.

4. *Vachanas*, sermons in Kan.: Rice, *KL.* 38; 40. ETr. of those attributed to Basava in MS. by Rao Sahib P. G. Halkatti, Bijapur.

c. 1350. Rāghavāṅka; 5. *Siddharāma P.*, Kan.: Rice, *KL.* 43.

14th c. Śiva-yogī; 6. *Siddhānta-śikhāmaṇi.* Tam. Tr., no. 8, p. 383, above.

1369. Bhīma Kavi; 7. *Basava P.*, Kan., based on No. 2: Rice, *KL.* 44: abridged ETr. Würth, *JBBRAS.* 1865-6; ETr. of one piece, Rice, *KL.* 47.

c. 1370. Mallanārya; 8. *Vīraśaivāmṛita.*, Kan.: Rice, *KL.* 49.

c. 1385. Padmanāṅka; 9. *Padmarāja P.*, Kan.: Rice, *KL.* 48.

c. 1400. Siṅgi-rāja; 10. *Mahā Basava Charitra*, Kan.: Rice, *KL.* 49. For Tel. Tr., see No. 17, below, and for Tam. Tr. see No. 24, below.

c. 1400. Maritoṇṭaḍārya; 11. Comm. on No. 6; 12. *Kaivalya-sāra.*

15th c. Channa Vṛishabhendra Svāmī; 13. *Vīra-Śaiva-sarvotkarsha-pradīpikā.*

15th c. Gurudeva; 14. *Vīra-Śaiva-āchāra-pradīpikā.*

15th c. Toṇṭaḍ Siddheśvara; 15. *Vīra-Śaiva-pradīpikā.*

c. 1460. Chāmarasa; 16. *Prabhu-liṅga-līlā*, Kan.: Rice, *KL.* 49: Tam. Tr., no. 7, p. 383, above. 17. Tel. Tr. of No. 10.

c. 1585. Virūpāksha; 18. *Channa Basava P.*, Kan.: Rice, *KL.* 49. Abridged ETr. Würth, *JBBRAS.* 1805-6.

17th c. Channa Sadāśiva Yogīśvara; 19. *Śiva-yoga-pradīpikā.*

17th c. Śiva-guṇa-yogī, or Nija-guṇa-Śiva-yogī; 20. *Viveka-chintāmaṇi*, Śaiva encyclopaedia; 21. Kan. Tr. of No. 20: Rice, *KL.* 68.

1657. Shaḍakshara Deva: Rice, *KL.* 62, 67; 22. *Rājaśekhara Vilāsa*, famous Kan. literary work; 23. *Śabara-Śaṅkara-vilāsa* (Kan.): Partial ETr. Barnett, *BSOSL.* 1918, p. 4.

17th c. Śiva Prakāśa; 24. Tamil Tr. of No. 10.

18th c. Monāppa; 25. *Vīra-Śaiva-āchāra-kaustubha.*

The dates of the following works seem to be uncertain:

Śrīpati Paṇḍitārādhya; 26. *Śrīkara Bhāshya* on *Vedānta-sūtras.* First half published in Telugu character at Secunderabad, 1893.

Svaprabhānanda Śivāchārya; 27. *Śivādvaita-mañjarī*: *Siddhānta Dīpikā*, xi. 128.

Nañjanāchārya; 28. *Vedasāra-Vīra-Śaiva-Chintāmaṇi.*

Nandikeśvara; 29. *Liṅga-dhāraṇā-chandrikā* (Semi-Liṅgāyat).

Siddhavīraṇa; 30. *Anādi-Vīra-Śaiva-sāra-saṅgraha.*

Both authors and dates of the following seem to be unknown.

31. *Vīra-Śaiva-mata-saṅgraha*; 32. *Vīra-Śaiva-chandrikā*; 33. *Vīra-Śaiva-dharma-śiromaṇi*; 34. *Vīra-Śaiva-mata-prakāśikā.*

6. THE SITTARS.

c. 16th. Patirakiriyar; 1. Hymns: ETr. Gover, *FSSI.* 158.

Paṭṭinattu Piḷḷai (?); 2. Hymns: ETrs. Gover, *FSSI.* 160.

c. 17th. 3. *Śiva-vākyam*: ETrs. Gover, *FSSI.* 170; Barnett, *HI.* 88.

17th c. Tattuva Rayar; 4. *Adaṅgan-muṟai.*

x. Literature of the Sect of Brahmā.

Mārkaṇḍeya P. xlv. 27–35; xlvi. 14–21. ETr. Pargiter, *MP.*
Padma P. i: see Wilson, *Works*, iii. 24.

xi. Śākta Literature.

Gen. Intro.: No historical intro. exists. The best intro. on the teaching and the cult is Avalon's Intro., *TGL.* See also his art. in *Mod. Rev.*, Aug. and Sept., 1917. On the literature, see an anonymous article in *SJM.* iii. 1897.

EARLY DOCUMENTS:

3rd or 4th. **1.** *MBH.* IV. vi: Mazumdar, *JRAS.* 1906, 355; Jacobi, *ERE.* v. 117. ETr. Avalon, *HG.* 69; **2.** *MBH.* VI. xxiii: ETrs. Avalon, *HG.* 115; Muir, *OST.* iv. 432.

4th c. **3.** *Harivaṁśa*, ch. lix: ETr. Avalon, *HG.* 82; **4.** *Harivaṁśa*, ch. clxvi.

5th or 6th c. **5.** *Chaṇḍī-māhātmya* in *Mārkaṇḍeya P.*: Vernac. versions: Bengālī, 16th c.; Punjābī, 17th c.; Malayalim, 17th c. ETr. Pargiter, *MP.*; Wortham, *JRAS.* xiii. 355.

Early 7th. Bāṇa; **6.** *Chaṇḍīśataka*: Text, ETr., &c., Quackenbos, *SPM.*

TANTRIK WORKS:

Gen. Intro.: Lists of 64 Tantras in *Vāmakeśvara T.*, *Kulachūḍāmaṇi T.*, and *Āgama-tattva-vilāsa*, with an extra list of 83 in the last-mentioned work; and a list in three sections, each containing 64, in *Mahāsiddhasāra T.*: Avalon, *TT.* I. ii; iv. 4; Dutt, *MT.* v. For early MSS., see H. P. Śāstrī, i and ii. For Śākta Yoga, see Avalon, *The Serpent Power*, London, 1919.

7th c. **7.** *Kubjikāmata T.*: H. P. Śāstrī, I. lxxxvii.

8. *Pārameśvaramata T.*: H. P. Śāstrī, I. lii, lxxvii; II. xxi.

Early 8th. Bhavabhūti; **9.** *Mālatī-Mādhava*: Rapson, *ERE.* iv. 886: ETr. Wilson, *TH.* II. i.

10. *Niśvāsatattva S.*: H. P. Śāstrī, I. lxxvii.

11. *Mahākaulajñāna-vinirṇaya*: H. P. Śāstrī, II. xviii.

12. *Rudra-yāmala T.*: H. P. Śāstrī, II. xxii; Wilson, *Sects*, 258 n.

13. *Vāmakeśvara T.*: said to be a part of the *Bhairava-yāmala T.* Bhandarkar, *R.* 1883–4, 87; Iyengar, *Outlines*, 142; H. P. Śāstrī, I. lxxiii; II. xxiii; Avalon, *TT.* iv. 4.

14. *Kulachūḍāmaṇi T.*: Text, intro., analysis, and ETrs. of two hymns, Avalon, *TT.* iv.

15. *Kālajñāna T.*: Analysis: H. P. Śāstrī, II. xx.

16. *Bhūtaḍāmara T.*: on magic: H. P. Śāstrī, II. xxvi.

17. *Kulārṇava*: Text and Intro., Avalon, *TT.* v.

18. *Prapañchasāra T.*: Text, intro., analysis, and ETrs. of three hymns, Avalon, *TT.* iii.

19. *Paraśurāma-Bhārgava-sūtras*: a text-book of the Kaula Mārga: *SJM.* iii, 1897.

20. *Subhagodaya*: ode in 52 stanzas attributed to Gauḍapāda: see R. A. Śāstrī, *Ānandalaharī*, 14; Iyengar, *Outlines*, 143, 173.

21. *Saundaryalaharī*: Partial ETr. Avalon, *Wave of Bliss*, London, 1917; Partial ETr. R. A. Śāstrī, *Ānandalaharī*.

11th c. Lakshmaṇa Deśika; **22.** *Śāradā-tilaka T.*: Intro. and analysis, Ewing, *JAOS.* xxiii. i. 65.

Śākta Upanishads: **23.** *Tripurātāpanīya*; **24.** *Devī*; **25.** *Tripurā*; **26.** *Bhāvanā*; **27.** *Kaula*; **28.** *Shaṭchakra*: see above, p. 364, Nos. 92, 93, 94, 96, 51, 122; and *Saktaic Literature, SJM.* iii, 1897.

Later Tantras written in Bengal:

29. *Kālikā T.*: ETr. of the Blood Chapter by Blaquière, *AR.* v. See *ERE.* ii. 134, 491.

1499. Pūrṇānanda Svāmī; **30.** *Śrītattvachintāmaṇi*: of this work part of Paṭala vi is called *Shaṭchakra Nirūpaṇa*: ETr., Intro. and comm., Avalon, *The Serpent Power*, London, 1919.

c. 16th. **31.** *Yoginī T.*: MS. ETr. Munro, in Macdonald MSS.

c. 16th. **32.** *Viśvasāra T.*

33. *Vārāhī T.*

34. *Kāmadhenu T.*: MS. ETr. Munro, in Macdonald MSS.

Late 18th. **35.** *Mahānirvāṇa T.*: ETr. of pt. i, Dutt, Calcutta, 1900; ETr. of pt. i, with valuable Intro. and Comm., Avalon, *TGL.*

36. *Mahāsiddhasāra T.*

37. *Āgama-tattva-vilāsa*: contains two lists of Tantras: Dutt, *MT.*, p. v.

38. *Mantrakośa*: MS. ETr. Munro, in Macdonald MSS.

1812. Kṛishṇānanda Vāgīśa; **39.** *Tantrasāra*: Partial ETr. Mac Culloch, in Macdonald MSS.

1821. **40.** *Prāṇatoshiṇī T.*

Brahmānanda Giri; **41.** *Śāktānanda-taraṅginī*: MS. analysis, Anderson, in Macdonald MSS.

Right-hand Literature:

42. *Devī Bhāgavata Upapurāṇa*: *SJM.* iii, 1897.

43. *Agastya-sūtra*: *SJM.* iii, 1897.

44. *Lalitopākhyāna* in *Brahmāṇḍa P.*

45. *Lalitātriśatī* in *Brahmāṇḍa P.*

46. *Lalitāsahasranāma* in *Brahmāṇḍa P.*: ETr. R. A. Śāstrī, *Lalitā.*

47. *Suta S.* in *Skanda P.*

48. *Kavacha*, 50 couplets; **49.** *Kīlaka*, 14 couplets; both from the *Varāha P.*

The five Saṁhitās; **50.** *Vasishṭha*; **51.** *Sanaka*; **52.** *Śuka*; **53.** *Sanandana*; **54.** *Sanatkumāra*: Iyengar, *Outlines*, 139; R. A. Śāstrī, *Ānandalaharī*, 5, 61.

c. 1300. Lakshmīdhara[1]; **55.** Comm. on No. 21.

15th or 16th. Bhaṭṭa Nīlakaṇṭha; **56.** *Tilaka*, Comm. on No. 42.

1589. Mahīdhara; **57.** *Mantramahodadhi*: *IOM.* 885.

c. 1600. Appaya Dīkshita; **58.** Comm. on No. 21.

Early 18th. Bhāskararāya; **59.** *Varivasyā-rahasya*: Bhandarkar, *R.* 1883-4, 88; **60.** *Bhāsya* on No. 46, written, A.D. 1729: ETr. R. A. Śāstrī, *Lalitā*; **61.** *Setubandha*, Comm. on No. 13, written, A.D. 1733; **62.** Comms. on Upanishads: see p. 365.

Mid 18th. Umānandanātha; **63.** Comm. on No. 19.

[1] Vidyābhūshaṇa says he flourished under Pratāparudra of Orissa, 1504-32: see art., *Calcutta Review*, July 1915.

Śākta Lit. in the Vernaculars:

Bengālī: Sen, *HBLL*. 119, 225, 252, 335, 342, 656, 662, 712, 1003. ETr. of a large part of Mukundarāma's *Chaṇḍī-maṅgal*, Cowell, *JASB*. Dec. 1902.

Gujarātī: Jhaveri, *MGL*. 46, 149, 192.

Marāṭhī: Acworth, *BM*. xxxiii.

xii. Saura Literature.

Gen. Intro.: Bhandarkar, *VS*. 151; Chanda, *IAR*. 160, 223.

1. The Gāyatrī: *Ṛik*. III. lxii. 10.

2. Many hymns to the Sun in the Vedas.

3rd or 4th. **3.** *MBH*. III. iii. 15–79; VI. xi. 35–8; VII. lxxxii. 14–16.

4. *Rāmāyaṇa*, vi. 106: called the *Āditya-hridaya*.

A.D. 473–4. **5**. Inscription at Mandasor: *CII*. iii. 80.

6. *Mārkaṇḍeya P.*, chs. cii–cx.

7. *Bhavishya P.*, Brāhma Parvan, chs. 139–41: Wilson, *VP*. v. 382; Bhandarkar, *VS*. 153.

c. A.D. 550. Varāha Mihira; **8.** *Bṛihat S.* lviii; lx. 19. ETr. Kern, *JRAS*. 1870, 430.

Early 7th. Mayūra; **9.** *Sūrya-śataka*: Quackenbos, *SPM*.

10. *Saura S.*: H. P. Śāstrī, I. lxxvi. Cf. Schrader, *IPAS*. 11, No. 203.

11. *Sāmba Upapurāṇa*: Alberuni, Sachau, i. 130; Bloch, *ZDMG*. lxiv. 733; Vasu, *Mayūrabhañja*, iii.

12. *Sūrya U.*: ETr. Kennedy, *HM*. 346.

A.D. 1137. Gaṅgādhara; **13.** Inscription at Gayā, *EI*. ii. 338.

14. *Brahma P.* xxi–xxviii.

15. Song to the Sun in Bengālī: Sen, *VSP*. i. 23–4; 164–71.

xiii. Gāṇapatya Literature.

Gen. Intro.: Bhandarkar, *VS*. 147; Grierson, *ERE*. vi. 175.

1. *Varadatāpanīya U.*: Jacob, *EAU*. 12: see No. 120, p. 364, above.

2. *Gaṇapati U.*: Weber, *HIL*. 170. ETr. Kennedy, *HM*. 493. See No. 101, p. 364, above.

3. *Agni P.*, chs. lxxi, cccxiii.

4. *Garuḍa P.*, ch. xxiv.

5. *Gaṇeśa Upapurāṇa*: Eggeling, *IOM*. 3349; Stevenson, *JRAS*. 1846, 319; Grierson, *ERE*. vi. 176.

6. *Mudgala Upapurāṇa*: Kṛishṇa Śāstrī, *SII*. 173; *IOM*., no. 3570 ff.

III. BUDDHIST LITERATURE.

i. Buddhism as a Whole.

Hackmann, *Buddhism as a Religion*, London, 1910; Saunders, *The Story of Buddhism*, London, 1916; Macdonell, *ERE*. vii. 209; Mādhava, *SDS*. ii: ETr. Cowell, 12.

1. Assam: Scott, *ERE*. iii. 37.

2. Burma: Scott, *ERE*. iii. 37; Bigandet, *Life or Legend of Gaudama*, London, 1914.

3. Cambodia: Cabaton, *ERE*. iii. 156.

4. Ceylon: Rhys Davids, *ERE.* iii. 331; Copplestone, *Buddhism Primitive and Present, in Magadha and Ceylon*, London, 1908.

5. China: de Groot, *ERE.* iii. 552. **The Canon**: Nanjio, Oxford, 1883; *JRAS.* 1911, 562.

6. Corea: Courant, *ERE.* vii. 757; Starr, *Korean Buddhism*, Boston, 1918.

7. Japan: Ashida, *ERE.* vii. 482; Griffis, *The Religions of Japan*, New York, 1904; Reischauer, *Studies in Japanese Buddhism*, New York, 1917.

8. Java: Kern, *ERE.* vii. 495.

9. Mongolia: Parker, *ERE.* viii. 807. **The Canon**: Waddell, *ERE.* vii. 786.

10. Orissa: Vasu, *The Archaeological Survey of Mayūrabhañj*, i, Calcutta, 1911; Vasu, *The Modern Buddhism and its Followers in Orissa*, Calcutta, 1911.

11. Sumatra: Kern, *ERE.* vii. 495.

12. Tibet: Waddell, *The Buddhism of Tibet*, London, 1895; *ERE.* vii. 784. Analysis of **the Canon**, Feer, *Annales du Musée Guimet*, ii. FTrs. from the Canon, Feer, *Annales du Musée Guimet*, v.

ii. Early Buddhism and the Pāli Canon.

Gen. Intro.: **Sketch of Early Buddhism**: Kern, *MIB.*; Rhys Davids, *HIB.* **The Founder**: Oldenberg, *Buddha*; Saint-Hilaire, *The Buddha and his Religion*, London, 1914; Kern, *MIB.*; Warren, *BT.*; Geden, *ERE.* ii. 881. **Connexions with Hinduism**: Oldenberg, *LU.*; Poussin, *Opinions*, ch. v. **System**: Poussin; *WN.*; Warren, *BT.*; Seidenstücker, *PBU.*; **Ascetic orders**: Oldenberg, *Buddha*, 332; Kern, *MIB.* **Councils**: Poussin, *ERE.* iv. 179.

PĀLI CANON: **History and Chronology**: Winternitz, II. i; Macdonell, *ERE.* viii. 85; Poussin, *Opinions*, ch. i; Keith, *JRAS.* 1909, 577; Waddell, *JRAS.* 1914, 661. **Anthologies** in ETr. Saunders, *The Heart of Buddhism*, London, 1915; Thomas, *Buddhist Scriptures*, London, 1913; in GTr. Neumann, *Buddhistische Anthologie*, Leiden, 1892.

I. VINAYA P.: Winternitz, ii. 1–17. **1.** *Suttavibhaṅga*; **2.** *Mahāvagga*; **3.** *Chullavagga*: Intro. and ETr. Rhys Davids and Oldenberg, *SBE.* xiii. xvii, xx. ETr. of sections, Warren, *BT.* **4.** *Parivāra*: Winternitz, II. i. 26; *SBE.* xiii. xxiv. Kern, *MIB.* 111.

II. SUTTA P.: Winternitz, II. i. 26; Rhys Davids, *SBB.* ii, Intro.; *SBE.* xi, Intro. The bulk in CTr.: Nanjio, cols. 127–80; a few suttas in Tibetan, *AMG.* ii. 288.

a. *Dīghanikāya*: 34 long sermons: Nos. 1–23 in ETr. with intros., Rhys Davids and Oldenberg, *SBB.* ii, iii; Nos. 1–13 in GTr. Neumann, München, 1907; Nos. 13, 16, 17 in ETr. Rhys Davids, *SBE.* xi. No. 22 in ETr. Warren, *BT.* 353; fragments of other suttas, ib.

b. *Majjhimanikāya*: 152 sermons and dialogues of medium length. Complete GTr. Neumann, 3 Bde., Leipzig, 1896–1902. Nos. 26, 63, 72 in ETr. Warren, *BT.* 331, 117, 123; also portions of 38, 44, pp. 183, 187, 303. Several suttas in ETr. Rhys Davids, *SBE.* xi. Suttas 1–50 in ETr. by the Bhikku Silachara, London.

c. *Saṁyuttanikāya* : 56 groups of discourses. Partial ETr. Mrs. Rhys Davids, *The Book of the Kindred Sayings*, Oxford, 1917 ; Nos. iv and v in GTr. Windisch, *Māra und Buddha* ; No. v in ETr. Mrs. Rhys Davids, *PEB*. i. 180–91 ; numerous portions in ETr. in Warreṅ, *BT*. ; No. LVI. ii in ETr. Rhys Davids, *SBE*. xi. 133 and in FTr. Feer, *Journal Asiatique*, 1870.

d. *Aṅguttaranikāya* : 2,008 discourses : in GTr. Bhikkhu Nanatiloka, Leipzig und Breslau, 1911. Three sections in ETr. Gooneratne, Galle, Ceylon, 1913. Many portions in ETr. Warren, *BT*.

e. *Khuddakanikāya* : 15 miscellaneous works.

1. *Khuddakapāṭha* : 9 short texts for neophyte monks : Intro. : Winternitz, II. i. 61. Text and ETr. Childers, *JRAS*. 1870, 309. GTr. Seidenstücker, Breslau, 1910.

2. *Dhammapada* : 423 stanzas on the ethical and religious life. Intro. : Winternitz, II. i. 63 ; Müller, *SBE*. x. ETr. Müller, *SBE*. x; ETr. Wagiswara and Saunders (*The Buddha's Way of Virtue*), London, 1912. GTr. Neumann (*Der Wahrheitspfad*), Leipzig, 1893 : GTr. Schultze, Leipzig, 1906 ; FTr. Fernando Hu, Paris, 1878 ; ITr. Pavolini, Milan, 1908.

3. *Udāna*, i. e. inspired utterances : 80 lofty verses, each preceded by a narrative as to how it came to be uttered. Intro. : Winternitz, II. i. 66. ETr. Strong, London, 1902. No. iv. 4 in ETr. Warren, *BT*. 313. ETr. of Tibetan *Udānavarga*, Rockhill, London, 1892.

4. *Itivuttaka*, i. e. utterances of the Buddha : Intro. : Winternitz, II. i. 68 ; ETr. Moore, New York, 1908.

5. *Suttanipāta* : verse. Contains some remnants of primitive Buddhism, Fausböll. Intro. : Winternitz, II. i. 71 ; Fausböll, *SBE*. x, pt. 2 ; Oldenberg, *Aus dem Alten Indien*, Berlin, 1910, 25 ; Keith, *JRAS*. 1910, 932 ; Hoernle, *JRAS*. 1917, 134. ETr. Fausböll, op. cit. ; GTr. Neumann, Leipzig, 1911 : GTr. Pfungst, Strassburg, 1889.

6. *Vimānavatthu*, i. e. stories of the palaces of the gods.

7. *Petavatthu*, i. e. ghost stories. These two are collections of late narratives, illustrating the working of karma.

8. *Theragāthā* : Hymns of the Monks ; and 9. *Therīgāthā* : Hymns of the Nuns : Intro. : Winternitz, II. i. 79 ; Oldenberg, *Literatur des Alten Indien*, 100. Intro. and ETr. Mrs. Rhys Davids, *PEB*. i and ii.

10. *Jātaka* : 547 previous lives of the Buddha. Intro. : Winternitz, II. i. 89 ; Cowell, *The Jātaka*, 6 vols., Cambridge, 1895–1907 ; Rhys Davids, *BI*. 189 ; Feer, *Journal Asiatique*, 1875, 1895, 1897. ETr. Cowell, op. cit. ; ETrs. Rhys Davids, *Buddhist Birth Stories*, London, 1880 ; Select Jātakas in ETr. : Francis and Thomas, *Jātaka Tales*, Cambridge, 1916. GTr. Dutoit, Leipzig. Nos. 68, 82, 189, 244, 316, in ETr. Warren, *BT*., pp. 267, 269, 262, 153, 274.

11. *Niddesa* : comm. to second part of No. 5.

12. *Paṭisambhidāmagga* : of the same character as the Abhidhamma : see below.

13. *Apadāna* : 590 legends of Buddhist saints : Intro. : Rhys Davids, *ERE*. i. 603 ; Winternitz, II. i. 128.

14. *Buddhavaṁsa* : Legends of the 24 Buddhas : Winternitz, II. i. 129.

15. *Chariyāpiṭaka* : 35 previous lives of the Buddha, meant to illustrate the virtues of the Buddhas.

III. Abhidhamma P. : Character : Mrs. Rhys Davids, *ERE*. i. 19 Winternitz, II. i. 134. Age and origin : Poussin, *Opinions*, 30–44 ; 166.

1. *Dhamma-saṅgaṇi* : classifies ethical and psychological facts. ETr. Mrs. Rhys Davids, *A Buddhist Manual of Psychological Ethics*, London, 1900.

2. *Vibhaṅga* : a continuation of No. 1.

3. *Kathāvatthu* : a manual of controversy for Buddhist monks, attributed to Tissa Moggaliputta of the 3rd cent. B.C. : Oldenberg, *ZDMG.* lii. 633 ; Poussin, *ERE.* iv. 184 ; *JRAS.* 1910, 413. Analysis, Rhys Davids, *JRAS.* 1892. ETr. Shwe Zan Aung and Mrs. Rhys Davids, *Points of Controversy*, London, 1915.

4. *Puggalapaññatti* : Winternitz, II. i. 135. GTr. Nyanatiloka, Breslau, 1910.

5. *Dhātu-kathā* : catechism of psychology.

6. *Yamaka* : book of double questions.

7. *Paṭṭhāna.*

iii. Later Sthavira Literature in Pāli.

Gen. Intro. : Winternitz, II. i. 146 ; Mabel Bode, *The Pāli Literature of Burma*, London, 1909.

1. *Milinda-pañha* : Intro. : Rhys Davids, *SBE.* xxxv ; *ERE.* viii. 631 ; Garbe, *Beiträge* (Berlin, 1903), p. 95 ; Schrader, *Die Fragen des Königs Menandros*, Berlin, 1905 ; Winternitz, II. i. 139. ETr. Rhys Davids, *SBE.* xxxv–vi ; Partial GTr. Schrader, op. cit. ; sections in ETr. Warren, *BT.*

2. *Nidānakathā* : first part of the comm. on the *Jātaka* of the Canon. Intro. : Winternitz, II. i. 149. ETrs. Rhys Davids, *BBS.* 5 ; two out of three sections in ETr. in Warren, *BT.* 5.

1st c. A.D. **3.** *Netti* : dogmatic : Winternitz, II. i. 163 ; Poussin, *Opinions*, 178, n. 2.

4th c. **4.** *Dīpavaṁsa.* Intro. : Geiger, *Dīpavaṁsa und Mahāvaṁsa*, Leipzig, 1905 ; Winternitz, II. i. 168. Intro. and ETr. Oldenberg, *Dīpavaṁsa*, London, 1879.

5th c. Buddhaghosha : Winternitz, II. i. 152 : **5.** *Visuddhimagga* : Intro. : Winternitz, II. i. 164. Full analysis, Warren, *JPTS.* 1891–3. Many passages in ETr. in Warren, *BT.* ; **6.** *Samantapāsādikā* : comm. on the Vinaya ; **7.** *Sumaṅgalavilāsinī* : comm. on the *Dīghanikāya* : Winternitz, II. i. 157 ; **8.** *Papañchasūdanī* : comm. on the *Majjhimanikāya* ; **9.** *Sāratthapakāsinī* : comm. on the *Saṁyuttanikāya* ; **10.** *Manorathapūraṇī* : comm. on the *Aṅguttaranikāya* : Winternitz, II. i. 158.

11. *Jātakaṭṭhavaṇṇanā* : comm. on the *Jātaka*-book, and **12.** Comm. on the *Dhammapada*, both ascribed to Buddhaghosha : Winternitz, II. i. 154.

Late 5th. Mahanāma ; **13.** *Mahāvaṁsa* : Intro. : Geiger, *Dīpavaṁsa und Mahāvaṁsa*, Leipzig, 1905 ; Winternitz, II. i. 170. ETr. Geiger and Mabel Bode, London, 1912.

Late 10th. Upatissa ; **14.** *Bodhivaṁsa*, history of the Bodhi tree ; Winternitz, II. i. 175.

12th c. Anuruddha, a Burmese monk ; **15.** *Abhidhammatthasaṁgaha* : a most important work on Buddhist psychology and ethics. Winternitz, II. i. 177. ETr. Shwe Zan Aung and Mrs. Rhys Davids, London, 1910.

13th c. Dhammakitti ; **16.** *Dāṭhāvaṁsa*, history of the Buddha's tooth. Winternitz, II. i. 175.

13th c. Vāchissara; **17.** *Thūpavaṁsa*, history of the Stupa. Winternitz, II. i. 176.

15th c. Sīlavaṁsa; **18.** *Buddhālaṁkāra*: founded on the story of Sumedha (Warren, *BT.* 5) in the *Nidānakathā*: Winternitz, II. i. 181.

18th c. **19.** *Yogāvāchāra*: ETr. Woodward, London, 1916.

1770. **20.** *Mahālaṁkāravatthu*, a biography of the Buddha. There is a Burmese Tr. of this work, of which Bigandet's *Life or Legend of Gaudama*, London, 1914, is an ETr.

iv. Hīnayāna Literature in Sanskrit or Mixed Sanskrit.

A. BUDDHIST SANSKRIT.

Intro.: Franke, *Pali und Sanskrit*, Strassburg, 1902: Review, Rhys Davids, *JRAS.* 1903, 398; Rapson, *JRAS.* 1904, 435; discussion, *JRAS.* 1904, 457. Senart, Intro. to *Mahāvastu*; Oldenberg, *Gött. Nach.*, 1912, Heft 2; Lévi, *JA.* 1912; Winternitz, II. i. 181.

B. MAHĀSĀṄGHIKAS.

Intro.: Winternitz, II. i. 187; Anesaki, *ERE.* iv. 836.

a. Vinaya P.: Nanjio, col. 386; Nos. 1119, 1150.

b. Sutta P., *Ekottarāgama*: Nanjio, 543; Anesaki, *ERE.* iv. 836.

C. MAHĪŚĀSAKAS.

a. Vinaya P.: Nanjio, 1122.

D. LOKOTTARAVĀDINS.

Intro.: Winternitz, II. i. 183, 187; Poussin, *ERE.* ii. 740.

a. VINAYA P.

1st c., *Mahāvastu*: Winternitz, II. i. 187; Poussin, *ERE.* viii. 328, 326 n.; *Opinions*, 265, 308; Mitra, 115.

E. SARVĀSTIVĀDINS.

Intro.: Poussin, *V. et Y.*; *Opinions*, 30, 166, 177; Winternitz, II. i. 186.

a. VINAYA P.: Nanjio, 1115, 1127, 1132, 1135, 1136, 1160, 1161, 1162. Nanjio, 1160: Sansk. text: *JA.* 1913, ii. 465; Hoernle, *MRBL.* 357, 358. Many Avadāna works are dependent on this Vinaya: Winternitz, II. i. 217, 222.

b. SUTTA P.: Hoernle, *MRBL.* 166.

c. ABHIDHARMA P.: Takakusu, *JPTS.* 1905, 67.

Kātyāyanīputra; **1.** *Jñānaprasthāna-śāstra*: Nanjio, 1273; comms., Nanjio, 1263, 1264.

Śāriputra; **2.** *Abhidharma-saṅgītiparyāyapāda*, Nanjio, 1276.
Vasumitra; **3.** *Abhidharma-prakaraṇapāda*, Nanjio, 1277.
Devaśarman; **4.** *Abhidharma-vijñānakāyapāda*, Nanjio, 1281.
Vasumitra; **5.** *Abhidharma-dhātukāyapāda*, Nanjio, 1282.
Mahāmaudgalyāyana; **6.** *Abhidharma-skandhapāda*, Nanjio, 1296.
Mahāmaudgalyāyana; **7.** *Prajñaptipāda-śāstra*, Nanjio, 1317.

On the first section of no. 7 are based three famous dependent works, namely:

Early 4th. Vasubandhu; **8.** *Abhidharma-kośa*, a set of verses, *Kārikās*, Nanjio, 1270, with a commentary, Nanjio, 1267, 1269. Poussin, *V. et Y.*; *ERE.* iv. 131; Lévi, *ERE.* i. 20; Winternitz, II. i. 257.

4th c. Saṅghabhadra; **9.** *Nyāyānusāra-śāstra*, a criticism of 8: Nanjio, 1265.

Yaśomitra; **10.** *Abidharma-kośa-vyākhyā*, a comm. on 8: Nanjio, 1267; Poussin, *V. et Y.*; *ERE.* iv. 131; Mitra, 3; Lévi, *ERE.* i. 20; Jacobi, *ERE.* ii. 201; Winternitz, II. i. 257.

F. MŪLASARVĀSTIVĀDINS.

VINAYA P.: Nanjio, col. 441.

Prātimoksha-sūtra: ETr. from the Tibetan, Vidyābhūshaṇa, *JASB.* 1915.

G. DHARMAGUPTAS.

VINAYA P.: Nanjio, 1117, 1128; Hoernle, *MRBL.* 4, 9. *Abhinishkramaṇa-sūtra*: Nanjio, 680; Winternitz, II. i. 194. ETr. of the Chinese Text, Beal, *The Romantic Legend of Sakya Buddha*, London, 1875.

H. SAMMITĪYAS.

VINAYA P.: Nanjio, 1139.

v. Literary Works, partly Hīnayāna, partly Mahāyāna.

c. 100. Mātricheṭa: Thomas, *ERE.* viii. 495; Vidyābhūshaṇa, *JASB.* 1910, 425; Winternitz, II. i. 211; **1.** *Varṇanārhavarṇana*, a hymn in 400 stanzas: Intro. and ETr. Thomas, *IA.* xxxiv. 145; **2.** *Śatapañchāśika-stotra*, a hymn in 150 stanzas: Nanjio, 1456; Hoernle, *MRBL.* 58; **3.** *Mahārājakanika-lekha*, a letter to King Kanishka. Other works: see *ERE.* viii. 495.

Early 2nd. Aśvaghosha: Anesaki, *ERE.* ii. 159; *JRAS.* 1914, 747; Winternitz, II. i. 201; Nanjio, col. 369; **4.** *Buddhacharita*: Intro. and ETr. Cowell, *SBE.* xlix; Nanjio, 1351; **5.** *Saundarānanda-Kāvya*: H. P. Śāstrī, *JASB.* 1904, 47; Winternitz, II. i. 206; **6.** *Sūtrālaṁkāra*: FTr. Hüber, Paris, 1908; Winternitz, II. i. 208; **7.** *Vajrasūchī* and **8.** *Mahāyānaśraddhotpāda*: of doubtful authenticity, Winternitz, II. i. 209.

2nd c. Nandīśvara; **9.** *Avadānaśataka*: Full summary, Mitra, 17: Winternitz, II. i. 216; Nanjio, 1324; *JRAS.* 1915, 505; *AMG.* ii. 284. FTr. *AMG.* xviii.

10. *Karmaśataka*: Winternitz, II. i. 221; *AMG.* ii. 282.

c. 200. **11.** *Aśokāvadāna*: Mitra, 6; Winternitz, II. i. 224; Nanjio, 1344.

3rd c. **12.** *Divyāvadāna*: Winternitz, II. i. 221.

4th c. Ārya-śūra; **13.** *Jātaka-mālā*: Winternitz, II. i. 212. ETr. Speyer, London, 1895.

11th c Kshemendra; **14.** *Avadānakalpalatā*: Full summary, Mitra, 57: Winternitz, II. i. 229. A number of the tales in ETr. *JBTS.* i–v.

vi. The Mahāyāna.

Gen. Intro.: Poussin, *ERE.* viii. 330; Suzuki, *Outlines of Mahāyāna Buddhism*, London, 1907; but see Poussin's Review, *JRAS.* 1908, 885. Avalokiteśvara: Poussin, *ERE.* ii. 256.

A. MAHĀYĀNA-SŪTRAS.

1. *Saddharma-puṇḍarīka*: Poussin, *ERE.* viii. 145; Winternitz, II. i. 230. Intro. and ETr. Kern, *SBE.* xxi; Anesaki, *ERE.* iv. 839; Nanjio, 134, 139; *AMG.* ii. 242.

2. *Lalitavistara*: Winternitz, II. i. 194; partial ETr. Mitra, Calcutta, 1881; FTr. Foucaux, Paris, 1892; Nanjio, 159, 160; *AMG.* ii. 223.

3. *Kāraṇḍavyūha* (prose): Poussin, *ERE.* i. 95; ii. 259; Winternitz, II. i. 238; Mitra, 101; Nanjio, 168, 782; *AMG.* ii. 246.

4. *Gaṇḍavyūha*, or *Buddhāvataṁsaka-sūtra*: Winternitz, II. i. 242; Mitra, 90; Nanjio, 87; *AMG.* ii. 208; Griffis, 232, 242.

5. *Karuṇāpuṇḍarīka*: Mitra, 285; Nanjio, 142; *AMG* ii. 242. Partial FTr. *AMG.* v. 78, 153.

6. *Megha-sūtra* (a rain-charm with many *dhāraṇīs*): Winternitz, II. i. 269; Bendall, *JRAS.* 1880, 386; Nanjio, 244; *AMG.* ii. 265.

7. *Laṅkāvatāra-sūtra*: Analysis: Vidyābhūshaṇa, *JASB.* 1905, 159; Winternitz, II. i. 243; Poussin, *Opinions*, 392; Mitra, 113; Nanjio, 175; *AMG.* ii. 237.

8. *Samādhirāja*: Winternitz, II. i. 244; full summary in Mitra, 207; *AMG.* ii. 249.

9. *Suvarṇaprabhāsa*: Winternitz, II. i. 245; Anesaki, *ERE.* iv. 839, 840; Mitra, 241; Nanjio, 126; *AMG.* ii. 315; Hoernle, *MRBL.* 108.

10. *Rāshṭrapālaparipṛichchhā*: Winternitz, II. i. 246; Nanjio, 23 (18); *AMG.* ii. 254.

11. *Mahāsannipāta-sūtra*: Nanjio, 61; Hoernle, *MRBL.* 100.

12. *Bhadracharyā*, propitious practice: Poussin, *ERE.* ii. 749 n.; Nanjio, 1142; *AMG.* ii. 212.

13. *Upāli-paripṛichchhā-sūtra*: Vinaya of the Mahāyāna; Poussin, *Opinions*, 334 n.; Nanjio, 1109; *AMG.* ii. 197–8. Parts in FTr. *AMG.* v. 81.

B. BOOKS ON THE TEN STAGES OF THE BODHISATTVA CAREER. See Poussin, *ERE.* ii. 743.

1. *Daśabhūmaka*: a chap. of the *Mahāvastu*: Poussin, *ERE.* viii. 329; ii. 744.

2. *Daśabhūmaka-sūtra* (Mādhyamaka): Poussin, *ERE.* ii. 745 n.; Nanjio, 110, 105, 87.

3. *Daśabhūmīśvara*: an enlarged edition of No. 2, found in Nepal, Mitra, 81; Winternitz, II. i. 244; Poussin, *ERE.* ii. 745 n.

4. *Bodhisattvabhūmi* (Yogāchāra): Poussin, *ERE.* ii. 745 n., 746, 747, 750; viii. 256. It is a portion of Asaṅga's *Yogāchārabhūmi-śāstra*: Nanjio, 1170; Winternitz, II. i. 255. Summarized in English in *Le Muséon*, N.S. vi. 38; vii. 213.

C. THE PARADISE MAHĀYĀNA.

1. *Sukhāvatīvyūha*: Winternitz, II. i. 240; Poussin, *Opinions*, 266–73; Intro. and ETr. Müller, *SBE.* xlix; Nanjio, 23 (5); *AMG.* ii. 214.

2. *Sukhāvatīvyūha* (the shorter text): Intro. and ETr. Müller, *SBE.* xlix; Nanjio, 200.

3. *Amitāyurdhyāna-sūtra*: Intro. Müller, *SBE.* xlix; ETr. from

Chinese, Takakusu, *SBE.* xlix. See also Poussin, *ERE.* ii. 257 n.; Nanjio, 198.

4. Vasubandhu, *Aparamitāyus-sūtra-śāstra*: Nanjio, 1204.

D. Mādhyamaka Literature.

Gen. Intro.: Poussin, *ERE.* viii. 235. For the Prajñā-pāramitā works, see Winternitz, II. i. 247, and for other works of the same class, see Nanjio, 1–22.

1. *The five-hundred Prajñā-Pāramitā-sūtra*: Nanjio, 16.

2. *The ten-thousand PP.*: Nanjio, 5.

3. *The twenty-five-thousand PP.*: Nanjio, 4.

4. *The Vajrachchhedikā PP.* (diamond-cutter): Nanjio, 10. Intro. and ETr. Müller, *SBE.* xlix; Hoernle, *MRBL.* 176, 178, 214.

5. *The Shorter*, and **6.** *The Longer PP. Hridaya*: Nanjio, 19, 935. Intro. and ETrs. Müller, *SBE.* XLIX; *Anecdota Oxon.*, i; Winternitz, II. i. 272.

Mid 2nd. Nāgārjuna: Anesaki, *ERE.* iv. 838; Winternitz, II. i. 250; Poussin, *ERE.* viii. 336; **7.** *Mūlamadhyamaka-kārikā*: Poussin, *ERE.* viii. 235; **8.** *Akutobhayā*, a comm. on 7 by the author: Winternitz, II. i. 251. GTr. from the Tibetan, Walleser, *Die mittlere Lehre des Nāgārjuna*, Heidelberg, 1911; **9.** *Yogāvatāra*: H. P. Śāstrī, II. xii. Other works: Nanjio, col. 370; Winternitz, II. i. 252; Vidyābhūshaṇa, *MSIL.* 70.

c. 300. Āryadeva: Winternitz, II. i. 254; Nanjio, col. 370; **10.** *Bodhisattvayogāchāra Chatuḥśataka*: H. P. Śāstrī, *JASB.* July, 1911; text, edited by H. P. Śāstrī, Calcutta, 1914: see *BSOSL.* 1918; **11.** *Svādhishṭhāna-prabheda*, H. P. Śāstrī, ii. xiii.

c. 600. Bhāvaviveka; **12.** *Prajñā-pradīpa*, comm. on No. 7: Nanjio, 1185; Feer, *Tandjour*, Mdo. xviii. 44–299; Poussin, *ERE.* viii. 235; **13.** *Tarkajvālā*, a criticism of the schools of philosophy: Walleser, *DAV.* 7; *AMG.* ii. 367.

Early 7th. Chandrakīrti; **14.** *Prasannapādā*, comm. on No. 7: Poussin, *ERE.* viii. 235; **15.** *Mādhyamakāvatāra* (gen. work on the Mahāyāna system): Winternitz, II. i. 251; Mitra, 1; Poussin, *Opinions*, 134; *ERE.* ii. 745, 748; viii. 332. FTr. from the Tibetan, Poussin, *Le Muséon*, viii ff.; **16.** Comm. on No. 10: text, H. P. Śāstrī, Calcutta, 1914.

7th c. Śāntideva; **17.** *Śikshāsamuchchhaya*: Winternitz, II. i. 260; Poussin, *Opinions*, 321; *ERE.* viii. 405, n. 2; **18.** *Bodhicharyāvatāra*: Intro. and ETr. Barnett, *The Path of Light*, London, 1909. FTr. Poussin, Paris, 1907. An old Bengālī version: Sen, *HBLL.* 5. See also Tawney, *JRAS.* 1908, 583; Winternitz, II. i. 263; Poussin, *ERE.* i. 97; ii. 184, 749.

8th c. Śāntarakshita; **19.** *Madhyamakālaṅkāra*: Walleser, *DAV.* 18. **20.** *Tattvasaṅgraha*, Vidyābhūshaṇa, *MSIL.* 125.

E. Vijñānavāda Literature.

Gen. Intro.: Poussin, *Opinions*, 186, 200; Lévi, Intro. to FTr. of *Mahāyāna-sūtrālaṁkāra*; Winternitz, II. i. 255.

c. 300. Asaṅga: Anesaki, *ERE.* ii. 62; Winternitz, II. i. 255; **1.** *Yogāchārabhūmiśāstra*: Nanjio, 1170, 1085; *AMG.* ii. 257. For the section called *Bodhisattvabhūmi*, see No. 4, p. 396; **2.** *Mahāyāna-sūtrālaṁkāra*: Nanjio, 1190. Intro. and FTr. Lévi, Paris, 1907, 1911; **3.** *Uttaratantra*: Nanjio, 1236: see Lévi, op. cit. i.

Early 4th. Vasubandhu: Winternitz, II. i. 256. Life in Chinese by Paramārtha, Nanjio, 1463: FTr. Takakusu in *T'oung Pao*, v, 1904; **4.** *Viṁsakārikāprakaraṇa*: 20 verses on the Vijñānavāda: FTr. from the Tibetan, Poussin, *Le Muséon*, 1912, 53; **5.** *Abhidharma kośa*: see No. 8, p. 395, above; **6.** *Paramārthasaptati*, a polemic against the Sāṅkhya: Winternitz, II. i. 258; Takakusu, *JRAS*. 1905, 16; Keith, *SS*. 87; **7.** *Gāthāsaṅgraha*: Winternitz, II. i. 257; ETr. Rockhill, *Udānavarga* (London, 1892), 213. Other works: Nanjio, cols. 371–2; Vidyābhūshaṇa, *MSIL*. 76.

8. *Mahāyāna-śraddhotpāda-śāstra*: Nanjio, 1249; Winternitz, II. i. 210; ETr. Suzuki, Chicago, 1900.

Early 7th. Chandragomin; **9.** *Śishyalekhadharma-kāvya*: Winternitz, II. i. 259; **10.** *Nyāyālokasiddhi*: Vidyābhūshaṇa, *MSIL*. 123.

Early 7th. Dharmakīrti: Keith, *JRAS*. 1916, 380.

vii. Śākta Buddhist Literature.

Gen. Intro.: Poussin, *Opinions*, 343, 378; Anesaki, *ERE*. iv. 840. Literature: Winternitz, II. i. 266; Mitra; H. P. Śāstrī, II. ii–xv; Nanjio, cols. 443–55; *AMG*. ii. 291–349; Waddell, *ERE*. vii. 785.

A. Tantras.

Early 7th. **1.** *Tathāgata-guhyaka* or *Guhya-samāja*: Winternitz, II. i. 274, 262; Mitra, 261; *AMG*. ii. 299.

7th c. **2.** *Suvarṇaprabhāsottamarāja*: *Catalogue of Hodgson MSS*. i. 8; iii. 10, 59; vi. 8; vii. 73; Mitra, 241; Nanjio, 126; *AMG*. ii. 315; Winternitz, II. i. 245; *ERE*. iv. 839. See no. 9, p. 396.

7th c. **3.** *Mahāvairochanābhisambodhi*: Anesaki, *ERE*. iv. 840; Nanjio, 530; *AMG*. ii. 307.

7th c. **4.** *Susiddhikāramahā T.*: Nanjio, 533; *AMG*. ii. 341.

7th and 8th cc. **5.** Tantras translated into Chinese by Amoghavajra: Nanjio, col. 446, esp. Nos. 1020, 1023, 1044, 1054, 1064.

Early 8th. **6.** *Vajra-mantra-dhirusanti-māra T.*: *AMG*. ii. 348.

7. *Guṇa-kāraṇḍavyūha* (verse): Mitra, 95; Winternitz, II. i. 238; Poussin, *ERE*. i. 95; ii. 259–60. See *Kāraṇḍavyūha*, above, p. 396.

8. *Mahākāla T.*: Winternitz, II. i. 274; Mitra, 172; *AMG*. ii. 298.

Prob. 9th c. **9.** *Pañchakrama*: Winternitz, II. i. 275; Poussin, *Études et Textes Tantriques*.

A.D. 965. **10.** *Śrīkālachakra T.*: Poussin, *ERE*. i. 95; Waddell, *ERE*. iv. 572; H. P. Śāstrī, II. ii; Winternitz, II. i. 275; *AMG*. ii. 292.

10th c. **11.** *He-vajra T.*: H. P. Śāstrī, II. xii; Nanjio, 1060; *AMG*. ii. 293; Getty, *GNB*. 125.

12. *Chaṇḍamahāroshaṇa T.*: H. P. Śāstrī, II. ix; *AMG*. ii. 298.

13. *Heruka T.*: H. P. Śāstrī, II. vii; *AMG*. ii. 347.

10th c. **14.** *Vajra-bhairava T.*: Nanjio, 1062; Getty, *GNB*. 146.

15. *Ḍākinī-jāla-sambara*: H. P. Śāstrī, II. xiii; *AMG*. ii. 292.

10th c. **16.** *Mañjuśrīmūla T.*: Winternitz, II. i. 275; Nanjio, 1056; *AMG*. ii. 313.

10th c. **17.** *Bhūtaḍāmara T.*: Nanjio, 1031; *AMG*. ii. 334.

B. Other Śākta Works.

10th c. Kāṇu Bhaṭṭa; **1.** *Charyācharya-viniśchaya*, Bengālī love-songs: Sen, *HBLL*. 38.

10th or 11th. **2.** *Dākārṇava*, a Bengālī aphoristic work: Sen, *HBLL.* 16.

3. *Jñānādi-sādhana*, a Sahajiyā polemical work in Bengālī: Sen, *VSP.* i. 26 ff.

12th or 13th. **4.** *Svayambhū P.*: Winternitz II. i. 267; Mitra, 249; Poussin, *ERE.* i. 94.

C. DHĀRAṆĪS.

1. The two Prajñā-pāramitā-hṛidaya sūtras: above, Nos. 5 and 6, p. 397.

2. *Ushṇīsha-vijaya Dh.*: Hoernle, *JRAS.* 1911, 460; Mitra, 267; Nanjio, 348, 1467; *AMG.* ii. 306.

3. *Aparājita-mahāpratyaṅgirā Dh.*: Hoernle, *JRAS.* 1911, 461; *MRBL.* 52; Mitra, 227; Nanjio, 1016.

4. *Aparimitāyur Dh.*, for long life: Mitra, 41; Hoernle, *MRBL.* 289; Getty, *GNB.* 9.

5. *Pañcharakshā*: Mitra, 164; Winternitz, II. i. 271.

6. *Durgati-pariśodhana Dh.*: Mitra, 84; *AMG.* ii. 306.

7. *Mahāmayūrī Dh.* against snake-poison: Mitra, 173; Winternitz, II. i. 271; Nanjio, 306; *AMG.* ii. 316.

8. *Parṇaśavarīnāma Dh.*: Mitra, 176; Nanjio, 973.

9. *Chundī-devī Dh.*: Nanjio, 344, 345, 346.

10. Eleven Tibetan Dhāraṇīs: FTr. *AMG.* v. 421.

D. STOTRA. Odes.

Intro.: Wilson, *Works*, II. ii; Winternitz, II. i. 267; Vidyābhūshaṇa, *Bauddhastotrasaṁgraha* (*BI.* 1908), Intro.

Early 6th. Chandragomin; **1.** *Tārāsādhanaśataka*: Winternitz, II. i. 269.

Mid 8th. Sarvajñamitra; **2.** *Āryatārāśragdharāstotra*: Mitra, 228; Winternitz, II. i. 268.

3. *Paramārthanāma-saṅgīti*, or *Mañjuśrīnāma-saṅgīti*; Mitra, 175; Nanjio, 1370; *AMG.* ii. 291; Poussin, *Opinions*, 399; *ERE.* viii. 405.

4. *Suprabhāta-stava*, 49 odes: Mitra, 239.

IV. JAIN LITERATURE.

Gen. Intro.: Mrs. Sinclair Stevenson, *The Heart of Jainism*, Oxford, 1915; Jacobi, *ERE.* vii. 465. **The system**: Mādhava, *SDS.* iii: Cowell, 36; Mrs. Stevenson, op. cit.; Jacobi, *Third Or. Cong.* ii. 59; *ERE*, ii. 199; vii. 467. **Cosmography**: Jacobi, *ERE.* iv. 160. **Biography**: Tank, *A Dictionary of Jaina Biography* (*A* only), Arrah, 1917. **Technical terms**: *The Jaina Gem Dictionary*, Jaini, Arrah, 1918.

LITERATURE: No history exists, but Guérinot's *Essai de Bibliographie Jaina*, Paris, 1906, contains full lists and indices of the books.

i. Śvetāmbara Literature.

THE CANON: Weber, *IA.* xvii–xxi; Jacobi, *SBE.* XXII. xxxv–xlvii; XLV. xl; *ERE.* vii. 467. Names in list given in Sanskrit, Prākṛit equivalents in brackets. The Canon is in Prākṛit. Later literature in Sanskrit, unless otherwise described.

A. Eleven AṄGA: **1.** Āchāra (Āyāra); **2.** Sūtrakṛita (Suyagaḍa); **3.** Sthāna (Thāṇa); **4.** Samavāya; **5.** Bhagavatī; **6.** Jñātadharmakathā

(Nāyadhammakahā) : **7**. Upāśakadaśā (Uvāsagadasāo) ; **8**. Antakṛitadaśā (Antagaḍadasāo) ; **9**. Anuttaraupapātikadaśā (Anuttarovavāiyadasāo) ; **10**. Praśnavyākaraṇa (Paṁhāvāgaraṇa) ; **11**. Vipāka (Vivāga) ; [12. Dṛishṭivāda : lost].

B. Twelve UPĀṄGA : **12**. Aupapātika (Ovāiya) ; **13**. Rājapraśnīya (Rāyapaseṇaiyya) ; **14**. Jīvābhigama ; **15**. Prajñāpanā (Paṇṇavaṇā) ; **16**. Jambudvīpaprajñapti (Jambuddīvapaṇṇatti) ; **17**. Chandraprajñapti (Chandapaṇṇatti) ; **18**. Sūryaprajñapti (Sūriyapaṇṇatti) ; **19**. Nirayāvalī (Nirayāvaliyāo) *or* Kalpika (Kappiyāo) ; **20**. Kalpāvataṁsikā (Kappāvadiṁsiāo) ; **21**. Pushpikā (Pupphiyāo) ; **22**. Pushpachūḍā (Pupphacūlao) ; **23**. Vṛishṇidaśā (Vaṅhidasāo).

C. Ten PRAKĪRṆA (Painna *or* Payanna) : **24**. Chatuḥśaraṇa (Chausaraṇa) ; **25**. Saṁstāra (Santhāra) ; **26**. Āturapratyākhyāna (Āurapachchakhāṇa) ; **27**. Bhaktaparijñā ; **28**. Taṇḍulavaitalika (Taṇḍulaveyāliya) ; **29**. Chandāviyyaya ; **30**. Devendrastava (Devindatthaa) ; **31**. Gaṇitavidyā (Gaṇiviyyā) ; **32**. Mahāpratyākhyāna ; **33**. Vīrastava (Vīratthaa).

D. Six CHHEDASŪTRA *or* CHHEDAGRANTHA : **34**. Niśītha ; **35**. Mahāniśītha ; **36**. Vyavahāra ; **37**. Daśāśrutaskandha, including **37** a. Kalpasūtra ; **38**. Bṛihatkalpa ; **39**. Pañchakalpa.

E. Two sūtras without a common name : **40**. Nandī ; **41**. Anuyogadvāra.

F. Four MŪLASUTRA *or* MŪLAGRANTHA : **42**. Uttarādhyayana ; **43**. Āvaśyaka ; **44**. Daśavaikālika ; **45**. Piṇḍaniryukti.

Note : For some variation in the canonical list, see Mrs. Stevenson, *HJ*. 13.

TRANSLATIONS : ETrs. of Nos. 1, 3, 37 a, and 42, Jacobi, *SBE*. xxii and xlv ; of No. 7, Hoernle, Calcutta, 1888 ; of Nos. 8 and 9, Barnett, *OTF*. London, 1907.

WRITERS :

Prajñāpanā, 15, is attributed to Ajjasāma (Weber, *IA*. xvii. 282) and also to *Kālakāchārya* (Guérinot, 176).

Chatuḥśarana, 24, is attributed to Vīrabhadra.

Vyavahāra, 36, *Daśāśrutaskhandha*, 37, including *Kalpa-sūtra*, 37 a, and *Bṛihatkalpa*, 38, are attributed to Bhadrabāhu, about 300 B.C.

Nandī-sūtra, 40, and part of the *Kalpa-sūtra*, 37 a, may possibly be by Devarddhi, who arranged the Canon : Weber, *IA*. xxi. 212.

Daśavaikālika, 44, is attributed to Sijjambhava.

EXTRA-CANONICAL LITERATURE.

300 B.C. Bhadrabāhu ; **46**. Niryuktis, i.e. brief comms. in Prākṛit verse, on Nos. 1, 2, 18, 36, 37, 42, 43, 44 ; **47**. *Upasargahara-stotra* (Prāk.), an ode to Pārśvanātha : text and ETr. Jacobi, *Kalpasūtra* (Leipzig, 1879), p. 12 n.

Kālakāchārya ; **48**. An old Jain astronomy : Guérinot, 22. Some say there were five Kālakāchāryas : Guérinot, 176.

3rd or 4th. Vimala Sūri ; **49**. *Paümachariya* (Prāk.) : a Jain Rāmāyaṇa. Jacobi, *Mod. Rev*. 1914, 574 ; *ERE*. vii. 467.

4th or 5th. Umāsvāti ; **50**. *Tattvārthādhigama-sūtra* : analysis in English, Mitra, *Notices*, vii. 187 ; Text, GTr., and notes, Jacobi, *ZDMG*. lx. 287 and 512 ; Text, Intro. ETr. and Comm., J. L. Jainī, Arrah, 1919.

4th or 5th. Siddhasena Divākara ; **51**. *Kalyāṇamandira-stotra*, ode to Pārśvanātha : Text and GTr. Jacobi, *I. St*. xiv. 375 ; **52**. *Nyāyāvatāra* (Logic) : Text and ETr. Vidyābhūshaṇa, Arrah, 1915.

A.D. 514. The Canon. Devarddhi presided, possibly author of the *Nandī-sūtra*, No. 40, and of part of the *Kalpa-sūtra*, No. 37 a.

Early 6th. Siddhasena Gaṇi; **53.** *Tattvārtha-ṭīkā*, a comm. on No. 50 **54.** A number of Prāk. bhāshyas, i.e. prose comms., on the canonica texts: see Leumann, *ZDMG.* xlvi. 581; Jacobi, *ZDMG.* lx. 289: Vidyābhūshaṇa, *MSIL.* 22; Guérinot, 156.

Early 7th. Mānatuṅga, Guérinot, 392; **55.** *Bhaktāmara-stotra*: Text and GTr. Jacobi, *I. St.* xiv. 359; Guérinot, 204; **56.** *Bhayahara-stotra*: Guérinot, 74, 372; Peterson, i. 52.

c. 800. Bappabhaṭṭi; **57.** *Sarasvatī-stotra*: Bhandarkar, *R.* 1883-4, 15; Duff, *CI.* 65.

8th or 9th. Jayavallabha; **58.** *Vajjālaggā* (Prāk.): Bhandarkar, *R.* 1883-4, 16; Konow and Lanman's *Karpūra-mañjarī* (*HOS.*), 193; Jacobi, *ERE.* vii. 467; *Mod. Rev.* 1914, 573; Guérinot, 67, 80, 84.

Early 9th. Mallavādin: Vidyābhūshaṇa, *MSIL.* 34; Peterson, iv. 4.

Late 9th. Haribhadra: Life and date, Pullé, *GSAI.* i. 47; viii. 159; ix. 1; xii. 225; **59.** Comms. on nos. 15, 16, 43, 44: Leumann, *ZDMG.* xlvi. 581; Guérinot, 56, 69, 144, 369, 433; **60.** *Shaḍdarśanasamuchchhaya*: Text and Intro.: Pullé, loc. cit. FTr. of last chapter, Suali, *Le Muséon*, 1908, ix. 277; **61.** *Samarāichchhakahā*: Prāk. tales: Jacobi, *ERE.* vii. 467; *Mod. Rev.* 1914, 576; Guérinot, 67.

Late 9th. Śīlāṅka: Leumann, *ZDMG.* xlvi. 581; **62.** Comm. on No. 1: A.D. 863: Guérinot, 79, 132; Peterson, iii. 36; **63.** Comm. on No. 2: Guérinot, 65, 133; **64.** Comm. on part of No. 43.

A.D. 906. Siddharshi: Life and date: Guérinot, 417; **65.** *Upamiti-bhava-prapañchākathā*: Prāk. allegory: Intro. and partial ITr. Ballini, *GSAI.* xvii and xviii: Guérinot, 150; Jacobi, *Mod. Rev.* 1914, 576; *ERE.* vii. 467.

66. *Kālakāchāryakathānaka* (Prāk.); Jacobi, *ZDMG.* xxxiv. 247; Guérinot, 176, 467.

Late 10th. Śobhana: Life, with text and GTr. of **67.** *Chaturviṁśati-jinastuti*: Jacobi, *ZDMG.* xxxii. 509.

Late 10th. Dhanapāla: Life, with text and GTr. of **68.** *Ṛishabha-pañchāśikā*: Klatt, *ZDMG.* xxxiii. 445; Guérinot, 56, 205; **69.** *Tilaka-mañjarī*: Jacobi, *ERE.* vii. 467; **70.** *Pāiyalachchhī*, A.D. 972, a Prāk. vocabulary: Text, Bühler, Göttingen, 1879.

10th c. **71.** *Jīvaka Chintāmaṇi*, romantic poem in Tam.: *BMCTB.* iv.

Died 1040. Śāntisūri; **72.** Prāk. comm. on No. 42: Jacobi, *AEM.*, Preface; **73.** *Jīvaviyāra*, Prāk. dogmatic work: text and FTr. Guérinot, *JA.* 1902, 231; Guérinot, 158.

Fl. 1069. Jinachandra (guru of Abhayadeva); **74.** *Saṁvegaraṅgaśālā*, a work on worship in 18,000 couplets: Duff, *CI.* 128; Peterson, *R.* V. xx.

Died 1078. Abhayadeva: Peterson, *R.* IV. iv; Leumann, *ZDMG.* xlvi. 582; **75.** Comms. on Nos. 3-12: Guérinot, 55, 66, 68, 69, 133, 134, 135, 138; **76.** *Jayatihuyaṇastotra*: Peterson, *R.* iii. 25; Guérinot, 79.

Fl. 1082. Guṇachandra; **77.** *Mahāvīracharita* (Prāk.): Duff, *CI.* 132.

1086-1169. Devabhadra: Peterson, *R.* IV. liv; Guérinot, 82; **78.** *Pārśvanāthacharitra*, A.D. 1112; **79.** *Vīracharitra*; **80.** *Saṁvegaraṅgaśālā*, on worship.

1089-1173. Hemachandra, Life: Bühler, *Ueber das Leben des Jaina-Mönches Hemachandra*, Vienna, 1889; Jacobi, *ERE.* vi. 591; Guérinot, 410; **81.** Comm. on No. 41; **82.** *Yogaśāstra*, or *Adhyātmopanishad*:

Intro., Analysis, and GTr. Windisch, *ZDMG*. xxviii. 185, 628; cf. also Garbe, *SY*. 39–40; **83**. *Vītarāgastuti*: Guérinot, 157, 410; **84**. *Pramāṇachintāmaṇi*: Jacobi, *ERE*. vi. 591; **85**. *Trishashṭiśalākāpurushacharita*: Analysis, Mitra, *Notices*, viii. 122; **86**. *Pariśishṭaparvan* (appendix to 85): Intro., Text, and Analysis, Jacobi, Calcutta, 1891. GTr. of the fables in this work, Hertel, *Ausgewählte Erzählungen aus Hemachandra's Pariśishṭaparvan*; **87**. *Mahāvīracharita* (last chapter of 85): Guérinot, 49, 82; **88**. *Vasudeva-Hiṇḍa* (Prāk.), Jacobi, *Mod. Rev*. 1914, 576; Peterson, *R*. i. 58; Guérinot, 75.

Fl. 1150. Malayagiri: Leumann, *ZDMG*. xlvi. 582; **89**. Comms. on Nos. 13, 14, 15, 17, 18, 36, 40: Guérinot, 69, 55, 65, 115, 69, 79.

Late 12th. Chandrasūri: Peterson, *R*. IV. xxvii; **90**. Prāk. comms. on Nos. 19, 43: Guérinot, 69, 398.

Fl. 1191. Āsaḍa; **91**. *Vivekamañjarī*: Duff, *CI*. 167; Peterson, *R*. IV. xii; **92**. *Upadeśakandalī*: Guérinot, 84.

Fl. 1220. Jinadattasūri: Duff, *CI*. 179; **93**. *Vivekavilāsa*: Bhandarkar, *R*. 1883–4, 156; Guérinot, 393.

Fl. 1230. Amarachandra: Duff, *CI*. 182; **94**. *Bālabhārata*: Guérinot, 184; **95**. *Padmanābhakāvya*: Guérinot, 75.

Fl. 1239. Tilakāchārya: Peterson, *R*. IV. xlviii; **96**. Comm. on No. 43.

c. 1250. Prabhāchandra (B); **97**. *Prabhāvakacharita*: Duff, *IC*. 202; Guérinot, 410.

Fl. 1271. Devendrasūri; **98**. Six *Karmagranthas* and comms. on the first five: Peterson, *R*. IV. lvii.

Fl. 1304. Merutuṅga; **99**. *Prabandhachintāmaṇi*: Intro. and ETr. Tawney, Calcutta, 1901; Duff, *CI*. 211; Guérinot, 77, 123, 391; **100**. *Mahāpurushacharitra*, or *Upadeśaśata*: Guérinot, 72, 85: **101**. *Shaḍdarśanavichāra* (a criticism of systems): Max Müller, *India, What?* 362; Guérinot, 393; **102**. *Muñjaprabandha* (Prāk.): Jhaveri, *MGL*. 19.

Fl. 1349. Rājaśekharasūri; **103**. *Prabandhakośa*: Guérinot, 109; **104**. *Antarakathāsaṅgraha*: Guérinot, 185.

Late 14th. Jñānasāgara; **105**. Comms. on Nos. 43, 45, the latter in 1383: Peterson, *R*. IV. xlvi; Duff, *CI*. 223.

c. 1372. Ratnaśekhara (A); **106**. *Śrīpālacharitra*: Peterson, *R*. IV. ciii; **107**. *Lagkukshetrasamāsa* (Mythical Geography): Guérinot, 432.

c. 1400. Guṇaratna; **108**. *Shaḍdarśanasamuchchhayaṭīkā*: comm. on No. 60: Guérinot, 68, 151.

109. Navatattva (date and author unknown): a popular statement, in varying recensions, of the nine Śvetāmbara categories: ETr. Stevenson, London, 1848.

1384–1443. Somasundara: Peterson, *R*. IV. cxxxvi; **110**. Comms. on Nos. 24, 43; **111**. Comm. on No. 36; **112** on the *Upadeśamālā*; **113**. on the *Navatattva*.

1380–1447. Munisundara; **114**. *Upadeśaratnākara*; **115**. *Mitrachatushkakathā*; **116**. *Adhyātmakalpadruma*; **117**. *Sahasranāmasmṛiti*: Peterson, *R*. IV. xcvii; Duff, *CI*. 230, 248.

Fl. 1436. Jinamaṇḍana; **118**. *Kumārapālaprabandha*: Duff, *CI*. 253; Guérinot, 410, 423.

Fl. 1438. Jinakīrti; **119**. *Champakaśreshṭhikathānaka* (A.D. 1400): Text and GTr. Weber, *Ueber das Champakaśreshṭhikathānakam*, Berlin, 1883; **120**. *Dhanyaśālicharitra*; **121**. *Dānakalpadruma*; **122**. *Śrīpālagopālakathā*: Peterson, *R*. IV. xxxiii; Duff, *CI*. 254; Guérinot, 177.

1401-61. Ratnaśekhara (B); **123.** Comms.: Peterson, *R.* IV. cii; Guérinot, 45, 71, 85, 376, 432.

Fl. 1464. Śubhaśīla; **124.** *Pañchaśatīprabodhasambandha*: Intro. and analysis in Italian, Ballini, *IOC.* xiii, Leyden, 1904; Guérinot, 183; **125.** *Bharatādikathā*, or *Kathākośa*: Guérinot, 65, 188; **126.** Comm. on No. 66: Bhau Daji, *JBBRAS.* ix. 139; Guérinot, 407.

Fl. 1526. Harisheṇa; **127.** *Jagatsundarīyogamālā*: Peterson, *R.* i. 52, 91; Guérinot, 74, 401; Duff, *CI.* 273.

Fl. 1573. Dharmasāgara; **128.** *Kupakshakauśikāditya*, or *Pravachanaparīkshā*: Weber, *SKPAW.* 1887; Bhandarkar, *R.* 1883-4, 150; Guérinot, 89, 175, 368.

Samayasundara: Peterson, iii. 3; **129.** *Kalpalatā*, comm. on 37 a; Guérinot, 65, 66; **130.** *Gāthāsahasrī*: 1,000 verse quotations: Peterson, iii. 3; Guérinot, 78; **131.** *Visaṁvādaśataka*: Guérinot, 78; **132.** *Sāmāchārīśataka*: *IA.* xxxiii. 169; Guérinot, 382, 83, 92.

1652. Vinayavijaya; **133.** *Lokaprakāśa*: an encyclopaedia of Jainism: Jacobi, *ERE.* vii. 467.

B. Digambara Literature.

Lit. in Sanskrit, unless otherwise described.

THE LOST CANON: see Bhandarkar, *R.* 1883-4, where an analysis of the account in Sakalakīrti's *Tattvārthasāradīpikā*, No. 204, below, is given; also Jaini, *Outlines of Jainism* (Cambridge, 1916), p. 135, where a fuller description may be read.

134. *Sūryaprajñapti*, Guérinot, 20, 139, 467; and **135.** *Chandraprajñapti*, Guérinot, 65, 69; both Prākṛit.

Vaṭṭakera; **136.** *Mūlāchāra*, Prāk.: Peterson, ii. 74; Guérinot, 20, 77, 99; **137.** *Trivarṇāchāra*, Prāk.: Bühler, *IA.* vii. 28; Guérinot, 20.

Kuṇḍakuṇḍa: Pāthak, *IA.* xiv. 14; Guérinot, 272. Cf. also Guérinot, 380. All works in Prāk.; **138.** *Shaṭprābhṛita*: Peterson, ii. 89; Guérinot, 77; **139.** *Ashṭaprābhṛita*: Guérinot, 99; **140.** *Samayasāraprābhṛita*; Analysis: Mitra, *Notices*, VII. 183; Bhandarkar, *R.* 1882-3; 42; Guérinot, 64, 86, 100, 140, 272; **141.** *Prābhṛitasāra*: Pāthak, *IA.* xiv. 15; Guérinot, 272; **142.** *Pravachanasāra*: full analysis, Bhandarkar, *R.* 1883-4, 91; Guérinot, 87; **143.** *Niyamasāra*: brief analysis, Bhandarkar, loc. cit. 102; Guérinot, 87; **144.** *Pañchāstikāya*, or *Pañchatthiyasaṁgahasutta*: Text, intro., and analysis in Italian: *Pavolini*, *GSAI.* xiv. 1; Guérinot, 157; **145.** *Rayaṇasāra*; and **146.** *Dvādaśānuprekshā*, Guérinot, 272.

c. 600. Samantabhadra: Pāthak, *IOC.* ix. 186; *JBBRAS.* 1894, 218; Guérinot, 415, 416; Vidyābhūshaṇa, *MSIL.* 22; **147.** *Gandhahastimahābhāshya*: comm. on No. 50: Vidyābhūshaṇa, *MSIL.* 22; **148.** *Āptamīmāṁsā* or *Devāgamastotra*: brief analysis, Vidyābhūshaṇa, 24; Sansk. analysis, Mitra, *Notices*, vi. 105; Guérinot, 63; its comms.: Pāthak, loc. cit.; Guérinot, 415; **149.** *Ratnakaraṇḍaśrāvakāchāra*: text and ETr. C. R. Jain, *The Householder's Dharma*, Arrah, 1917; Guérinot, 85, 476; **150.** *Yuktyanuśāsana*: Guérinot, 476; **151.** *Svayambhūstotra*; and **152.** *Chaturviṁśati-jina-stuti*: Vidyābhūshaṇa, *MSIL.* 23. Other works: Rice, *JRAS.* 1883, 395; Guérinot, 403.

Fl. 643. Ravikīrti; **153.** *Jinakathe* (Kan.): Guérinot, 96, 227, 483; Rice, *JRAS.* 1890, 245: Guérinot, 405.

Fl. 660. Ravisheṇa: Duff, *CI.* 55; **154.** *Padma Purāṇa*: Bhandarkar, *IOC.* vii. 30; Guérinot, 394.

c. 700. Pūjyapāda; **155.** *Sarvārthasiddhi*: comm. on No. 50: Rice, *JRAS.* 1883, 397; Guérinot, 403.

c. 700–70. Akalaṅka: Pāthak, *IOC.* ix. 1, 186; Guérinot, 270, 298, 415; **156.** *Akalaṅkastotra*; Guérinot, 19; **157.** *Ashṭaśatī*: comm. on No. 148: Pāthak, loc. cit.; Guérinot, 416; **158.** *Jainavarṇāśrama* (on conduct): Guérinot, 96; **159.** *Tattvārthaṭīkāvyākhyālaṅkāra*: comm. on No. 50: Peterson, ii. 78; Guérinot, 77. For these and other works, see Vidyābhūshaṇa, *MSIL.* 25.

8th c. **160.** *Rājavārttika*: comm. on No. 50: Guérinot, 35.

8th c. **161.** *Nālaḍiyār* (Tamil verse): Barnett, *BMCTB.* iv.

Fl. 783. Jinasena; **162.** *Harivaṁśapurāna*: full analysis, Mitra, *Notices*, vi. 74; Guérinot, 63.

c. 800. Vidyānanda; **163.** *Ślokavārtika* or *Jainaślokavārtika*, comm. on No. 50; Vidyābhūshaṇa, *MSIL.* 27; Guérinot, 416; **164.** *Ashṭasahasrī*, or *Āptamīmāṁsālaṅkāra*: a super-comm. on No. 148, following up No. 157: Vidyābhūsaṇa, *MSIL.* 27; **165.** *Āptaparīkshā*, Guérinot, 63, 415; **166.** *Pramāṇaparīkshā*: Vidyābhūshaṇa, *MSIL.* 27.

Śrīvarddhadeva; **167.** *Chūḍāmaṇi* (Kan.): Rice, *KL.* 24.

c. 800. Māṇikyanandin; **168.** *Parīkshāmukha*: Vidyābhūshaṇa, *MSIL.* 28.

c. 825. Prabhāchandra (A); **169.** *Prameyakamalamārtaṇḍa* on No. 168: Vidyābhūshaṇa, *MSIL.* 33.

A.D. 837. **170.** *Jayadhavalā*: Bhandarkar, *EHD.* 68; Guérinot, 394; Pāthak, *JEBRAS.* 1894, 226.

9th c. Jinasena; **171.** *Ādipurāṇa* or *Trishashṭilakshaṇamahāpurāṇa*: brief analysis, Bhandarkar, *R.* 1883–4, 118; Guérinot, 88; **172.** *Pārshvābhudaya*: Pāthak, *JBBRAS.* 1894, 224; Guérinot, 99.

9th c. Guṇabhadra; **173.** completed Jinasena's *Ādipurāṇa*: Pāthak, *JBBRAS.* 1894, 225; **174.** *Uttarapurāṇa*: Bhandarkar, *R.* 1883–4, 119; Guérinot, 88, **175.** *Ātmānuśāsana*: Guérinot, 476.

9th c. Amoghavarsha I; **176.** *Praśnottaramālā*: Bhandarkar, *EHD.* 68.

Fl. 905. Amṛitachandra: Duff, *CI.* 83; **177.** Comm. on No. 140: Guérinot, 77; **178.** Comm. on No. 142: Peterson, IV. ix.; **179.** Comm. on No. 144: Guérinot, 157; **180.** *Tattvārthasāra*: Guérinot, 476; **181.** *Purushārthasiddhyupāya*: *Bodleian Catal.* ii. 226; Guérinot, 45, 476.

Fl. 941. Pampa; **182.** *Ādipurāṇa*, Kan.: Guérinot, 414; Rice *KL.* 27; **183.** *Pampa Bhārata* or *Vikramārjunaviyaja*, Kan.: Rice, *KL.* 26.

Fl. 950. Ponna; **184.** *Sānti Purāṇa*, Kan., on the 16th Tīrthakara: Rice, *KL.* 28; **185.** *Jināksharamāle*, Kan., an acrostic in praise of the Tīrthakaras: Rice, *KL.* 28.

Fl. 960. Somadeva; **186.** *Yaśastilaka*: full analysis, Peterson, ii. 33; Guérinot, 76; **187.** *Nītivākyāmrita*: Guérinot, 108.

Fl. 980. Ranna; **188.** *Ajita Purāṇa*, Kan., on the 2nd Tīrthakara: Rice, *KL.* 28; **189.** *Sāhasa Bhīma Vijaya*, Kan., Rice, *KL.* 28.

Prob. 10th c. **190.** *Jīvaka-chintāmaṇi*, a Tamil artistic romance: Frazer, *ERE.* viii. 91.

c. 980. Chāmuṇḍarāya (Kan. Chāvuṇḍarāya); **191.** *Chāvuṇḍarāya-purāṇa*, Kan.: Rice *KL.* 28; Ghoshal, *Davva Saṁgaha* (see next entry), Intro., xx.

c. 980. Nemichandra; **192.** *Dravya-saṁgraha* (Prāk.): Text, Intro., ETr. and comm., Ghoshal, *Davva Saṁgaha*, Arrah, 1917; **193.**

Trilokasāra: Ghoshal, op. cit. xlii; analysis, Mitra, *Notices*, vi. 97; Guérinot, 20; **194**. *Gommatasāra* (written for Chāmuṇḍarāya): Ghoshal, xl; **195**. *Labdhisāra* (on attainment): Ghoshal, xii; **196**. *Kshapaṇasāra*: Ghoshal, xlii.

c. 1100. Abhinava Pampa; **197**. *Mallināthapurana*, Kan.: Rice, xl. 30; **198**. *Pampa Rāmāyaṇa*, Kan., Rice, *KL*. 30.

c. 1120. Bālachandra (A); **199**. Comm. on No. 141: Guérinot, 272, 404; **200**. *Tattvaratnadīpikā*: Guérinot, 404.

1200–50. Āśādhara; **201**. *Dharmāmṛita*; **202**. *Trishashṭismṛiti*: and many other works. Life, analysis of the *Dharmāmṛita* and list of works: Bhandarkar, *R*. 1883–4, 103.

Śrī Yogindra; **203**. *Paramātmaprakāśa*: ETr. R. U. Jain, Arrah, 1915.

Fl. 1464. Sakalakīrti; **204**. *Tattvarthasāradīpikā*; **205**. *Praśnottaropāsakāchāra*: Bhandarkar, *R*. 1883–4, 116; **206**. *Śāntināthacharita*; and **207**. *Pārśvanāthacharita*: analysis, Bhandarkar, 106, 116, 122; **208**. *Vardhamānapurāṇa*: Guérinot, 100.

End 15th. Śrutasāgara: Peterson, IV. cxxiii; **209**. *Jinasaṁhitā* (on the building of temples, making images, and worship): Bhandarkar, *R*. 1883–4, 117; **210**. Comm. on No. 138; Guérinot, 77; **211**. *Tattvārthadīpikā*: Bhandarkar, 117.

Fl. 1528. Nemidatta; **212**. *Śrīpālacharitra*; **213**. *Nemijinapurāṇa*; **214**. *Dhanyakumāracharitra*; **215**. *Arādhanākathākośa*: Guérinot, 83, 83, 88; **216**. *Śrāvakāchāra*: Peterson, V. xl.

16th c. Śubhachandra; **217**. *Pāṇḍava P.*, and many other works: Peterson, V. lxxiii.

c. 1626. Ratnachandra; **218**. *Subhaumacharitra*: Bhandarkar, *R*. 1883–4, 124; **219**. *Pradyumnacharitra*: Guérinot, 73.

1630–50. Banārasī Dās; works in Hindī verse; **220**. *Sādhubandanā*; **221**. *Mokshamārgapaiḍī*; **222**. *Samayasāranaṭīkā*: Guérinot, 101, 148, 208.

INDEX